Computer-aided Drawing and Design

Computer-aided Drawing and Design

B.L. DAVIES
Senior Lecturer in Engineering Drawing,
Design and CAD/CAM at Imperial College, London

A.J. ROBOTHAM
Senior Lecturer in the Department of Mechanical
Engineering and Manufacturing Systems at Coventry Polytechnic
and

A. YARWOOD
Registered Applications Developer for AutoCAD with
AutoDesk (UK) Ltd

SPRINGER-SCIENCE+BUSINESS MEDIA, B.V.

First edition 1986
Revised edition 1991

© 1986 B.L. Davies and A. Yarwood; 1991 B.L. Davies, A.J. Robotham, A. Yarwood
Originally published by Chapman & Hall in 1986

Typeset in 10/12pt Palatino by Excel Typesetters Company

British Library Cataloguing in Publication Data
Davies, B.L. (Brian L)
  Computer-aided Drawing and Design.
  1. Engineering. Design. Applications of computer graphics
  I. Title II. Robotham, A.J. III. Yarwood, A.
  620.00420285

ISBN 978-0-412-34230-1   ISBN 978-94-011-3074-5 (eBook)
DOI 10.1007/978-94-011-3074-5

Library of Congress Cataloging-in-Publication Data
Davies, B.L. (Brian L.)
  Computer-aided Drawing and Design / B.L.
  Davies, A.J. Robotham, A. Yarwood.
      p.   cm.

  1. Computer graphics. 2. Computer-aided design. I. Robotham.
A.J. II. Yarwood, A. (Alf) III. Title.
T385D39   1991
620'.0042'0285—dc20   90-37458
                                                     CIP

This book is dedicated to our wives and families in appreciation of their encouragement and support.

Contents

Acknowledgements

The authors wish to record their appreciation of the help given by representatives of the following organizations who have granted permission to reproduce copyright illustrations:

Autodesk Limited (Fig. 1.1, Fig. 4.13, Plate 2 and Plates 12 to 14)
Tektronix (UK) Limited (Fig. 2.11, Fig. 2.18, Fig. 2.21, Plate 1, Plate 21 and cover illustration)
Benson Electronics Limited (Fig. 2.14a and Fig. 2.16)
Roland Digital Group (Fig. 2.19 and Fig. 2.20)
Compaq Computer Limited (Fig. 2.23 and Fig. 2.24)
Deltacam Systems Limited (Fig. 4.14, Figs. 11.42 to 11.52)
PAFEC Limited (Fig. 9.3, Fig. 11.9, Plate 15 and cover illustration)
Structural Dynamics Research Corporation (Fig. 10.35, Fig. 10.39, Fig. 11.6 and Figs. 11.27 to 11.41)
The School of Industrial Design, Royal College of Art, London (Fig. 10.37, Fig. 10.38 and Fig. 10.40)
Prime Computer Limited (Fig. 11.1, Fig. 11.25, Plate 18 and cover illustration)
Pathtrace Engineering Systems (Fig. 11.7 and Fig. 11.8)
Schlumberger Technologies (Fig. 11.10, Fig. 11.23 and Fig. 11.26)
BYG Systems Limited (Fig. 11.11 and Plate 17)
Intergraph (UK) Limited (Fig. 11.24, Plate 19 and Plate 20)

The authors would also like to acknowledge the following companies for use of their trademarks:

Autodesk Limited (AEC Architectural, AutoCAD, AutoLISP, AutoShade, Auto-Sketch and AutoSolid)
BYG Systems Limited (GRASP)
Cad Centre (GNC)
Deltacam Systems Limited (DUCT)
International Business Machine Corporation (IBM)
Microsoft Corporation (MS.DOS)
PAFEC Limited (BOXER, DOGS, DOGS-PC, PAFEC-FE, PIGS and DOGS derivatives)
Pathtrace Engineering Systems (Pathcam)
Prime Computer Limited (SAMMIE)
Schlumberger Technologies (BRAVO 3 and BravoNC)
Structural Dynamics Research Corporation (I-DEAS, GEOMOD, GEODRAW and SUPERTAB)
Swanson Analysis Systems (ANSYS and ANSYS-PC)

Preface

This book is intended for engineers, computer scientists, managers and all those concerned with computer graphics, computer-aided design and computer-aided manufacture. While it is primarily intended for students, lecturers and teachers, it will also appeal to those practising in industry. Its emphasis on applications will make it easier for those not currently concerned with computers to understand the basic concepts of computer-aided graphics and design.

In a previous text (*Engineering Drawing and Computer Graphics*), two of the authors introduced the basic principles of engineering drawing and showed how these were related to the fundamentals of computer graphics. In this new text, the authors attempt to give a basic understanding of the principles of computer graphics and to show how these affect the process of engineering drawing. This text therefore assumes that the reader already has a basic knowledge of engineering drawing, and aims to help develop that understanding through the medium of computer graphics and by the use of a number of computer graphics exercises. The text starts by giving an overview of the basics of hardware and software for CAD and then shows how these principles are applied, in practice, in the use of a number of graphics packages of different levels of complexity. The use of a graphical database and the implications for computer-aided design and manufacture are also discussed.

This book is unique in its applications approach to computer graphics. It gives sufficient detail to explain the fundamentals of the computer graphics hardware and software, without adopting the usual computer specialist approach that can confuse a newcomer to this area. The book assumes no prior computing knowledge. It concentrates on the wider aspects of the applications of computer graphics. The text will be ideal for those who have bought, or are about to buy, a CAD package and want to know what underlies the 'button pressing' activities that are given in most instruction manuals of packages. Similarly, those who are now familiar with the basic concepts of engineering drawing can supplement their knowledge by undertaking exercises in computer graphics whilst learning about CAD principles. Those managers and industrialists who wish to gain a quick overview in a jargon-free, readily understandable way, will find this an ideal text. It is not our intention that this text will give sufficient detailed knowledge about any single package to make a user's manual redundant. Rather it will supplement such manuals by explaining the generic principles underlying many of the procedures and which are common to a number of different systems.

The sequence of the book starts with an overview of CAD/CAM and its benefits. There is then a discussion of the various forms of hardware and software, underlying the majority of CAD systems. The graphics process and how a computer draws lines on the display screen are then considered.

Next the methods of generating features in two dimensions are reviewed, e.g. how to draw a line, square or circle, and leading on to the construction of simple block types of objects. The use of 2-D packages for industry are then considered, together with their advantages and disadvantages. Examples are then given of the use and capabilities of a number of packages, ranging from the simple to the more complex PC-based systems. The use of simpler 3-D modelling packages, as typified by AutoCAD (Release II), are then discussed. After looking at the extension of such systems to 2½-D objects, such as are found in simple milling and turning, the full range of 3-D modelling is considered. The various methods of generating the full solid geometry are reviewed.

Finally, a number of examples are given of the benefits to be expected from integrating the whole range of CAD and CAM processes into a total CAE system. Examples are also given of the various analysis and manufacturing processes which benefit from the use of a 3-D computer database. The problems and benefits of introducing CAD into an industrial company are also discussed. Exercises are provided throughout the text which will be of benefit to both teachers and students.

We believe that this text will fulfill an important role since it bridges the gap between texts of a theoretical computer science nature and those which are user manuals for a single CAD package. The applications orientation should be useful to a wide range of engineers and managers in giving them an understanding of the generic principles of computer-aided drawing, graphics and design.

Introduction

1.1 THE ENGINEER AND COMPUTER-AIDED ENGINEERING

An engineer can be defined as a person who is concerned with the many processes leading to the production of artefacts which will aid mankind. These processes include a span of activities which start with the inception of the idea, pass through the design and manufacture phases and finish with the safe scrapping of the product.

Traditionally, the engineering drawing has played a crucial role in these processes, because its graphical form is ideal for quickly conveying complex ideas in an unambiguous manner. It is used by a variety of specialist engineers, for example the designer who, as he sketches and draws, carries on a conversation with himself and others to refine his design ideas step by step. The analyst and the researcher define from drawings the precise geometry of parts for mathematical analysis. Managers in industry discuss aspects such as length of manufacturing times, costs of manufacturing parts, material requirements and other such details with the aid of sets of engineering drawings. The draughtsman will use a range of drawings to ensure that parts are correct in shape and form, have the correct dimensions and tolerances and will assemble together properly into a working device. Engineering drawings, therefore, provide an essential means of communication between a wide variety of types of engineer.

In order to communicate as much information as possible in a concise form, a system of drawing views known as **orthographic projection** has been developed. Orthographic projections show single views of faces alongside other views seen from directions which are at right angles to each other. The views of individual component parts can be drawn and fully dimensioned to specify their precise geometry, size, shape and form. However, it is necessary for those using orthographic projection to build up in their minds a three-dimensional visualization of the parts shown in the various views of the drawing. They have to interrelate the separate two-dimensional views. The ability to read and understand engineering drawings remains an essential part of any engineer's skills.

More recently, however, all the processes leading to the production of an artefact have been aided by the use of the computer, but most notably computer-aided manufacture (CAM) and computer-aided design (CAD). Both CAD and CAM depend upon an accurate definition of the geometry of the product within the computer database. This is achieved by a range of computer graphics activities, but depends mostly upon a good three-dimensional modelling system and upon a good computer-aided draughting system. In computer graphics it is now relatively easy to generate a number of pictorial views of a part seen from a variety of directions. These show more than one face in a single view and quickly give a better overall impression of the three-dimensional nature of a part. Such pictorial views are generated from the data in the computer that holds all the geometry of the part being displayed. As the use of computer becomes more widespread, it is likely that the use of pictorial views will eventually result in orthographic projection (and hence the traditional engineering drawing) diminishing in importance.

The last decade has seen an explosion in the use of CAD, CAM and computer-aided draughting. The reduction in hardware and software costs, together with their ever increasing sophistication, has resulted in facilities which are now used by the average engineer which a decade ago were available to only a few specialist CAD companies. The engineer today has available at his desk as much computing power and capability as the specialist CAD software house of the late 1970s. It is for this reason that it is important for every student or professional engineer, no matter which branch of the discipline that is being followed, to become thoroughy familiar with the basic principles and the capabilities of CAD, computer-aided drawing and computer graphics. The whole range of computer graphics activity in engineering is dealt with in this text, gradually building towards utilizing computer-aided drawings and three-dimensional models to integrate together all the design, analysis, manufacture and management processes into a single computer-aided engineering (CAE) system. As will be seen from later chapters, it is from this integration of the range of engineering activities that the maximum benefit can be obtained.

1.2 THE ROLE OF COMPUTER-AIDED DESIGN AND ITS IMPLICATIONS FOR ENGINEERING DESIGN

Engineering design is a decision-making process which requires a wide range of knowledge and expertise. Early design activities, in which all calculations were performed manually, required that the models being analysed were greatly simplified in order that the mathematics involved was sufficiently simple to allow standard techniques of analysis to be applied. However, the simplifications were often so extreme that the resulting mathematical model bore little relationship to the reality. With the tremendous processing power of computers as an aid to the design process, the models can now be much more complex. In fact some analytical techniques, such as finite element analysis, can only be effectively carried out by using a computer. Thus, until recently, it has been the calculation power of the computer which has had the most impact on the process of engineering analysis and design. The introduction of the low-cost microcomputer, available on the desk of the majority of engineers, has meant that the computer is available for a number of calculations requiring relatively small programs with simple graphics output, e.g. graphs and diagrams to represent shear force and bending moments. The storage of data and standard codes of practice on a computer disk, together with purpose-written programs, can give the engineer the guidance and step-by-step advice at his computer terminal that was previously only obtainable from specialist consultants.

Until quite recently, graphical computing aids for the engineer were restricted to graphs and 2-D draughting systems. The 2-D draughting systems were comparatively simple and contained no intrinsic knowledge of the geometry of the part to be drawn. An example of the output from a popular system of this type, which is often used in education, is shown in Fig. 1.1. Many of the cheaper microcomputer-based systems contain only 2-D draughting systems with this level of complexity. These systems display the views of an object on a graphics screen in just the same way as an engineering drawing on paper. However, because all points and lines are held in computer memory, changes to the drawing can easily be carried out without having to re-enter all the data by hand. Only those lines which are to be modified need be re-entered and all the rest can then be automatically regenerated on the screen. However, individual views are drawn using the lines on the screen, but there is no facility for representing the three-dimensional (3-D) nature of the part. It was therefore necessary for the designer to be able to specify, for example, hidden features by showing them by hidden detail lines or by showing cross-hatching lines for sectioned planes.

The advent of a type of 3-D computer graphics, known as 2½-D has improved this situation. The dramatic reduction in the computer graphics hardware costs has also helped. A 2½-D system is one which is used only for shapes where a

Fig. 1.1 *AutoSKETCH: a typical PC-based 2-D draughting system.*

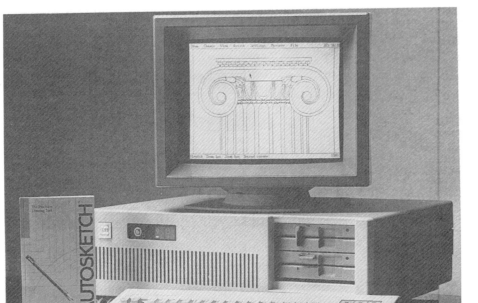

2-D profile is translated linearly by a small distance to make a 3-D object of constant depth. Alternatively a 2-D profile of an object can be rotated through 360° to make a roughly cylindrical type of 2½-D component. These shapes are of particular value because they are of a type often used in engineering and are relatively easy to produce on a simple numerically controlled lathe or milling machine. The programs can now be provided on relatively small and cheap microcomputers and graphical displays. The use of 2½-D facilities in 2-D draughting has meant that many design offices have been able to show savings of a factor of three or four on productivity.

The process of modelling, in a computer, a complex engineering component in three dimensions is difficult. It requires both sophisticated computer programs and special computer hardware for the graphical display systems. The topic of **solid modelling** is one in which a full 3-D representation of the product can be constructed. This is an area that has only recently been developed on a large scale, partly because the previously high cost of computer hardware has recently come down to more acceptable levels, and partly because of advances in computer programs which have produced many new techniques. It is this area of computer graphics that has the greatest potential for changing the way that products are designed. The ability to produce a full solid model, or an outline of an object as a **wire frame**, means that the full 3-D geometry of a part is available as a database. This data-based geometry is then available, not only to produce 2-D drawings of an assembly and its constituent parts, but is also available for transmission to other computer programs for design, analysis and manufacture. This central nature of the geometric database, together with the manner in which it integrates with a range of design and manufacture activities, is shown in Fig. 1.2. This figure shows that it is the graphics display screen which now readily enables the geometry of the part to be specified. The 3-D geometry can then be used in design and analysis, for example to pass to a finite element pre-processor which breaks down the geometry into a mesh which can then be analysed by a further program. The other major area where the geometric database is used, is in manufacture and management activities. Not only is the information of value for the automatic generation of numerical control machine tool motions, for example so that a computer numerically controlled lathe can produce turned objects, but also for such activities as scheduling the motions of robots and automated guided vehicles. The total computer information is also available for management activities in planning production and maintenance, in costing, sales and marketing. Although any single one of these activities may only have a marginal cost advantage taken on its own, by bringing them all together, the whole process becomes very cost effective. The result is that the engineer is relieved of many routine tasks and can use his time more creatively.

The availability of specially written programs means that a small business can have access to information, expertise and guidance which was previously available only to larger corporations. This process is likely to change the skills required of the engineer. The knowledge of a large number of detailed standards and procedures will no longer be necessary as they can be accessed directly from a computer. The emphasis on analytical ability is also likely to decrease for the generalist engineer, who will rely more on the standard analytical tools available

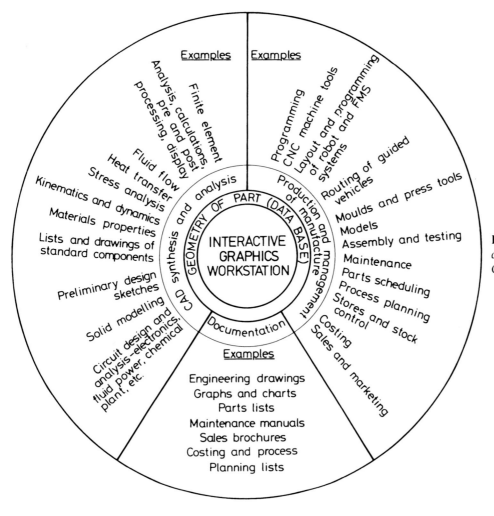

Fig. 1.2 *The central role of computer graphics in CAD/CAM.*

on the computer. For a small number of mathematicians and researchers, who will be responsible for developing or updating computer programs, the mathematical process will remain important. For the average engineer, however, the main activity is likely to become one of using the computer as a synthesis tool to enhance creativity. This reliance on the use of standard computer programs implies that their integrity must be fully verified and that the limitations of their application are well documented and understood. Until the time when totally integrated sophisticated computer graphics systems are in widespread use, it is generally thought necessary for every engineer to understand at least the basic analytical principles of a range of engineering subjects and to be able to understand the type of thinking and processes that underlie existing computer programs.

The recent trends in computer graphics have shown that there is a greater availability of larger systems with more memory and faster operation at very competitive prices. Thus, computer-aided design systems similar to those being used by the larger companies a few years ago, are currently being produced at a cost which is affordable by smaller companies and colleges. If the use of the computer graphics continues to expand as these recent trends imply, then it is essential for all those who have a knowledge of the more traditional engineering drawing processes to become familiar with computer graphics terminology and techniques.

It is this need for a fundamental undertanding of the graphics hardware, software and methods of application which has resulted in the provision of this book. It is hoped that this book will provide an introduction to computer-aided drawing and graphics in a way that those with a general knowledge of engineering drawing will be able to understand. The subjects of computing and computer graphics are full of terminology (often contradictory) which makes it difficult for the beginner to be able to read even an introductory text and understand what is happening; these texts often require a knowlege of procedures which is beyond the experience of the normal beginner. The constraints and reasons for a particular type of hardware or software system and the wider context issues are also seldom discussed in such texts. It is hoped that this book will give a sound appreciation of the basic principles and processes which are used in most computer graphics systems. The text has been written with the assumption that the reader is not well versed in any particular computer language. Similarly, the text has not been based upon any particular computer hardware system, but covers a range of categories from the simple to the complex. It is hoped that this text will be of interest to those about to use computer-aided drawing and graphics for the first time and also to those who wish to extend their existing knowledge beyond the smaller microcomputer-based systems. However, the text will also benefit all those who wish to see how a 3-D graphical model can lead to the integration and improvement in the design, manufacture and management of all products.

NOTE

We have already seen that computer graphics is at the heart of computer-aided design (CAD) and of computer-aided manufacture (CAM). There is much confusion about the use of the term CAD because for many years computer graphics systems were purely concerned with draughting and so the term CAD has mistakenly been used in some texts to mean computer-aided draughting. In this text, CAD is taken to refer to the application of computers in the whole design process.

Computer graphics hardware

2.1 HARDWARE FOR INTERACTIVE GRAPHICAL SYSTEMS

The term 'hardware' is used to cover all those pieces of equipment which are used to implement computer programs. The computer programs themselves are referred to as 'software' and are considered in detail in Chapter 3. A third term 'firmware' covers those software instructions which have been implemented permanently into the electronic hardware, usually to enable increased speed of computation to be achieved.

The division into hardware and software reflects the way that most companies organize their responsibilities, and it is now very rare to find a company which not only manufactures hardware but also originates software. A manufacturer, for example, of intelligent work stations, will enter into an arrangement with a number of software suppliers who will adapt their software to the requirements of his particular CAD equipment. Thus there are often a number of draughting and modelling programs available which will run on a particular CAD hardware system. Because the majority of CAD users are more interested in the application of software to a number of problems than they are in the hardware that drives the system, most users will approach the software company initially. The software company will then recommend a particular hardware system and generally take responsibility for seeing that the hardware and software will operate well together and perform to the customer's requirements.

Hardware includes the computer with its memory and central processing unit (CPU), the means of storing programs on disk or magnetic tape, the display screens, various devices for inputting instructions to the computer, e.g. keyboards, digitizers and tablets, and the output devices which can give 'hard copy', e.g. printers and plotters. We will look at each device in turn before considering how these elements are brought together to form a typical CAD system.

2.2 THE COMPUTER

The term 'computer' is often liberally used with reference to all the hardware components of a CAD system. Here, we use the term computer to refer to the processor which controls the operation of the CAD system. In this sense, the computer is only one part of the system. Depending upon the complexity of the system, the computer required to operate a comprehensive range of CAD applications software may vary from a small personal computer with a memory size of 640 Kb, to an intelligent work station with up to 10 Mb memory, or to a larger machine with up to 30 Mb of memory. In all cases the computer processor operates in a similar way.

It is not necessary completely to understand how a computer functions to operate a CAD system, but a basic knowledge of the fundamentals of how a computer works is essential for selecting hardware and software for your system, and to ensure the equipment and programs are used to best effect. The computer itself is often the most 'remote' component of the CAD system, inasmuch as the operations it carries out are 'invisible' to the user. Every computer has an **operating system** to control the flow of information between the computer processor and the various peripheral devices to which it is connected, i.e. keyboards, display screens, printers, plotters and other computers. The operating system provides the user with a command language to control these devices and to manage the storage of information on the system. Applications software allow specific tasks such as draughting, modelling, analysis, simulation or machine tool control to be carried out. Without either an operating system or applications software, which are considered further in Chapter 3, the computer is of little practical value to the operator.

Although computer technology has developed rapidly over recent years, the fundamental principles of operation of the processor itself, which were defined by John Von Neumann in the 1940s, have not changed. The sequential operation of the central processing unit, whereby instructions are processed in series, is the basis of the microprocessor used in most CAD computers. While **reduced instruction set computing** (RISC) technology currently gives a higher performance, by making more effective use of the processor, it is **parallel processing**, whereby a number of instructions are carried out simultaneously by the same processor, that will significantly improve the performance of future computers in CAD systems. This will be especially true in applications where interactive computer graphics play a major role. Although these processors have recently attained commercial maturity, they are not readily available for use in all current CAD systems, but the larger processing power per unit cost of these devices will surely secure their place in future CAD technology.

2.2.1 CENTRAL PROCESSING UNIT

The central processing unit (CPU) is the key element of the computer; it is the microprocessor at the heart of all modern computers. The central processing unit regulates the action of the computer, controlling the input, storage, manipulation and output of all information and data. The information received from input devices or retrieved from secondary storage media is temporarily held in the computer's memory; this is know as **main memory** or **internal memory**. The **arithmetic logic unit** (ALU) of the CPU performs four tasks: addition, subtraction, comparison and data transfer between itself and the main memory.

Instructions, numbers and characters are stored in memory and manipulated by the ALU as binary coded **words.** A word consists of a series of binary digits, or **bits**, each of which has two states, '1' or '0'. These states are represented in the microprocessor as 'on' or 'off'. Since instructions, numbers and characters will be stored as a series of noughts and ones, the computer is only able to recognize what type of code is being handled by its location in the memory. The CPU allocates part of its memory for instructions, part for numbers and part for characters.

Program instructions held in the main memory are followed in sequential order. The ALU retrieves data from specific locations in the memory and performs either an addition, subtraction or comparison calculation as instructed. The result is stored in memory before another instruction is retrieved and executed. The speed at which instructions are carried out is a measure of the 'power' of the computer. Processor speeds of 1 to 26 million instructions per second (mips) are usual for the processors used in today's CAD systems. The results of a whole sequence of instructions are output from memory to the various display, hard copy, and secondary storage devices under the control of the CPU. The control of the computer microprocessor and the way it communicates with the input and output devices are organized by the operating system software, and program instructions are converted into binary code by a **compiler** or an **interpreter**.

The word length used by a computer depends upon the microprocessor selected for the CPU. The small home computer typically has a word length of eight bits, the personal computer 16 bits, and the larger, business computer 32 bits. The word length affects the power and speed of instructions. A 16-bit word can be used to represent a large number to a certain precision which is expressed by the number of places after the decimal point. To obtain improved accuracy, or 'double precision', two 16-bit words would be required. However, if a computer with a 32-bit word is used, the same high precision can be obtained in a single word. This gives advantages in speed of processing. Since CAD graphics work requires both large numbers and high precision, 32-bit computers in modern systems give considerable speed advantages.

The word length of a microprocessor also determines how large the internal memory will be. Size of memory is measured in **bytes** (from the expression **by eight**), e.g. 64 Kb. However, a 64 Kb memory does not represent 64 000 bytes because in computer terminology K does not refer to 1000 but to 1024. Each byte is made up of eight bits, and thus a 64 Kb memory will give:

$$64 \times 1024 \times 8 = 524\,288 \text{ bits of memory.}$$

The term for half a byte, representing four bits is a **nybble**. Thus, although a word varies in size depending upon the computer being used, a bit, byte and nybble are all fixed in size.

The number of memory locations that can be addressed directly by the CPU depends upon the word length of the microprocessor. A 16-bit microprocessor can only address 65 536 memory locations (64 Kbyte of memory), whereas a 32-bit processor can address several Mbyte of memory. The operating system software and compiler or interpreter occupy space in the memory, reducing the space available to store other programs and data. The internal memory of a 16-bit computer can be expanded using additional 64 Kbyte memory units, but the

CPU is only able to address one memory unit at a time. Switching control between different memory units effectively enlarges the memory space available to the user, but slows down the operating speed of the computer.

Internal memory is either **volatile**, i.e. all stored data is lost when the computer is switched off, or **non-volatile**, i.e. all data is permanently stored in the memory. Read-only memory (ROM) is non-volatile memory which is used permanently to store instructions. When the computer is switched off, the instructions remain in memory ready for use the next time the computer is switched on. Instructions held in ROM cannot be overwritten or erased, so it is common practice to store rudimentary operating system software in ROM. In this way, when the computer is switched on, the computer has sufficient instructions to enable the processor to react to the initial instructions received from the operator and to control devices such as a disk drive and the display screen.

Eraseable programmable ROM (EPROM) also allow instructions to be stored in the computer in non-volatile memory. Unlike an ordinary ROM, however, the instructions held in an EPROM may be erased and overwritten, but this requires the processor to be removed from the computer and modified using a special machine. An EPROM allows the computer to respond immediately to the instructions it contains as soon as the system is switched on, yet gives the operator the facility occasionally to modify the software.

Random-access memory (RAM) is volatile memory suitable for storing a variety of information, provided the computer remains switched on. It is RAM that gives the computer its flexibility, allowing the user to operate applications software and temporarily store data in the computer. However, as soon as the computer is switched off, all the information contained in RAM will be lost. Therefore any information that has to be retained for later use must be stored in an alternative medium. To avoid these difficulties battery power is sometimes used to protect the more vital areas of RAM from being lost when the mains power is switched off.

2.3 SECONDARY STORAGE MEDIA

Although the computer stores programs in its memory, generally the program in its memory will be lost when the computer is switched off. In order to ensure that a program can be used on a subsequent occasion, it must be transferred from the computer's memory into a secondary storage medium to enable it to be loaded back into the computer when required. A further reason for needing such a storage medium is that most graphics application packages are too long to be totally stored in a computer's memory and sections of it will need to be loaded in and out of memory while the program is running. The most common secondary storage is on magnetic disk, but there are alternative media that will also be considered.

2.3.1 MAGNETIC DISKS

The disks are coated with magnetic oxide and revolve at very high speed in the disk drives. Magnetic sensors are tracked radially across the surface of the disk to **read** the binary information which is coded magnetically in specific locations, or **sectors**, on the disk. The **disk directory** lists the locations of all the files stored on the disk, enabling the read head to move quickly to a specific sector to access the start of a file. This is known as **direct access**. The information on the disk can be erased or overwritten, allowing old files to be deleted or current files to be modified.

The read and record head rides so closely above the disk surface that any dust or smoke particles will cause damage to the disk or the heads. For this reason cleanliness is essential and, on larger installations, a filtered air-conditioning system is advisable to improve hardware reliability. There are two types of disk commonly available; floppy and fixed-head.

Floppy Disks

These are small thin disks of flexible mylar, typically 89 mm (3.5 in), 133 mm (5.25 in) or 205 mm (8.0 in) diameter. The small 89 mm diameter floppy disks are protected by a stiff plastic outer casing, and so are not truly floppy. Often, to further protect the disk, a shuttered aperture in the outer casing allows the magnetic disk to be exposed only when it is inserted in the disk drive. The density with which information can be stored on the disk varies with quality and cost. Single, double and high density options are available, the high-density 133 mm disks being able to store up to 1.44 Mb of information for little more than £1 each.

Information that is stored on the disk can be protected from accidental erasure or overwriting in two ways. Individual files can be labelled on the disk using a disk operating system command, or the floppy disk itself can be protected by covering a **write-protect hole** that is moulded into the outer casing. In either case, the information is protected from accidental erasure or overwriting, yet may still be read without difficulty.

The cheapness of floppy disks enables each user to store programs and data on his or her own disks. It is good practice to make several copies of programs and data on separate floppy disks. If one disk should in any way become corrupted, i.e. destroyed or distorted in such a way that it is longer a correct record of the program or data, the information may be retrieved from a back-up copy of the original disk.

Fixed-head Disks

Fixed-head disks are generally used in large computer systems to store vast amounts of information (10 Mb up to 650 Mb) in a single fixed unit attached to a work station. Precision bearings in a fully sealed unit enables the rigid disks to be rotated very rapidly and so ensure an improved time to access information. Smaller fixed-head drives (often referred to as Winchester disks or hard disks) with a storage capacity of up to 120 Mb are often used in small CAD work stations. The high cost of fixed-head disks precludes their use for 'back-up' copying of files to a second such disk; a cheaper storage medium is usually used.

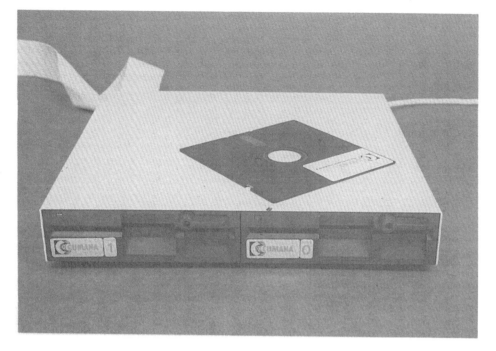

Fig. 2.1 *Floppy disks and disk drive.*

2.3.2 MAGNETIC TAPE

An alternative secondary storage medium is magnetic tape, which is much cheaper than disks. However, because a tape has to be unwound serially to find a particular piece of information (**sequential access**), accessing data is much slower than when using a disk (typically 200 times longer). Magnetic tape is therefore used in all but the very cheapest computer systems as a means of **archiving**, i.e. storing programs and data which are seldom needed and when storing on valuable disk space is not justified. Magnetic tapes are often used as back-up storage for fixed-head disks because of their large storage capacity.

Streamers

Streamers use audio cassettes to store data on either 3.81 mm (0.15 in) or 6.35 mm (0.25 in) magnetic tape. The 3.81 mm cassettes (commonly used in dictation machines) are capable of storing 10 to 60 Mb of information, and the 6.35 mm cassette upto 150 Mb. These devices are most convenient for copying information stored on small-capacity fixed-head disk drives. For instance, a 30 Mb disk can be backed up in approximately six minutes using a streamer, whereas it could take approximately 30 minutes to complete this operation using floppy disks.

2.3.3 OPTICAL DISKS

The optical disk is a more recent addition to the range of secondary storage media, and is considered highly suitable for CAD systems where large amounts of information need to be stored. Although times to access information are longer than for fixed-head drives of a similar physical size, the large volumes of information that can be stored on an optical disk prompted its adaption to computer applications. Optical disks fall into one of two distinct categories.

'Write Once Read Many' Disks

The **write once read many** (WORM) optical disk employs the same technology used for audio compact discs, and therefore is sometimes known as a CD ROM (compact disk read-only memory). The WORM disk is made of clear polycarbonate, coated with a material which changes when heated by a laser. The change to the coating is permanent, offering a greater robustness and reliability over magnetic storage media. The write once nature of WORM disks, though, restricts their usage to those applications where information does not need to be modified or erased. The digital information stored on the WORM disk is read using an optical read head that moves close to the disk surface. Random access to data ensures information is quickly retrieved from the disk.

Magneto-optic Disks

The magneto-optic (MO) disk uses the heat of a laser in the locality of a small bias magnetic field to alter the magnetic polarity of the coating material. During a disk read, laser light reflected from the disk is polarized, the direction of polarization depending upon the local magnetic polarity of the coating material. The direction of polarization is sensed in the reading head and interpreted as a 0 or 1. The magnetic polarity of the coating can be reversed by reversing the bias magnetic field when heating the material with the laser. In this way, information can be erased from a MO disk as easily as it can be stored. The MO disk therefore offers the same record/erase facility as other magnetic storage media and present 133 mm (5.25 in) disks hold about 600 Mb of information.

2.4 GRAPHICS DISPLAY SCREENS

At the heart of the CAD system is the graphical display screen or graphics unit. Its quality is important to the operator because it will be a big factor in how easy it is to use the CAD system. The basis of most currently used screens is the **cathode ray tube** (CRT) that is found in the home TV set. Figure 2.2 shows the elements of a cathode ray tube. An electron gun produces a stream of electrons which are accelerated towards a phosphor-coated screen. On the way, the electron stream passes through a focusing system which converges the electrons to a point on the screen. The electrons are deflected to a particular location on the screen by vertical and horizontal deflection plates with variable charge.

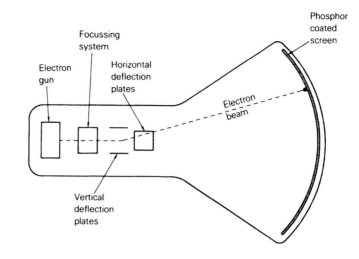

Fig. 2.2 *Basic operation of cathode ray tube.*

Where electrons hit the screen, the phosphor coating glows as a visible spot of light. Since the image quickly decays it has to be refreshed continually. Provided the refresh rate is greater than around 25 times a second, the image will not appear to flicker. On some displays the intensity of the image can be varied to

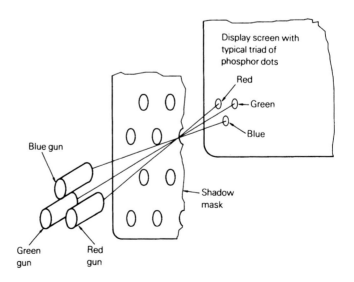

Fig. 2.3 *Basic operation of colour cathode ray tube.*

give a **grey-tone scale** of a number of levels from white through to black, so that a picture can be generated rather like a half-tone photograph.

Colour can also be generated on a CAD screen, just as in a domestic TV set, as shown in Fig. 2.3. To generate colour, the cathode ray tube contains three electron guns, giving red, blue or green signals. The phosphor screen is coated with red, blue and green dots, arranged in thousands of triangular patterns. A shadow mask of fine holes is placed in front of the phosphor screen. The three guns fire electrons through the holes in the mask illuminating some of the dots on the screen. The holes in the mask are spaced so that dots are only hit by the correct gun. The intensity of each beam is variable, so that when seen from a distance, each triad of spots merges together and takes on a particular colour, depending upon how strongly each of the red, blue and green spots is being excited.

Although, as we shall see later, a colour display requires more computing memory than monochrome, the quality in terms of number of points displayed (or **resolution**), may be lower to achieve the same level of ability to discriminate easily between adjacent lines on the screen. There is also some debate as to whether high-resolution monochrome or a similarly priced medium-resolution colour display should be used for computer graphics. Monochrome displays are generally recommended for 2-D draughting work, while more complex 3-D solid modelling of components benefits from the use of colour for adjacent features. Colour is particularly useful where objects are overlapped and it would be difficult to determine which line was which using a monochrome display.

Three types of display are in common use: raster scan, direct beam refresh and storage tube.

2.4.1 RASTER SCAN

This type of display is being employed increasingly in CAD system. Figure 2.4 shows the concept in which an electron beam traces a zig-zag pattern across the screen similar to that on a TV screen. However, a TV set uses an analogue signal, while a computer graphics screen uses a digital signal, which can be either on or off, provided by the computer. As shown in Fig. 2.4, the beam starts at the top left-hand corner and traverses from left to right of the screen. At the right-hand end of the screen the beam moves back along the dotted path to the left-hand end and starts to refresh the next line. This process continues until the bottom right corner of the screen is reached, when the beam flies back to the top left corner to start all over again. As the beam traverses along the line the computer continually turns the beam on or off to create the desired picture. The greater the number of points on the screen, the better the quality (or **resolution**) of the picture.

A low-resolution professional CAD screen has typically 256 lines of information and 312 addressable points on each line. The 312×256 matrix creates over

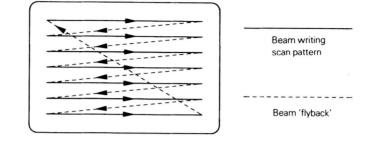

Fig. 2.4 *A raster scan display screen.*

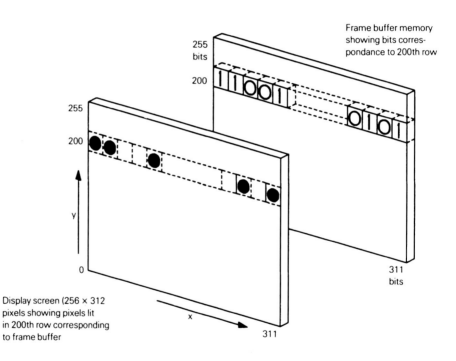

Fig. 2.5 *A frame buffer and display screen.*

79 000 bits of information corresponding to the number of picture elements or **pixels**, each of which can either be turned on or off. Each pixel is stored in a special location in the memory and is scanned through every 1/30 s or 1/60 s. When the screen is refreshed at this rate (greater than around 1/25 s) the persistence of vision of the eye causes the image to appear steady and without flicker. Each pixel is stored in the computer in such a way that the screen is 'mapped' successively into the computer memory with a memory location for each pixel in the *xy* plane of the screen. Each of the memory locations will contain either a 1 if the pixel is to be turned on, or a 0 if the pixel is to remain dark.

Each time the raster scans across the screen from top to bottom, it consults every location in the mapped memory to decide which pixels should be turned on to create the required picture. Figure 2.5 shows the memory, called a **frame** (or **refresh**) buffer, in relation to a diagrammatic representation of a screen. Larger CAD systems have a separate frame buffer memory for mapping the pixels, which can give faster access than a normal microprocessor memory, leading to very rapid refresh rates. These systems are known as **bit mapped** displays.

Medium-resolution displays for industrial CAD systems have around 512×512 pixels; high-resolution displays have 1024×1024 pixels; while a very high-resolution system could have 4096×4096. Using 1024×1024 pixels would require over one million locations or bits of computer memory. On a computer having eight bits to each byte this would require 128 Kb just for the refresh buffer. (One Kb of memory is usually 1024 bits.) The number of bits is further increased if a variety of intensity levels or colour is used. To provide a reasonable grey-scale picture, eight levels of intensity are generally needed which require three bits per pixel; three binary bits are needed to represent the eight levels because we can show decimal 0 by the binary number 000, decimal 1 by binary 001, and so on through to decimal 7 represented by the three binary bits 111. Applying colour shading is more complex because each shade requires three guns: red, blue and green. If, as is common in a professional CAD system, 16 levels of shade for each colour are used, then the number 16 will require four binary bits for each gun. Thus for the three guns, each pixel will need a 12-bit word to define the 16 levels for red, blue and green. A typical arrangement is shown in Fig. 2.6. Here every pixel represented in the frame buffer requires not just the 0 or 1 (off or on) shown in Fig. 2.5, but a number of binary bits capable of differentiating a range of colours for each pixel. The eight binary bits are capable

Fig. 2.6 *Organization of a programmable colour display screen.*

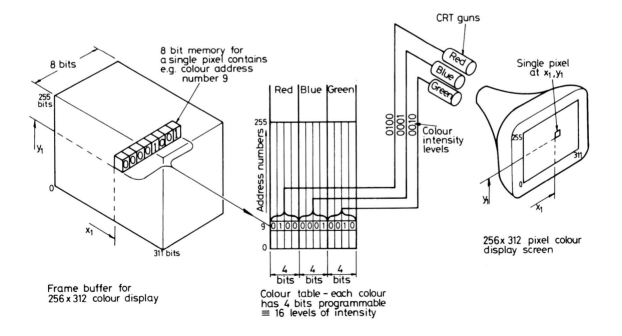

Frame buffer for
256 x 312 colour display

Colour table – each colour
has 4 bits programmable
≡ 16 levels of intensity

256x 312 pixel colour
display screen

of giving up to 256 separate levels. While these levels could be fed straight to the colour guns of the display screen this would limit the range of colours to 256. Instead, larger CAD systems use a **colour table** (or **colour map**) as an additional memory between the refresh buffer and the cathode ray tube guns. The eight bits in the frame buffer now give a number from 0 to 255 which is an **address** of a location in the colour table. Each location in the colour table contains a further memory of 12 bits: four for the red gun, four for the blue and four for the green. Since four bits can represent from 0 to 15 hues, the three guns can represent $16 \times 16 \times 16 = 4096$ variations in colour. If the colour table memory can not only be read but can also be rewritten (i.e. it has read/write memory), then any of the 256 locations in the colour table can be reprogrammed to show any of the 4096 colours. The display screen can at one time show any of the 256 colours which may be selected from a **palette** of 4096.

An alternative method of organizing the refresh buffer is to use the number of bits per pixel to represent differentiated display screens or **planes** that can be superimposed, one over the other. Thus in the example of Fig. 2.6, two planes, each of four bits could be represented by the same eight bits per pixel. The two screens could then be used to aid animation. As a simple example, a clock, including the minute and hour hand, could be shown on one screen while the second hand on its own could be shown on an overlapping screen. The first screen with all its detail need only be updated every minute, while the second hand, on its own, can be updated on its screen after every second. These multiple-plane-bit-mapped displays require a great deal of memory.

Costs of computer memory have fallen dramatically in recent years. This, together with the fact that raster CAD systems benefit from similar components to those in TV sets (and thus benefit from the cheaper costs of large-scale manufacture), has resulted recently in raster screens being the most popular type of CAD display. Even when a great deal of information is displayed, the image does not flicker because the refresh rate is fast and constant. Also it is easy for a part of the picture selectively to be erased or changed.

2.4.2 DIRECTED-BEAM REFRESH DISPLAYS

These are also called stroke-writing, vector-writing or line-drawing refresh displays. In this system only the line segments, making up the image, are generated in turn by the directed beam. Curves are approximated by a number of straight-line segments. Figure 2.7 shows a typical sequence. After the image is drawn, the picture is refreshed by repeating the sequence. Thus the more detailed the image, the longer it is before the next refresh. Since the eye has a persistence of vision lasting around 1/25 s, if the refresh frequency is less than around 30 Hz the image flickers and is unpleasant to view. Refresh displays only require memory locations for the end points of a line in terms of the x and y coordinates on the screen. Thus for fairly simple objects, the size of memory required is much smaller than for a raster display, and consequently is cheaper. Refresh displays preceded the design of raster-scan displays, but because the cost of memory has fallen so dramatically in recent years, raster scan is now the

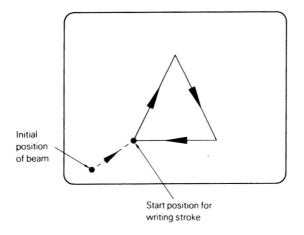

Fig. 2.7 *A directed beam refresh display.*

preferred system and the refresh display has been reduced to an historical item, found only in a few drawing offices.

2.4.3 DIRECT-VIEW STORAGE TUBE

This system uses vector writing, from one co-ordinate to another, just as in a directed-beam refresh display, but the use of a long-persistent phosphor on the screen prevents the need for the screen to be refreshed continually. An additional electron gun, called a **flood gun**, is used in the cathode-ray tube to create a **fog** of electrons which keep the phosphor elements glowing once they have been illuminated by the stroke-writing electron beam. Thus, once the picture is drawn and stored on the screen, it does not need to be refreshed until a change is required. The screen is therefore flicker-free, even when a large amount of data is stored. High-resolution screens are generally adopted so that curves can be displayed almost free from steps or zig-zags, giving a high quality picture. The problem with this type of display is that if a single line is altered, the whole picture must be erased and re-drawn with the new line in position and this can be quite slow. The display of dynamic images is therefore not possible on a storage tube. Although storage tubes can have more than one brightness level, they cannot use colour.

2.4.4 ALPHANUMERIC DISPLAYS

In order to display images on the screen it is usual to select what you require from a **menu**. This is the name given to a list containing the types of lines, views, scales, etc., which can be chosen. While the menu could be part of a **tablet** on the desk in front of the screen, it is often more convenient for it to be part of the display screen. Frequently the menu is displayed along the edge or bottom of

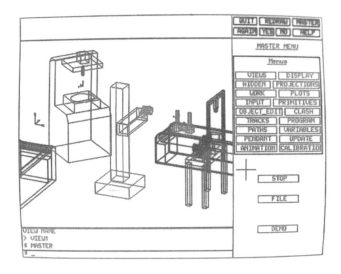

Fig. 2.8 *A graphics menu on a display screen.*

the graphics screen and a cursor is used to point at whichever instruction is required. Figure 2.8 shows a typical arrangement. A number of menus can be listed on the screen, one replacing another so that a large number of instructions can be accessed. While it is convenient to view the menu on the screen alongside the picture to which it refers, the graphics area is thereby reduced. On large systems it is therefore usual to have a separate display screen for instructions. Since only letters and numbers are required, this is called an **alphanumeric** screen and is often known as a **visual display unit** (VDU).

NOTE

To overcome the need for a separate alphanumeric display, modern CAD systems that use raster scan displays have adopted pull-down menus for inputting instructions. This type of menu is displayed on the graphics screen only while the user is deciding which instruction to select. When the selection has been made, the menu of options disappears, revealing the full graphics screen once more.

2.4.5 DYNAMIC DISPLAYS

The development of the graphics display screen is today moving further and further away from the 'dumb' terminal used in earlier CAD systems. Manufacturers are producing graphics displays that allow the user to manipulate the screen image using processing facilities contained in the display itself. Using local pan and zoom, the user may select an area of the screen and enlarge it so that it fills the whole of the graphics area. The local processing power of the display allows this to be done without further use of the host computer and, therefore, the operation is completed quickly. More importantly, the original image can be restored to the screen and the pan and zoom operation repeated as required.

Where three-dimensional component models are being viewed, more advanced local facilities might include hidden line removal, surface shading, dynamic motion, and even stereoscopic viewing. In all cases, the local processing power of the display is being used to modify the screen image first generated by the host computer and the applications software.

While the displays that support these features are a lot more expensive than their dumb counterparts, the speed and ease with which the screen image can be modified significantly eases visualization problems. For instance, dynamic motion allows either wire-frame, hidden-line removed, or colour-shaded images of the model to be viewed from a variety of positions. The screen image of the computer model is controlled either by thumbwheels or by position dials. Their movement corresponds to the movement of the observer around the object. In this way, engineering components, architectural structures, chemical molecular models, can be viewed as if the computer model was realized as a scale model in your hands.

2.4.6   STEPPING OR ALIASING OF LINES

Because images on a display screen are generated by turning pixels on or off, the greater the number of pixels, the greater the quality of the picture and the better the resolution. Figure 2.9 shows the difference between a high- and low-resolution image. Each screen is rectangular with the vertical dimension three-quarters of the horizontal so that each pixel is rectangular. This is the normal ratio for most TV screens and is known as the **aspect ratio**. The screen shown in Fig. 2.9(b) has four times the resolution of that shown in Fig. 2.9(a) but each has similar features displayed. The difference between high and low resolution is not very noticeable with lines near the horizontal or vertical. However, diagonal or curved lines on a low-resolution screen can be difficult to interpret if there are a large number of lines.

In practice the steps or **aliasing** (sometimes called **zig-zags** or **jaggies**) are not as severe as shown in the illustration because the intensity of the spot of light from the pixel causes light to diffuse from its centre to overlap with its neighbours.

On a simple graphics screen, the computer works out which pixel is crossed by the centre of a thick line and then puts a 1 into the refresh buffer for only that pixel to be illuminated. In a more expensive system, the stepping effect can be minimized by looking at the pixels adjacent to the centre of a thick line in a technique called **anti-aliasing**. This concept is shown in Fig. 2.10 where part of a thick line has crossed four pixels A, B, C, D. Pixel B is totally covered by the line and is fully lit. Pixel C is only one-third covered by the line and would, on a cheap graphics system, not be lit. An anti-aliasing technique would, however, illuminate pixel C but with an intensity only one-third that of B. Similarly A would have 80% of the intensity of B, while D has 10% intensity of B. The effect

Fig. 2.9 *Aliasing effects on high- and low-resolution screens.*

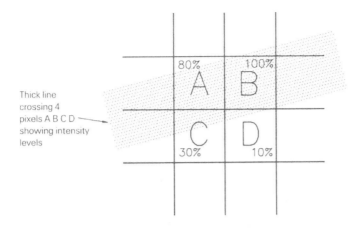

Thick line crossing 4 pixels A B C D showing intensity levels

Fig. 2.10 *An anti-aliasing technique.*

is that the edges of the line become diffused, lose their 'step' and are easier to interpret. However, the line also becomes less crisp. Anti-aliasing requires more memory and therefore requires more time and cost to generate a particular image. Each pixel would require several levels of intensity to be mapped, but the overall result is only one level of intensity for the line as a whole. Special anti-aliasing electronic hardware is being introduced to reduce costs, but at the present time it is still cheaper to minimize the step problem by opting for a high-resolution screen. Stroke generated screens have the added disadvantage that anti-aliasing requires a much larger number of pixels to be accessed, increasing the overall refresh time and promoting flicker.

2.5 INPUT SYSTEMS

In order to use the graphics programs which have been loaded into the computer from disk or magnetic tape, it is necessary to interact with the programs by inputting data on to the display screen. To get this information into the computer via the graphics display screen, some type of input device is needed.

On very simple graphics systems the computer keyboard is used by the operator to input data. Using a simple program, it is possible to draw a straight line between two points on the display screen. The *x* and *y* co-ordinates of each point can be specified by typing their values using the keyboard. This type of input system is slow and tedious for complex drawings and other, easier, methods are used to input data and commands on a professional CAD system. However, the ability to type co-ordinates on a keyboard, with whatever degree of precision is required, makes this a preferred method when a high degree of accuracy is necessary.

One of the most common input systems uses a menu of drawing commands as discussed in section 2.4.4. The advantage of this system is that it is possible to have a hierarchy of menus nested one inside the other. Thus selecting, for example the instruction 'draw' on one menu will automatically cause the next menu to be displayed containing a list of features to be drawn (lines, arcs, circles, etc.). Selecting one of these could then access another menu from which the type of line or its co-ordinates can be selected.

To select an instruction it is necessary to point to the menu command, typically by having some control over the x and y co-ordinates of a pointer or cursor. The cursor is often displayed as a flashing point or cross. To confirm that this is the desired location, a separate button must be pressed. The movement of the cursor can be controlled by the cursor-control keys on the keyboard, but again this method is slow and tedious. The other devices used to select the x and y co-ordinates of the cursor work from a continually varying electric signal (or analogue signal) which has to be converted inside the computer into a digital (binary) signal. This process is carried out by a piece of electronic hardware called an **analogue to digital converter** (A/D converter). The movement of the cursor on the display screen can be controlled by any one of the following devices.

2.5.1 JOYSTICK OR PADDLE

Essentially, a joystick consists of two electrical potentiometers, one controlling the x co-ordinate and the other the y co-ordinate, which position the cursor anywhere on the screen. A button on top of the joystick is used to confirm that this is the required point, whose co-ordinates are then entered into the computer.

2.5.2 THUMBWHEELS AND TRACKERBALL

Instead of a joystick it is possible to use two potentiometers, each controlled by a thumbwheel fixed mutually at right angles on the keyboard so that they protude slightly from the surface. Each thumbwheel controls respectively the x and y motions of the cursor. One of the keyboard buttons, usually the space-bar, is used to confirm the menu selection.

A variation of this device called a **trackerball** consists of a trapped ball with just the surface protuding. The ball drives a pair of potentiometers on the underside. This has the advantage that diagonal motions of the trackerball adjust the two potentiometers simultaneously, making it easier to use than thumbwheels.

2.5.3 MOUSE (Fig. 2.11)

This is a small block with a roller ball underneath which drives two potentiometers, placed mutually at right angles, to record the x and y motions of the mouse on the table. Wires from the mouse feed the signals to the computer. The mouse is free to move across the table in front of the user and does not have to be associated with any specific area on the table. The advantage of a mouse over a thumbwheel system is that, like the trackerball, diagonal movements

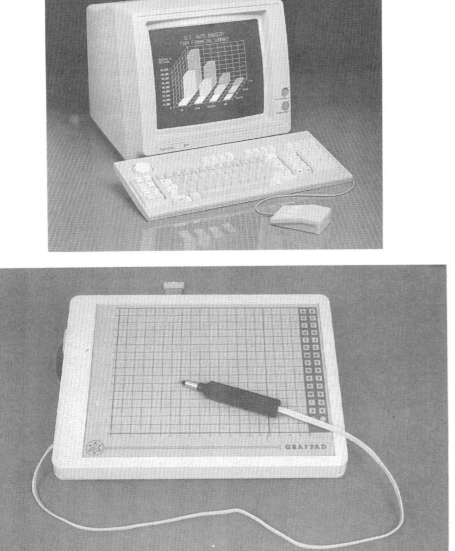

Fig. 2.11 *A graphics screen with mouse input system in foreground.*

Fig. 2.12 *A graphics tablet.*

of the mouse result in diagonal movements of the cursor on the screen. This is easier to control than driving the thumbwheel x and y potentiometers separately.

2.6 GRAPHICS TABLET SYSTEMS (Fig. 2.12)

The graphics tablet is a board that can be placed on the table in front of a display screen so that it acts as a mimic of the screen area. Selecting a position on the tablet provides a signal to the computer so that the cursor is driven to a corresponding position on the display screen. The advantage of this approach is that the tablet can have its whole surface covered with menu instructions while leaving the screen free for drawing pictures. The disadvantage of the tablet system is that you have to look down at the tablet and up at the screen alternatively and so it is easy to lose your place on the menu. Also, successive menus have to be overlaid by physically fixing separate menu sheets on to the tablet. The tablet's x and y co-ordinates are represented as analogue values and so an A/D converter is required. A variety of methods can be used to obtain the x and y locations on the tablet. The following sections represent some common systems.

2.6.1. PANTOGRAPH (Fig. 2.13)

This is like a small draughting machine with two jointed links, which is clamped to the tablet at one end and a pointer moved over the board at the other. Potentiometers clamped to the joints can be calibrated, using a simple trigonometric program in the computer, to give the x and y co-ordinates of the pointer in terms of the angles θ and ϕ. Pantograph systems need very precise potentiometers to obtain even average accuracy of the pointer and so are only used for cheaper CAD systems.

2.6.2 STYLUS AND PUCK (Fig. 2.14)

In this device the pen-like **stylus** is used to point at a location on the tablet. Wires are buried under the tablet surface and create a magnetic field that is sensed by a receiver built into the stylus. On quality systems it is possible to resolve positions to better that 100 μm. An additional switch on the stylus confirms the position. The **puck** is similar to the stylus but uses a magnifying glass for accuracy. A cheaper version of the tablet uses two wires looped back and forth

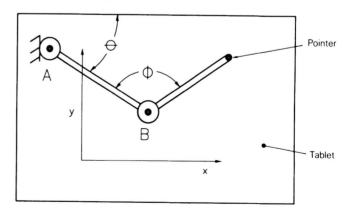

Fig. 2.13 *A pantograph.*

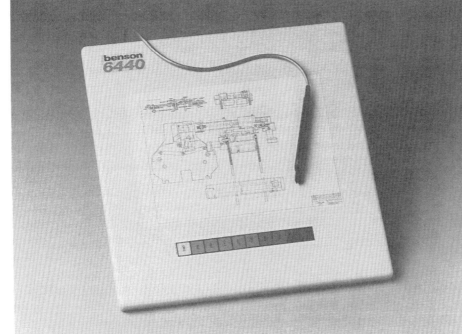

Fig. 2.14a *A stylus input device.*

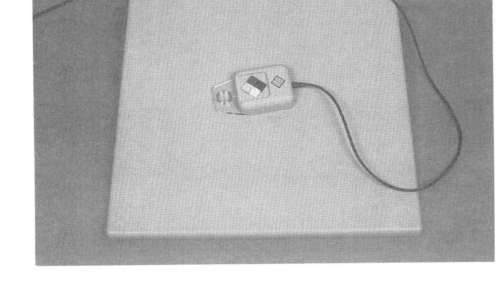

Fig. 2.14b *A puck input device.*

across the tablet surface so that they cross at right angles. The wires are held slightly apart by semi-conducting foil. Touching the tablet surface with an ordinary pen presses the two wires together, altering the resistance of each so that the contact point can be located approximately.

2.6.3 LIGHT PEN (Fig. 2.15)

This is a small pen-sized device with a light-sensitive diode at its tip. It is connected to the computer by a cable. If the pen is pointed at a glowing spot on the display screen, the diode can detect this and passes a signal to the computer. Since the beam refreshes at a constant rate, the time for the refresh beam to traverse from the screen origin to the light pen can be used to give the address of the pixels being indicated. In this way the selected feature can be identified. Similarly the pen can be used to point at a cursor so movement of the pen causes the cursor to be dragged with it and re-positioned. However, the speed at which the cursor can be dragged is limited by the refresh rate and the area scanned by the pen. Thus it is easy for the pen to lose track of the cursor. The illumination level of the screen and the angle at which the pen contacts the screen are both critical to successful use of the pen. Also, where two features are adjacent to each other, it is easy to pick the wrong one. For all these reasons, light pens are being replaced by the tablet as the preferred system for inputting data.

2.6.4 DIGITIZERS (Fig. 2.16)

The small tablet and stylus (or puck) detailed in section 2.6.2 can also be used to input data from existing drawings as well as the menu commands previously described. Because the x and y co-ordinates of a position on the tablet are captured using the stylus, the stylus can be used to trace over a drawing and input lines to the computer as a series of vectors stored in digital form. When used in this way the tablet is described as a **digitizing tablet**. Professional digitizers tend to be expensive large systems, capable of reading drawings up to

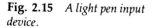

Fig. 2.15 *A light pen input device.*

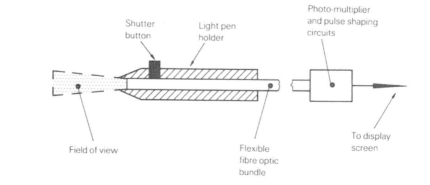

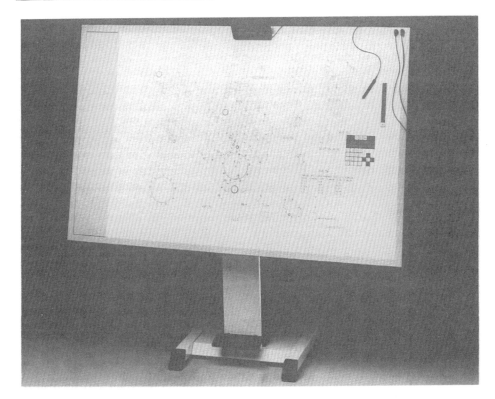

Fig. 2.16 *A digitizer.*

A0 size with great accuracy. To input data, a puck, consisting of a glass lens with cross hairs, is passed over the existing drawing by hand. Each time the cross hairs are positioned over a point, its co-ordinates can be stored in the computer by pressing a button alongside the cross hairs. Additional text and features such as arrowheads are added from a keyboard.

Using a digitizer in this manner to store existing drawings is a lengthy process requiring extensive checking to ensure that the computerized drawing is free of errors. The data held in the computer by digitizing will only be a record of the drawing and will not represent the geometry of the object. To provide a solid model from such data would require a very expensive system and considerable further user input to define the object geometry. For these reasons it is not thought worth while to input existing drawings into a CAD base, unless they are part of a product range that is expected to have a long life and require frequent modifications. Most companies are content to implement CAD only for their new products.

The introduction of automatic line-following systems, or **auto-vectorizers**, has helped to automate the process of digitizing. An auto-vectorizer employs a vision system which detects the contrast of ink lines on paper and will then automatically track along the line entering the points as it moves. Special software ensures that raster style data for each pixel is converted to a series of vectors while the drawing is being scanned. This results in much smaller memory storage. At this stage, the image will consist of a series of often wavy lines, representing vectors and text, together with the smudges and folds of the paper. To improve the quality and remove unwanted features, separate graphics **structuring software** is necessary. This enables the user to point to features which should be represented by straight lines and have them straightened automatically to their average line positions and entered into the computer as single vectors represented by their end points, instead of being entered as thousands of small vectors. Similarly the text and circular arcs can be regenerated from their vector representations and stored as separate hardware text characters or as **primitives** in which, for circles, only centres and radii are stored. Not only does this clean up the quality of text and arcs, but their representation by hardware as distinct entities or primitives requires a smaller memory than if stored as a large number of vectors. Even using such automatic digitizing techniques, however, digitizing of existing drawings remains a lengthy and costly process.

2.7 OUTPUT SYSTEMS

In addition to displaying drawings on a graphics screen, it is often necessary to have a permanent record or **hard copy** of a drawing. One form of hard copy is in the form of a photograph taken directly from the screen and either enlarged for display or miniaturized as a **microfiche** for filing as a record of the drawing. Microfiche filing, while useful for the storage of a large number of drawings in a small space, not only requires miniaturizing systems for producing the microfiches, but also requires special enlargers or viewing the drawings. Despite this microfiche is becoming a common form of record keeping in industry, not only of computer graphics, but also of conventionally produced engineering drawings.

The most common form of hard copy still remains ink on paper. A number of devices are available for transferring the data from a computer on to paper.

2.7.1 PRINTERS

The traditional method of producing hard copy from a computer is by using a printer. **Daisy-wheel** printers produce letter-quality output of a standard equivalent to the typewriter. The characters available with such a printer limit its use to text and symbolic output, and these printers are therefore of little use for CAD work. **Dot-matrix** printers are capable of quickly printing text and graphics hard copy. Because this type of printer prints in a series of dots, the resulting graphics will not be of as high a quality as hard copy from a plotter. The results are adequate for a reasonable representation of what is seen on the screen in a process known as a **screen dump**. In this process every pixel on the screen is mapped on to the printer by a binary 1 when a dot is printed, or as a 0 when a dot is blank. This pixel mapping technique is used by many other forms of printer, allowing both single-colour or multiple-colour hard-copy records of the screen image to be made.

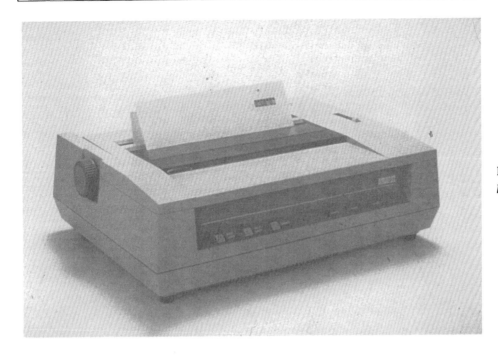

Fig. 2.17 *A dot matrix printer.*

Dot-matrix Printers (Fig. 2.17)

These are the most common type of printer, in particular for use on small CAD systems. The text quality is not as good as that obtained from a typewriter, but the print rate is considerably faster. Dot-matrix printers operate by impacting a character on to a carbon ribbon which in turn prints on the paper in the same way as that in which typewriters print. Unlike typewriters, however, which use a ready-formed letterpress print character, a dot-matrix printer sets up the appropriate characters as and when they are required. Typically, the printer head consists of a vertical row of nine pins which can move independently so that dots are printed as the head traverses the paper, to build up characters in much the same way as pixels on a raster screen. The appropriate pins forming the character are selected by the computer and pushed out by a number of tiny solenoids to strike the ribbon in the correct sequence as the head moves over the page. Typically, each character consists of a matrix of dots, seven high by eight wide. Because of the similarity between the dot-matrix and the screen pixels, the program for a graphics screen dump is relatively simple. A limited range of colours can be added by using a printer with a series of rapidly moving coloured ink ribbons, but such devices are expensive.

The quality of the text can be improved to that of a typewriter by printing each letter twice, with the dots offset by a fraction of a millimetre on the second pass. This blurs the crisp image of the dots slightly, but improves the overall quality of the print, so that it appears similar to that of a typewriter. This is known as **near letter quality** (NLQ).

Fig. 2.18 *An ink jet plotter with graphics screens.*

Ink-jet Printers (Fig. 2.18)

These are similar to dot-matrix printers except that each dot is formed from a tiny jet of ink squirted through a hole and not by striking through a ribbon. Since the printer head does not strike the paper, ink-jet printers are quieter than dot-matrix printers during printing. Differently coloured, fast-drying inks can be used. These come either in a liquid form or a solid form that is melted in the jet head. The blending together of different coloured dots gives a good range of colours. These printers are most suitable for recording images which use large patches of colour such as a shaded image of a solid model.

Electrostatic Printers

Electrostatic printers are fitted with an array of fine nibs that form electrostatically charged dots on the surface of the paper. Toner is placed on the charged surface and adheres to the dots to form the images. The image is then baked on by heating. Electrostatic printers can produce either monochrome or colour hard copy.

Thermal Printers

Thermal printers use either a laser or a hot dot device to transfer wax toner from a film on to the paper. Using a single black film allows monochrome images to be produced quickly. These thermal printers are suitable for a variety of hard-copy applications including screen dump. Using a series of coloured films gives a high-quality coloured image. Thermal printer output has a photographic quality once complete because the wax forms a glossy surface texture on the paper.

2.7.2 PLOTTERS

Small x, y plotters have been in use for a long time for drawing graphs, but plotters working to the same principles can be used for producing high-quality engineering drawings. Of all the hard-copy devices available, plotters produce the most accurate reproductions of computer drawings by using a direct pen-on-paper approach. All lines, arcs and text are reproduced by moving the pen across the surface of the paper. The information required to drive a plotter must be in a **vector** format, that is to say, the start and end positions of all lines, arcs and text must be defined in order for the pen to be moved across the paper. Different widths of pen and colours of inks may be inserted by the operator, or a group of pens may be held in a rack and be selected automatically when a different width or colour of line is required during the drawing process. Firmware routines for creating different line styles (e.g. solid, dashed, chain dashed or wavy) and different text fonts (e.g. standard, Roman or italic) ensure these features can be reproduced quickly and efficiently.

Flat-bed Plotters (Fig. 2.19)

With these plotters, the paper is held on a flat bed either by suction or by electrostatic attraction. An x motion is given to a vertical bar that moves the length of the bed. A pen moves on a separate carriage up and down the vertical bar to produce an independent y motion. By driving the two motions in this manner, the pen can reach any position on the paper fixed to the flat bed. The direct-current motors driving the plotter axes require analogue signals and thus

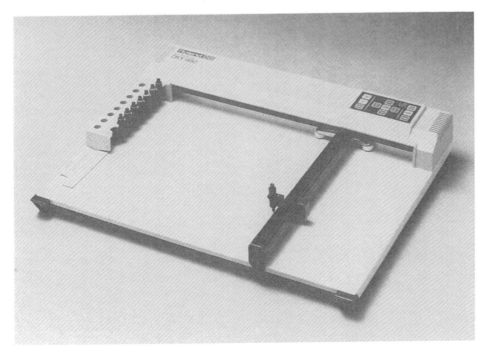

Fig. 2.19 *A flat bed plotter.*

a **digital-to-analogue** (D/A) converter is necessary to transform the digital signals from the computer to suit the analogue motors. The up and down motion of the pen is controlled by a solenoid determining when a line is to be drawn or a space is to occur. An alternative arrangement is to employ a stepper motor to drive the x and y motions, in which case a D/A converter is not necessary, because the computer digital signals can pulse the motors directly.

Large versions of x, y plotters of A0 size, but also up to E size, are used in industry for the production of quality engineering drawings, and have an accuracy of about 0.1 mm.

Drum Plotters (Fig. 2.20)

In this configuration, a pen moves backwards and forwards along a bar placed along the length of a drum to form the y motion. Paper is wound around the drum and the drum is rotated to give the x motion. Because the paper is wound around the drum, virtually unlimited lengths of drawings can be produced.

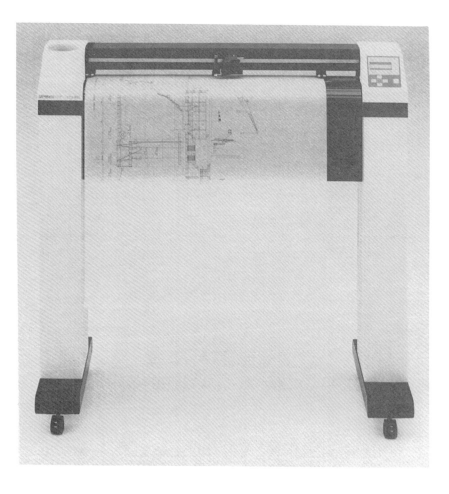

Fig. 2.20 *A drum plotter.*

Drum plotters occupy much less floor space than large flat-bed plotters, so they are more suitable where space in the room is limited.

NOTE

The need for hard copy of engineering drawings usually occurs at an interim stage in the implementation of CAD. In those industries where CAD/CAM is well advanced, with a sufficient number of graphics terminals in both the design office and factory, hard copy is not needed. This is because all the data required can be accessed directly from the computer system using the graphic displays. Some automotive manufacturers have announced the paperless factory in which all traditional drawing boards are replaced by graphics screens and all drawings in the factory are viewed on display screens. However, the implications of this approach are that small sub-contractors supplying components to the main company should also have their product drawings stored on CAD systems. This would not be a problem if the sub-contractors could afford to install a large CAD system similar to that installed in the main company to enable the two systems to communicate directly with each other. A series of internationally agreed standards are required for both hardware and software before such systems can intercommunicate. This is the reason why attempts are being made to formulate international graphics standards.

2.8 CHOOSING HARDWARE FOR CAD SYSTEMS

We have looked at individual pieces of hardware for CAD systems in some depth. However, we have considered each device in isolation, paying little attention to how they might be used together in a CAD system. As we have already mentioned, it is more usual for a CAD user to select appropriate software for his CAD activities before purchasing the computer hardware. However, both CAD software and hardware are being improved continually, and it is often difficult to predict what facilities may be offered either by the software suppliers or by the hardware manufacturers in the future. It is therefore important to choose computer hardware that has the flexibility to take advantage of the modifications made to the software or the advances made in hardware technology.

Industry standards for hardware enable devices such as display screens, printers, plotters, disk drives and computer processors to be readily interchanged with similar devices from other manufacturers. Theoretically, the CAD system vendor is therefore able to choose devices from a wide range of manufacturers knowing that they will operate successfully with the devices made by other manufacturers. This enables the CAD system to be built from hardware made by specialist manufacturers that includes state-of-the-art technology. In practice, however, each manufacturer offers a number of non-standard features peculiar to their own product, often specially designed to link with other devices in their own product range. Taking full advantage of these features may require all CAD hardware to be purchased from a single manufacturer. Device **emulation** is a popular way of achieving the performance of a superior product on a cheaper device. However, care is needed to ensure that all the required facilities have been successfully emulated. Alternatively, a **turnkey system** will come with both CAD software and hardware devices selected and integrated. In such systems, the software and hardware are often customized to take full advantage of the facilities offered by both.

2.8.1 HOW CAD SYSTEMS ARE CHANGING

Until the late 1970s, computer analysis programs were usually run on large computers which were excellent at performing a lot of computation in batches, but not very good at allowing a number of users to interact directly with their own programs in **real time**. Graphics facilities were generally limited to simple display screens which required a continual dialogue with the computer to process data. To display even simple objects, computer graphics require large amounts of data to be transferred back and forth between the computer and display screen. The display of complex graphics images was therefore slow, particularly if the central computer was also processing a large analysis program. As computer memory and electronic hardware get cheaper, some of the 'intelligence' for processing graphics images has been added to the graphics terminals to allow such features as hidden line removal and shading, both of which can be time consuming, to be performed quickly at the local terminal.

Fig. 2.21 *Tektronix intelligent graphics workstations.*

A central computer can host several graphics screens, each of which has additional hardware to speed up some of the display functions. When modelling complex objects and performing large analysis programs, for which many lengthy calculations are required, it is usual to submit the program to the computer to run in batch mode, often overnight. When a program is run in batch mode, it is in general not possible to modify it until the run is completed.

In the last few years, the process of transferring more and more computer power to the graphics terminal has culminated in the **intelligent workstation**, an example of which is shown in Fig. 2.21. This process has been brought about by the advent of cheaper miniaturized computing hardware which allows both the computer memory and the computer disk, which stores programs, to be sited alongside the graphics display screen to provide a self-contained CAD workstation. Several workstations can be linked, or **networked**, together to allow information to be interchanged between them. There is also the possibility of linking each workstation to a large computer which has a huge memory and central processing unit (CPU) for processing very large computer analysis programs.

2.8.2   AN OVERVIEW OF A TYPICAL CAD FACILITY

A typical configuration of a large-scale industrial CAD system is shown in Fig. 2.22. This shows a central computing facility linked to local workstations at which the CAD users would sit.

Fig. 2.22 *Typical large scale CAD facility.*

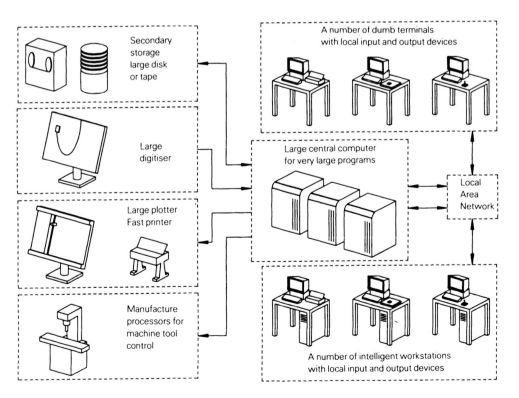

The central facility will have a very large central processing unit which can be used to process large programs. The large CPU may be a single mainframe computer or a number of minicomputers clustered together. The larger programs, and applications data, can be stored on a central fixed-head disk storage system which can quickly access a vast amount of stored information. Magnetic tape is also frequently used as an additional storage back-up in case of disk failure. Expensive output devices (e.g. plotters of A0 size) are connected to the large CPU and shared amongst the system users. These devices work in batch mode, producing drawings in turn as submitted by the users. In this way, the CPU controls the transmission of drawing information to the output device without impeding the user in his work of plotting drawings. Other expensive output devices like colour printers can be placed similarly. Expensive input devices like a digitizer which can be used to input information about the x and y co-ordinates of existing engineering drawings, maps or printed circuit layouts, would also be centrally located. The central facility will also provide the links to other areas of the factory (e.g. manufacturing workshops) or other computers in the organization.

The CAD workstations would be connected to the central facility using a network system. Dumb terminals can be linked directly to the central computer for interaction with programs being processed on this machine. These terminals may have both alphanumeric and graphics display capabilities, in which case CAD activity can be undertaken at these terminals. However, since the central facility is being shared with other users, the speed of processor response may be slow. This is undesirable in CAD work, because interaction with the computer is continuous and large amounts of information need to be exchanged. If large programs are to be processed centrally, then the number of system users must be restricted if a quick response is required continually. The computer also has associated with it a local storage facility in the form of a floppy disk or a Winchester hard disk, smaller and slower than the expensive central facility. The local computer has sufficient memory to run both the graphics programs and the applications programs. Using intelligent workstations, the CAD user has a computing facility dedicated to his work. Therefore, the speed of response is limited only by the quality of the local processor. Alternatively, the intelligent workstation contains a local computer and display screen. The intelligent workstation interacts with the central facility only when the use of centrally located devices is necessary. Each workstation has associated with it a number of devices which enable information to be input to the computer (e.g. tablet, mouse, joystick or light pen) and at least one local system which allows information to be output from the computer as hard copy (e.g. a small plotter and printer).

As we have already noted, graphics displays increasingly often have additional graphics processors consisting of a variety of electronic devices which speed up the display process. With local pan, zoom, hidden-line removal, surface shading, dynamic motion, and stereoscopic viewing facilities, the dumb terminal is no longer solely dependent upon the host computer to generate all its graphics information. Modern terminals with these local display features significantly reduce the amount of interaction required with the host computer during visualization exercises, releasing it to work more quickly on other users' work. There is currently some debate about whether the additional cost of local computing power is justified where terminals with local graphics facilities may suffice. Certainly where the workstation is being used for a diversity of computing tasks, it can be argued that a local computer may not be fully utilized at all times (e.g. during documentation preparation using a word processor). In these situations spare processor capacity cannot be accessed by other users, which can be done in a shared central facility. On the other hand, a shared computing facility must be organized so that the number of processes occurring at any one time does not adversely affect its response, especially for interactive graphics work.

The type of large-scale CAD system described here is very expensive and beyond the finances of many colleges and small firms. A central computer connected to three workstations, each of which has three display screens, would cost around £¾ million including CAD software. However, a more limited single workstation facility could be purchased for around £75 000, with a limited modelling and draughting package.

The type of simple CAD facility that can be found in many small firms and colleges is shown in Fig. 2.23. This is a small personal computer (PC) based system with a supplementary memory and keyboard. A medium-quality display screen and floppy disk drive are provided. This system can be enhanced by a

Fig. 2.23 *Personal computer based CAD system.*

tablet for inputting information and a screen for displaying numbers and characters. Such a system, together with software, could be provided for around £10 000 with small printer and plotter, but would have a very limited three-dimensional modelling capability. However, as the costs of both computer memory and displays fall, the capabilities of these small systems is rising to equal those provided by today's small intelligent workstation.

2.8.3　HARDWARE STANDARDS

The history of computer technology shows that particular manufacturers have developed hardware devices that have become standards for others to attain. For instance, when Tektronix invented the first direct-view storage display, their model 4010 and 4014 displays became industry standards for graphics terminals. During the 1970s, these models provided a measure of graphics display performance against which all other displays were compared. Importantly, software suppliers were able to adapt their software to take full advantage of the facilities offered by these displays. In order to use these programs a Tek 4010 series display, or equivalent, was needed. When the first raster scan displays were developed, they were designed to emulate the Tek 4010 devices so that they could replace them in a CAD system without modification to the existing software or hardware. In some cases the green on black display characteristic of the Tek 4010 devices was retained, even though other monochromic colour combinations were possible. The rise of the multi-colour raster scan display has led to other display models becoming industry standards. However, software suppliers are keen to support as wide a range of hardware devices as possible, and good quality CAD software will contain many **device drivers**, allowing the software to be operated using a variety of devices, including terminals, from different manufacturers. This approach is known as **open-architecture computing**.

Other terminal standards include Digital Equipment Corporation's VT52, VT100 and VT220 alphanumeric terminal types. These terminals offer an on-screen file-editing facility for which the keyboard is defined with standard file-editing functions.

In a similar vein, the IBM-PC and its XT and AT variants have become industry standards for personal computing. This computer has become the measure of performance, all other personal computers claiming IBM compatability. Using the ubiquitous MS-DOS operating system software (see Chapter 3), IBM's rival companies have produced personal computers that are able to operate all the software developed for the original IBM-PC range. The colour graphics capability of these machines can be enhanced using standard graphics adaptors, e.g. VGA (video graphics array) and EGA (enhanced graphics adaptor) standards (Fig. 2.24), and with additional electronic devices (e.g. a maths co-processor or extended RAM memory) these computers become very powerful CAD tools. However, care must be taken to ensure that the most appropriate screen, graphics cards and co-processors are selected for the intended CAD software system. On a more fundamental level, the performance of the personal computer is highly dependent upon the make and model of its

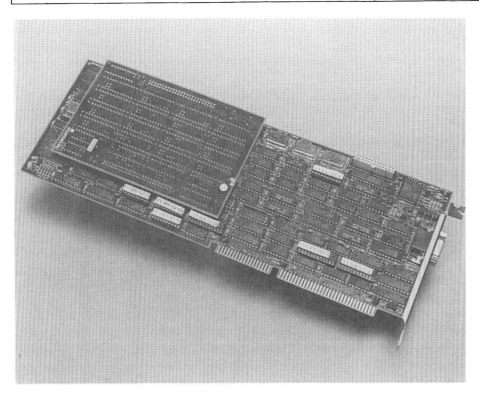

microprocessor where the number of variants is much smaller. Many current PC-based CAD systems use the 16-bit Intel 80286 microprocessor to ensure compatability with IBM-PC products, while the 32-bit Intel 80386 microprocessor is common in first level entry intelligent work stations.

Fig. 2.24 Advanced graphics adaptor board.

The exchange of data between devices must be completed without the receiving device corrupting any of the information sent by the sending device. To ensure that devices are correctly interfaced and that data is completely understood by sending and receiving devices, various protocols for interfacing hardware have been established. A popular interface between the computer and the terminal is RS232. This connection sends information in a **serial** format at a controlled transfer speed known as **baud rate** (bits per second). Both devices must be set up to receive and send signals at the same baud rate, otherwise the information will be misinterpreted on reception. Serial transfer can be slow (e.g. 9600 baud), which is especially tedious in CAD applications where a graphics image may consist of several hundred kbytes of information.

Parallel interfaces allow information to be exchanged simultaneously via a number of connection lines. Centronics interfaces are usually used for printer connections, enabling data to be transferred at up to 30 000 bytes per second. Where data transfer rates are high, data is usually stored in a **buffer memory** to allow the exchange to be completed as quickly as possible. Data stored in the buffer memory will be processed gradually by the host device, while the sending device is free to continue with other CAD activities.

Exchange of data between computers and other hardware devices can occur at very high rates using a **local area network** (LAN). In a LAN, a group of workstations may use a common **file server** to communicate with each other or other devices connected to the system. A LAN would be used in the CAD system considered earlier, to connect the workstations to the central facility. An important feature of a LAN is that each device has a unique hardware address which prevents data for that device interacting with data from another. A LAN also controls access to a device, preventing data being transmitted if the receiving device is busy. Ethernet is a well-established industry local area network standard supported by many hardware manufacturers. A **wide area network** (WAN) would be used to communicate between different CAD systems where the exchange of data is less frequent and where distances are generally larger.

Industry standards in hardware allow the CAD user to use different manufacturers' products to build up a CAD system. These standards have generally evolved because of a single manufacturer establishing a worthy hardware solution to a particular problem and establishing a market lead in that technology. The product becomes a *de facto* standard because other manufacturers recognize the worthiness of the solution and design their own products to interact with it or to operate using the same basic principles. Unfortunately, choosing an emulation of a *de facto* hardware standard cannot guarantee that the copy will operate in exactly the same way as the original product. However, the establishment of further hardware standards will help ensure that open architecture computing can be truly achieved.

EXERCISES

1. How are instructions, numbers and characters stored in the CPU? How does the CPU distinguish numbers from characters or instructions?
2. Why is it that although simple computer draughting systems have a small CPU memory and eight-bit word structure, for larger CAD systems considerable memory and a 32-bit word structure are usually necessary?
3. Some CPU memory is volatile and some non-volatile. Discuss the differences between these memory types, and identify what sort of information would be stored in each.
4. What are the functions of secondary storage systems for CAD? Distinguish between their relative merits.
5. A small company wishes to purchase a number of raster displays for computer draughting and solid modelling. Discuss the benefits of using colour or monochrome displays and high- and low-resolution screens.
6. A raster scan monochrome 256×256 display is to be used for CAD. An image is to be displayed in which the central four pixels are turned *on*. These are surrounded by a band, two pixels wide, which is *off*. These in turn are surrounded by a further band, two pixels wide, which is turned *on*.
   (a) Sketch the frame buffer for such a display indicating the bit pattern in the central region.
   (b) How many bytes are needed for such a display?
7. The screen in Exercise 6 is now a colour display in which four bits per pixel

are used for addressing a colour map having nine bits per address. In addition there are two bit planes used for animation.

(a) Sketch the arrangement of frame buffer, colour maps and screen.

(b) How many shades of colour can be represented on the screen?

(c) Calculate the new memory requirements for the display.

8. Discuss the relative merits of raster scan, line drawing refresh and storage tube displays.

9. A series of concentric circles, each represented by 32 facets is to be displayed on a vector refresh display. If the average time per vector is 30 microseconds, how many flicker-free circles can be displayed?

10. A 128×128 raster display has a line one pixel wide drawn diagonally across the centre of the screen at 30° to the horizontal.

(a) Show the aliasing effect on the screen's central 16 pixels.

(b) If the anti-aliasing techniques were used, indicate the percentage brightness for the central 16 pixels.

(c) If the brightness level, including on and off were controlled by only two bits, draw the new anti-aliased screen image.

11. What local graphics features distinguishes a dynamic display from a dumb display? What advantages do these local graphics features offer in CAD applications?

12. Contrast the uses of a mouse on its own with that of a mouse used with a tablet. Why is a mouse superior to a pair of thumbwheels on a keyboard for most applications? When are the thumbwheels preferable?

13. Why do most input systems have at least one switch associated with them?

14. Why are companies generally not digitizing their existing drawings on paper?

15. Auto-vectorizers generally store primitives and their attributes rather than digitized vectors. Why is this?

16. A small company with a cheaper CAD installation may well use an ink-jet printer as a screen dump, rather than say, a drawing plotter. Why is this? What disadvantages would it have compared with a drawing plotter?

17. Why is it that plotters and printers are likely to disappear from use in the long term? What problems must first be overcome?

18. It is proposed to purchase a large central computer, together with a number of dumb graphics terminals for the full range of CAD activity. Discuss the advantages and disadvantages of this type of system.

19. A CAD system comprises a number of intelligent work stations linked to a large central computer as shown in Fig. 2.22.

(a) Distinguish between the role of the CPU in the central computer from that of the intelligent workstations

(b) Contrast the role of the central magnetic tape facility with that of the workstation's floppy disks.

20. Discuss the merits of open architecture computing. Why are industry standards for hardware required if this approach to CAD system design is to be successful?

3

Computer graphics software

3.1 AN INTRODUCTION TO BASIC ASPECTS OF PROGRAMMING

Before discussing concepts specifically concerned with graphics software and how graphics programs operate, it is necessary to consider some of the more general concepts involved in all computer programming. Thus some preliminary information is included on operating systems, languages and filing systems with a level of detail that will be helpful to graphics users.

3.1.1 OPERATING SYSTEMS

The operating system is the software link between the computer hardware and software. Without operating system software, a computer system would merely be a collection of electronic devices without purpose and unable to function. The operating system manages the flow of information between the various system devices, providing the user with a communications link to the computer system, organizing the storage of data on secondary storage media, organizing the retrieval of data, and facilitating the operation of applications software on the system. Without the correct operating system for a particular machine, the computer would not even load its own programs when first switched on. The operating system provides the utilities essential for the full exploitation of the computer hardware by the user and the applications software.

The operating system provides a command language which allows the computer to be instructed to perform many tasks. As a CAD user, the applications software you use will usually provide all the necessary commands satisfactorily to operate the computer system, so only a rudimentary knowledge of the operating system command language would be required. However, this knowledge should include the commands for organizing and storing applications software and data in files on disk. A file is a group of related data or information that is identified by a unique filename. Typically, a CAD system operator should fully understand the operating system commands for the following tasks:

1. running applications software;
2. creating a file;
3. copying a file;

4. deleting a file;
5. renaming a file;
6. finding the size of a file;
7. listing the directory of files;
8. listing a file;
9. printing a file.

The number of operating system commands you understand and use will depend upon the way you wish to operate the computer system and your role as a computer operator.

Historically, operating system software has been developed for a specific computer. This approach creates a number of problems when data created and stored on one computer needs to be transferred to a second computer with a different operating system. One way of overcoming this problem, is to reorganize the data into a format understood by both computers. However, if the two computers used the same operating system, transfer can take place immediately. Thus computers using the same operating system can interchange information quickly and simply. Standardization of operating system software has meant that CAD computer systems now operate using one, or more, of a limited number of standard operating systems. If a computer system uses an industry standard operating system, (e.g. MS-DOS or UNIX) it will behave in exactly the same way as another system using the same operating system. This allows programs to operate on a variety of computer systems without modification, and data and information can easily be transferred between different CAD facilities. A user who is familiar with a particular operating system will be able to operate any computer system using the same operating system, irrespective of the equipment being used. Often, though, computer manufacturers provide additional operating system commands and facilities that exploit the particular characteristics of their own computer system. These non-standard utilities are often unavailable on other manufacturers' equipment, and if information is to be transferred between different systems, their use must be avoided, otherwise the organization (or **format**) of the file will be altered.

Traditionally, operating system commands are entered using a rigourously defined command sequence (**syntax**). Each command requires specific information to be entered via the keyboard in a particular order. It is very easy to make mistakes while entering commands in this way. A typing mistake may invalidate the command, requiring the whole sequence to be re-entered. A syntax error may execute an unwanted operation, which may have a significantly different result than the one intended. The typed input nature of these commands can become very tedious during lengthy file management exercises, and the user becomes more prone to error as he tires. Newer operating systems (e.g. X-Windows) exploit **WIMP** (window, icon, mouse, pop-down menus) techniques to minimize the amount of information entered via the keyboard. Here, commands are represented by small graphics pictures (icons) which can be selected using the cursor, mouse or similar. Once a particular icon has been selected, additional information is supplied in sequence in response to prompts from the operating system. Where a selection has to be made from a list, a menu of options will be displayed temporarily (or popped down) until a choice is made. In this way, the user may carry out file management tasks using a minimal amount of typed input, thereby minimizing the likelihood of typing or syntax errors. The operating system icons and menus are displayed as graphic images in discrete areas of the screen (windows). In this way only the window area has to be redrawn when information needs to be updated. A graphics display device is essential for this type of operating system.

MS-DOS

Microsoft Disk Operating System (MS-DOS) is currently the industry standard operating system for the personal computer (PC). It is almost identical to the DOS operating system used by IBM for their range of PCs. The computers that use MS-DOS are often called IBM 'clones' because they operate in the same way as the IBM-PC. Using MS-DOS enables programs suitable for use on the IBM-PC to be run on any IBM-PC compatible personal computer.

The operating system software is supplied on a disk and must be loaded into the computer memory each time it is switched on. If the computer has a hard disk, it is usual practice to copy the operating software on to the hard disk, so that the software is automatically loaded when the computer is switched on, a process known as 'boot-up'. When the software has been fully installed, the operating system prompt will appear on the screen. The usual MS-DOS prompt is 'A>' which informs you that the computer is waiting to receive an operating system command. There are two types of MS-DOS command, **internal** and **external**. Internal commands, e.g. DIRectory, COPY, ERASE, RENAME, TYPE, can be carried out immediately because these commands have already been loaded into computer memory during boot-up. External commands (e.g. FORMAT, DISKCOPY, COMPile, DISKCOMPile, SELECT) need the MS-DOS disk to be placed in the disk drive before they can be carried out. The operating system software for external commands is read from the MS-DOS disk as and when it is required.

The A> prompt also informs you that the **default disk drive** is drive A. This means that any disk drive operation (e.g. load a file) will be carried out on drive A, unless otherwise indicated. The default drive can be set by typed instruction to other disk drives, e.g. drive B, the second disk drive, or drive C, the hard disk. MS-DOS also provides a facility to use part of the computer memory as if it were a disk drive, known as a **virtual disk**. Using computer memory to simulate a disk drive allows fast access to the information stored in the virtual disk. However, when the computer is switched off, all the information will be lost. More than one virtual disk can be created, the size of each being specified by the user, and they may be assigned **drive specifiers** such as C (if a hard disk is not fitted), D, E or F.

The way information is stored in a file and how files are organized on disk are controlled by the MS-DOS operating software. Information is stored on disk in files. Each file is identified by a unique filename which can be up to eight characters in length. Each file will have a **file extension**, which helps to identify what sort of information is stored in the file, and a drive specifier, which specifies which disk the file is stored on. The drive specifier is optional, and if omitted, MS-DOS assumes the file to be on the default drive. Each disk will have a **directory** which lists all the files stored on the disk. The directory also maintains a record of the position of each file on the disk. Therefore, the read head (see Chapter 2) can move directly to the track and sector location of a single file without searching from the start of the disk. A disk can be split into a number of sub-directories, enabling the user to organize the file space in an ordered manner, separating different file types into different sub-directories if necessary. The amount of space available on a disk depends upon the floppy disk used and the way it is formatted. A single-sided, single-density disk can store up to 180 Kb of information, whereas a double-sided, high-density disk will be able to store up to 1.44 Mb of information. Since MS-DOS uses a well-defined file-storage format, the floppy disk can be used in any MS-DOS based computer system. Information can readily be transferred between computer systems simply by exchanging copies of files on floppy disk, provided the disk format is compatible with the type of drive fitted in the computer.

MS-DOS also provides a **line editor** which allows the user to modify text files. The line editor is used for creating program listings and data files, or for amending information in existing files. A large number of editing facilities are provided which enables text changes to be made very quickly.

UNIX

UNIX operating system software differs from MS-DOS in many ways, but its most notable difference is its 'multi-tasking' capability, enabling computers that operate UNIX to perform several tasks at once. UNIX also has a 'multi-user' capability, allowing more than one user to use the computer system at the same time. With these features, UNIX enables a number of different applications programs to be operated at the same time by a number of users. This is important for CAD activities where groups of people will need to use the same information at the same time, or where expensive computing facilities need to be used for a variety of tasks. UNIX is particularly popular amongst CAD users with 32-bit computers, and is fast becoming the accepted industry standard for these types of computer because of its suitability for CAE applications.

UNIX software consists of three distinct parts: the **kernel**; the **file system**; and the **shell**. The kernel is the part of the operating system that manages the system hardware, organizing the exchange of information between the various peripheral devices. Its operation is invisible to the user. The file system defines the structure of information and data stored on the computer system, organizing how the files are stored on disk. Files are arranged in directories, which can be divided into sub-directories any number of times. This hierarchical filing facility allows the user to organize the file space in a convenient and controlled way specific to his own needs. The shell provides the user interface to the operating system software and acts as the command interpreter, translating user commands into operating system actions. The shell is the most visible part of UNIX to the system user, and in some cases, has been adapted to interpret MS-

DOS commands into UNIX commands, though the conversion of commands to UNIX equivalents slows its speed of operation. However, such a shell would allow a user to type in familiar MS-DOS commands and yet be able to utilize all the facilities of an UNIX system.

To use a computer operating UNIX, you will require a username. The username is needed for 'signing on' to the computer system, a process also known as logging in or logging on. This is because UNIX is structured to allow several users to have access to the same piece of software and only permitted users can progress. A terminal that is ready for use will display the UNIX prompt 'login:'. Typing your username will start the signing on process. To complete the signing on process, you will be required to type a password. The password is a set of characters only known to you and is provided to prevent other people using your username account. As an added measure of security, the password is not displayed on the screen as it is being typed. Once signed on to the computer system a whole variety of tasks can be undertaken, but once complete you should always 'sign off' (or 'log out' or 'log off'), e.g. by typing 'CTRL D'.

Amongst its set of operating system commands, UNIX has various utilities for manipulating text files, printing text, creating documents, and developing applications software using programming languages. UNIX also has a number of utilities for finding out what the computer system is doing, or who is using it. These are provided to ensure that the computer system is being operated effectively at all times. A **mail** facility allows messages to be sent to and received from other users on the system.

UNIX was originally devised by AT&T Bell Laboratories over twenty years ago, and has since been developed by several different manufacturers. As a result of this diversified development history, there are currently some twenty versions of the UNIX operating system software. The need to unify to a single industry standard is recognized by the computer industry and the International Standards Organization (ISO).

3.2 LANGUAGES

As discussed in Chapter 2, a program (or algorithm) is a sequence of instructions which are carried out sequentially by the computer hardware. Chapter 2 also explained how the computer memory consists of a series of binary bits which are programmed to be either ON or OFF. Bits are combined together in groups to form instructions called a **machine code**. A machine code numbering system can present difficulties to the newcomer because it is based not on a decimal notation (i.e. to the base 10), but on a hexadecimal notation (i.e. to the base 16). A hexadecimal notation is used because it is convenient to store numbers in groups of four binary bits (e.g. 1111) which can represent 16 numbers from 0 to 15. The 16 numbers of the hexadecimal system are represented from 0 to 9, then the letters A, B, C, D, E and F represent 10 to 15. In order to ensure that everyone knows that a hexadecimal system is being employed, a prefix or suffix is used with the number. A number of alternatives are used. In the Acorn BBC micro, a prefix & is used, i.e. &A24 represents in hexadecimal, the decimal number:

$$10(16)^2 + 2(16)^1 + 4(16)^0 = 2560 + 32 + 4 = 2596.$$

Other commonly used hexadecimal formats for the number A24 are \$A24; A24H; $A24_{16}$.

If a complex program were written as a series of instructions in machine code, it would be carried out very speedily and efficiently by the computer. This is because machine code is based in binary bits and the computer works on binary bits. However, the overall program would be very lengthy to write and would be difficult to understand. The next highest level of coding in which it is possible to write long programs is in a language called **assembler**. Assembler programs also run in the computer speedily and efficiently. Assembler statements consist of instructions such as LDA#2 (load a temporary memory store or **accumulator** with the number 2); STA &1FF (take the contents of the accumulator and store them in a memory address whose location is hex1FF). From assembler programs both instructions and data can automatically be translated or **compiled** by the computer into the hexadecimal machine code form. The assembler program is known as the **source code**, while the compiled form is called the **object code**. Although assembler is very efficient, it is still cumbersome to write and to understand and is known as a **low-level language**.

For complex programs it is usual to write in a **high-level language**. The language called BASIC (beginner's all-purpose symbolic instruction code) is one of the most easily understood high-level languages because it contains a number of English-style statements. It is frequently used in schools and colleges for the more simple types of computer graphics. The following illustrates a simple BASIC program for drawing a square.

```
 10 REM. PROG 1. THIS PROGRAM DRAWS A SQUARE
 20 X=200
 30 Y=250
 40 L=50
 50 MOVE X, Y
 60 DRAW X, Y+L
 70 DRAW X+L, Y+L
 80 DRAW X+L, Y
 90 DRAW X, Y
100 END
```

Each line of the program is numbered. The REM statement is not acted upon. It is a remark to aid the understanding of the program. Lines 20 to 40 provide the data for the program, with lines 20 and 30 stating the x and y co-ordinates, referred to the screen origin in absolute co-ordinates. Line 40 states the required length of the sides of the square. The 'MOVE' command moves the cursor to a location without making a mark, whilst the 'DRAW' command makes a mark on the screen from the current location to a new location given by the co-ordinates following the draw command. Thus line 50 moves the cursor to the start point for drawing the square. Lines 60 to 90 draw the square of side length L in a clockwise direction, starting with the vertical line. Line 100 ends the program.

Typing RUN into the computer keyboard would result in the BASIC program

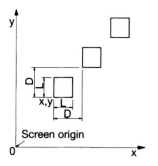

Fig. 3.1 *Three squares resulting from Program 2, drawn together with axes and dimensions.*

being compiled into object code while running and the square would then be drawn on the display screen. To modify the size of the square, it would only be necessary to change L in line 40. The square could be positioned anywhere on the screen by changing the values of *x* and *y* in lines 20 and 30. The strength of BASIC is that it is easy to use, e.g. to set up conditional logic statements using commands such as IF . . . THEN . . ., this instruction could allow the sequence of commands being executed to branch off into a side loop until a particular condition is met, when the program could once again continue its sequence. The effect of introducing conditional logic can be seen in an amplification of the previous program for drawing a square to one in which three squares are drawn offset from the first as shown in Fig. 3.1. The BASIC program is as follows.

```
10 REM. PROG 2. THIS PROGRAM DRAWS 3 SQUARES
20 X=200
30 Y=250
40 L=50
50 D=100
60 N=3
70 C=1
80 MOVE X, Y
90 DRAW X, Y+L
100 DRAW X+L, Y+L
110 DRAW X+L, Y
120 DRAW X, Y
130 IF C=N THEN END
140 C=C+1
150 X=X+D
160 Y=Y+D
170 GOTO 80
180 END
```

Program 2 uses program 1 to draw the square as before but, in addition, uses a count 'C' which is initially set to 1 in line 70. Having drawn the square in lines 80 to 120 , line 130 then checks the count to see if C=N (i.e. 3). If it does then the program ends. If it does not, then line 140 is carried out and the count C is incremented by 1. The values of X and Y are then incremented by a displacement value D before the program returns to line 80 to draw a new square. This process is then repeated a third time, so that now C=N and hence in line 130 the program ends.

The structure of program 2 is now rather awkward and could be tidied up to become easier to follow. Because program 2 uses the simple routine of program 1 to draw a square over and over again, it would be easier if we called program 1 as a separate **procedure**. The Acorn BBC microcomputer is an example of a system which has a powerful procedure routine. Program 3 shows how program 2 would appear on an Acorn BBC micro using a procedure called PROC-SQUARE to draw the square which can be separately defined at lines 90 to 150. The use of the procedure makes the program easier to follow. Because program 3 is designed for use on an Acorn BBC micro, the resolution and colours available on the screen must first be defined by line 15. Mode 1 defines a particular graphics screen mode in which the screen has a resolution of 320 pixels horizontally by 256 vertically and four colours are available for each pixel. If programs 1 and 2 are also to be run on the Acorn BBC micro, then the programs will each require the insertion of an additional line: 15 MODE 1.

```
10    REM. PROG 3. USING PROCEDURES
15    MODE 1
20    X=200: Y=250: L=50: D=100: N=3
30    FOR C=1 TO N
40    PROCSQUARE
50    X=X+D
60    Y=Y+D
70    NEXT C
80    END
90    DEF PROCSQUARE
100   MOVE X, Y
110   DRAW X, Y+L
120   DRAW X+L, Y+L
130   DRAW X+L, Y
140   DRAW X, Y
150   ENDPROC
```

Line 20 gives a string of data. Lines 30 and 70 control the number of repetitions of drawing the square. Line 40 calls for a specific procedure called PROCSQUARE which is defined in lines 90 to 150.

While BASIC, like other high-level languages, is easy to write and understand, it is quite slow to run because the compiled version will usually contain a large number of redundant statements. If it is necessary for small sections of the program to run quickly, e.g. for a dynamic display, then it is quite usual to have that section written in assembler code and called up from the main BASIC program.

Another popular high level language called FORTRAN is slightly further removed from everyday English than is BASIC. However, it is much more suitable for calculating mathematical formulae. Since complex drawings involve many calculations, a large number of the professional CAD systems were programmed in FORTRAN. FORTRAN statements do not require line numbers and are thus easily distinguished from BASIC. FORTRAN source statements must be compiled into object code as a separate activity prior to running the program. This makes editing the program into its final form a little more tedious but improves the time required for the computer to execute the program.

Unlike BASIC, FORTRAN does not have graphics commands like MOVE and DRAW as part of its programming language. To generate graphics output using FORTRAN requires the use of a **library** of special pre-defined graphical routines. These are discrete FORTRAN programs similar in their use to the BASIC procedures already considered. These discrete FORTRAN programs are known as subroutines. These can be linked to the object code of a FORTRAN program when the program is being compiled into its machine code form. Subroutines are invoked using a CALL statement in the main program, and the values of any variables in the subroutines are defined by the values of the **arguments** in the call statement. Some manufacturers display devices (e.g. Tektronix) can be used directly from a FORTRAN program using the manufacturers own graphical routines (e.g. PLOT 10). Another popular library of graphical routines is GINO-F, devised and developed by CADCentre Limited. GINO-F routines, which are discussed in more detail later in this chapter, are device independent, that is to say they are suitable for any computer or graphical output device. However, the output device must be defined at the start of the program. The following is a simple FORTRAN program for drawing three squares which illustrates the use of GINO-F routines in a FORTRAN program.

```
C PROG 4. FORTRAN PROGRAM TO DRAW 3 SQUARES
      X=200
      Y=250
      L=50
      D=100
      N=3
      I=1
      CALL GINO
      CALL 4014
      CALL WINDOW (2)
      CALL MOVTO2 (X, Y)
      CALL LINTO2 (X, Y+L)
      CALL LINTO2 (X+L, Y+L)
      CALL LINTO2 (X+L, Y)
      CALL LINTO2 (X, Y)
      IF (I. EQ. N) THEN
         CALL GINEND
      ELSE
         I+I+1
         X=X+D
         Y=Y+D
         GOTO 1
      END IF
      STOP
      END
```

Program 4 is essentially a FORTRAN equivalent of program 2, but using a count 'I' and the conditional statements IF . . . THEN . . . ELSE . . . END IF. The CALL statements all invoke GINO-F subroutines which are external to the program. The first three GINO-F CALL subroutines initialize a two-dimensional graphics workspace, organizing the graphics output for a Tektronix 4014 display. The MOVTO2 and LINTO2 subroutines are for moving to, and drawing, a straight line to the x, y co-ordinates specified in the call arguments. The IF . . . THEN . . . statement checks to see if all three squares have been drawn. If not, then the ELSE statement is used to increment the counter and move to the next square before repeating the sequence from statement 1. Once the three squares have been drawn, the GINEND subroutine terminates the graphics activity.

Subroutines can also be defined internally, which allows a more elegant program structure to be created. The following FORTRAN program uses both internal and external subroutines, and presents an improved version of program 4.

```
C PROG 5. FORTRAN PROGRAM TO DRAW 3 SQUARES
C USING AN INTERNAL SUBROUTINE
      DATA X, Y, L, D, N, I/200, 250, 50, 100, 3, 1/
      CALL GINO
      CALL 4014
      CALL WINDOW (2)
      DO 1 I=1, N
        CALL SQUARE (X, Y, L)
        X=X+D
        Y=Y+D
      END DO
      CALL GINEND
      STOP
      END
C SUBROUTINE FOR DRAWING A SQUARE
      SUBROUTINE SQUARE (X, Y, L)
      CALL MOVTO2 (X, Y)
      CALL LINTO2 (X, Y+L)
      CALL LINTO2 (X+L, Y+L)
      CALL LINTO2 (X+L, Y)
      CALL LINTO2 (X, Y)
      RETURN
      END
```

Here the subroutine SQUARE draws a single square whose size and position is defined by the arguments X, Y and L. The DO loop in the main program controls the number of repetitions of this drawing subroutine.

Program 5 is similar to program 3 in its structure, and shows just some of the differences between BASIC and FORTRAN. The syntax of each language is different, but the programmer's approach to creating simple graphics programs is similar. The use of procedures and subroutines enables complex programs to be compiled from a series of tried and tested routines linked by calls from the main program, each routine being developed in isolation and available for use in other graphics programs. The GINO-F graphics routines allow the FORTRAN programmer to use computer graphics in his own programs, without having to devise the drawing routines himself.

Other high level languages which are becoming popular for complex graphics programs are called C and PASCAL. These have a highly structured approach which is well suited to graphics programming because there are often a number of **nested** routines which are placed one inside another and have many different **branch** and **return** loops. The structure which is imposed by these languages makes it less likely that the programmer will have a loop return to the wrong location. This could be a condition which would not show up for some time until, when the particular branch is called, the program fails to do what was intended, often with disconcerting results whose cause can be difficult to locate and remedy.

3.3 FILING SYSTEMS

Because graphics software is lengthy, particularly when the applications data is also included, it is often necessary to have sections of programs repeatedly transferred from disk into the computer memory and then back to the disk again. Indeed, in smaller microcomputer-based systems, a different floppy disk is used to hold each part of the program. The following separate files are used in many smaller graphics systems.

3.3.1 GRAPHICS SYSTEM SOFTWARE

This file will contain most of the standard software required to prepare a particular drawing and will include routines for drawing lines, arcs, circles, etc., in different colours and line types, to a variety of scales, etc. This is usually loaded into the computer memory. The additional software that is required is in the form of a read-only memory (ROM) chip. This is a dedicated microchip which will allow those routines which are used most frequently to run much more quickly than if they were programmed in software.

3.3.2 THE WORKING FILE

In order to build up a picture of a drawing, it is necessary to use the graphics system software to create a series of lines which are stored in a working file (or **work page**) which is held in the computer memory. By referring to a series of menu commands, it is possible to move the cursor around the work page on the screen, draw lines of several types and colours, delete any part of the drawing, etc., in order to build up the final version of your drawing on the work page.

3.3.3 LIBRARY FILES

Having created the required drawings, it is possible to store them on a separate disk called a library file. Most small CAD systems allow the user to store a number of pictures in separate library files. In this way a series of simple drawings can be filed separately and then called up to be combined to form a more complex drawing on the work page, which can in turn be filed in the library. In this way drawings of considerable complexity can gradually be built up. It is usually possible to display the library files as pictures on the display screen because they are stored in the file as scaled down images. This allows the user to identify quickly the various files without having to remember what name they are filed under. Having finally completed a drawing, it is possible to then store it on a separate **archive disk** which is used only for finished drawings.

3.3.4 A BUFFER DISK

During the process of producing the finalized drawing of a work page, particularly on the smaller micro-based CAD systems, occasions will arise when the computer memory is too small to contain both the full system software and the work page contents. In this instance a **buffer disk** is employed as a temporary storage to swop programs backwards and forwards as a drawing is being compiled.

3.4 GENERATING BASIC GRAPHICAL ELEMENTS

3.4.1 STRAIGHT LINES

As shown in program 1, a line from (x_1, y_1) to (x_2, y_2) can be drawn on a microcomputer-based system using an instruction such as DRAW X_1, Y_1, X_2, Y_2. We have seen, however, in Chapter 2 that by using either raster scan or refresh display, the computer must generate a series of points between the two ends of the line corresponding to each pixel that needs to be turned on. Thus an additional series of calculations is required to find all the appropriate pixels that must be lit between the two ends of the line. There are a number of methods of doing this, all based on the definition of a line.

The general definition of a line in 2-D space is

$$ay = bx + c.$$

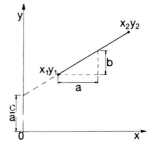

Fig. 3.2 *General definition of the line* ay = bx + c.

In the graph (Fig. 3.2) b/a is the tangent of the angle made by the line with the positive x-axis and c/a is the constant value of the y intercept at which the line crosses the y-axis. Making use of this equation, it would be possible to increment in the x direction by Δx, a pixel at a time and calculate the corresponding increment in Δy in the y direction. However, because the slope b/a becomes very large as the line moves towards the vertical, computational accuracy is poor unless a series of special cases is invoked, e.g. changing over to use the slope referred to the y axis when the angle of the line moves above 45°.

An alternative and more usual treatment is to consider the line from (x_1, y_1) to (x_2, y_2) as containing a generalized point (x, y). A ratio p can now be defined as in Fig. 3.3 as

$$P = \frac{\text{distance of } (x, y) \text{ from } (x_1, y_1)}{\text{distance of } (x, y) \text{ from } (x_2, y_2)} = \frac{l}{R}.$$

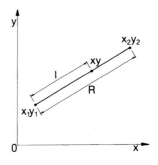

Fig. 3.3 *Definition of a point lying on a line.*

The generalized point then has the co-ordinates

$$x = [(1 - p)x_1 + px_2]$$
$$y = [(1 - p)y_1 + py_2].$$

These equations can be simplified to the parametric form:

$$x = x_1 + (x_2 - x_1)p$$
$$y = y_1 + (y_2 - y_1)p.$$

If the value of p lies between 0 and 1 then the generalized point lies between (x_1, y_1) and (x_2, y_2). If p is less than 0, the point lies on the opposite side of (x_1, y_1) from (x_2, y_2). If p is greater than 1, then the point lies on the opposite side of (x_2, y_2) from (x_1, y_1). This last concept is particularly useful if the line is to be enlarged.

When calculating which pixels need to be lit to display the line on the graphics screen, the values of Δy and Δx can now be calculated simply by varying the parameter p in increments Δp. The size of Δp can be optimized by inspection of (x_1, y_1) and (x_2, y_2) to minimize the number of calculations required while ensuring all the pixels between the two points are lit. This type of calculation takes place whenever a line is drawn. However, because this is a time-consuming process, calculations at this level are usually carried out in a special-purpose microchip which is part of the graphics processor contained in displays with graphics capability. Hence this calculation, and the associated pixel fill, are performed whenever a command such as DRAW is given.

The **parametric form** of expression for a line is also particularly convenient in 2-D draughting systems. Here a line can be defined uniquely by the position of its two endpoints (often referred to as **control points**). Using the parametric form of equation, the position of intermediate points along the line can easily be determined by setting a value to the parameter p, i.e. the position of the midpoint of the line can be calculated by setting $p=0.5$. The length and position of the line can be altered by simply modifying the position of its control points.

It can be seen that many of the tasks which are quite simple for the draughtsman (e.g. drawing a line between two points) are more complicated when carried out by a computer and often require a mathematical expression to be generated. The intuitive procedures of a draughtsman are replaced by detailed mathematical processes within the computer. Thus a study of computer graphics needs to include some mathematics concerned with the description and transformation of graphical primitives. However, these expressions are kept at a relatively simple level in this chapter.

Circles, arcs of circle and other curve forms are similarly required to have their own software routines. Again parametric forms of equation are sought to ensure all cases can be uniquely defined.

3.4.2 COMPLETE CIRCLES

The equation for a circle with axes located at the circle centre, as shown in Fig. 3.4, is

$$y = \sqrt{(R^2 - x^2)}.$$

Although this form strictly gives two possible values of y for each value of x (the square root could be positive or negative), when it is calculated on a computer system, the positive value of y is always given. Therefore this equation is known as an **explicit form** in which there is only one y value for each x value. However, since the circle is a closed form, the point $\theta=0$ is also the point $\theta=2\pi$ radians, and for multiple rotations $\theta=4\pi$, etc. In order to deal with this closed-value condition, the equation must be changed to an **implicit form**. The implicit form of the circle shown in Fig. 3.5 is

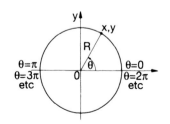

Fig. 3.4 *Multiple rotations resulting from the definition of a circle.*

$$(x - x_1)^2 + (y - y_1)^2 - R^2 = 0.$$

Hence the correct point on the implicit curve can be found by calculating the roots of the algebraic equation.

A difficulty with this form of equation is that, if the increments of x are equal and the corresponding values of y are calculated, the dots shown in Fig. 3.5 are produced. Since the dots are not equispaced around the circle, joining them with a series of straight lines would result in a form giving a poor representation of a circle. This form of algebraic expression is known as non-parametric. Non-parametric curves are very dependent upon the choice of axes for their ease of use.

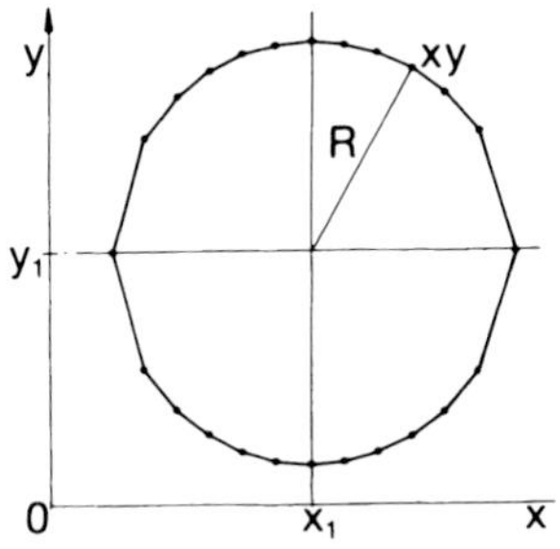

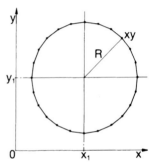

Fig. 3.5 *Non-parametric representation of a circle by 24 points.*

A more accurate representation of a circle, as shown in Fig. 3.6 employs a parametric form

$$x = x_1 + R \cos \theta$$
$$y = y_1 + R \sin \theta.$$

Here the circle is represented in polar form using the parameter θ, i.e. the angle subtended at the centre of the circle. This leads to a good representation of a circle if equal increments of the angle θ are chosen and the points joined by a series of straight lines. Also, since θ can be readily set to angles greater than 2π radians, the parametric form is ideal for dynamic representations such as the continuous rotation of a wheel. Just as for straight lines, programs similar to the above are part of a special graphics microchip. Some devices, such as expensive plotters and refresh displays, have circle generators built into them at a hardware level. Not only do these produce fast and efficient plots, but they also plot a large number of points, giving high-quality circles. For most cheaper displays, however, the circle is approximated by a number of straight lines. To ensure adequate definition of larger diameter circles, it is necessary to plot more points to ensure that the chords stay at a constant length. This is automatically adjusted in most drawing routines.

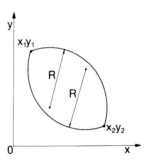

Fig. 3.6 *Parametric representation of a circle by 24 points.*

As before for a straight line, the parametric form of expression for a complete circle is particularly convenient in 2-D draughting systems. Here it is usual to define a complete circle by the positions of two control points, the first being the centre of the circle (x_1, y_1) and the second being a point anywhere on the circumference of the circle (x_2, y_2). The radius of the circle R can be calculated using the equation

$$R = \sqrt{[(x_2 - x_1)^2 + (y_2 - y_1)^2]}.$$

In this way, a complete circle can be defined uniquely by the position of the two control points. The radius and position of the circle can be altered simply by modifying the position of its control points.

3.4.3 CIRCULAR ARCS

If a circular arc were represented solely by its end points and its radius an ambiguity would arise, since the curve could be either concave or convex (Fig. 3.7). This can be avoided by attaching a convention sign to the radius, but would still lead to ambiguity if the arc angle were greater than 180°. Also the points of

Fig. 3.7 *Two interpretations of an arc using end points and radius.*

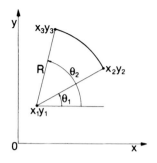

Fig. 3.8 *An alternative representation of an arc.*

the arc have to be less than $2R$ apart. It is often easier and more useful if the arc centre, radius and angles corresponding to the two end points can be specified as in Fig. 3.8. This representation uses the same parametric form as for a full circle, where the end points are given by

$$x_2 = x_1 + R \cos \theta_1$$
$$y_2 = y_1 + R \sin \theta_1$$

and

$$x_3 = x_1 + R \cos \theta_2$$
$$y_3 = y_1 + R \sin \theta_2.$$

In a 2-D draughting system, the values of R, θ_1 and θ_2 frequently are not defined by the user. It is common practise to define just the positions of the three control points (x_1, y_1), (x_2, y_2) and (x_3, y_3). The radius of the arc would then be calculated using the same expression defined above for the radius of a full circle, and the two parameters θ_1 and θ_2 can be determined by observation, i.e.

$$\tan \theta_1 = \frac{(y_2 - y_1)}{(x_2 - x_1)}$$

$$\tan \theta_2 = \frac{(y_3 - y_1)}{(x_3 - x_1)}.$$

The draughting routines for circular arcs often assume the sense of the arc, typically defining the segment of a circle in a clockwise direction between the second and third control points. Professional quality draughting systems provide a number of alternative methods for defining circles and circular arcs. These will be considered in later chapters where the use of draughting packages is discussed in some depth; however, these alternative construction methods merely allow the user to define the position and size of the arc in the most convenient manner. Once the arc has been constructed, the positions of the control points, if not explicitly defined, will be calculated by the software and used to display the circle or arc using a generalized display routine.

3.4.4 CUBIC CURVES

Although the implicit form can be employed to represent exactly such features as circles, free-form curves and surfaces which are often required in geometrical modelling cannot be represented precisely. To obtain precise representation a parametric polynomial is required.

To draw through a pair of end points and pass near to other points (the control points) a generalized curve is needed. If we also need to join two curve segments smoothly, then the slopes at the meeting point need to be the same. The third-order cubic curve is the lowest-order curve that will satisfy all these criteria.

A 2-D curve will require two third-order equations, one in x and one in y. This can be expressed in terms of a parameter t varying from 0 to 1. This is expressed mathematically as

$$x = a_x t^3 + b_x t^2 + c_x t + d_x$$
$$y = a_y t^3 + b_y t^2 + c_y t + d_y ,$$

where $0 \leqslant t \leqslant 1$. The slopes of the curves are ratios of the tangent vector components, e.g.

$$\frac{dy}{dx} = \frac{dy/dt}{dx/dt}$$

where

$$\frac{dx}{dt} = 3a_x t^2 + 2b_x t + c_x , \text{ etc.}$$

The tangent vectors are more useful than the slopes because slopes can become infinite, whereas tangent vectors need never be infinite.

There are many ways of defining a cubic parametric curve. The most frequently encountered are the Bezier and B-spline curves.

Bezier Curves

The Bezier curve has the positions of the start and end points of the curve segment defined by two position vectors, and uses the two control points not on the curve to define the tangents at the ends. The four position vectors used to define the shape of a Bezier curve segment form the characteristic polygon $P_0 P_1 P_2 P_3$. The x and y co-ordinates of a point on the curve segment are defined in terms of the x and y co-ordinates of $P_0 P_1 P_2 P_3$ as follows

$$x(t) = (1 - t)^3 x_0 + 3t(1 - t)^2 x_1 + 3t^2(1 - t)x_2 + t^3 x_3$$
$$y(t) = (1 - t)^3 y_0 + 3t(1 - t)^2 y_1 + 3t^2(1 - t)y_2 + t^3 y_3$$

where $0 \leqslant t \leqslant 1$. Figure 3.9 shows three separate Bezier curve segments (a), (b) and (c) that typify the range of curve shapes that can be generated using this curve form. In each case the vectors P_0 and P_3 define the positions of the start and end points of the curve segment. At these positions the parameter t has the values $t = 0$ and $t = 1$ respectively. The control points P_1 and P_2 may be moved by the designer and the curve segment will smoothly modify to suit, allowing the designer to check if this is better suited to his purpose. The tangent vectors at the end of each segment are controlled by $P_0 P_1$ and $P_2 P_3$.

Bezier curve segments can be linked together into a continuous curve provided the end points of the adjacent curve segments are coincident. Figure 3.9(d) shows three curve segments linked together in this way. The position vectors A_3 and B_0 are identical, as are B_3 and C_0. Also note that $A_2 A_3 B_0 B_1$ are co-linear. This condition ensures that the slope of the curve remains continuous between the first two segments. This is not the case, however, for points $B_2 B_3 C_0 C_1$, therefore there is an abrupt change in the slope of the curve between the second and third segments. The slope of the curve is said to be **discontinuous** at $B_3 C_0$.

The Bezier curve has a notable property, known as the **convex hull property**, which is particularly useful in graphics applications. The convex hull property tells us that the curve segment will always be contained within the bounds of

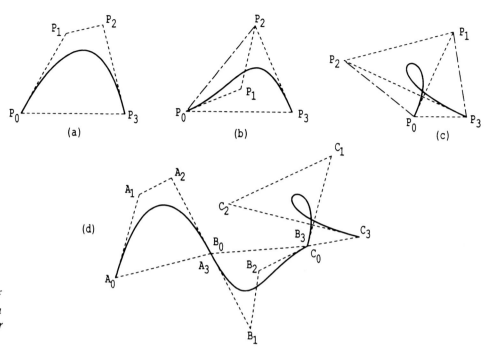

Fig. 3.9 *Three examples of Bezier cubic segments and an example of a composite Bezier cubic curve.*

the characteristic polygon, as seen in Fig. 3.9(a). The extreme limits of this boundary are shown by the chain-dashed lines in Fig. 3.9(b) and Fig. 3.9(c). This property is most useful for quickly testing whether the curve segment is likely to intersect another line or curve, or whether it is close to the screen position of the cursor. For instance, if the characteristic polygons of two Bezier curve segments overlap, it is possible that the curves will intersect. However, a more rigorous and lengthy test is required to determine whether the curve segments actually intersect or not. If the two characteristic polygons do not overlap, the convex hull property tells us that the two curves segments will not intersect, so there is no need to apply the more rigorous test, thus saving computation time and effort. Similarly, when using the cursor to select a line or curve, if its screen co-ordinates lie within the bounds of the characteristic polygon of a particular Bezier curve segment, then the curve is likely to be the one being chosen. Again, though, a more rigorous and lengthy test is required to check whether the curve is the one actually being indicated with the cursor. If the screen co-ordinates of the cursor lie outside the bounds of the characteristic polygon, the curve segment is clearly not the one being chosen.

B-spline Curves

The B-spline approximates, rather than matches, the curve segment end points but allows the slope and curvature of the curve to be continuous at these points. Bezier curves can only have slope continuity and so B-splines tend to have a smoother form of curve. The x and y co-ordinates of a point on the curve segment are defined in terms of the x and y co-ordinates of $P_0P_1P_2P_3$ as follows

$$x(t) = \tfrac{1}{6}(1 - 3t + 3t^2 - t^3)x_0 + \tfrac{1}{6}(4 - 6t^2 + 3t^3)x_1 + \tfrac{1}{6}(1 + 3t + 3t^2 - 3t^3)x_2 + \tfrac{1}{6}t^3x_3$$
$$y(t) = \tfrac{1}{6}(1 - 3t + 3t^2 - t^3)y_0 + \tfrac{1}{6}(4 - 6t^2 + 3t^3)y_1 + \tfrac{1}{6}(1 + 3t + 3t^2 - 3t^3)y_2 + \tfrac{1}{6}t^3y_3$$

where $0 \leq t \leq 1$. Figure 3.10 shows ten B-spline segments linked together to form a continuous curve. To ensure curve continuity, each successive curve segment has three control points common with the previous segment, i.e. $P_0P_1P_2P_3$, $P_1P_2P_3P_4$, $P_2P_3P_4P_5$, etc. The ends of each curve segment, known as a **span**, are clearly marked by circles. The control points for the first three spans are all distinct, whereas the other spans have at least two control points, if not three, that are coincident. Where a span has four distinct control points, the curve will satisfy both conditions of curvature continuity and slope continuity at the segment ends. If, however, two control points are coincident, e.g. P_5P_6, only the slope of the curve will be continuous at both ends of the segment; curvature will be discontinuous at one end, and possibly both. In the case where three control points are coincident, e.g. $P_8P_9P_{10}$, the curve segment will be discontinuous in both slope and curvature at one end. These conditions are all illustrated by the example in Fig. 3.10.

B-spline curves, like Bezier curves, also possess the convex hull property. However, neither B-spline nor Bezier curves can be employed for representing precisely conic or circular curves. Thus in practical CAD systems, curves are often modelled on a hybrid of cubic splines and implicit curves. In more sophisticated CAD systems the **non-uniform rational B-spline** (NURB) is popular for representing all forms of curve. NURBs are a variant of the B-spline described above whose mathematical formulation includes additional weighting coefficients. These can be chosen to control the form of the resultant B-spline segment, even when the same control points are being used. With this curve form, conic curves (i.e. circle, ellipse, parabola, hyperbola) and cubic curves can be represented using a single curve formulation.

Fig. 3.10 *A B-spline cubic curve with ten segments.*

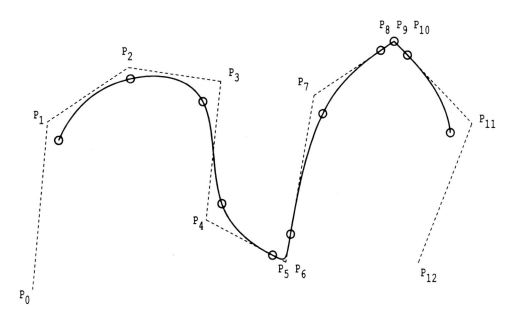

3.5 TWO-DIMENSIONAL (2-D) DRAUGHTING SYSTEMS

The main purpose for using a CAD system is to generate a computer-based representation of an object. One approach is to draw a picture of the object on the graphics screen using a **pixel painting** technique. Here the colour intensity of each pixel is defined individually by the user. Pixel painting graphics packages have a number of facilities for drawing pictures quickly on the screen, often utilizing input devices such as a mouse, stylus or light pen for spreading colour across the screen in a freehand manner. This technique is highly suitable for technical illustration where the user is more likely to be an artist rather than a draughtsman or engineer. In the colour section, the picture of the cross-section of an internal combustion engine is a good example of technical illustration using pixel painting, showing that a high level of realism can be achieved with this technique. However, this approach for representing an object is extremely limited. For instance, a line or curve drawn on the screen is not represented in a parametric form as described earlier, but merely as a series of adjacent pixels that display the same colour intensity. To modify the shape or size of a line or curve represented in this way, requires each pixel to be modified in turn, which is a slow and tedious operation.

An alternative method for representing objects on a CAD system adopts a far more structured approach (a vector-based system), utilizing the software routines discussed earlier for generating lines and curves. In order to represent 2-D (two-dimensional) objects, the graphics screen can be used quite simply to represent the two axes of the object, employing the vertical screen direction as the y-axis and the horizontal direction as the x-axis. As discussed in Chapter 2, even with a simple CAD system, the (x, y) co-ordinates of a point on the screen can be defined either by typing the numerical values of each ordinate, or by fixing the position of the cursor. The position of the cursor is controlled by an additional input device (joystick, mouse, etc.) and its position is fixed by pressing a button. The use of the cursor is often preferred, but where precise control of the position of a point is required, then typed input must be used. Alternatively, a lightly drawn grid, whose mesh size can be defined beforehand, can be used to aid positioning of the cursor. In graphics software the basic building blocks used to generate images are known as primitives. Lines, circles, arcs and curves are typical primitives provided by most graphics software, but some systems include additional primitives such as rectangles and prisms, which speed up the process of generating the image.

A line drawing of an object can be constructed using lines, circles, arcs and cubic curves for which the (x, y) co-ordinates of the control points are defined for each. For instance, to draw a straight line, the CAD user need only define the screen positions of its end points. The graphics software will automatically calculate which pixels are to be illuminated to display the line fully. Similarly, if the graphics software includes Bezier curves, the user need only define the screen positions of the four control points of the characteristic polygon to display the cubic curve segment. Furthermore, graphics software usually provides a number of alternative methods for constructing lines and curves which do not require the user to define explicitly the position of all the control points, e.g. for constructing a line that is tangent to an existing circle or arc. However, when the control points are not defined explicitly by the user, they must be calculated by the computer as part of the construction process. Using this approach, the object is constructed as a series of discretely defined lines, circles, arcs, and curves, which are collectively known as **edges**, whose position, size and shape are defined by the positions of the control points, known as **vertices**.

When creating a line drawing of an object in this way, the graphics software generates two sets of data. One set is a list of control points known as the vertex list, the other is a list of lines, circles, arcs, and curves known as the edge list. The vertex list records the (x, y) co-ordinates of all the control points and gives each point a unique vertex number. The edge list records the vertex numbers of the control points required to define each edge fully. The screen co-ordinates of the control points of a specific edge may be determined by cross-referencing the vertex numbers stored in the edge list to the (x, y) co-ordinates stored in the vertex list. Figure 3.11(a) shows a simple object constructed from eight straight lines. The vertex and edge lists for this object are shown in Fig. 3.11(b). In this example, the edge list shows that edge E_3 has two endpoints: vertices V_3 and V_4. The vertex list shows these two points to have the (x, y) co-ordinates (50, 70) and (65, 100), respectively.

The object drawn in Fig. 3.11 has been constructed with its edges linked together to form a continuous boundary. To form this structure, the end points of adjacent edges must be shared, and if the first and last edges of the boundary are linked, the object is considered to be **closed**. The significance of closure will

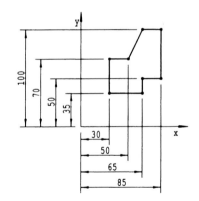

Fig. 3.11 *A 2-D object drawn together with axes, dimensions, edge list and vertex list.*

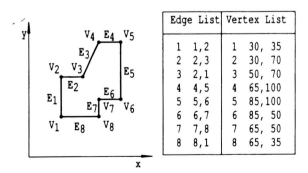

Edge List		Vertex List	
1	1,2	1	30, 35
2	2,3	2	30, 70
3	2,1	3	50, 70
4	4,5	4	65,100
5	5,6	5	85,100
6	6,7	6	85, 50
7	7,8	7	65, 50
8	8,1	8	65, 35

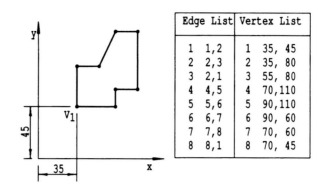

Edge List		Vertex List	
1	1,2	1	35, 45
2	2,3	2	35, 80
3	2,1	3	55, 80
4	4,5	4	70,110
5	5,6	5	90,110
6	6,7	6	90, 60
7	7,8	7	70, 60
8	8,1	8	70, 45

Fig. 3.12 *The 2-D object translated (5, 10) showing the changes to the vertex list.*

be discussed later, however, at this stage it is important to observe that where two edges share a common point, the (x, y) co-ordinates of that point are recorded only once in the vertex list. The two edge definitions in the edge list will each include a reference to the same vertex, rather than reference two separate vertices with the same (x, y) co-ordinates (e.g. Fig. 3.11(b) shows edges E_4 and E_5 sharing vertex V_5). To construct an object of this type, the start point of each edge must be defined by using the cursor to 'snap' on to the endpoint of an existing edge. Cursor snapping, which is discussed in more detail later in this chapter, ensures that a particular screen position will be defined only once in the vertex list.

One of the benefits of the edge–vertex approach of representing an object is the ease with which the image can be modified. All graphics software provide **transformation** facilities for moving, rotating, or scaling the drawn object. Figure 3.12 shows the example object moved five units in the x-direction and 10 units in the y-direction. The (x, y) co-ordinates of V_1 are changed to (35, 45) by this movement. Modifying the position or size of the object in part or as a whole using a transformation is discussed in more detail later in this chapter. At this stage, however, it is important to appreciate that transformations only affect the data in the vertex list where the new (x, y) co-ordinates of the transformed vertices will be stored.

Alternatively, modifications to the design of the object may require new edges being defined or existing ones being deleted. Where a new edge is defined, an addition to the edge list will be made, though whether further additions are made to the vertex list depends upon whether or not the new edge is constructed using existing vertices. Figure 3.13 shows the example object modified by the addition of edge E_9. No additions to the vertex list have been made because the endpoints of the new edge already exist.

Where an existing edge is deleted, the edge definition will simply be erased from the edge list. Figure 3.14 shows the example object modified by the deletion of edges E_6 and E_7. Vertex V_7 is redundant and often is deleted automatically from the vertex list. Here, however, its definition remains in the list. During the buildup of a complex image, a number of edges might be deleted before the drawing is finalized. This will leave a number of gaps in the edge

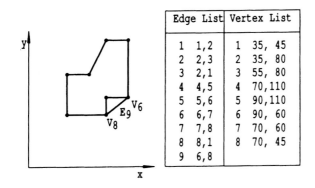

Edge List	Vertex List
1 1,2	1 35, 45
2 2,3	2 35, 80
3 2,1	3 55, 80
4 4,5	4 70,110
5 5,6	5 90,110
6 6,7	6 90, 60
7 7,8	7 70, 60
8 8,1	8 70, 45
9 6,8	

Fig. 3.13 *The 2-D object modified with an additional edge.*

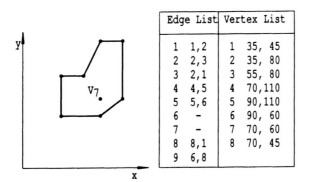

Edge List	Vertex List
1 1,2	1 35, 45
2 2,3	2 35, 80
3 2,1	3 55, 80
4 4,5	4 70,110
5 5,6	5 90,110
6 -	6 90, 60
7 -	7 70, 60
8 8,1	8 70, 45
9 6,8	

Fig. 3.14 *The 2-D object with two edges deleted.*

list where edges have been deleted (Fig. 3.14) so a facility for compacting the edge list is often provided. This process simply reorganizes the edge definitions to fill the gaps, so reducing the apparent number of edge definitions in the list. Figure 3.15 shows how the edge list is modified so that E_8 becomes E_6 and E_9 becomes E_7. Similarly the vertex list can be reorganized to erase the redundant vertex. This process is complicated by the need to modify the entries in the edge list where the vertex identity numbers are changed, i.e. since V_8 becomes V_7, all edges using V_8 will have their edge list entry modified from 8 to 7, i.e. E_6 and E_7.

Each edge can be assigned what is known as an attribute. Thus a line may be a continuous thick line, a dashed line to represent hidden detail, or a chain dashed line for a centre line. Similarly each line may have an attribute of a specific colour, chosen from a palette of those available. In some of the cheaper

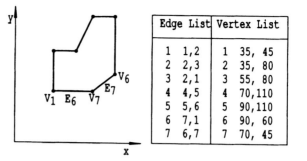

Edge List		Vertex List	
1	1,2	1	35, 45
2	2,3	2	35, 80
3	2,1	3	55, 80
4	4,5	4	70,110
5	5,6	5	90,110
6	7,1	6	90, 60
7	6,7	7	70, 45

Fig. 3.15 *The 2-D object with its edge and vertex list reorganized.*

systems, the attributes of line type are not fully available on the graphics screen but can be reproduced when plotted out on paper so that, for example, a hidden detail line can be generated by a series of pen up/pen down commands to the plotter. Similarly line thickness and colour could be varied by choosing the appropriate pen for the plotter. Attributes are retained in an attributes list as a code which defines the style and colour intensity of each edge.

Having built up a view of an object it is often advisable to file it away on to a library disk or other storage medium. This will not only ensure a back-up copy should the view be erased accidently, but will also allow the view to be called up and modified for use on another drawing. Only the data in the edge, vertex and attributes lists need be stored on file because the graphics screen image can be regenerated from this information alone.

The view of the object can be positioned on the work page to enable other views to be projected from it in orthographic projection. The use of a grid is particularly useful at this stage in enabling the views to be projected accurately. The features in the other views can be built up gradually by enlarging the portion containing the view currently drawn until it fills the work page in order to achieve a reasonable accuracy of drawing. In addition to orthographic views, it is also possible to generate isometric views by laying down a dotted isometric grid to facilitate setting out distances along directions parallel to the three isometric axes.

It should be emphasized at this stage that the isometric and orthographic views held in the computer which result from the use of a 2-D graphics program do not have any information about the 3-D nature of the part being drawn. In the same way that a conventional draughtsman will specify a plan view from the front view using his knowledge of the 3-D nature of the part, so it is necessary for the CAD user to interpret the 3-D nature of the part shown on the screen. In this sense the computer and graphics screen are only acting as a substitute for the traditional drawing board and no 3-D properties (e.g. volume or centre of gravity) can be obtained. Indeed, except in some limited cases where a plane is specified as parallel to the plane of projection, it is not possible to determine 2-D properties (e.g. areas and centres of areas). However, although a 2-D graphics program does not offer any information about the 3-D nature of the part, computer-aided drawing does provide the CAD user with a number of facilities that speed up the process of generating an image.

3.6   ADDITIONAL 2-D FACILITIES

In this section a number of terms and features are introduced that are found in most CAD systems, ranging from the small educational systems through to the largest professional systems. Rather than give a very detailed description of a specific system, at this stage the discussion will be kept fairly general. A more detailed treatment of applications packages is given in later chapters.

3.6.1   SNAPPING

The object drawn in Fig. 3.15 has seven straight edges. If the position of the each edge end point was defined using typed input, the (x, y) co-ordinates of fourteen vertices would be stored in the vertex list, even though each would be coincident with one other vertex. When using the cursor, however, the graphics software searches through the (x, y) co-ordinates in the vertex list to check whether the cursor co-ordinates are close to those of an existing vertex. If the cursor is found to be in close proximity to an existing vertex, this vertex will be used to define the position of the edge endpoint, and so a new vertex will not have to be created. Since the object in Fig. 3.15 is closed, in using this technique only seven vertices have been defined for the seven edges.

At a more general level, whenever the cursor is used to select a position on the screen, the graphics software will always use the (x, y) co-ordinates of an existing vertex in preference to the actual cursor co-ordinates, provided they are in close proximity to each other. This facility has many uses in interactive CAD systems which will be demonstrated in the later chapters of this book. The maximum allowable difference between the co-ordinates of the cursor and the vertex to which it snaps can usually be controlled by the CAD user, and if necessary, cursor snapping can be switched off so that the cursor position is taken as the true position of the point being defined.

3.6.2   COPY

The copy command enables the CAD user to replicate drawn parts on the work page. The parts may be drawn already on the work page or exist as a separate drawing on the library disk. The ability to store an image on the library disk enables a view to be called up several times over. The image can be scaled appropriately and then copied into several locations on the work page. The ability to copy is a useful feature for repetitive items, e.g. nuts and bolts, which can be stored as standard files, often referred to as **symbol files**. In some systems, such items are provided as primitives which can be scaled and positioned appropriately to fit the drawing.

3.6.3 MIRROR

A further command frequently used in drawings is the mirror (or reflect) command which enables a part to be drawn using only one half and a centre line. If the part is then identified by a rectangular box, the mirror command will enable the missing half of the view to be drawn about the centre line, saving considerable time.

3.6.4 TWEENING

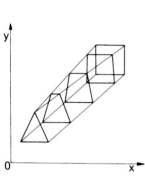

Fig. 3.16 *In-betweening.*

A process called tweening (or in-betweening) can be found in some systems, particularly for animation work. The computer can take an initial and final view and generate a specified number of in-between stages. Figure 3.16 shows the transition of a triangle into a square using a series of three in-between images.

3.6.5 AREA FILLING

Graphical routines for area filling enable enclosed parts of the drawing to be quickly filled with colour, patterns, or hatching. For engineering applications, the most common use of area filling is for hatching to indicate where an object has been cut by a sectioning plane. This drawing facility requires the boundary of the area to be closed. If the boundary is not closed, the area filling routine usually fails.

3.6.6 DIMENSIONING

Once all the views of an object have been completed, in all but the simplest 2-D packages, the CAD user is able to add dimensions to the line drawing using special drawing routines. Since the edge–vertex representation of the object includes geometrical data about the position of vertices, the distance between features, e.g. two parallel edges, can easily be calculated. The cursor is used in dimensioning routines to indicate the feature being dimensioned and the position of the dimension text on the drawing. Using this information, the routine not only calculates the size of feature being dimensioned, but automatically generates the leader lines, dimension line with arrowheads, and the dimension text itself.

3.6.7 TEXT

In addition to graphical information and dimensions, an engineering drawing contains written information that specifies particular features that cannot be represented in any other way (material type, draughtsman's name, etc.). All CAD systems have routines for annotating drawings with text, usually using the default character style (font) of the display or plotting device. The size and style of the text often can be changed, but where special character fonts are used, the text has to be generated using special drawing routines which are very slow. Editing facilities vary with the quality of 2-D packages. Some have text editors which are just as good as those in word processor packages.

3.7 TWO-DIMENSIONAL TRANSFORMATIONS

As part of the process of displaying an object on the screen, it is often necessary to change (or **transform**) a whole group of picture features, points, lines or planes. The most frequent types of transformations are: **translations**, in which the group of features is moved linearly with reference to the origin; **rotation**, in which all picture features are rotated about the origin; and **scaling**, in which the whole group is enlarged or reduced with reference to the origin.

The principles underlying these transformations are illustrated graphically in this section and the mathematical process is explained. However, the majority of 2-D draughting systems employ a mathematical technique for representing the picture features called a **matrix representation**. All matrices can be manipulated in a standard way so that the various transformation processes, individually and in combination, can be calculated quickly using a standardized procedure. For those who have a knowledge of matrices, the matrix approach to transformation is included as Appendix A. However, it is recommended that the following section be read first, since this deals with the underlying principles of the process which are often not apparent when dealing with matrices. While the process of total transformation of a line is often intuitively obvious, the mathematical definition of the process demands a regularized procedure in which everything proceeds step by step and all transformations take place with reference to the origin.

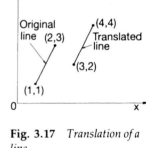

Fig. 3.17 *Translation of a line.*

3.7.1 TRANSLATION

An example is given in Fig. 3.17 of a line translated by two units in the x direction and one unit in the y direction with respect to the origin. The start of the line is translated from (1, 1) to (3, 2). Because the translation values for both ends of the line are the same, the new line will be parallel to the old. In general mathematical terms translation can be represented by

$$x_1 = x + \Delta x$$
$$y_1 = y + \Delta y$$

where x_1, y_1 are the co-ordinates of the translated point, x and y are the original co-ordinates, and Δx and Δy are the translation displacement values. Thus translation involves a process of addition (or subtraction).

3.7.2 SCALING

If the line (1, 1) to (2, 3) is now scaled by doubling its length, the result is as shown in Fig. 3.18. As can be seen in this figure the process of scaling also changes the position of both ends of the line. Scaling therefore also involves

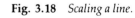

Fig. 3.18 *Scaling a line.*

a process of translation. The new line is also parallel to the original line. Quite often it is necessary to enlarge an object while keeping a corner fixed relative to the origin.

This process would be similar to doubling the length of the line in Fig. 3.18 while keeping the end (1, 1) in its original position. Because all processes take place with respect to the origin, a sequence of transformations is required. This sequence would involve a translation by $(-1, -1)$ for the whole line followed by a scaling and then a re-translation by (1, 1) to bring the lowest end of the line back to its earlier position. The mathematical expressions for scaling are:

$$x_1 = x \times S_x$$
$$y_1 = y \times S_y ,$$

where S_x and S_y are the scale factors for x and y. Scaling thus involves a process of multiplication. Theoretically there is no reason why the values S_x and S_y need to be the same. Thus the drawing can be stretched in the x direction by an amount different to that in the y direction. This is a useful facility when drawing an ellipse.

3.7.3 ROTATION

A point P_1 at (4, 3) is to be rotated about the origin by $+30°$ (i.e. anti-clockwise). The result is readily constructed as shown in Fig. 3.19. The mathematical expression of the new co-ordinates is

$$
\begin{aligned}
x' = 0x_2 &= OA = BD - CD \\
&= OD \cos\theta - DP_2 \sin\theta \\
&= x_1 \cos\theta - y_1 \sin\theta \\
y' = 0y_2 &= AP_2 = AC + CP_2 \\
&= OB + CP_2 \\
&= OD \sin\theta + DP_2 \cos\theta \\
&= x_1 \sin\theta + y_1 \cos\theta
\end{aligned}
$$

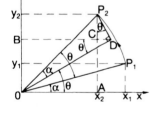

Fig. 3.19 *Rotation of a point.*

where θ is the angle by which the point is rotated. If the rotation of $60°$ is applied to the line (1, 1) to (2, 3) then the result is as shown in Fig. 3.20. Because the rotation is about the origin, the process results also in the line being translated. If the line were to be purely rotated about the end (1, 1) by $60°$, then for the mathematical process, it would first be necessary to translate the line to the origin as shown in Fig. 3.21(a), then rotate about the origin by $60°$ (Fig. 3.21(b)) and finally re-translate back to the original end point (1, 1) as shown in Fig. 3.21(c).

As a general rule the process of translation can be seen to involve addition, while both scaling and rotation are processes of multiplication. This has implications for the matrix manipulation described in Appendix A, and is the reason for introducing there the concept of **homogeneous co-ordinates**. A further implication for the matrix manipulation is in the fact that the order of a sequence of transformation is important. This can be seen clearly in Fig. 3.21 where the

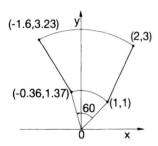

Fig. 3.20 *Rotation of a line about the origin.*

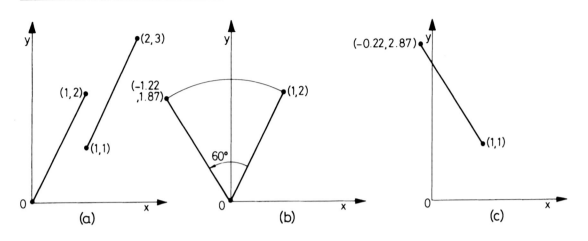

Fig. 3.21 *Sequence of transformations for rotation of a line about one end.*

sequence is translate, rotate, translate. Had the sequence been translate, translate, rotate, then the first two translations would cancel out, leaving a pure rotation about the origin instead of one about the end of the line.

3.8 TWO-DIMENSIONAL DISPLAY CONTROL FACILITIES

The small size of the screen of a graphics display does not allow the drawing to be displayed at full size nor enable the screen co-ordinates to represent the true dimensions of the object. Consequently, the displayed image must be scaled from true dimensions to fit the bounds of the graphics area. All CAD systems have facilities to control the displayed image, enabling the CAD user to define the (x, y) co-ordinates of the object at real size, using true dimensions.

3.8.1 SCALE AND ZOOM

It is not only possible to scale on overall drawing but, in most systems, the x direction can be scaled separately from the y. In addition to being able to define a scale for the drawing, most systems have a **zoom** facility. This enables a particular part lying at the centre of the drawing to be continuously enlarged or shrunk at the press of a button. This is particularly useful in checking that two lines actually meet. The part to be enlarged can also be identified by placing it in a rectangular frame. Pressing a button will then enlarge the frame to fill the screen. However, if the part to be enlarged is off to one side at the start of the zoom, it will be quickly lost from view as the image magnifies.

3.8.2 PAN

Under these circumstances it is necessary to use the **pan** (or **shift**) command. This has the effect of moving the screen across the work page as if it were a moving window.

3.8.3 WINDOWS AND VIEWPORTS

Let us assume that the end of a long shaft is to be drawn on a graphics screen. The shaft exists in what are called the user's (or **world**) co-ordinates. The end of the shaft to be displayed represents a small **window** on the world and parts lying outside that window are **clipped** so that no attempt will be made to display them on any device. The device (e.g. printer, plotter, display screen) has a viewing surface on to which the image is to be mapped. The view surface can be scaled so that its maximum co-ordinates are represented by a square ranging from (0, 0) to (1, 0) in both the x and y directions. This is known as **normalized device co-ordinates** because it can represent any output device. The normalized device co-ordinates could be converted, in turn, into the particular device co-ordinates – e.g. the number of pixels on a display screen. Since the screen is rectangular, using normalized device co-ordinates, the right hand part will not be used for graphics display and can be used for computer error messages, etc. The **viewport** containing the end portion of the shaft is shown as appearing in the top left section of the screen. This allows space on the screen for other viewports which are mapped from the world co-ordinate systems and can contain, for example, parts which are to be assembled on to the shaft, or associated text. The viewports can be of any size and in any location on the screen. Unfortunately many modern business systems where the screen is partitioned into several sections use the term window incorrectly when, according to International Standard definitions, the term viewport should be used. This misnomer is so widespread that it is likely that the Standard will have to be revised.

3.8.4 CLIPPING

The process of clipping is applied to a window to ensure that the display device does not attempt to draw parts which lie outside the window. Fig. 3.22(a) shows an attempt to draw a line from point 1 to point 2, where point 2 lies outside the screen. The analogue values equivalent to the distance of 2 from the right-hand edge of the screen x would be interpreted as an x value and the actual view that is drawn would be as shown in Fig. 3.22(b). This effect is known as **wraparound**.

There are several possible routines for clipping. The most common, ascribed to Cohen and Sutherland, is shown in relation to a series of lines in Fig. 3.23. The total drawing represents a world co-ordinate system which is to be clipped to a window represented by the central square. The 'world' is divided into eight separate regions lying around the central window. Each of these regions is assigned a value as a block of four bits in the computer. The lowest (right-hand) bit is set to 1 if the region lies to the left of the central window. The second bit is set if the region is to the right of the window, the third bit is set if below the window and the fourth bit if above the window. Thus, if a line is drawn across the regions and both ends are zero, then the line is entirely within the central window. If the line is totally outside the central region, it will be found that each end of the line will have the same corresponding bit set to 1. Hence a horizontal line from the top left to the top right corner will have ends 1001 and 1010 re-

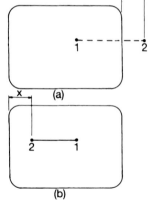

Fig. 3.22 'Wraparound' effects.

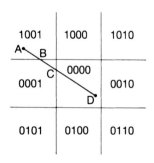

Fig. 3.23 Clipping a line.

spectively, i.e. the left-hand bit will be a 1 in each case. This test can be applied to reject all lines lying outside the centre. A line such as AD in Fig. 3.23 can be subdivided at B. The section AB is tested by the above criteria and discarded as totally outside the centre. The line BD is now tested and found that it cannot easily be rejected. BD is further divided at C and the line CD found to lie entirely within the central window so that BC can be rejected. Clipping routines of this type can be set up in special-purpose graphics chips and operate extremely quickly.

SUMMARY

In this chapter we have considered the basic principles of representing straight lines, circles, circular arcs and curves on a computer system. We have also seen how these principles are used to create a structured representation of an object in a simple 2-D CAD system. Methods for modifying the database and controlling the displayed image have been introduced.

While these techniques are useful for computer-aided draughting, mimicking conventional manual drawing does not take full advantage of the capabilities offered by CAD systems. In the next chapter, we will consider the principles of representing the full three-dimensional nature of an object.

EXERCISES

1. What are the main functions of a computer operating system. Why is the standardization of operating system software important?
2. Discuss the relative merits of MS-DOS and UNIX operating systems. Describe how information is stored and organized on disk.
3. What are the differences between low- and high-level computer languages? Why must programs written using these languages be translated into machine code?
4. Starting with the graphics source program, discuss the sequence of files, menu and system activities required to build up and archive a simple assembly drawing.
5. What is the function of a library file in a simple 2-D draughting system?
6. Using PROGRAM 1, p. 49, as a guide, create a BASIC program which will draw an equilateral triangle of side length 50, starting at position (50, 50) with one side horizontal. The computer software uses the line command MOVE X, Y to move the cursor to a position (x, y) and LINE X, Y to draw a line from the current location of the cursor to a position (x, y).
7. Using the concepts in PROGRAM 3, p. 51, as a guide, write a BASIC program to draw an S shape consisting of two tangential semicircles each of radius 50. Using the same concepts, write BASIC programs to draw all the upper-case letters of the alphabet using a standard letter height of 100 units.
8. How might the programs created in exercise 7 be modified to draw letters using a variable character height?
9. Is the expression $y = mx + c$ implicit or explicit? What is a parametric form of

this equation? Use the parametric form to generate a series of radial lines 50 long and at 30° increments from the point (100, 100).

10. Discuss the relative merits of Bezier and B-spline curves. What is the convex hull property?

11. Describe how a 2-D object would be represented by an edge–vertex listing in a 2-D draughting system. Why is this a convenient method for representing objects on a CAD system?

12. A simple 2-D draughting system can be used for drawing isometric views but it is not thought of as a 3-D system. Why is this?

13. Discuss, with the aid of diagrams, how the small end bearing of a car engine connecting rod can be mapped from world co-ordinates to be displayed as a viewport (in screen pixels) on a 256×312 pixel display screen.

14. A line from (0, 0) to (200, 150) is to be clipped to a square viewport located from 50 to 100 in x and from 50 to 100 in y. Determine the sequence of clipping operations using the Cohen and Sutherland technique.

Three-dimensional modelling software

The general way in which three-dimensional modelling works and how it differs from 2-D systems will now be discussed.

4.1 THREE-DIMENSIONAL (3-D) MODELLING

While the majority of small CAD systems have only a 2-D capability, it is becoming increasingly necessary for larger, professional CAD systems to have an ability to model in three dimensions. The progression from 2-D to 3-D CAD is by no means straightforward and requires significantly more complex software to be used. No longer can the graphics screen be used to simply represent just two axes of an object. The graphics screen must now represent all three axes. This necessarily involves three distinct processes in generating a screen image of a 3-D object.

1. Edges must be represented by lines and curves defined in 3-D space. The software routines used to generate the 2-D parametric definitions of lines and curves must be adapted to 3-D space by including a third axis, the z-axis. Routines are also required for representing surface geometry. These routines allow each face of an object to be described by a surface whose bounds are usually defined by a group of edges.
2. Techniques for creating object models in three dimensions are required. The basis of these modelling techniques will be the parametric edge and surface definitions of 1. The full co-ordinate geometry of an object can then be stored, together with spatial relationships and all resulting properties such as volumes and centres of gravity. Three-dimensional transformations must be defined to enable the object geometry to be manipulated in 3-D space.
3. The 3-D description of an object can be used to create plan, front and end views by the embodiment of the 'rules' of orthographic projection into the graphics display software. A convention for representing the x-, y- and z-axes on the screen must be adopted and understood by all. Similarly, perspective views can be generated from pre-defined viewpoints, or if surface information is included in the 3-D model, pictorial views with hidden edges omitted can be generated. Advanced display software includes a variety of colour rendering techniques enabling photographic quality images to be generated.

The reader should be warned that some packages that appear to have a 3-D modelling capability, in fact have no 3-D database. Some of the simpler packages incorporate pictorial views which involve simply setting dimensions of an object along three axes, e.g. in an isometric view. Such a pictorial view, however, requires the user to interpret the 3-D nature of the object. In such cases there is no 3-D data to allow, for example, a rotated view or 3-D properties, such as centre of gravity, to be obtained.

Once a 3-D representation of an object has been created and stored on the CAD system, the geometric and topological information used to describe the item can be utilized in many other activities of the engineering design and manufacture process. For instance, the 3-D model can be used to generate suitable views for use with a draughting package to produce fully dimensioned engineering drawings. Here the orthographic views are produced automatically from the information stored in the 3-D model database. The CAD draughtsman is relieved of the task of drawing each view himself, saving time and minimizing the likelihood of drawing error. Similarly, if the model contains information about the surface shape of the object, this can be used to assist the programming of computer numerically controlled (CNC) machine tools for manufacturing the item. The information stored in the 3-D model database is used to generate **cutter paths** for the CNC machine tool to follow. These two examples of the use of 3-D representations of objects in computer-aided engineering serve merely to illustrate the importance of 3-D modelling in CAD and how the information created by the designer can be used to integrate design with various other engineering activities. This aspect of CAD is considered further in later chapters, but at this stage it is important to appreciate the need to find a 3-D modelling approach that will allow readily the integration of CAD with other computer aided tasks.

4.2   THREE-DIMENSIONAL LINES AND CURVES

The principles of representing lines, circles, circular arcs and cubic curves in 3-D space are essentially similar to those used for 2-D lines and curves. The addition of a third degree of freedom has little effect on the parametric formulations for straight lines and cubic curves considered earlier, since these curve types are defined explicitly in terms of the position vectors of their respective control points. The parametric representation of a circle and circular arc can only be used in 3-D space, however, if the plane of the curve is uniquely defined.

4.2.1   STRAIGHT LINES

A straight line in 3-D space can be represented using the same parametric expression defined for a 2-D line, based upon the positions of the two end points (x_1, y_1, z_1) and (x_2, y_2, z_2).

The position of a generalized point (x, y, z) on the line can be determined in terms of the parameter p, where

$$x = x_1 + (x_2 - x_1)p$$

$$y = y_1 + (y_2 - y_1)p$$
$$z = z_1 + (z_2 - z_1)p.$$

The parameter p has the same significance in 3-D space as it has in 2-D space, i.e. if the value of p lies between 0 and 1 then the generalized point lies between (x_1, y_1, z_1) and (x_2, y_2, z_2).

4.2.2 COMPLETE CIRCLES

A complete circle cannot be uniquely defined in 3-D space by the positions of its centre (x_1, y_1, z_1) and a point on its circumference (x_2, y_2, z_2) alone. An infinite number of circles could be defined using just two control points, so the plane in which the 3-D circle lies must be specified before it can be fully represented. The simplest method for doing this is to define the position of a third control point (x_3, y_3, z_3) which lies in the plane of the circle, though it is not necessary that this point actually lies on the circle itself. Provided the three points are not colinear, they can be used to uniquely define the plane of the circle

$$ax + by + cz + d = 0.$$

A generalized point on this plane can be defined in terms of two parameters s and t and the position vectors of the three control points

$$x = (1 - s - t)x_1 + sx_2 + tx_3$$
$$y = (1 - s - t)y_1 + sy_2 + ty_3$$
$$z = (1 - s - t)z_1 + sz_2 + tz_3.$$

The parameters s and t can take any value and define a point in the plane of the circle, but in general do not represent an orthogonal co-ordinate system in the plane. It is therefore not possible to represent the complete 3-D circle using a 2-D parametric circle drawn in (s, t) space.

With the plane of the circle fully defined, the 3-D transformation required to relocate the three control points in the plane $z = 0$, so that (x_1, y_1, z_1) is transformed to $(0, 0, 0)$ and (x_2, y_2, z_2) to $(R, 0, 0)$, can be determined. Using the inverse transformation, points from a circle radius R centred on $(0, 0, 0)$ and lying in the $z = 0$ plane can be mapped to the plane of the required circle. The transformation between planes would involve 3-D translation and rotation; such transformations are considered later in this chapter.

4.2.3 CIRCULAR ARCS

The same technique for defining a complete circle in 3-D space can be used to define a circular arc. Here the three control points defining the arc centre and the two end points can be used to define the plane of the arc, provided the three are not colinear. If the three control points are colinear, the plane of the arc must be defined by another means, or the arc defined as two separate segments joined using a common end point. The transformation technique discussed for full circles can also be applied to circular arcs.

4.2.4 CUBIC CURVES

A 3-D cubic curve will require three third-order equations; one in x, one in y and one in z. The parametric form of the 3-D cubic curve takes the form

$$x = a_x t^3 + b_x t^2 + c_x t + d_x$$
$$y = a_y t^3 + b_y t^2 + c_y t + d_y$$
$$z = a_z t^3 + b_z t^2 + c_z t + d_z,$$

where $0 \leqslant t \leqslant 1$. The slopes of the curves are ratios of the tangent vector components as before, but can be defined with respect to each axis, e.g.

$$\frac{dy}{dx} = \frac{dy/dt}{dx/dt}$$
$$\frac{dz}{dy} = \frac{dz/dt}{dy/dt}$$
$$\frac{dx}{dz} = \frac{dx/dt}{dz/dt}$$

where

$$\frac{dx}{dt} = 3a_x t^2 + 2b_x t + c_x, \text{ etc.}$$

The 3-D Bezier and B-spline curves use four control points defined in 3-D space to define the shape of the curve segment. The four control points define the corners of the **characteristic tetrahedron** in which the curve segment will be totally enclosed. Thus the convex hull property is applicable in 3-D space because the curve is bounded by the volume of the characteristic tetrahedron.

4.3 SURFACE REPRESENTATIONS

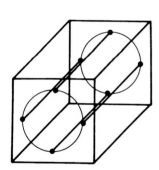

Fig. 4.1 *Wire-frame object.*

A 3-D model of an object can be made up of a series of linked 3-D edges which, when displayed, give the observer an impression of its size and shape. Such models are known as **wire-frame** models. Figure 4.1 shows a simple wire-frame model that is made up of a series of straight lines and circular arcs. The model represents a block with a through hole. The surfaces of the object are not defined, so the observer must interpret for himself what the object would look like in reality. His interpretation of the displayed image may be incorrect, e.g. is the object in Fig. 4.1 being observed from above or below? In some cases, the interpretation of the wire-frame model may be ambiguous, e.g. Fig. 4.2, where it is not clear if some surfaces are plane or have a surface cut away. In these cases, the surface geometry of the object must be represented so that more realistic images can be generated by the computer.

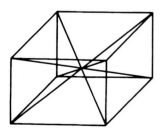

Fig. 4.2 *Ambiguous wire-frame object.*

Parametric surface representations use the two parameters s and t to define the position of a generalized point (x, y, z) on the surface. The parameters s and t are independent variables, so can be considered to represent a 2-D co-ordinate system on the surface. When used to represent the face of an object the range of values taken by s and t is usually restricted to $0 \leqslant s \leqslant 1$ and $0 \leqslant t \leqslant 1$. This generates a **patch** which defines a curved surface with four boundary lines and four corners. The boundary lines are often selected from the list of edges in the wire-frame model, in which case the shape of the surface patch will be determined by the shape of the selected edges.

4.3.1 PLANAR SURFACES

The co-ordinates of a generalized point (x, y, z) on the planar surface will satisfy the equation

$$ax + by + cz + d = 0.$$

A parametric definition of the planar surface can be defined in terms of the parameters s and t and the position vectors of three control points P_{00}, P_{10} and P_{01}. A generalized point on the surface P_{st} is given by

$$P_{st} = (1 - s - t)P_{00} + sP_{10} + tP_{01}.$$

The parameters s and t can take any value, though if their values are restricted to $0 \leqslant s \leqslant 1$ and $0 \leqslant t \leqslant 1$ a planar surface patch is defined. The parameters s and t form a 2-D co-ordinate system which enable lines of constant s or t to be drawn across the surface. Figure 4.3 shows lines of constant s and t running parallel to $P_{00}P_{01}$ and $P_{00}P_{10}$, respectively. The positions of P_{00}, P_{10} and P_{01} are usually defined by the endpoints of two straight lines. In this way the faces of a wire-frame model can be represented by a series of planar surface patches bounded by the edges of the model.

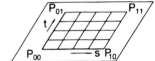

Fig. 4.3 *Parametric planar surface.*

Since the planar surface is completely defined by the positions of the three control points, the planar surface will be moved likewise if these points are transformed in any way. This obviates the need to redefine the position of a plane each time the position of an object is changed.

4.3.2 RULED SURFACES

A restriction in the use of the planar surface is that the two edges used to define the position of the three control points must be straight and share a common endpoint. However, where the edges are straight but not linked by a common endpoint, or where one or both of the edges are not straight, it is not possible, in the general case, to define a planar surface between the edges.

A **ruled surface** uses linear interpolation to generate a surface patch bounded by two edges whose endpoints are connected by straight lines. The edges may take any 3-D parametric form including straight lines, circular arcs or cubic curves. The parameter s is varied along each edge within the range $0 \leqslant s \leqslant 1$. Positions of constant s on each curve are used to define the endpoints of a parametric straight line which connects them. The parameter t varies from 0 to 1 along each of these lines.

If the position of a point on the first edge is $P_0(s)$ and the second $P_1(s)$, then the position of a generalized point P_{st} in (s, t) space is given by

$$P_{st} = P_0(s) + [P_1(s) - P_0(s)]t.$$

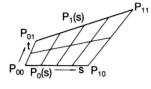

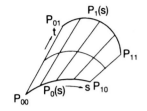

Fig. 4.4 *Two examples of ruled surface patches.*

The corners of the patch are given by P_{00}, P_{10}, P_{01} and P_{11}, where $P_{00} = P_0(0)$, $P_{10} = P_0(1)$, $P_{01} = P_1(0)$, and $P_{11} = P_1(1)$.

Figure 4.4(a) shows a ruled surface patch where both edges are straight, and so in this specific case

$$P_0(s) = P_{00} + (P_{10} - P_{00})s$$
$$P_1(s) = P_{01} + (P_{11} - P_{01})s$$

and

$$P_{st} = P_{00} + (P_{10} - P_{00})s + (P_{01} - P_{00})t + (P_{00} + P_{11} - P_{10} - P_{01})st.$$

Figure 4.4(b) shows a generalized case where a ruled surface patch has been created between two curved edges.

Where ruled surface patches are linked together to form a composite surface, the curvature of the surface at each edge will be discontinuous. A smoother transition between surfaces can be achieved by replacing the linear interpolation between the two edges with a higher order interpolating function. One type, called **Hermite interpolation**, uses a cubic interpolating polynomial to join the two edges. Using this method, the slope of the surface across each edge can be controlled, enabling a smoother transition between adjacent surface patches to be created by the designer.

4.3.3 BOUNDED SURFACES

Planar and ruled surfaces use just two edge definitions to specify the surface over all (s, t) space. The boundaries of the surface patch are defined by limiting the range of values that can be taken by s and t. As a result, two of the four edges on the boundary of the patch are defined by the computer software. The position and shape of these edges are dependent upon the position and shape of the other two edges. This is not always convenient for the designer, who may wish to control the position and shape of all four edges independently. If this is the case, he must then use a parametric surface definition for which the boundary of the patch is specified by the four edges. The endpoints of adjacent edges must be common so that the surface patch is defined by a closed boundary. The shape of the surface can then be defined by interpolation of the curves across (s, t) space in the range $0 \leqslant s \leqslant 1$ and $0 \leqslant t \leqslant 1$ (Fig. 4.5).

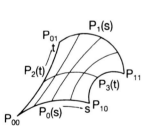

Fig. 4.5 *A bounded parametric surface patch.*

Bilinear Interpolation

Using the same notation as before, the position of the points $P_0(s)$ and $P_1(s)$ on two of the boundary edges are defined in terms of the parameter s. Similarly, the positions of the points $P_2(t)$ and $P_3(t)$ on the other two boundary edges are defined in terms of the parameter t. The corners of the patch are $P_{00} = P_0(0) = P_2(0)$, $P_{10} = P_0(1) = P_3(0)$, etc. The position of the point P_{st} on the surface is given by

$$P_{st} = (1 - t)P_0(s) + tP_1(s) + (1 - s)P_2(t) + sP_3(t) - (1 - s)(1 - t)P_{00}$$
$$- s(1 - t)P_{10} - t(1 - s)P_{01} - stP_{11}.$$

This surface definition can be used for any mixture of parametric curves used to define the four edges. Patches can be linked together to form composite surfaces, though whether the curvature of the surface across the patch boundary remains continuous across an edge depends upon whether edge continuity is maintained between joined edges.

Bicubic Interpolation

Bicubic interpolating surfaces make use of cubic equations to determine the shape of the curve within the boundary of the four edges. A general mathematical expression for these types of curved surface would be

$$P_{st} = a_{11}s^3t^3 + a_{12}s^3t^2 + a_{13}s^3t + a_{14}s^3 + a_{21}s^2t^3 + a_{22}s^2t^2 + a_{23}s^2t + a_{24}s^2$$
$$+ a_{31}st^3 + a_{32}st^2 + a_{33}st + a_{34}s + a_{41}t^3 + a_{42}t^2 + a_{43}t + a_{44},$$

where a_{ij} is a series of constants defined in terms of the surface patch boundary curves, the four corner points and three slopes at each corner.

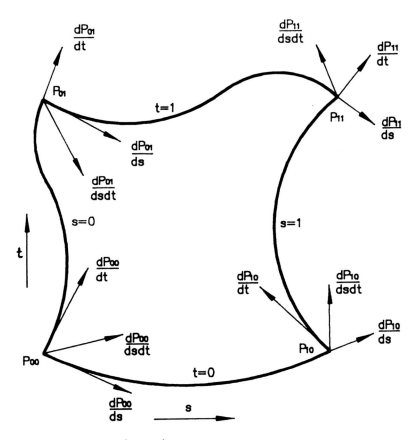

Fig. 4.6 *A typical Coons surface patch.*

Figure 4.6 shows an arrangement of a bicubic surface patch which is frequently used in CAD surface generation. It is known as the **Coons patch** after its orginator, Stephen Coons. The four boundary curves are cubic curves for which the slope of the curve is defined at each endpoint in a 3-D vector form. At each corner of the patch there are two slopes defined in this way. A third slope vector is given in terms of a partial derivative in both s and t and defines the degree of twist at the corner of the surface patch. Composite surfaces can be defined by placing adjacent patches in a position to match exactly the edges and their slopes, so giving a smooth surface profile between adjacent patches.

Similar curved surface forms can be generated using bicubic interpolation of other specific curve types, e.g. Bezier, uniform cubic B-spline, non-uniform cubic B-spline, etc. A generalized curved surface using Hermite interpolation, though, allows a mixture of curve types to be used for the boundary edges.

4.4   TECHNIQUES FOR 3-D MODELLING

4.4.1   WIRE FRAME

The wire-frame method of representing the 3-D geometry of the edges and vertices of an object simply extends the 2-D draughting approach discussed earlier into 3-D space. The model is constructed from a collection of 3-D line and curve segments and has the appearance of a frame constructed from wire because none of the faces of the object are fully represented.

The object in Fig. 4.7 is shown as a wire frame with only straight lines and semi-circular arcs. Each straight line is fully defined by two endpoints, while the semi-circular arcs require three control points to define their position and size fully. The geometry of the model is represented by the (x, y, z) co-ordinates of each of the control points. This data is stored in the vertex list. The topology of the model is represented by the entries in the edge list. This list records the vertex identities of the control points required to define each edge fully. The position and orientation of the model in 3-D space may be altered using 3-D transformations (e.g. translation, rotation about the x-axis, scaling). Modifications to the position or orientation of the 3-D model only affect the geometrical data stored in the vertex list, whereas if the structure itself is altered (e.g. an edge is deleted), then the topological data stored in the edge list will be modified appropriately. The simplicity of this modelling technique allows the 3-D model to be manipulated easily and the result can be displayed quickly. For this reason, wire-frame models are often used with surface and solid modellers to give a quick viewing of the object without waiting for a complete surface representation, which can take a long time to generate.

A difficulty with a wire-frame model is that hidden lines cannot be removed. For complex items, or where a number of items are being displayed simultaneously, the resulting screen image can be a jumble of lines that is impossible to determine. The use of colour, however, to differentiate between items or edges

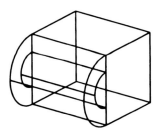

Fig. 4.7 *Wire-frame model consisting of lines and semi-circular arcs.*

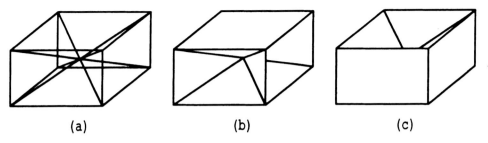

(a)   (b)   (c)

Fig. 4.8 *Ambiguous wire-frame model with two inter-pretations of its surface geometry.*

can significantly improve the understanding of a complex wire-frame image (see section 4.6.4).

Similarly, because surface features are not represented there are no contour lines and so the surface can be ambiguous and the resulting interpretation of the object open to question. The block drawn in Fig. 4.8(a) is a wire-frame model in which it is not clear which of the surfaces are plane and which re-entrant. Figures 4.8(b) and Fig. 4.8(c) show two interpretations of the wire-frame model and illustrate the ambiguous nature of this model. This latter problem is partic-ularly significant in CAD where the primary objective is to generate an object model that can be understood completely by all users without misinterpretation.

2½-D Objects

The term 2½-D is used for those parts which are either flat objects with a constant depth (extruded parts) or for solids of revolution. This limited class of 3-D entities can be generated on smaller CAD systems. Flat objects can be considered as 2-D shapes which are translated, swept or extruded, into the z dimension. Figure 4.9 shows a typical example. Using the 2½-D concept, the groove can be set to a shorter depth than the rest of the object to produce the recess. Revolute objects can also be produced by sweeping a 2-D profile through 360° as shown in Fig. 4.10. The amount of storage needed for 2½-D objects can be minimized by displaying in a wire-frame or faceted form.

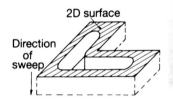

Fig. 4.9 *2½-D extruded shape.*

4.4.2 SURFACE MODELS

Surface models utilize the edge–vertex definitions of the wire-frame model as the basis for defining the geometry of the surface patches used to represent the faces of an object. The surface model will have an additional list, the **face list**, in which the identities of the edges used to define each surface patch will be stored. Figure 4.11 shows a wire-frame image of a block with its associated face–edge–vertex listing. This model comprises eight vertices, 12 straight-line edges and six faces. The type of surface used to represent the faces will depend upon the sophistication of the modelling software and the accuracy of the representation required. The faces of the object in Fig. 4.11 are each bounded by four edges, and so a bounded surface patch with bilinear interpolation will represent the surfaces of this item with suitable accuracy.

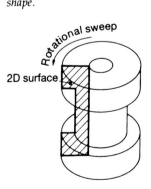

Fig. 4.10 *2½-D rotational shape.*

Fig. 4.11 *A wire-frame model of a block with its associated face–edge–vertex listing.*

faces	edges	vertices
1 1,2,3,4	1 1,2	1 0, 0,60
2 4,5,12,8	2 2,3	2 0, 0, 0
3 1,5,9,6	3 3,4	3 45, 0, 0
4 2,6,10,7	4 4,1	4 45, 0,60
5 3,7,11,8	5 1,5	5 0,25,60
6 9,10,11,12	6 2,6	6 0,25, 0
	7 3,7	7 45,25, 0
	8 4,8	8 45,25,60
	9 5,6	
	10 6,7	
	11 7,8	
	12 8,1	

Once the faces of an object have been represented using surface patches, it is possible to display the object with hidden edges removed. Where edges are curved, the silhouette outline of the object can be determined and so a more realistic image is displayed. The software routines for determining which edges can be seen and which are hidden involve many repeated calculations and so generating such images takes significantly longer than generating the wire-frame image. However, the calculations can be undertaken by even the smallest of business computers and so all 3-D CAD systems generally provide this display option. Furthermore, the hidden line removal image can be augmented by shading patterns and colour tone to increase its realism. This necessarily involves additional calculation by the computer, but as Fig. 4.12 shows, an Acorn BBC microcomputer with no additional memory is capable of generating this type of image.

The CAD user may wish to display a whole series of object models simultaneously to test their spatial relationships to each other. If one of the objects is to be moved to a new position, rather than identify the vertices needed to be moved (remembering the positions of the edges and surface patches will be modified automatically) it would be more convenient to identify just the object itself. To allow this **object-orientated manipulation** of the 3-D database, a **volume list** is created. The entries in the volume list identify the faces in the face list which are used to construct a single object. Thus, identifying the volume to be moved allows the computer to interrogate the volume–face–edge–vertex listing and identify automatically all the vertices whose positions need to be changed.

Low-level entry surface modelling systems use only the simplest of surface representations, i.e. planar surface patches. Where a curved surface is to be modelled, its shape can be approximated using a series of planar surface patches located around the curved edge. This type of representation is known as a **faceted model** (Fig. 4.12). A problem with faceted models is the large size of the face–edge–vertex listing required to represent curved surfaces, e.g. a

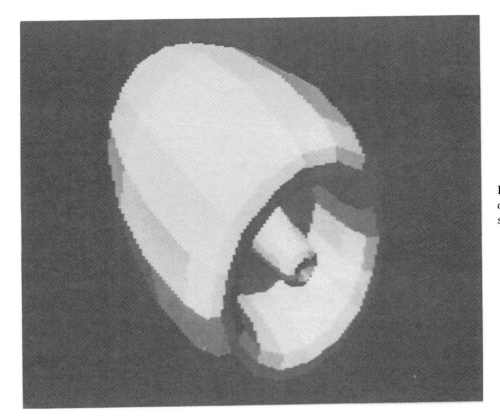

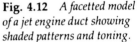

Fig. 4.12 *A facetted model of a jet engine duct showing shaded patterns and toning.*

cylinder that is represented by 12 facets around its surface requires 24 vertices, 36 edges and 12 faces to be defined. The accuracy of the representation is improved by increasing the number of facets (Fig. 4.13), but the size of the surface model database will be larger and the computer will take a longer time to manipulate the data and calculate the hidden line removed images. When using a faceted modeller, the CAD user will always have to make a compromise between accuracy of representation and speed of operation.

High-level entry surface-modelling systems utilize high-order polynomial curve types and bicubic interpolating surface patches to achieve highly accurate representations of complex surface shapes. Figure 4.14 shows the engine exhaust manifold of a motor car modelled using an industrial quality CAD system that has been devised for modelling doubly curved surfaces (e.g. aeroplane fuselages, boat hulls, telephone handsets, motor car bodyshells), where the shape of the surface is continually changing in all three axes. This type of application is probably the most complex of all 3-D modelling tasks. To achieve a good representation of a complex shape requires the designer to have a good understanding of the geometry of the object he is trying to create. Surface-modelling systems for these applications frequently provide a number of automatic surface-creation routines that generate surface representations from a small number of key surface profiles.

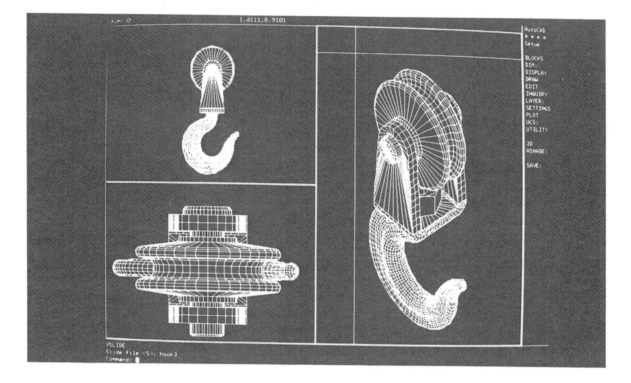

Fig. 4.13 *Three views of a multi-facetted model of a hook and pulley.*

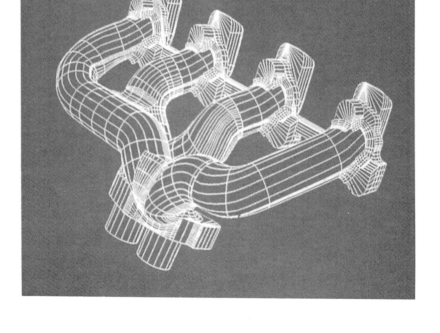

Fig. 4.14 *A surface model of an engine exhaust manifold.*

4.4.3 SOLID MODELLING

Solid modelling is a technique for 3-D object representation that is becoming more frequently used for CAD, especially in engineering applications. Not only does the solid model represent the full surface geometry of an item, but the internal 'material' not explicitly represented by an edge or surface is also considered as part of the model. So, if a solid model of an object is cut in half as if the item was being fully sectioned, the cut solid model would display new faces where the sectioning plane had cut through the 'solid material'. If the same operation had been carried out with a surface model of the object, only a series of new edges would have created where surface patches had been cut by the sectioning plane (e.g. an analogy to this process would be cutting the finger tips off a rubber glove with a pair of scissors).

The quality of image produced by a full solid modeller, with highlights and shadows, is often so good that it can be confused with photographs taken of the real object. Alternatively an abbreviated form can be displayed, which shows cylinders as multi-faceted surfaces with no hidden lines removed. The two most common methods of fully modelling solids are **boundary representation** and **constructive solid geometry**. In practice, most commercial solid modellers employ a combination of these two approaches, the most appropriate being chosen for a particular task. Spatial enumeration is suitable for use with small computers.

Constructive Solid Geometry (CSG)

This technique uses a series of standard 3-D building blocks, often referred to as primitives, which are used to build composite solid models. Standard CSG primitives include rectangular blocks, cylinders, cones and spheres whose shape, size and orientation can be defined from just a few describing parameters, e.g. a sphere is fully defined by its centre position and radius. Primitives are combined mathematically by a process known as **Boolean algebra** using processes of **union** ($\cup$), **difference** ($-$) and **intersection** ($\cap$).

Figure 4.15 shows the construction of a crank using just rectangular blocks and cylinders combined using a series of union and difference processes. Figure 4.15(a) shows the five primitives A, B, C, D and E in their correct positions with respect to each other. Figure 4.15(b) shows an intermediate object F that has been created using a union process, e.g. $F = A \cup B \cup C \cup D \cup E$. Three more cylinders G, H and I are shown in Fig. 4.15(c). Finally, the process of difference is used to form the object J ($J = F - G - H - I$) shown in Fig. 4.15(d). The full Boolean operation is

$$J = (A \cup B \cup C \cup D \cup E) - G - H - I.$$

Figure 4.15 illustrates two of the Boolean processes. The process of union clearly fuses the primitives into a new object, while the process of difference is one of subtraction as when drilling a hole. The Boolean process of intersection is illustrated in Fig. 4.16, where the primitives A and B have been combined to form object C (e.g. $C = A \cap B$). This Boolean process results in an object whose

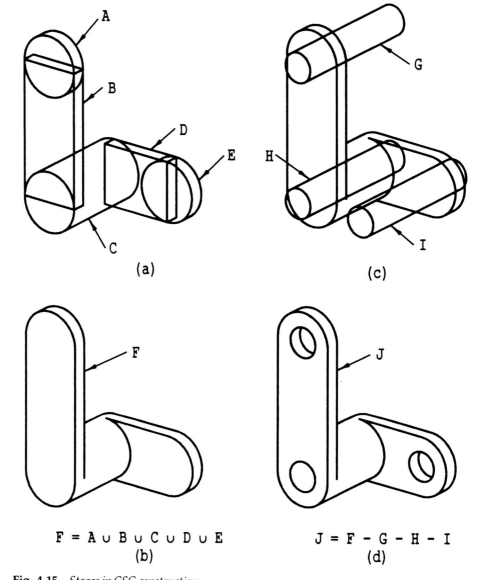

A

B

D

E

C

(a)

G

H

I

(c)

F

$F = A \cup B \cup C \cup D \cup E$

(b)

J

$J = F - G - H - I$

(d)

Fig. 4.15 *Stages in CSG construction.*

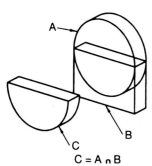

A

C

B

$C = A \cap B$

Fig. 4.16 *An example of CSG intersection.*

volume is common to the primitives so combined. It is of value for checking interference between two or more solid models.

The database for models using CSG is a combination of data and of logical procedures for merging the various primitives. It is compact to store, but lengthy to build. If only the CSG **tree** is kept, comprising which primitives are used, how they are connected and their sizes, then storage is very compact. This form of database is called **unevaluated**. The slow task of finding face and edge intersections is generally left to the end of the model build, prior to which the model can easily be amended by changing the tree. Once the full surface representation has been calculated (i.e. an **evaluated** state) and stored, the data storage advantages are largely lost, but the model can quickly be displayed. Surfaces are stored in their algebraic form, usually as quadrics (e.g. unbounded planes, cylinders, cones and spheres) which must have a closed form of topology. CSG cannot deal with parametrically described sculptured surfaces. These must be approximated by a combination of solids having quadric surfaces.

Boundary Representation (B-Rep)

B-Rep stores a description of the object in terms of its faces, edges and vertices in a similar manner to the surface modeller. Since the boundary information is kept at all times as an explicit definition (i.e. evaluated), it is quicker to build the model than using CSG, but the database that must be stored is larger. Boundary representation is very compatible with wire-frame models, but modifications are more difficult to make than when using CSG. Boundary representation is a useful technique for non-standard shapes, e.g. aircraft fuselage and wing shapes and for car body styling. Boundary representation modellers usually come with a variety of construction facilities and frequently include Boolean processes to generate objects from B-Rep primitives. The results of these combinations are immediately calculated and the object database amended to include the new structure.

Spatial Enumeration

In this technique, 3-D space is divided up into a number of small 3-D **cells**. The process is simple to program and can be implemented in a hardware chip. The intersection of two solids can be found easily by looking for the common spatial properties in each of the two sets of 3-D cells. However, an exact definition of the boundary, or intersection curve, is difficult to display and to change. Also surface definition is generally poor. A small increase in cell resolution leads to a vast increase in data storage.

4.5 THREE-DIMENSIONAL TRANSFORMATIONS

The addition of a third dimension to the previously defined 2-D transformations adds some complications, particularly for rotations. Figure 4.17 shows the positive rotation directions in relation to a right hand set of positive Cartesian axes.

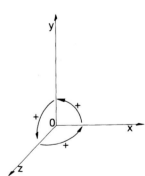

Fig. 4.17 *Positive rotation conventions.*

4.5.1 TRANSLATION

Pure linear transformation is little affected by the introduction of the z-axis. The triangle in Fig. 4.18 shows an example of 3-D translation for which

$$x_1 = x + \Delta x$$
$$y_1 = y + \Delta y$$
$$z_1 = z + \Delta z,$$

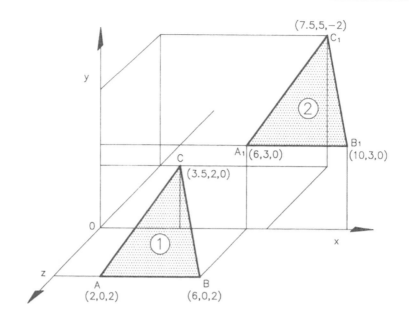

Fig. 4.18 *An example of 3-D translation.*

i.e. the separate translation values Δx, Δy and Δz can be added independently to each axis to achieve the new translated co-ordinates (x_1, y_1, z_1) for each of the corners of the triangle ABC.

4.5.2 SCALING

Similarly, the scaling can be applied to each axis independently, i.e.

$$x_1 = x \times S_x$$
$$y_1 = y \times S_y$$
$$z_1 = z \times S_z,$$

where S_x, S_y and S_z are the scale factors in each axis direction. Normally an overall, constant scale factor applies in which $S_x = S_y = S_z$.

4.5.3 ROTATIONS

Rotations are similarly treated. This reduces a 3-D rotation to a sequence of 2-D rotations. The rotation about the z-axis is as previously described for a 2-D rotation, i.e. for R_z

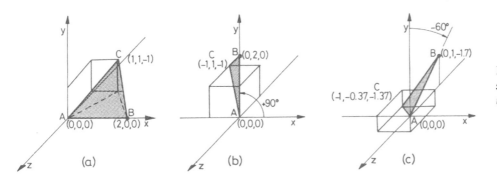

Fig. 4.19 *An example of successive rotations of a triangle.*

$$x_1 = x \cos\theta - y \sin\theta$$
$$y_1 = y \cos\theta + x \sin\theta$$
$$z_1 = z.$$

there is no change in the z co-ordinate due to rotation about the z-axis. For R_y

$$x_1 = x \cos\theta + z \sin\theta$$
$$y_1 = y$$
$$z_1 = x \cos\theta - x \sin\theta$$

and for R_x

$$x_1 = x$$
$$y_1 = y \cos\theta - z \sin\theta$$
$$z_1 = z \cos\theta + y \sin\theta$$

Figure 4.19 shows an example of successive rotations in which a triangle (Fig. 4.19(a)) with AB coincident with the x-axis, is to be successively rotated about the 0z-axis by $+90°$ (Fig. 4.19(b)) and they by $-60°$ about the 0x axis to give the final view as shown in Fig. 4.19(c). Each of the corners A, B and C would have x', y' and z' co-ordinates which can be calculated from the previously given equations after each rotation. See also 3-D transformations in Appendix A.

4.6   THREE-DIMENSIONAL DISPLAY CONTROL FACILITIES

The display of 3-D models requires some specialized software routines for generating the screen image of the object. Like so many of the 2-D display control routines, the calculations for many of the 3-D display routines discussed below are carried out by graphics processors local to the graphics display. These processors are able to use the information in the 3-D model database to generate the screen image very quickly.

4.6.1   ORTHOGRAPHIC PROJECTION

In 2-D draughting systems the graphics screen is used quite simply to represent the x- and y-axes of the draughting plane. Difficulties arise when defining 3-D objects which require a third z-axis because of a number of conventions. The

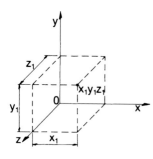

Fig. 4.20 *Positive axes in a right hand Cartesian co-ordinate system.*

most common convention adopted in texts on geometry is known as the right-hand Cartesian co-ordinate axis system. This is illustrated in Fig. 4.20. In this system the x and y-axes are as in the 2-D system and the positive z-axis is shown as if coming out of the graphics screen. Thus a point in 3-D space is defined by the Cartesian co-ordinate dimensions (x_1, y_1, z_1). Further confusion can arise because some texts describe a left-hand Cartesian co-ordinate axis system as shown in Fig. 4.21. Using this convention, the positive z-axis is going into the graphics screen away from the observer. This method is favoured where it is thought to be more 'natural' for the depth of an object (along the z-axis) to recede away from the observer.

In this text we will adopt the convention of employing a right-hand set of Cartesian axes with the motion of an object shown with reference to a fixed set of axes. Also we will consider the plane of the graphics screen to have its own 2-D co-ordinate system with the horizontal screen direction as the x'-axis and the vertical screen direction as the y'-axis.

An orthographic projection of a 3-D object can be developed by calculating the corresponding positions of each vertex on the plane of the graphics screen. A 2-D vertex list for (x', y') space will be generated and the screen image of the

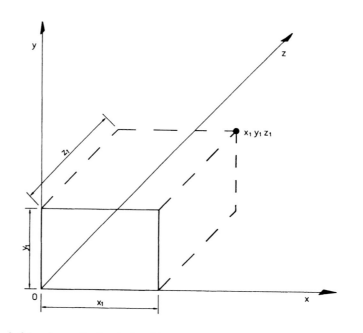

Fig. 4.21 *Left hand co-ordinate set of positive axes.*

object can be drawn by simply following a 2-D draughting routine. In the case where the observer is positioned at some point on the positive z-axis looking along the axis towards the origin (the **focal point**), the screen image can be generated simply by ignoring all z co-ordinates and using the x and y co-ordinates to define the position of each vertex on the graphics screen, i.e.

$$x' = x$$
$$y' = y.$$

In this case a z-orthographic projection will be obtained. Zoom and pan processes can be used to ensure the object is fully displayed in the graphics viewport.

The z-orthographic projection can be considered to give a front elevation of the 3-D object. Alternatively, a plan elevation can be created using a y-orthographic projection, where

$$x' = x$$
$$y' = -z,$$

or an end elevation by using an x-orthographic projection, where

$$x' = -z$$
$$y' = y.$$

However, it is not always convenient to use these projection systems because at any one time only two of the three axes are displayed. Displaying views of each projection simultaneously will give the graphics screen the appearance of a conventional engineering drawing, but the observer must then interpret the views to discern for himself what object is being displayed. Other problems with this approach include the additional time required to generate all three views, and the reduction in size of the image on the screen.

A more convenient way of displaying the 3-D object is to use a pictorial image, e.g. isometric projection, where all three axes are displayed simultaneously in a single image. In this case, the observer can be considered to be positioned at the viewpoint (x_E, y_E, z_E) looking towards the origin. To obtain an orthographic projection of the 3-D model requires both the model and the observer to be rotated in 3-D space so that the viewpoint is transformed from (x_E, y_E, z_E) to $(0, 0, s)$, where

$$s^2 = x_E^2 + y_E^2 + z_E^2.$$

The new position of the viewpoint lies on the positive z-axis so that a z-orthographic projection can be obtained by using the new vertex co-ordinates of the 3-D model. The transformation process involves two rotations. The first rotation is about the z-axis, where the angle of rotation is calculated to move the viewpoint into the z, x plane. The second rotation is about the y-axis, where the angle of rotation is calculated to move the intermediate position of the viewpoint on to the z-axis. The co-ordinates of all the vertices are transformed in the same way.

A further display option offered by 3-D CAD systems enables the positions of both the viewpoint (x_E, y_E, z_E) and the focal point (x_F, y_F, z_F) to be defined. In this case, the 3-D model and the viewpoint must be translated in 3-D space so that the focal point is transformed from (x_F, y_F, z_F) to $(0, 0, 0)$ before the rotational transformation described above can take place.

In all the cases considered, the positions of the viewpoint and the focal point serve only to determine the direction from which the object is being observed. The distance of the observer from the object plays no part in determining the screen image of an orthographic projection. If more 'natural' images are to be developed, this distance must be considered.

4.6.2 PERSPECTIVE VIEWS

A means of displaying realism and depth is to project objects as perspective views. To obtain a single-point perspective view let us consider the object has been transformed for orthographic projection purposes and so the viewpoint is positioned on the positive z-axis. Figure 4.22 shows the eye looking at a cube so that the z-axis passes through the eye and the object. A perspective plane (the plane of the graphic screen) is placed between the eye and the object. Rays, drawn from the eye to the corners of the block, will pass through the projection plane and create the image. Corners nearest to the eye, e.g. A, will appear larger than corner B which is further from the eye.

To find the perspective view co-ordinates, we need to find the x' and y' co-ordinates of points such as B_1. These can be found by considering Fig. 4.23 which shows a side view of Fig. 4.22. In the sided view, from similar triangles, it can be seen that the ratio

$$\frac{z_1}{y_1} = \frac{z_2}{y_2},$$

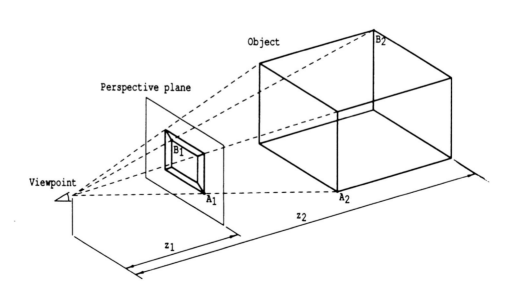

Fig. 4.22 *Perspective projection.*

from which

$$y_1 = \frac{y_2 z_1}{z_2}.$$

Similarly, horizontal ratios will be preserved as

$$\frac{z_1}{x_1} = \frac{z_2}{x_2},$$

from which

$$x_1 = \frac{x_2 z_1}{z_2}.$$

Hence the screen co-ordinates of B_1 are

$$x' = \frac{x_2 z_1}{z_2}$$

$$y' = \frac{y_2 z_1}{z_2}.$$

The values of z_1 and z_2 are absolute values and represent the z-axis distances from the viewpoint to the projection plane, which is fixed, and from the view-

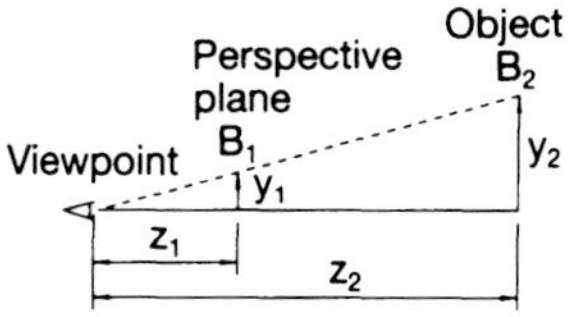

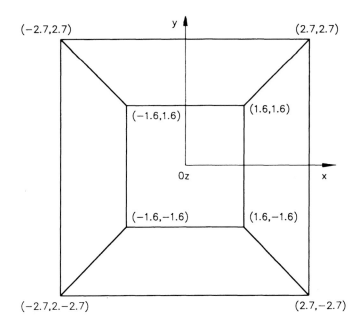

Fig. 4.23 *Side view of perspective projection.*

Fig. 4.24 *Single-point perspective view of a cube.*

point to the point being projected, e.g. B_2, which varies between vertices.

The resultant view of a cube is shown in Fig. 4.24. The cube is of side length 4, centrally viewed from a distance of 8 from the viewpoint at the cube centroid and also to the projection plane, i.e. $z_1 = 8$. The effect is a vanishing point at $0z$, i.e. the viewpoint. As the viewpoint is moved closer to the screen, the convergence effect will increase. If the object is moved further from the projection plane, it also moves further from the viewpoint and so the converging effect is diminished. The advantage of perspective views is that they enable the user to 'fly around' an object to view it from many different angles; a facility that is of particular advantage to architects.

4.6.3 HIDDEN LINES

Because wire-frame figures are confusing when all the hidden edges are left in, it is useful to be able to erase, or dot, those which are hidden behind the nearer surfaces. There are many programs for deleting hidden lines. The more general purpose are extremely complex and require both a large memory and a considerable time to execute. One of the simpler strategies can handle only convex bodies. A body is defined as convex if, when any two points on the body are joined by a line, all parts of the line lie within the body. Figure 4.25 shows examples of convex and concave bodies. The program checks whether lines lie behind plane surface patches (or facets). A surface test is used in which a line of sight is drawn to the object surface from the projection origin. A further line is drawn as a normal outward from the surface of the object. If the angle between the two lines is less than 90°, then the face and all its edges are visible. Figure 4.26 shows a rectangle projected on to a plane. The normals to the centres of the four surfaces are N_1 through to N_4 and the angles made between the line of sight and these normals are θ_1 to θ_4. Since θ_1 and θ_2 are both less than 90°, faces 1 and 2 are seen in full. θ_3 and θ_4 are both greater than 90° and so represent hidden surfaces.

This simple hidden surface removal test is often used to remove back faces before more rigorous hidden line tests are made. With concave objects, or where more than one object is being displayed, a surface may be partially obscured by another surface. In this case, the boundary edges of the surface may themselves be completely or partially obscured. A lengthy calculation procedure is required to determine the part of the edge that can be seen. How-

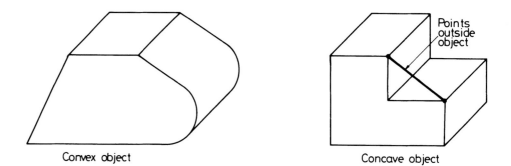

Fig. 4.25 *Examples of concave and convex objects.*

Convex object

Concave object

Points outside object

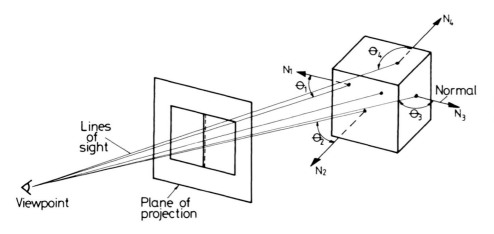

Fig. 4.26 *General hidden-surface test.*

ever, by removing back faces first, the number of surfaces that need testing in this way can be reduced. Where curved surfaces are displayed, the silhouette edges must defined to ensure a realistic outline of the object is displayed.

4.6.4 COLOUR SHADING

Additional realism can be achieved if the appearance of an object with hidden surface removed can be shaded with colour. There are many established techniques for colour shading. However, even the simplest of these routines involves a large amount of computational effort and the generation of such images takes considerably longer than those for hidden surface methods. The final appearance of the object is dependent both on the properties of its surface, and on the position and illumination characteristics of the light.

It is usual for the object to be lit from two sources: one the ambient light and the other from one or more point sources. Ambient light comes from all directions and gives a diffuse reflection off a surface. The object will appear to be shaded uniformly over its whole surface when only ambient illumination is used. A point source, however, provides a directional light which will illuminate some surface areas and leave others unlit, consequently the appearance of each facet of the object must be considered separately. The colour seen reflected from a surface illuminated by a point source will depend upon the colour intensity I_s of the source light, its angle of incidence φ relative to the surface normal, and the reflectance k of the surface. If the surface has a low reflectance, a diffuse light will be reflected whose intensity I_d is calculated using Lambert's cosine law

$$I_d = I_s k \cos \varphi.$$

If the surface has a high reflectance, light will be reflected in a single direction. This is known as **specular light** and has the same colour as its source. The colour intensity seen reflected from the facet is the sum of specular and diffuse reflections from all the point sources, plus the diffuse reflection from the ambient source.

The results achieved using the above technique give single-value colour intensities for each visible facet or surface patch of the 3-D model. This approach is suitable for models with planar surfaces, but is limited for models with curved surfaces. The observed colour intensity of a curved surface will, in reality, vary continually across the surface patch. This can be simulated by using average surface normals to calculate the colour intensity value at each corner vertex of the facet or patch. These values are then used to interpolate intermediate intensity values across the surface. This technique, attributed to Gourand, will give a curved surface a smooth colour shaded appearance. An improved technique, developed by Phong, interpolates surface normals across the surface patch, allowing the intensity of light from point sources to be determined at each intermediate position.

Ray tracing is the most comprehensive technique for producing colour shaded images. It is based upon simple principles, but the very large number of repetitive calculations involved restricts its use to the more powerful computer systems where dedicated hardware is often used for the calculations. Ray tracing considers each pixel of the graphics screen in turn, tracing back the path of light incident upon the pixel to its original source. Using this technique, surface reflections, transparency, refraction and cast shadows can be considered, giving a very realistic final image.

4.7 GRAPHICS STANDARDS

The engineering design and manufacture process requires a continual interchange of information between the synthesis and analysis and production and management of manufacture phases of the product development cycle as shown in Chapter 1. Traditionally, information has been exchanged using hard-copy documentation (e.g. engineering drawings, parts lists). However, the existence of a computer-based description of the geometry of a part allows this information to be transferred numerically between computer systems. In practice, engineering companies have found that this exchange of data has reduced design times, improved the accuracy of information exchange and its understanding, consequently reducing the time required to complete the product development cycle. However, if the exchange of geometrical information between users is to be completely successful, it is essential that the information is organized into a format understood by each computer system involved in the exchange process. This is especially true where the computer systems involved use different software and hardware configurations. Two approaches to this problem are briefly discussed. Finally, we will consider the graphics kernel system (GKS) which is not truly an exchange standard for engineering applications *per se* but a graphics standard to allow graphics software to operate on any graphics hardware with the minimum of adaptation.

4.7.1 DATA EXCHANGE BY DIRECT TRANSLATION

In this approach, information created in CAD system A is reorganized and translated into a format understood by another CAD system, CAD system B.

This requires A to have a translator for converting information generated by A into the database format used by B. Similarly, if information from B is be sent to A, then B must have a translator to convert information generated by B into the database format used by A. In principle this technique works well because the translation converts database information into a format that can immediately be used by the receiving system, but the exchange of information can only be between these two systems. If a third system was involved, CAD system C, then A would require two translators: one for A to B translation, the other for A to C translation. Likewise, systems B and C would each require two translators to ensure that a complete interchange of information between the three systems can be achieved. Difficulties arise when information has to be exchanged between a large number of different systems. In this situation, direct translation is not always feasible because a suitable translator may not exist, or the current translator has not been modified to prepare files suitable for use with newer versions of the receiving software.

4.7.3 DATA EXCHANGE USING NEUTRAL FORMATS

In this approach, information created in CAD system A is translated into a neutral format that can be used by any other CAD system. However, the receiving system, CAD system B, must first convert the neutral format into its own format before it can use the data. To exchange information from B to A requires B to generate the neutral format file and A to convert this information into its own data structure. Using this method, each system must have a **pre-processor** for converting information from its own database into the neutral format and a **post-processor** for converting information in a neutral format file into its own structure. The advantage here, is that a CAD system need only have pre- and post-processors to enable a full exchange of information to occur between it and many other systems that use the neutral file format exchange. Currently there are a number of neutral file formats being used in CAD. Some (e.g. IGES, SET, VDA-FS) have been established as national standards, others (e.g. DXF) are software vendors' own standards. No international standard for neutral format files exists as yet, but the International Standards Organization (ISO) has begun development of a standard known as STEP.

Initial Graphics Exchange Specification (IGES)

IGES is the most common neutral format standard in use for general engineering applications and is supported by all major CAD systems, though in many cases the standard is not fully implemented. The standard is comprehensive in its treatment of 2-D and 3-D engineering data, with IGES 4.0 supporting CSG solid model geometry and a later version supporting B-rep solid model information. Data is stored as coded entities in an ASCII file. In 2-D draughting, codes for circular arcs (100), lines (110), diameter dimensions (206) and linear dimensions (216) are typical of the entities supported by this standard. While IGES is in common use commercially, it has yet to take on the status of an International Standard.

SET

This is a neutral format standard developed in France by Aérospatiale and so is in common use in the aerospace industry in that country. It is similar to IGES in that it offers a complete exchange standard for all engineering information.

VDA-FS

This is a German neutral file standard whose use is restricted just to surface data exchange and used primarily in the motor car industry.

Standard for the Exchange of Product Model Data (STEP)

In 1985 ISO initiated the development of this International Standard. The aim is to produce a standard that can be used throughout the product development cycle, so the applications for which the standard is being developed are very broad, e.g. draughting, 3-D modelling, finite-element modelling, mechanical parts, electronic parts and architecture. A first draft of this standard was released in 1988, and therefore this standard has yet to achieve widespread use amongst CAD users.

Data Exchange File (DXF)

This is a neutral file format developed by Autodesk for use with their range of CAD software, most notably AutoCAD. This file allows information to be transferred readily between Autodesk products, or exchanged with other CAD systems that support this neutral format. Its use is common amongst PC-based CAD systems because of the importance AutoCAD retains in this CAD sector.

4.7.4 GRAPHICS KERNEL SYSTEM (GKS)

The need for an international graphics standard has arisen because, without a common standard, each time a new hardware vendor attempts to use graphics software, a major rewrite of the graphics programs is necessary. The process of formulating an International Standard started in the mid-1970s and was adopted by ISO in 1982. The difficulty has been that each hardware and software supplier has had its own standards within the company and so each has attempted to ensure that its own features appear in the standards. It has thus taken a number of years to achieve a concensus on which features should be adopted.

A difficulty occurs because the standard must cater for a whole range of equipment and the coding must adopt many features which are not required in any single hardware/software combination. This leads to more memory and longer run times than would otherwise be necessary. The result is that often only a minimal subset of GKS is implemented, which is then further modified by the company. The result is that each company's version of GKS is slightly different.

GKS is a set of procedures for standardizing subroutine interfaces so that any hardware configuration of input and output devices can be used with any software package. GKS uses many of the concepts listed in this chapter, including features such as world and normalized device co-ordinates. It attempts to ensure that the applications package is unaffected by any peculiarities of the hardware by defining standard classes of input and standard output primitives. The device independence of GKS is introduced by defining a concept of an abstract workstation. This workstation is rather different from that of the intelligent workstation discussed in Chapter 2. The GKS workstation utilizes a single display device which can be a plotter, printer, or storage tube, refresh or raster display. If a separate display device is used, this will be identified as a separate workstation. Thus there are input workstations (keyboard, tablet, light pen, etc.), output work stations and input/output work stations. The output primitives are abstractions of basic actions that a basic device can perform. The six basic primitives are:

1. polyline – a set of connected lines defined by their sequence of points,
2. polymarker – symbols located at a given position,
3. text – strings of characters at a given position,
4. fill areas – polygons which may be hollow or filled with colour, pattern or style of hatching,
5. pixel array – arrays of pixels, each with its own colours, and
6. generalized drawing primitives – circular and elliptical arcs, splines, etc., characterized by a means of identification, a number of points and additional data, e.g. radii or angles of arc.

Each output primitive has two groups of attributes. One group is an attribute fixed when the primitive is created, e.g. text size and spacing, pattern size for filling areas. The other group is a workstation attribute that can identify, for example, the type of line, line width, colour. This latter facility would, for example, allow a line to be output on to one workstation, consisting of a display screen, as a particular colour and when input to another workstation, consisting of a plotter, convert the line to a particular type, e.g. centre line. GKS also defines **metafiles** for use in the long-term filing of graphical information between systems or from one place to another, e.g. by the use of magnetic tape.

SUMMARY

In this chapter we have considered more of the fundamental principles of computer software for CAD. We have discussed in depth some of the underlying mathematical concepts used to model objects in 3-D CAD systems, building upon the 2-D CAD principles discussed in Chapter 3. This gives an understanding of the basic processes which are utilized in most commercial CAD software systems. The discussion has been generalized as it is the principles of the approach that were of importance at this stage, not the reality of how it is implemented into the software. However, in the following chapters we will look at the use of commercial CAD systems and consider in detail how object models are created in both 2-D and 3-D systems. In these chapters we will be concerned with the way the designer has to interact with the CAD system to achieve the desired result.

EXERCISES

1. Discuss the differences between the 3-D and 2-D parametric representations of straight lines, circles, circular arcs and curves. If the three control points specifying a 3-D circular arc are colinear, what additional information must be supplied before the arc can be defined uniquely?
2. Why may a wire-frame model cause the observer some difficulty with interpretation? Sketch some alternative interpretations of Fig. 4.2.
3. Discuss the relative merits of ruled and bounded surfaces.
4. How many separate parameters are needed for the definition of four adjacent Coons patches for a smoothly intersecting 3-D curved surface?
5. Discuss the relative merits of wire-frame and surface-modelling techniques.
6. Discuss the relative merits of constructive solid geometry and boundary representation solid modelling techniques.
7. In CSG modelling, what are primitives? What Boolean operations are used to construct more elaborate solid models? Sketch the results of applying these modelling operations to a cylinder and rectangular block.
8. The triangle shown in Fig. 4.19 is to be translated by -1 in the z direction, then rotated $+60°$ about $0z$ and finally rotated $+30°$ about $0y$. Draw the positions of the triangle after each transformation and give the corner A in each case, as functions of x and y.
9. Use a boundary representation to describe a cube.
10. What are the advantages and disadvantages of using a wire-frame construction for the block shown in Fig. 4.11?
11. Using Figs. 4.22 to 4.24 as a guide, construct the perspective views of the end of a cylinder $\phi40$ by 60 long centrally viewed with a distance of 60 from the viewpoint to the front face of the cylinder. The projection plane is 50 from the viewpoint.
12. A cube of side length 40 is viewed along its diagonal. Describe how you would check which surfaces are hidden. Assume the picture plane is vertical and the diagonal is horizontal inclined at $45°$ to the picture plane.
13. Discuss the relative merits of data exchange by direct translation and data exchange using neutral formats.
14. Contrast the aims of the functions of the GKS Standard with that of the IGES.

Two-dimensional shape generation

5.1 INTRODUCTION

Chapter 3 gave a general overview of CAD and computer software packages, together with examples of the detailed coding underlying the facilities of a package. The basic principles of 2-D drawing were given in Chapter 3 in order to show how they related to computer graphics as a whole. In this chapter and the following Chapters 6 and 7, a more detailed description of 2-D drawing is given describing how to start using a computer to generate shapes, together with the features and difficulties found in some commercial CAD packages.

It must be emphasized that the objects shown in drawings in these three chapters are two-dimensional (2-D) and not three-dimensional (3-D). As such, no 3-D database is formed for representing the object. Only a series of lines (lines, arcs, circles, etc) are displayed on screen. The viewer must interpret and interconnect these lines in order to visualize the object. In the case of one package referred to (AutoCAD), there is a facility for generating 3-D databases, but this is not described in these three chapters. The 3-D facility of AutoCAD is described in Chapter 8.

When generating 2-D drawings by CAD, the computer, its peripherals and software, replace the drawing board, instruments and pens or pencils which are used when drawing 2-D shapes by manual methods.

5.2 ADVANTAGES OF CAD OVER MANUAL DRAWING

1. Speed. The speed at which accurate drawings can be produced is greatly increased. The increase depends upon the item being processed. Outlines can be produced four or five times as quickly; CAD dimensioning is much faster than when using manual methods; hatching can be as much as twenty times as fast.
2. More interesting. Boring and repetitive tasks such as dimensioning, printing, hatching are reduced – CAD does them automatically.
3. Amendments. An original drawing can be recalled to screen, amendments made as required and the amended drawing saved to a file on disk. Both the original and the amended drawings can be retained for recall when needed. Many companies draw products which are variations on a basic theme. Once the first computer drawing is produced, subsequent amendments can be

made quickly. This is an important commercial justification for computer drawing.

4. Storage. There is no need to store large numbers of drawings on paper. CAD drawings can be stored electronically, e.g. on disks or tapes in drawing files.

5. Distribution. Any size or scale of a drawing can be plotted as required without having to make new drawings to different scales. Drawings of the same items to different scales can be plotted from the same drawing file for distribution to those requiring them.

6. Additions. Details from drawing or text files can be added to existing computer drawings with ease.

7. Lines. Lines of differing thicknesses and/or colours can be included in drawings by changing pens on the plotter in use. Some CAD software packages contain commands which alter line thicknesses on screen, or alter the type of a line, e.g. change a centre line to an outline line.

8. Circuits. Speed is noticeably increased when drawing circuit diagrams with CAD. All symbols for such circuits can be kept in library files to be recalled for adding into circuits as and when needed.

5.2.1 GENERAL NOTE ABOUT THE USE OF CAD

When using CAD packages there are two important concepts that should be practised.

1. Never draw the same detail twice. CAD packages always contain facilities allowing details to be copied, moved, mirrored, rotated around a given position, copied in arrays or stored as separate details to be recalled to other drawings. These facilities should be used as often as possible.

2. CAD drawings should be drawn to the relevant British Standards.

5.3 STARTING UP YOUR TERMINAL FOR CAD

5.3.1 SOME POINTS TO NOTE WHEN STARTING TO USE CAD

1. When you switch on, either the computer will have been programmed to start up with the CAD software you will be using; or

2. You will have to load the software from:
   (a) the computer's hard disk, or;
   (b) floppy disks.

3. Check that you have a manual covering the operation of the software at hand in case you get into difficulties.

4. Check that you have a formatted floppy disk in the disk drive to take backup copies of your drawing files, even if they will also load into the hard disk. Always work with backup disks to avoid corrupting the original disks. Save your work on the floppy disk at regular intervals – if a fault occurs while you are working, you will at least have some of it saved to be reloaded when the fault is cleared.

5. When you start up or when you load the CAD software, the program may

automatically load the required drawing sheet size, with various limits and commands ready for use; check that this is appropriate to your requirements.

6. If the sheet size is not so loaded, you may have to set the drawing limits and other commands to the required sheet size, linetypes, measurement units, etc., before commencing drawing (Chapter 6).

Note: The details given in this chapter and Chapter 6 assume that an A2, A3 or A4 sheet size file, with their necessary units and layers (see Chapter 6) has already been loaded into the computer.

5.3.2 UNDERSTAND YOUR WORK STATION

Try to understand the various parts of the workstation you are using:

1. the microcomputer – its type, and its memory size in Kbytes or Mbytes;
2. how to use the keyboard; where certain constantly used keys are; the meanings of some keys which may not be familiar to you;
3. where the floppy disk drive slot is; which lights indicate the hard and floppy disks being on; the memory capacity of the floppy disks; whether the floppies you are using contain the correct directories;
4. how to use the pointing device you will be using for the CAD system – mouse, trackerball, puck, stylus, graphics tablet;
5. the menu and command system of the CAD software package being used.

5.4 CAD SOFTWARE PACKAGES

There are a large number of CAD software packages for 2-D drawing. In order to show features common to these, references in Chapters 5 to 7 will largely be restricted to three CAD packages. This does not mean that other packages have less facilities than these three. There is a large variety of packages available which makes it difficult to include details of more than a few representative types. For further details of CAD packages, see Appendix C. Our three representative packages used in Chapters 5–8 are given below.

5.4.1 AUTOSKETCH

This is a simple and inexpensive 2-D CAD package developed for IBM-type microcomputers. It is also available for the Acorn Archimedes microcomputer. It is purchased as either a single disk or as two disks (depending on your computer setup) which can be loaded on to a hard disk, or used from the floppy disks.

5.4.2 TECHSOFT DESIGNER

This is a 2-D CAD package for use with the range of Acorn BBC computers – B, B+, Master, Master Compact and Archimedes. It is widely used in schools and is also suitable for light industrial use. It is available on several floppy disks for all but the Archimedes, for which it comes on one disk. It can be loaded on to a hard disk.

5.4.3 AUTOCAD

This is available for the IBM, Apple, Macintosh and some mini computers; it is the most widely used CAD package. It is used throughout the world in educational and industrial systems. AutoCAD is capable of many more features than the other two packages and involves a much more complex menu and command structure. It is more difficult to use and requires considerable practice before its full value as a draughting package is mastered. It is a much more expensive package both as to software and hardware requirements. It is usually operated from a hard disk.

5.5 FEATURES COMMON TO CAD SOFTWARE PACKAGES

The features common to these three packages are typical of most other CAD packages.

5.5.1 CO-ORDINATES

Two-dimensional co-ordinate geometry is the normal method used in CAD software for indicating the positions of points within the screen drawing area. With some CAD software it is necessary to impose **limits** to the maximum co-ordinates available horizontally (x) and vertically (y) for the screen drawing area. In other software the user is asked whether A4, A3, A2 or other drawing area is required before commencing drawing. In some software the (0, 0) position is at the bottom left of the drawing area, in others (0, 0) is central to the drawing area. Each coordinate unit can be regarded as a drawing unit, thus CAD users can work in millimetres, kilometres, inches, feet or whatever other unit they require, on the assumption that the units for drawing correspond to the co-ordinate units, providing they have been chosen correctly.

5.5.2 MENUS AND COMMANDS

Features of particular importance, common to most CAD software packages, are systems of menus and commands for providing easy-to-operate methods by which the parts of drawings will be executed. Although the positioning of menus and the actual wording of commands within menus varies between CAD packages, there is a good degree of comparability, with many commands being similar in different packages. The main common feature of the menus is that they are words, short phrases, or icons which can be understood quickly and easily with reference to the task they are designed to operate.

Many of the menu commands contain sub-menus also consisting of words, phrases or icons. In addition most commands call up prompt words and phrases which appear at the top or at the bottom of the screen (in some cases both at top and bottom) which allow the commands to be understood and the steps needed to perform the tasks controlled by the commands. In fact one important detail to remember when using CAD software is to make sure you read such prompts before taking action on them.

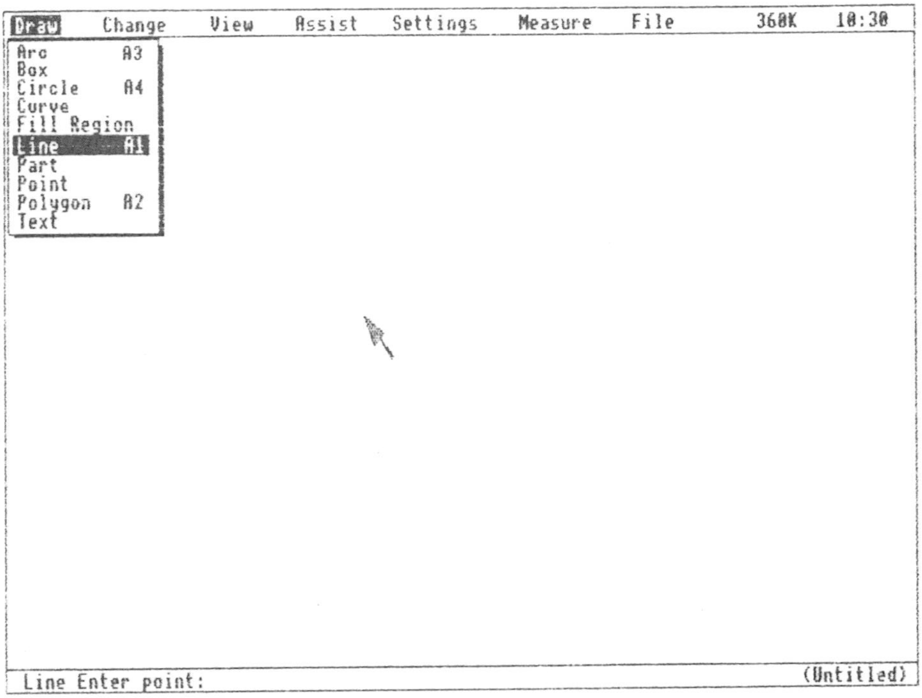

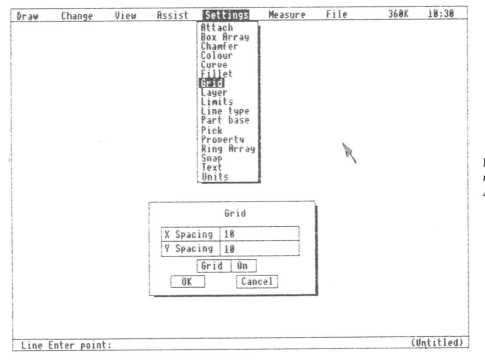

Fig. 5.1 *A pull-down menu from AutoSketch.*

Fig. 5.2 *A pull-down menu and dialogue box from AutoSketch.*

Parts of the menus appear on screen when the CAD software is loaded into the computer. These may be on one side (left or right) of the screen, or operated as pull-down menus (Figs. 5.1 and 5.2) by pointing at menu headings along the top of the screen. The menus of some CAD software appear in the centre of the screen, to disappear when a command from the menu is selected. Pointing at a menu command usually highlights the word or phrase of the command and causes the software program appropriate to the highlighted command to be selected and ready to operate. Selection may be carried out using cursor keys on the keyboard, by pointing a pointer arrow or a cursor on the screen at the required command with the aid of a mouse, puck, stylus, joystick, or trackerball or by pointing at the command on a graphics tablet. When a command from a menu is selected, a sub-menu may appear for further selection of details appropriate to the selected command. In addition prompts at top and/or bottom of the screen appear to assist the user in operating the command.

In addition to the menus and their commands, a work space will appear on the screen within which drawings are built up. Some systems (e.g. AutoCad) allow the optional use of two monitor screens, one for showing the menus and commands, the other to be used as a drawing screen. The obvious advantage of this is that a larger screen area is available for drawing.

5.5.3 EXAMPLES OF CAD MENUS

Figures 5.1 to 5.8 illustrate some of the variety of menus and commands used with CAD software.

AutoSketch (Figs. 5.1 and 5.2)

When AutoSketch is loaded, a number of menu headings appear along the top of the screen. If a menu heading is highlighted by pointing at it with the aid of a mouse or by pointing with the aid of keyboard cursor keys, the menu appropriate to that heading is pulled down (it appears on screen as shown in the figures). Commands from the menus are also selected by a pointer controlled by a mouse or by the cursor keys, following which prompts appear at the bottom of the screen. Some menu commands will cause sub-menus to appear in the centre of the screen. Figure 5.2 shows the sub-menu (or dialogue box) by which grid spacing can be set.

Techsoft Designer (Figs. 5.3 and 5.4)

When Techsoft Designer is loaded, a menu appears on the right of the screen as shown in Fig. 5.3, together with details at the bottom of the screen of the cursor position with respect to the screen centre. Details of scale, grid, element, marker and linetype also appear at the bottom of the screen. With this software there are four sets of menus numbered 1 to 4. Figure 5.4 shows menu 2, selected by pointing with the mouse at the 2 in the menu command rectangle (top of menu list). Also in Fig. 5.4 the command CIRCLE has been selected, and detailed

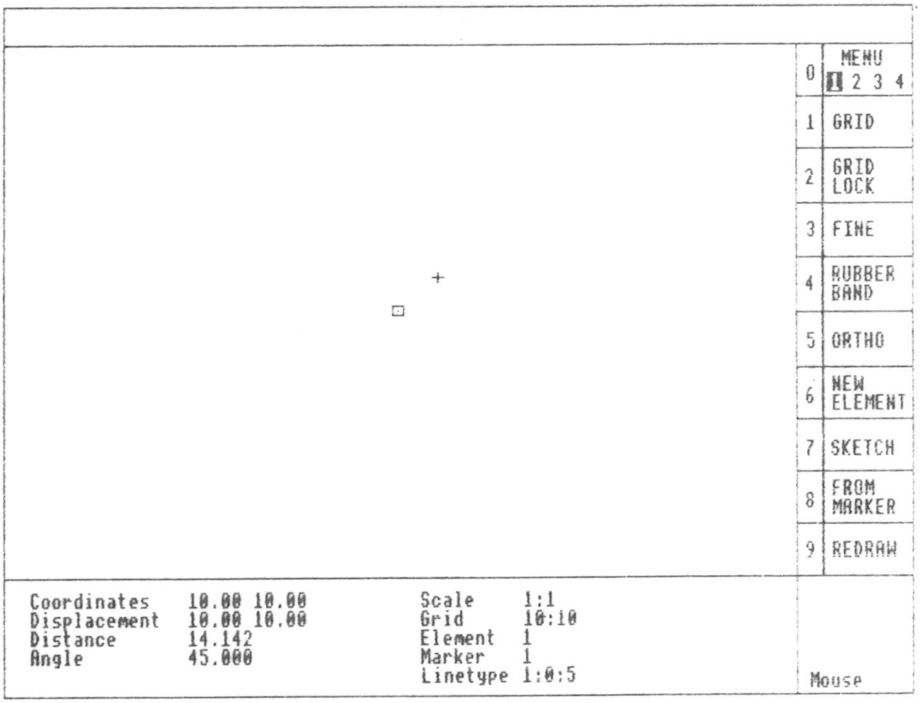

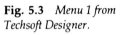

	MENU
0	**1** 2 3 4
1	GRID
2	GRID LOCK
3	FINE
4	RUBBER BAND
5	ORTHO
6	NEW ELEMENT
7	SKETCH
8	FROM MARKER
9	REDRAW

Coordinates	10.00 10.00	Scale	1:1
Displacement	10.00 10.00	Grid	10:10
Distance	14.142	Element	1
Angle	45.000	Marker	1
		Linetype	1:0:5

Mouse

Fig. 5.3 *Menu 1 from Techsoft Designer.*

Select (1-9)

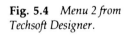

	MENU
0	1 **2** 3 4
1	MOVE
2	MIRROR IMAGE
3	ROTATE
4	ALTER SIZE
5	**CIRCLE**
6	TANGENT NORMAL
7	ARC
8	S.LINE/ CURVES
9	HATCH

CIRCLE

1 Centre, Radius	6 Radius, Touch Two Points
2 Centre, Point	7 Three Points
3 Radius, Touch Two Lines	8 Radius, Point, Touch Line
4 Radius, Touch Line, Arc/Circle	9 Radius, Point, Touch Arc/Circle
5 Radius, Touch Two Arc/Circle	

Mouse

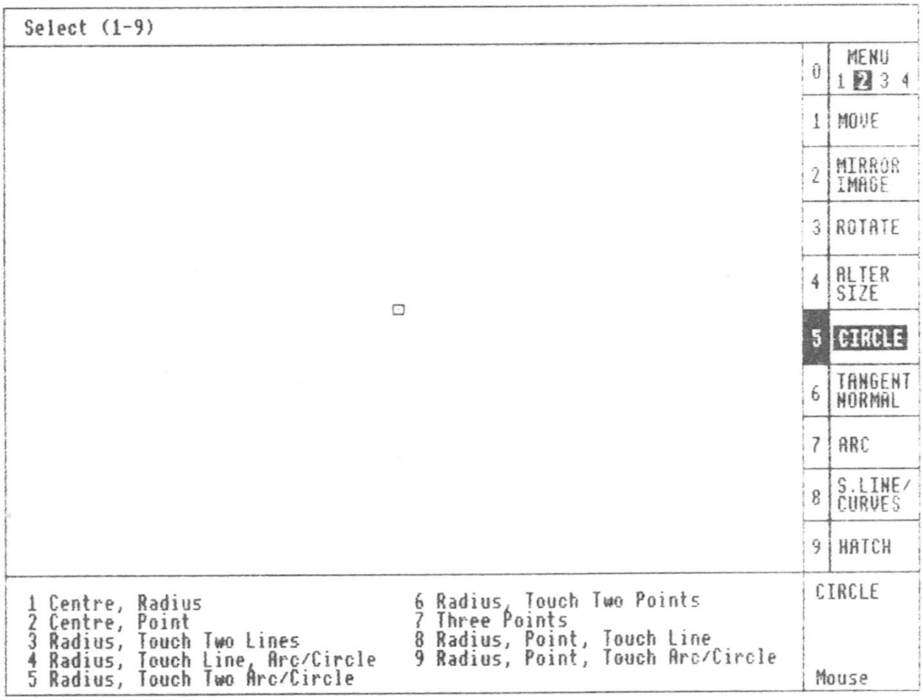

Fig. 5.4 *Menu 2 from Techsoft Designer.*

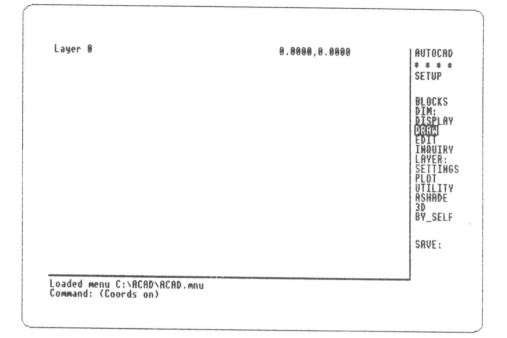

Fig. 5.5 *An example of a main menu from AutoCAD.*

prompts concerning the drawing of circles on screen appear both at the top and at the bottom of the screen.

This software can be operated by mouse, trackerball or cursor keys. Note that in Figs. 5.4 and 5.5 these particular screen illustrations show that a mouse is being used in this case (bottom right corner).

AutoCAD (Figs. 5.5 to 5.8)

The complete menus, sub-menus, commands and prompts systems of this software are much more complex that those of the preceding two items of software. When AutoCAD is loaded the screen could appear as in Fig. 5.5. The actual screen your particular AutoCAD programs will show will depend partly on the version you are using. It will also depend upon how your software has been programmed. The menu headings and commands may appear on a separate screen if the system being used has been set up to allow for this.

The menus generally appear on the right of the screen, with notes top left and co-ordinate details top right. The main command prompt area is at the bottom left of the screen, below the drawing work area.

Figure 5.6 shows the screen when the DRAW sub-menu has been selected and the LINE command selected from the DRAW menu. Note the change in the prompts at the bottom of the screen and the cursor cross-hairs on the screen. The intersection of these cross-hairs can be positioned by whatever pointing device is being used. Note also the small cross showing where the start of a line has been selected by pointing with the pointing device.

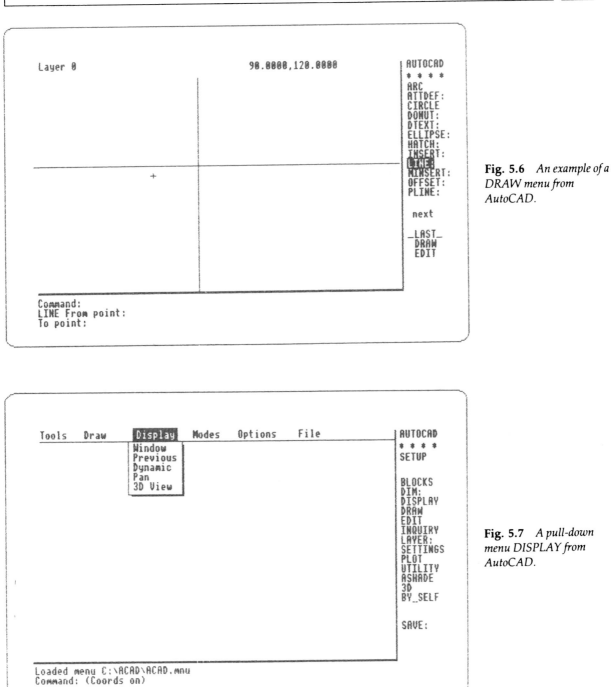

Fig. 5.6 *An example of a DRAW menu from AutoCAD.*

Fig. 5.7 *A pull-down menu DISPLAY from AutoCAD.*

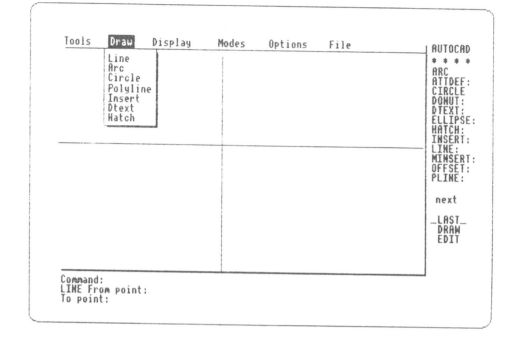

Fig. 5.8 *A pull-down menu DRAW from AutoCAD.*

If your computer is fitted with an enhanced graphic adaptor (EGA) or a video graphics adaptor (VGA) card (or the equivalent) and an EGA or VGA screen and you have at least a version 9 release of AutoCAD, you will be able to use pull-down menus, similar to those of AutoSketch on EGA or VGA. Figures 5.7 and 5.8 show two of the menus after their headings have been selected by pointing. Sub-menus are extensively used with this pull-down menu system, these appearing as dialogue boxes, some with icons, in the centre of the screen.

Pointing to a command or a position on the screen using AutoCAD can be by one of a number of methods. That commonly adopted is by using a graphics tablet together with a puck or stylus for selecting the required command from the tablet. Figure 5.9 shows such a tablet. However, the software can also be operated from the keyboard, by using a mouse or with other forms of pointing device.

AutoCAD is generally operated by using a puck or stylus with a graphics tablet in conjunction with the keyboard, although using a mouse in place of a graphics tablet is another popular method of control.

5.6 COMMON COMMANDS IN CAD SOFTWARE

Many of the command names and phrases used in CAD are common to many of the available software packages. The list below, of some of the more frequently used commands from the three CAD software packages given above, shows this. However space does not permit us to give here a complete analysis of the similarities between the menus and commands systems from these three packages.

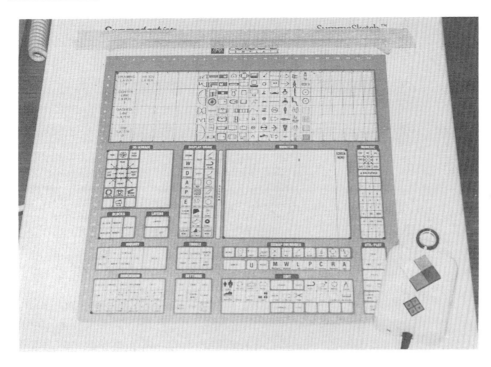

Fig. 5.9 *A graphic tablet and puck (AutoCAD).*

1. The menus and commands systems from AutoCAD are much more complex and cover many more possible situations than do the other two.
2. The way in which commands with the same name are used to obtain the expected drawing results varies between the three packages although, in general, the results are similar.

This is not really a problem because with all three packages, when commands are called for, prompts appear at top/bottom of the screen drawing area to assist the user in obtaining the drawing result aimed for.

Although excellent 2-D drawings of a complicated nature can be obtained from the use of any CAD software, a word of advice is needed here. In order to get the most out of your software and to gain the full potential of the possibilities offered by each of the menus and their commands, it is advisable to read those parts of the manual accompanying the software which apply to the drawings being attempted. This may appear daunting to the novice, because of the large volume of written material available. It is best for the beginner to concentrate only on those sections required to complete the job in hand.

5.6.1 SOME COMMANDS COMMON TO THREE CAD PACKAGES

Note: Similar common commands will be found in CAD software other than the three packages shown in Table 5.1.
We will now discuss in more detail some of the more frequently used commands from the above list.

Table 5.1 Common commands in CAD software

AutoCAD	AutoSketch	Techsoft designer
ARC	ARC	ARC
ARRAY (Polar)	RING ARRAY	ROTATE
ARRAY (Rectangular)	BOX ARRAY	
BLOCK	PART	ELEMENT
BREAK	BREAK	
CIRCLE	CIRCLE	CIRCLE
COPY	COPY	MOVE
DIM	DIMENSION	DIM LINE
ERASE	ERASE	DELETE
GRID	GRID	GRID
LINE	LINE	RUBBER BAND
LINETYPE	LINETYPE	LINETYPE
MIRROR	MIRROR	MIRROR IMAGE
MOVE	MOVE	MOVE
POINT	POINT	
REDRAW		REDRAW
SNAP	SNAP	GRID LOCK
TEXT	TEXT	TEXT
WINDOW	WINDOW	WINDOW
ZOOM	VIEW	ZOOM

LINE and CIRCLE

Lines and circles form a major part of most 2-D drawings whether drawn using manual methods or using CAD methods. Simple examples of the use of the LINE and the CIRCLE commands from AutoCAD are given in Figs. 5.10 to 5.13. In these examples, depending on the set-up being employed, Return indicates that:

1. the Return key on the keyboard is to be pressed; or
2. the Return or Next Command area on a graphics tablet is to be selected; or
3. the Return button on a puck is to be pressed.

Example 5.1 LINE Command (Fig. 5.10)
The LINE command has been selected from the DRAW menu by pointing. The command **LINE** appears on the prompt line. When the prompts **From line**: and **To line**: appear after Return is pressed, the x, y co-ordinates of the corners of the required rectangle are typed in from the keyboard. The command **close** (c) automatically completes the rectangle.

Example 5.2 LINE Command (Fig. 5.11)
The line command has been typed in from the keyboard in response to the **Command**: prompt. In this example **relative co-ordinates** are typed in response to the **From point**: and **To point**: prompts.

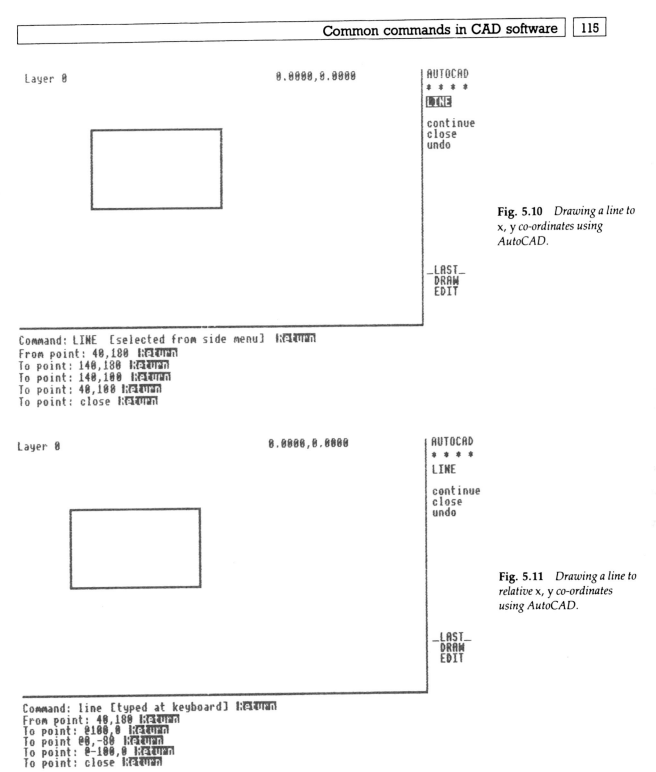

Layer 0   0.0000,0.0000

AUTOCAD
* * * *
LINE

continue
close
undo

LAST
DRAW
EDIT

Command: LINE [selected from side menu] Return
From point: 40,180 Return
To point: 140,180 Return
To point: 140,100 Return
To point: 40,100 Return
To point: close Return

Fig. 5.10 *Drawing a line to x, y co-ordinates using AutoCAD.*

Layer 0   0.0000,0.0000

AUTOCAD
* * * *
LINE

continue
close
undo

LAST
DRAW
EDIT

Command: line [typed at keyboard] Return
From point: 40,180 Return
To point: @100,0 Return
To point @0,-80 Return
To point: @-100,0 Return
To point: close Return

Fig. 5.11 *Drawing a line to relative x, y co-ordinates using AutoCAD.*

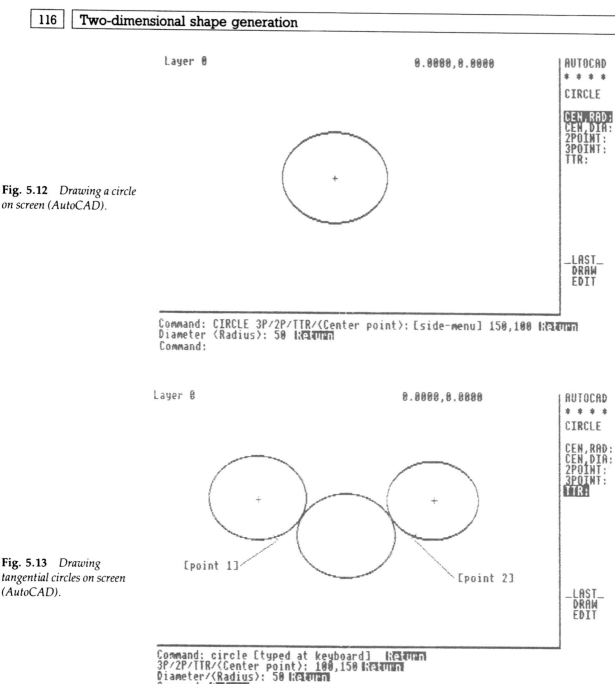

Fig. 5.12 *Drawing a circle on screen (AutoCAD).*

Fig. 5.13 *Drawing tangential circles on screen (AutoCAD).*

Relative co-ordinates allow the drawing of lines whose lengths are governed by x and y co-ordinates. If, as in the examples given, each co-ordinate unit is equal to 1 mm when plotted, the exact required sizes of the rectangle can be produced without having to calculate the co-ordinate position of each corner. Relative co-ordinates take the form @100,0 or @0,100 to give horizontal and vertical lines respectively of 100 units long, from a selected point. Note the use of negative figures in the co-ordinates when drawing to the left or downwards.

Example 5.3   CIRCLE Command (Fig. 5.12)
The **CIRCLE** command has been selected from the side menu by pointing. Note that when a prompt requires a selection from a variety of sub-commands – in this case whether the circle is to pass through two points (2P), three points (3P), be tangential (TTR) or the centre point is required – it is the sub-command in brackets which is operative (in this example ⟨Center point⟩). Similarly the **Diameter ⟨Radius⟩**: prompt is asking for the radius. If the diameter is required a D must be typed in at this prompt.

Example 5.4   CIRCLE Command (Fig. 5.13)
The CIRCLE command has been typed in from the keyboard. After responding to the prompts to draw the two circles the TTR sub-command is typed in answer to the **CIRCLE** prompt. A circle of the required radius and tangential to the first two is then automatically drawn when the required information is typed in from the keyboard in answer to the further prompts.

Notes on the above Examples
In all four examples given above, the positions of the ends of the lines, the circle centre and the radius of the circle could have been positioned by pointing with the pointing device. Alternatively, some could have been selected by pointing and others by keying in co-ordinate positions through the keyboard.

In general, the more complex and sophisticated the capabilities of the package, the greater will be the choice of commands available at any one moment.

ERASE (DELETE), ZOOM

One of the most frequently used CAD commands will be **ERASE** or **DELETE**, often used in conjunction with windows formed by **ZOOM**ing on to small parts of a drawing screen in order to ensure that accuracy of erasure is correct. Figures 5.14 and 5.15 show examples of the use of these commands. These two drawings are examples using Techsoft Designer software.

As can be seen in Fig. 5.14, two small errors were made when the original drawing was being constructed. The first, a line on the right of the drawing was drawn in the wrong place. By pointing at the **DELETE** command in **MENU 3** the prompts at top and bottom of the drawing screen appeared. When prompt **2. Line** was selected, the following prompts appeared at the top of the screen.

> **Locate line** [line selected with cursor by mouse]
> [line flashes]

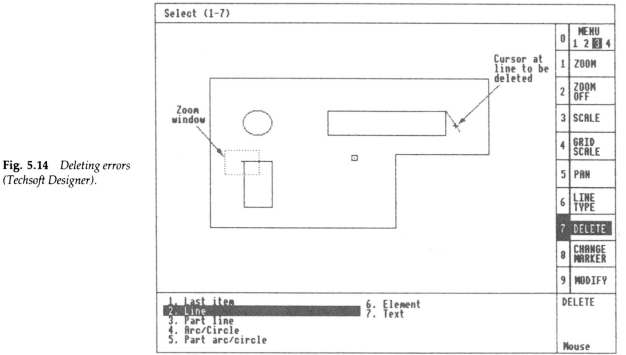

Fig. 5.14 *Deleting errors (Techsoft Designer).*

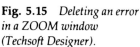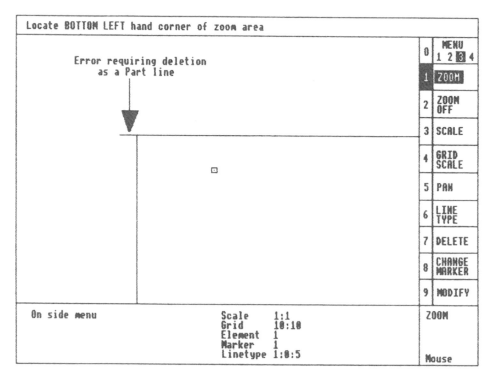

Fig. 5.15 *Deleting an error in a ZOOM window (Techsoft Designer).*

Delete this line? (Y/N) [Keyboard – Y]
      [line deleted]
Another (Y/N)? [keyboard – N]

To delete the smaller error, the **ZOOM** command was selected from MENU 3 and the prompts as seen in Fig. 5.15 appeared at top and bottom of the screen. The **WINDOW** shown in Fig. 5.14 was selected with the aid of the mouse and the screen then appeared as in Fig. 5.15. To select a **ZOOM** window, point at one of its corners with the aid of the mouse, then point at its far corner and DRAG that corner of the rectangle to the size required using the mouse. Selection of the **DELETE** command and the **3. Part line** prompt, then allowed the error to be deleted.

Note: in other CAD software, the term **ERASE** is more common. Another command **BREAK** is often used to delete parts of details in drawings. Prompts associated with these commands in other software assist the user in achieving what is required. Lines can also be **TRIM**med when using some packages.

In all these CAD packages, the entities are defined in the computer as a series of vectors which are stored as a series of separate lines and arcs, which can be deleted in their entirety. In some systems (e.g. Techsoft) small sections of a line can be selected and deleted without the need to delete the whole of the line as originally entered. This vector (or object orientated) approach to storing entities as used in CAD packages is different from the concept in many of the packages using PAINT commands (e.g. Mac Paint). In these the entities are mapped on to a region of the screen as a series of illuminated pixels instead of as vectors. Thus deleting a line in a paint program involves selecting an icon of a rubber and then using the mouse to move the rubber over the pixels to delete the required region of the screen.

MOVE, COPY, MIRROR, ARRAY (ROTATE)

Another group of commands frequently used to speed up the production of drawings is **MOVE, COPY, MIRROR** and **ARRAY**. In some CAD, **ARRAY** will be called **ROTATE, RING ARRAY** or similar, although the **ARRAY** command in AutoCAD allows both polar and rectangular co-ordinates to be used, **ROTATE** in Techsoft Designer only allows polar arrays, **RING ARRAY** in AutoSketch is for polar and **BOX ARRAY** is for rectangular. Figures 5.16 to 5.21 show applications of these commands. These commands are usually fairly general to CAD software.

MOVE Command (Fig. 5.16)

When the shape 1 had been drawn on the screen, the draughtsman realized that the rectangle A had been drawn in the wrong position. It was therefore **MOVE**d by first placing a window around it and then **DRAG**ging the window, containing the rectangle to its new position B as shown in 2. The **MOVE** command is particularly useful for positioning **TEXT**, for repositioning numbers, for allowing details to be constructed in a convenient part of the screen and then **MOVE**d into their final positions relative to other parts of a drawing.

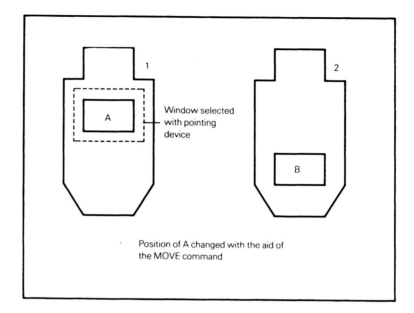

Fig. 5.16 *An example of using the MOVE command.*

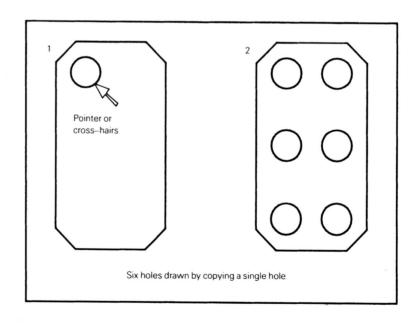

Fig. 5.17 *An example of using the COPY command.*

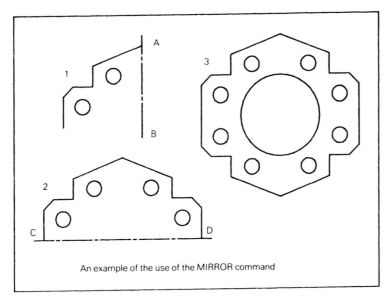

An example of the use of the MIRROR command

Fig. 5.18 *An example of using the MIRROR command.*

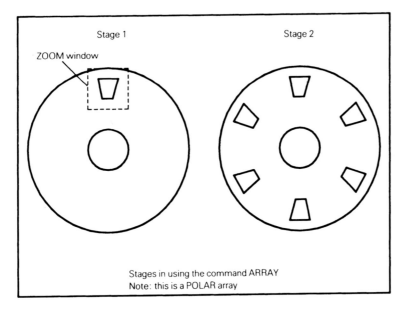

Stages in using the command ARRAY
Note: this is a POLAR array

Fig. 5.19 *An example of using the ARRAY (polar) command.*

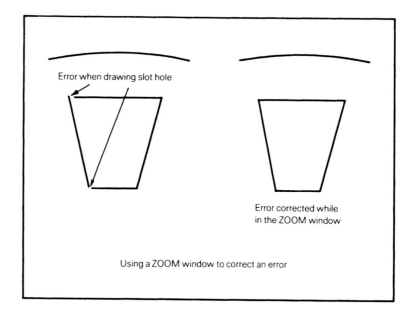

Fig. 5.20   *An example of using a ZOOM window to correct errors.*

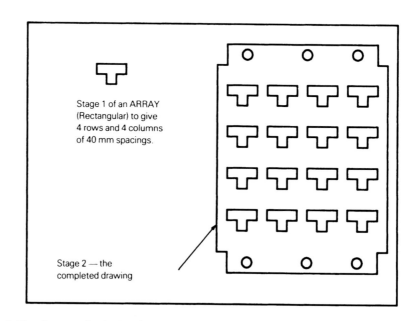

Fig. 5.21   *An example of using the ARRAY (rectangular) command.*

COPY Command (Fig. 5.17)

To draw the 6 holes of the shape 2, the shape 1 with its single hole was first drawn. **COPY** was selected from its menu, the circle of 1 pointed at with the pointing device and then **DRAG**ged to a second position. This was repeated a further four times to position all six holes. With some software, several repetitions of a detail can be **COPY**ed after pointing once at the original detail, the software being programmed to keep the detail in RAM until **COPY**ing is completed. If the detail being **COPY**ed contains more than a single item, e.g. several lines, then the detail must be placed in a window before it can be **COPY**ed.

MIRROR Command (Fig. 5.18)

This command allows rapid drawing of details which are symmetrical about axes. In the example given the following actions were performed.

1. The top left-hand quarter of the detail was drawn. This was **MIRROR**ed about the line AB to produce
2. which was then **MIRROR**ed about line CD to give
3. the required outline. The hole of 3 was added after the two **MIRROR** operations had been completed, because it is easier to draw a single circle rather than to draw and then mirror a quarter-circle twice.

ARRAY Command

The **ARRAY** command in AutoCAD allows rapid copying of details in both polar form (around a central point) and rectangular form (in columns and rows). Other CAD software uses the command **ROTATE, RING ARRAY** or a similar word to perform polar repetitions (in AutoCAD, polar repetitions are a specified number of repeats of a detail at required angles in a circular direction around a central point). Comparing our items of software we see the following.

1. AutoCAD: **ARRAY** allows both polar (P) and rectangular (R) repeats.
2. AutoSketch: **RING ARRAY** allows polar repeats around a central point. **BOX ARRAY** command allows rectangular arrays in rows and columns.
3. Techsoft Designer: **ROTATE** allows a specified number of repeats at required angles around a centre point. There is no **ARRAY** command.

ARRAY (Polar) (Fig. 5.19)

Stage 1: The slot hole was drawn in its position within the large circle. Because the original slot hole detail did not appear to be correct when it had been drawn on screen, a window containing the slot hole was **ZOOM**ed, an error found and corrected by **ERASE**ing the line and redrawing it while still in the **ZOOM** window (Fig. 5.20).

Stage 2: The **ARRAY** command was selected from its menu, the polar form chosen and six repeats requested within 360° in response to screen prompts by keying in the required information. This resulted in the other five slot holes appearing on position in the screen.

ARRAY (Rectangular) (Fig. 5.21)

Stage 1: The shape to be repeated in the ARRAY was drawn.

Stage 2: The **ARRAY** command was then selected from its menu, the Rectangular form chosen and four rows at 40 mm and four columns at 40 mm requested by typing in the information as prompts appeared on screen. The results of this ARRAY are shown in Fig. 5.21. The drawing of the outline of the surrounding plate with its attachment holes was drawn around the rows and columns after the ARRAY had been completed.

Examples of these Commands in Engineering Drawings

The examples given below include orthographic projections containing different types of lines. The production of this type of drawing by CAD means is covered in Chapter 6. The drawings given below show how the commands described above can be used in CAD engineering drawing.

Example 5.5   Pump Cover (Fig. 5.22)
The four stages in obtaining this drawing are described in Fig. 5.23.

Stage 1: The circle of the flange and one of the the keyed slots have been drawn. While drawing the keyed slot small errors were noted. These were corrected by **ZOOM**ing a window around the slot and correcting the errors, mainly by **MOVE**ing lines to correct positions, together with some **DELETE**ing of unwanted lines (Fig. 5.24).

Stage 2: The six slots required were **ROTATE**d around the centre of the flange circle.

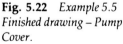

Fig. 5.22 *Example 5.5 Finished drawing – Pump Cover.*

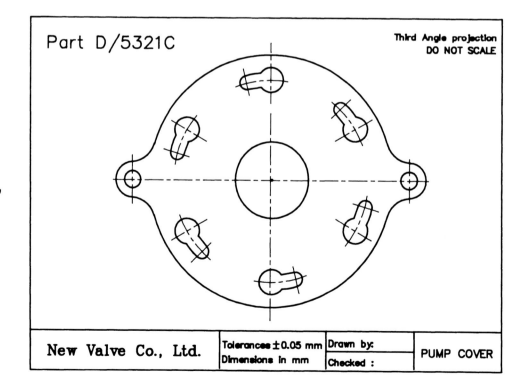

Part D/5321C

Third Angle projection
DO NOT SCALE

| New Valve Co., Ltd. | Tolerances ±0.05 mm | Drawn by: | PUMP COVER |
| | Dimensions in mm | Checked : | |

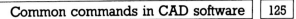

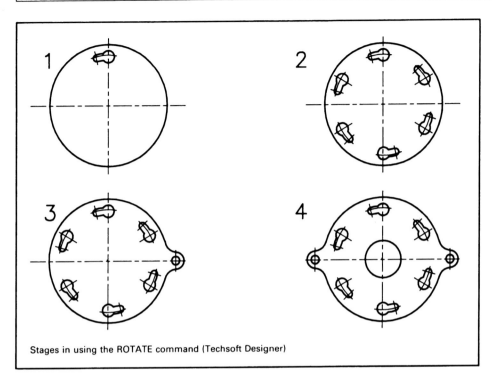

Stages in using the ROTATE command (Techsoft Designer)

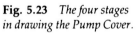

Fig. 5.23 *The four stages in drawing the Pump Cover.*

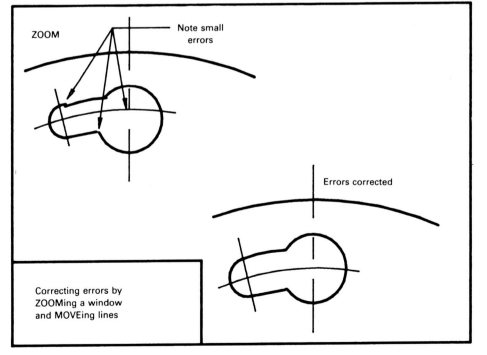

Fig. 5.24 *ZOOMing to correct an error.*

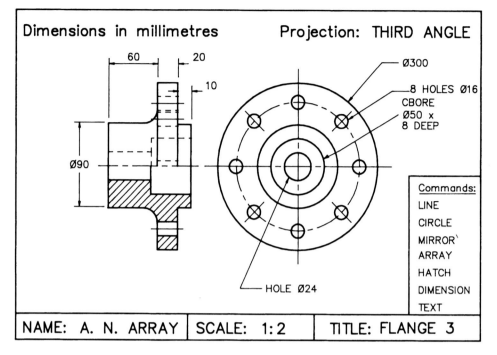

Fig. 5.25 *Example 5.6 Finished drawing – Flange 3.*

Stage 3: The hole on the right of the flange was then drawn; this involved some **DELETE**ing.

Stage 4: The right-hand hole was ROTATEd from the first around the flange circle.

Example 5.6   Flange 3 (Fig. 5.25)
This drawing involved the use of **MIRROR** and **ARRAY** as well as the commands needed to construct the outlines of the views.

The first stage in producing this drawing is shown in Fig. 5.26.

Example 5.7   Part 6 (Fig. 5.27)
The stages in producing the final drawing are shown in Fig. 5.28 and 5.29.

Stage 1: As this drawing required **MIRROR**ing in two directions, only one quarter of the front view was drawn.

Stage 2: The front view was then obtained by **MIRROR**ing below and to the right to obtain the full view. Note that some **ERASE**ing was needed before the final drawing could be completed. However, despite this, the use of the **MIRROR** command in this example made for speedy drawing.

Note on the Given Examples

A number of small details in these examples could only be drawn accurately by making full use of windows resulting from **ZOOM**ing. The capability of the **ZOOM** command is one of the most frequently used facilities of CAD.

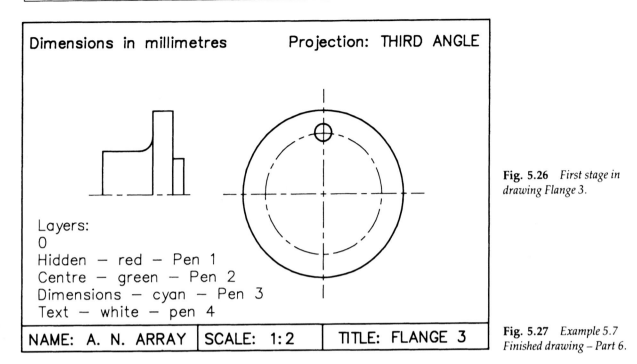

Dimensions in millimetres   Projection: THIRD ANGLE

Layers:
0
Hidden — red — Pen 1
Centre — green — Pen 2
Dimensions — cyan — Pen 3
Text — white — pen 4

| NAME: A. N. ARRAY | SCALE: 1:2 | TITLE: FLANGE 3 |

Fig. 5.26 *First stage in drawing Flange 3.*

Fig. 5.27 *Example 5.7 Finished drawing – Part 6.*

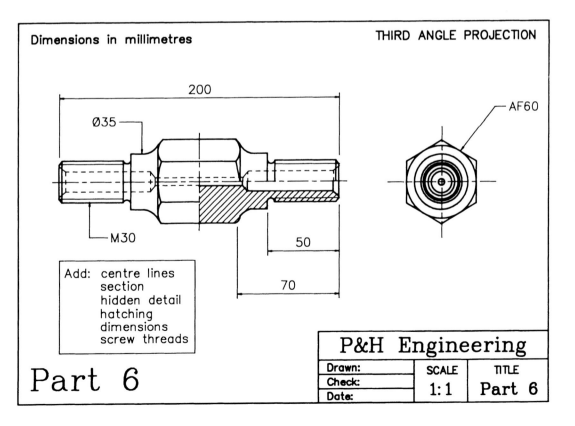

Dimensions in millimetres   THIRD ANGLE PROJECTION

200

Ø35

AF60

M30

50

70

Add: centre lines
     section
     hidden detail
     hatching
     dimensions
     screw threads

Part 6

P&H Engineering		
Drawn:	SCALE	TITLE
Check:	1:1	Part 6
Date:		

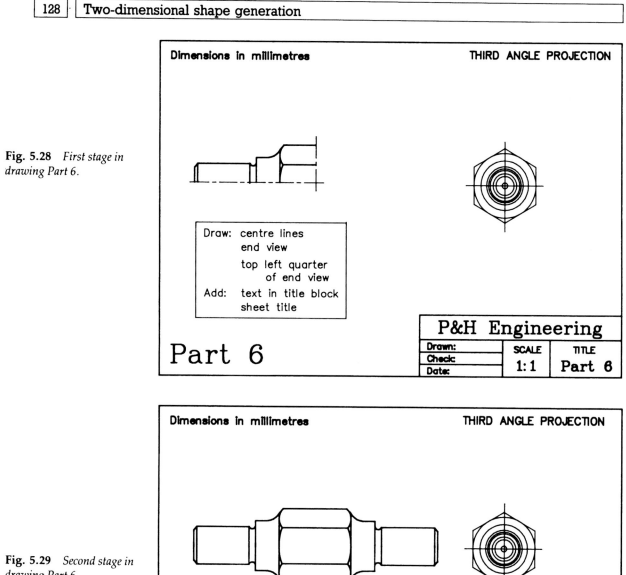

Fig. 5.28 *First stage in drawing Part 6.*

Fig. 5.29 *Second stage in drawing Part 6.*

Practically any size of window can be **ZOOM**ed, allowing even the smallest of inaccuracies to be checked for and corrected.

GRID and SNAP

When **GRID** is on, a pattern of dots or of faint lines appears on screen. Grid patterns can be vertical and horizontal, or at angles. Angular grids are for generating isometric, oblique or planometric types of pictorial drawings. The dot positions can be modified as required by setting them to a prescribed number of units apart. Grids assist drawing to correct sizes on screen.

The command **SNAP, GRID LOCK**, or similar allows the positioning of the screen cursor precisely on points on the screen in positions determined by the setting (in units) of the SNAP (or GRID LOCK) spacings.

SNAP can also be modified to form an imaginary grid, either the same as or different from the GRID pattern. When SNAP is on, the cursor can automatically be locked on to these grid points. SNAP allows precise positioning of points (ends of lines, circle centres, etc.) by **SNAP**ping the cursor on to points of the SNAP grid.

Figure 5.30 shows a screen with a 10 mm square grid for an A4 size sheet. The grid dots do not appear when a drawing is printed or plotted.

If the ends of lines (or similar features) are located with **SNAP**, no gap will occur between joining lines. If however, **SNAP** is not used in such situations, small gaps will inevitably occur at joins. It is virtually impossible to guess the

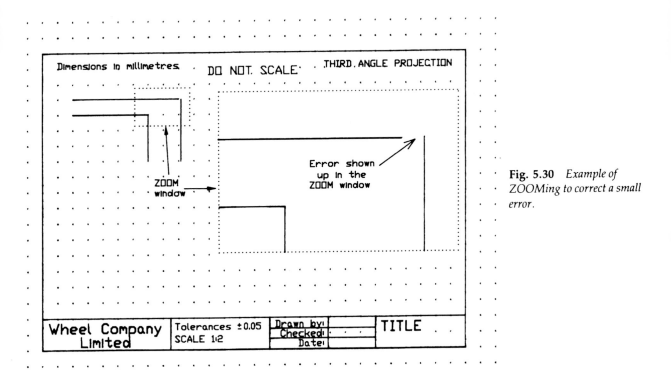

Fig. 5.30 *Example of ZOOMing to correct a small error.*

exact position of the cursor when locating ends of features without the aid of **SNAP**. Some CAD software also allows exact positioning of joining features by the use of commands such as **OSNAP** or **ATTACH** (depending on the software used). The **ZOOM** window included in Fig. 5.30 shows this problem. An alternative is to fill in the missing sections of lines when enlarged under **ZOOM**, although the use of **SNAP, OSNAP** or similar is still recommended.

ARC

Arcs of differing sizes are important in 2-D geometrical drawing. Compare ARC as a command from our three packages.

AutoSketch

When the **ARC** command is selected, three prompts appear at the screen bottom, one after the other (since three points are required completely to define the arc):

> **Arc First point:** [point with pointing device];
> **Arc Point on arc:** [point];
> **Arc End point:** [point].

Techsoft Designer

When **ARC** is selected from its menu, prompts appear at the screen bottom:

1 Fillet	6 Radius, Touch Two Points
2 Centre, Point, Angle	7 Three Points
3 Radius, Touch Two Lines	8 Radius, Point, Touch Line
4 Radius, Touch Line, Arc/Circle	9 Radius, Point, Touch Arc/Circle
5 Radius, Touch Two Arc/Circles	

At the top of the screen a further prompt appears: **Select (1–9)**. These nine prompts cover most of the methods by which circles or arcs can be defined uniquely.

To draw a **Fillet**, type 1. The bottom of the screen clears and prompts appear at the screen top one after the other as the item requested is pointed at:

> **Locate contact point on first line (approx)** [point]
> **Locate contact point on second line (approx)** [point]
> **Radius:** [type in radius at keyboard]

Then prompts at the screen bottom ask:

1 **Major arc**
2 **Minor arc**

Upon choosing 2 the fillet arc is drawn and further prompts appear at the screen top as each redundant line flashes in turn.

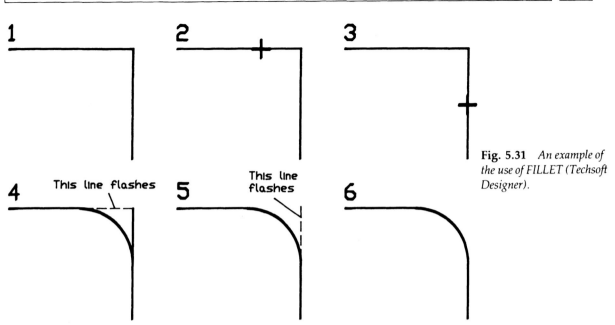

Fig. 5.31 *An example of the use of FILLET (Techsoft Designer).*

Delete? (Y/N)

When Y is keyed in, the redundant line disappears.

The drawings 1 to 6 of Figure 5.31 show this sequence.

Note: The **FILLET** command here is a special case of the method 6, which requires a radius and two points.

AutoCAD

In AutoCAD, **FILLET** is treated as a command separate from **ARC**. Redundant lines are automatically erased without assistance from the operator when the fillet appears on screen.

The **ARC** command allows the following methods of defining an arc.

3-point:

S,C,E:	Start, Centre, End
S,C,A:	Start, Centre, Angle (inclusive)
S,C,L:	Start, Centre, Length (of chord)
S,E,A:	Start, End, Angle (included)
S,E,R:	Start, End, Radius
S,E,D:	Start, End, Direction (of centre from start)
C,S,E:	Centre, Start, End
C,S,A:	Centre, Start, Angle (inclusive)
C,S,L:	Centre, Start, Length (of chord)
CONTINUE:	Continue from an arc

When any one of these are chosen, prompts (bottom left of screen) inform the operator of the action required in order to draw the required arc on the screen.

Figure 5.32 shows the results of each of these forms of arc from AutoCAD.

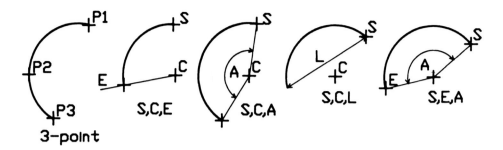

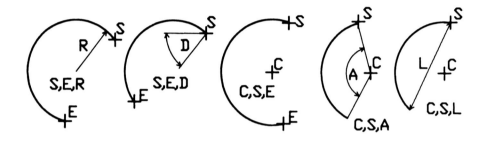

Fig. 5.32 *The type of ARC available in AutoCAD.*

CHAMFER

In AutoCAD, **CHAMFER** has a result similar to FILLET, except that **CHAMFER** draws a straight line between two other lines at a corner rather than an arc and then goes on automatically to erase the parts of the lines not required to form the chamfer at the corner. Figure 5.33 shows examples of chamfers.

UNDO and REDO

UNDO and **REDO** in AutoSketch and AutoCAD give the user the opportunity to correct errors by reversing the results of previous commands(s) – **UNDO** by deleting the effects of previous commands(s) and **REDO** by reversing the effects of an **UNDO**. You cannot **REDO** anything that has not previously been **UNDO**ne.

QUIT and END

Be careful when using these two commands. **QUIT** usually means that you wish to come out of the CAD software program and you will lose your drawing unless it has first been **SAVE**d to disk. **END** in AutoCAD means you automatically **SAVE** the drawing being worked. Because these two commands can cause difficulties in what is being **SAVE**d or not **SAVE**d to disk, prompts usually appear on screen to advise the user, so that all is not inadvertently lost.

EXERCISES

Note: Different types of screen cursors are used in various CAD software packages. Some examples are given in Fig. 5.34:

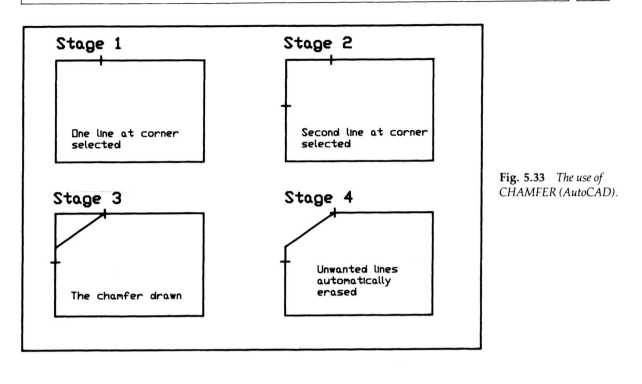

Fig. 5.33 *The use of CHAMFER (AutoCAD).*

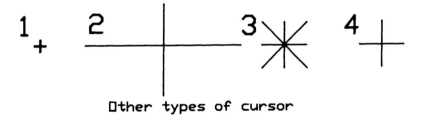

Other types of cursor

Fig. 5.34 *Types of screen cursor found in CAD packages.*

1. the Techsoft Designer screen cursor;
2. the cursor of AutoCAD consists of vertical and horizontal lines of drawing area height and width; when a point has been selected a small cross (similar to 1) appears on the screen; this can be suppressed if desired;
3. a cursor common on other CAD packages;
4. another commonly used cursor.

Note: Fig. 5.35 shows the mouse pointer and its cursor from AutoSketch.

Exercise Example
The exercises 5.1, 5.2 and 5.3 below are given here to allow the reader to have elementary practice in using the commands so far described. Figure 5.35 is an example of how to start to answer these exercises. This example has been drawn with AutoSketch.

The process of drawing the shape 4 in Fig. 5.35 is as follows.

Other types of cursor

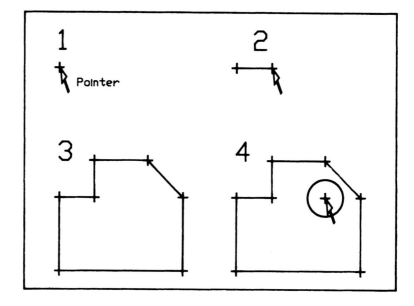

Fig. 5.35 *Exercise – an example.*

1. Select the **LINE** command from its menu. With the aid of the mouse (or keyboard cursor keys) point at the first corner of the shape on screen. Press Return or the equivalent mouse button.
2. Drag the line with the pointer to a second position and press Return (or mouse key).
3. Continue pointing and pressing the mouse button at each corner to complete the shape.
4. Select the **CIRCLE** command from its menu, point to the circle centre and draw the required circle.

Note: The actual methods of producing the required shapes in the following exercises may follow a different pattern depending on the software you are using.

Exercise 5.1 (Fig. 5.36)
With the **LINE** or **RUBBER BAND** command draw each of the shapes 1 to 7 in Fig. 5.34 to any suitable sizes and proportions.

Exercise 5.2 (Fig. 5.37)
Use the **CIRCLE** command to draw the arcs of these shapes. The parts of the circles not needed can be erased using **BREAK** or the **PART LINE** (from **DELETE**) or a similar command peculiar to the software being used. Copy the shapes 1 to 8 to any convenient sizes and proportions.

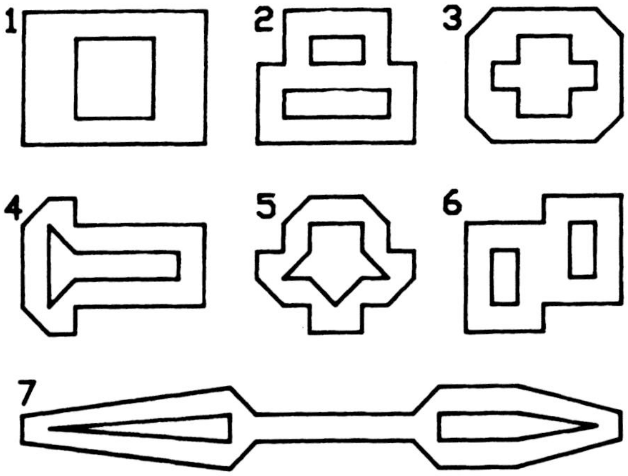

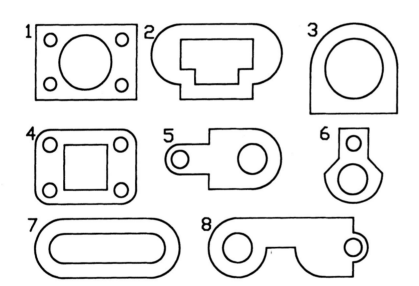

Fig. 5.36 *Exercise 5.1.*

Fig. 5.37 *Exercise 5.2.*

Exercise 5.3 (Fig. 5.38)
This exercise requires you to use the co-ordinates of your software package to ensure the shapes are drawn to the given sizes, either by planning the co-ordinate positions of each point, or by the typing in of relative co-ordinates (see p. 114) if your software allows this. Do not include dimensions in your drawings.

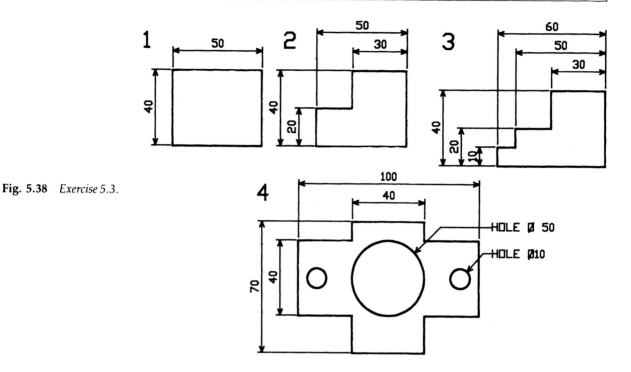

Fig. 5.38 *Exercise 5.3.*

Exercise 5.4 (Fig. 5.39)

Drawing 1. Draw the left-hand half of the outline. **MIRROR** the right half.

Drawing 2: Draw one half. **MIRROR** the other half.

Drawing 3: Draw half. **MIRROR** the other half. Add the central circle last.

Drawing 4: Draw half of the outline. **MIRROR** the other half. Draw the square A. **MOVE** A into other positions within the outline.

Drawing 5: Draw the outline. Draw cross B within the outline. **COPY** the cross so that there are three rows of three crosses (nine in all) within the outline. If you have suitable software the crosses may be **ARRAY**ed.

Drawing 6: Draw one quarter of the outline. **MIRROR** both to the right and downwards to obtain the full outline. Draw the square C. **COPY** C into the other three corners.

Exercise 5.5 (Fig. 5.40)

Drawing 1: Draw the outer circle. Draw the top small circle. Either **ROTATE** or **ARRAY** (polar) the small circle at 45° positions (eight in all). Draw the inner circle.

Drawing 2: Draw the outer circle. Draw the cross (enlarged at A). **ARRAY** (polar) or **ROTATE** the cross into its other positions around the drawing with 30° spacing (12 in all).

Drawing 3: Draw the rectangle. Draw one of the shapes within the rectangle (enlarged at B). Either **COPY** or **ARRAY** (Rectangular) the shape B to complete the drawing.

Fig. 5.39 *Exercise 5.4.*

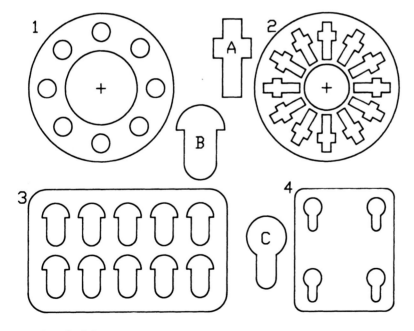

Fig. 5.40 *Exercise 5.5.*

Fig. 5.41 *Exercise 5.6.*

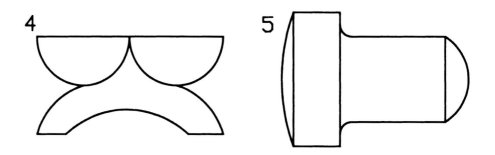

Drawing 4: Draw the rectangle. Draw the keyhole (enlarged at C) within the rectangle shape. Either **COPY** or **ARRAY** the shape C.

Exercise 5.6 (Fig. 5.41)
The exact command used for these drawings will depend upon the CAD software being used. Copy the given five drawings with the aid of commands such as: **LINE, CIRCLE, FILLET, ARC**. The commands **BREAK** and/or **DELETE (ERASE)** may also be required.

Orthographic projection | 6

Orthographic projection is probably the most common form of drawing in engineering (mechanical, civil, chemical, electronic, electrical), building, architecture, etc.

Most CAD software is designed for industrial use and contains many features specifically included to speedily produce accurate orthographic projections, in accordance with the appropriate British Standard:

1. **GRID** and **SNAP, GRID LOCK** (or equivalent), with facilities to change grid and snap point spacings;
2. **ORTHO** (or similar), allowing lines to be drawn only horizontally and vertically;
3. **LINETYPE** to draw different types of lines (outlines, centre lines, hidden detail, etc.);
4. **LAYER** (or similar), see below, on which only details of specified lines, colours, or types of feature are drawn;
5. **LIMITS** to determine the screen co-ordinate limits suitable for drawing sheet sizes;
6. **SCALE** to allow drawing to a selected scale;
7. **HATCH** for hatching sectional views;
8. **DIM** or **DIMENSION**s for automatic dimensioning of a variety of types (horizontal, vertical, at angles);
9. **BLOCK**s, **WBLOCK**s, **PART**s, **ELEMENT**s (and similar) by which details occurring frequently in drawings can be inserted on to the screen from libraries held on disk;
10. **TEXT** for adding text and notes to drawings;
11. **CHAMFER** and **FILLET** because such features frequently occur in orthographic drawings.

6.1 LAYERS

Figure 6.1 shows the idea behind the **LAYER**s system. Each layer is as if it were a tracing on which only one type of line, dimensions, text, hatching, etc., is drawn. Each layer fits precisely in position over others. There are several advantages in using the **LAYER** system.

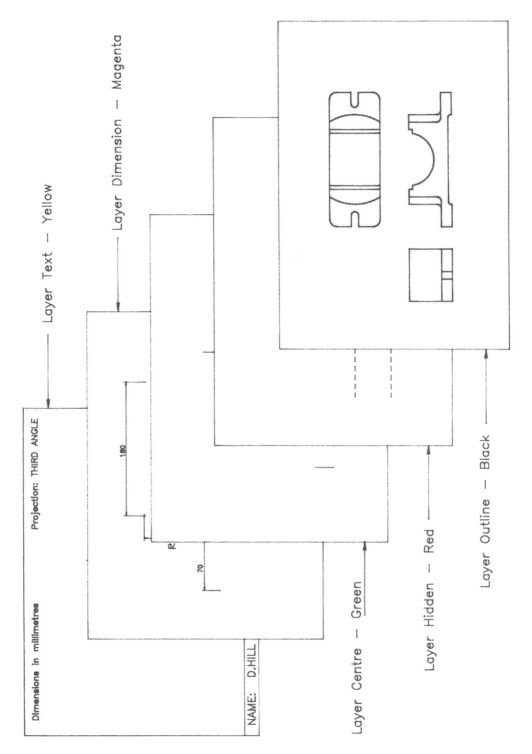

Fig. 6.1 *The idea behind the CAD LAYER system.*

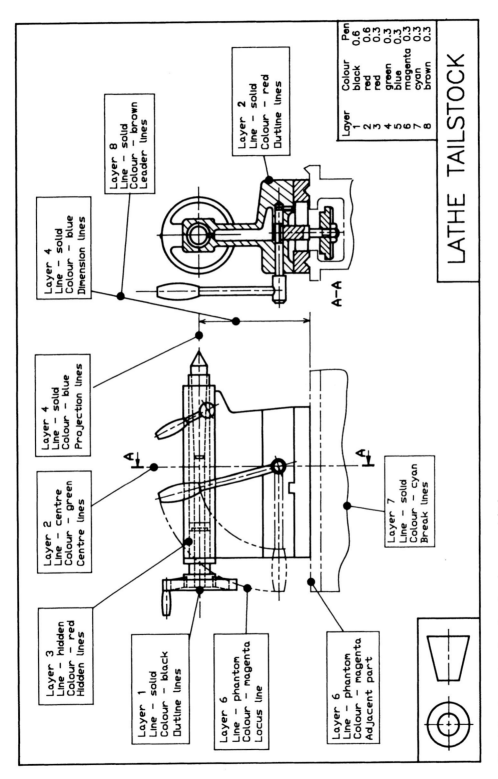

Fig. 6.2 An engineering drawing drawn on eight layers.

1. The drawing on screen is much easier to understand and to construct if different colours are allocated to different layers.
2. Layers can be **OFF**, so that they do not show on screen. This allows details of complicated drawings to be seen more easily as they are being developed.
3. A number of different line thicknesses can be plotted by allocating pens of different widths to different layers.
4. Coloured drawings can be plotted by allocating differently coloured pens to different layers when plotting.

Figure 6.2 shows how a variety of lines on eight layers can be built up. When plotted Layers 1 and 2 would be allocated a wider pen in the plotter than all the other layers. If plotted in colour, Layer 1 would be allocated a wide pen with black ink and Layer 2 a wide pen with red ink. Other layers would be allocated thinner pens with inks of the colours indicated in the drawing. The software used for this drawing was AutoSketch loaded into a computer with a colour monitor. In AutoSketch Layers are built up as required by following prompts in menus which appear centrally on screen when commands such as **Layer, Linetype, Color** are pointed at.

Note: Do not worry about the spellings of some commands in some CAD software. The spelling will often be American.

6.2 DRAWING SHEET SIZES

When some CAD software packages are loaded for 2-D drawing, the screen drawing area is assumed to represent the size of one of the A series of drawing sheets (A0, A1, A2, A3 or A4). The actual sheet size required can be varied by the user.

If one is drawing to a scale of full size, the co-ordinates of such screens can be read off directly in millimetres from the dynamic co-ordinate numbers which may be displayed at top or bottom of the screen. Even when drawing to other scales, sizes can be drawn accurately by making full use of the co-ordinate numbers, whether the co-ordinate (0, 0) is bottom left or central to the screen. The Techsoft Designer package is one such item of CAD software.

In other CAD packages the user must set up his own screen to represent the sheet size required. When configuring the drawing area of screens for such CAD packages, each co-ordinate point is assumed to represent the unit being worked in (inches, millimetres, etc.). The other two CAD packages in our three samples, AutoSketch and AutoCAD, are of this type.

6.2.1 A SIZE DRAWING SCREEN AREA FILES

When setting up a drawing sheet file, the following features can be set, so that when the required sheet file is loaded, the user can immediately commence constructing a drawing within a sheet of the chosen A size:

1. Sheet size: with the aid of command **LIMITS**;
2. Linetypes: with the aid of commands **LAYER** and **LINETYPE**;

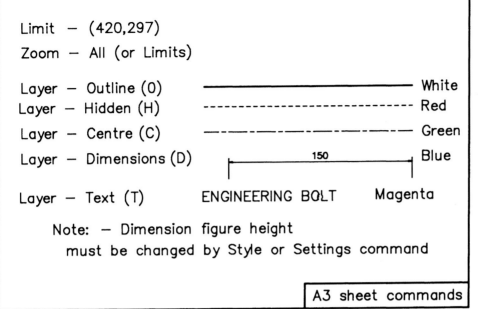

Fig. 6.3 *The commands to form an A3 sheet file.*

3. Colours: if working with a colour monitor, each layer can use a different colour;
4. Dimensioning; with the aid of command **DIM**;
5. Grid and Snap spacings: with the aid of commands **GRID** and **SNAP**.

Example 6.1   A3 Sheet File AutoCAD
The following examples are included here to show that when one is compiling a sheet file, the prompts of the software give considerable assistance.
    The rectangle of an A3 sheet is 420 mm by 297 mm. The first stage is to set the LIMITS of the screen co-ordinates to these numbers:

Command: LIMITS [typed at keyboard or selected with pointer] Return
ON/OFF/⟨Lower left corner⟩⟨0.0000, 0.0000⟩: Return [given co-ordinates accepted]
Upper right corner ⟨12.0000, 9.0000⟩: 420, 297 [typed at keyboard] Return
Command: ZOOM [typed at keyboard] Return
All/Centre/Dynamic/Extents/Left/Previous/Window/⟨Scale(X)⟩: All [typed at keyboard] Return
Regenerating drawing.
Command:

    The following shows the setting of the LAYER CENTRE on which centre lines of a red colour will be drawn, by requesting in sequence: New (n) with name centre; Ltype (l); with name centre; Color (c) with name r (red), in response to the requests appearing on screen.

Command: layer [keyed in or selected with pointer]
?/Make/Set/New/ON/OFF/Color/Ltype/Freeze/Thaw. n [typed from keyboard] Return
New layer name: centre [typed at keyboard] Return
?/Make/Set/New/ON/OFF/Color/Ltype/Freeze/Thaw. l [typed from keyboard] Return
Linetype (or?) ⟨CONTINUOUS⟩: centre [typed from keyboard] Return
Layer name(s) for linetype CENTRE ⟨0⟩: centre [typed from keyboard] Return
?/Make/Set/New/ON/OFF/Color/Ltype/Freeze/Thaw. c [typed from keyboard] Return
Color: r [typed from keyboard] Return
Layer name(s) for color 1 (red) ⟨0⟩: centre [typed from keyboard] Return
?/Make/Set/New/ON/OFF/Color/Ltype/Freeze/Thaw. Return
Command:

The layer CENTRE has now been formed. To set the LAYER CENTRE key in S in answer to the Layer queries and type in centre, followed by Return (twice).

Before being able to include linetypes in this file, the linetype centre and another, hidden, will have to be created and loaded into the software. Although this is not shown here, there are sufficient prompts given by the software for these linetypes to be created and loaded.

The last layer required to complete our A3 sheet is the DIMENSIONS layer. The various DIMENSIONs characteristic will also need to be set. Once again sufficient prompts are given to assist in this task.

GRID set to (10,10) and **SNAP** also set to (10,10) could also be added to this file. The numbers in brackets are units, in this case millimetres.

Finally, the file should be **SAVE**d. A suitable filename would be A3sheet. Before **SAVE**ing, a title block and margins could be added if wished.

Several sheet files (e.g. A4, A3, A2) could be compiled and **SAVE**d, to be **LOAD**ed when required.

The above detailed method of compiling sheet files appears rather tedious, but it only needs to be done once for each size sheet. After that the required sheet file can be recalled from the sheet files saved on disk.

6.3 AN ORTHOGRAPHIC PROJECTION WITH CAD

Although different methods might have to be used with different software, the following shows how the features of the menu/commands systems of CAD can be used to advantage in producing orthographic drawings accurately and quickly. Users of CAD software tend to develop their own methods, depending on their software and hardware and partly on the way in which they wish to operate their equipment.

Figure 6.4 is an isometric drawing of a bracket. Figure 6.5 and 6.6 show the stages of producing an orthographic projection of the bracket using CAD methods.

Before commencing drawing load an A4 sheet file if you have one on disk. This file should be set up to have at least:

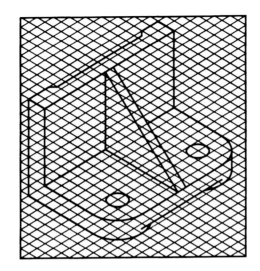

Fig. 6.4 *An isometric drawing of a bracket.*

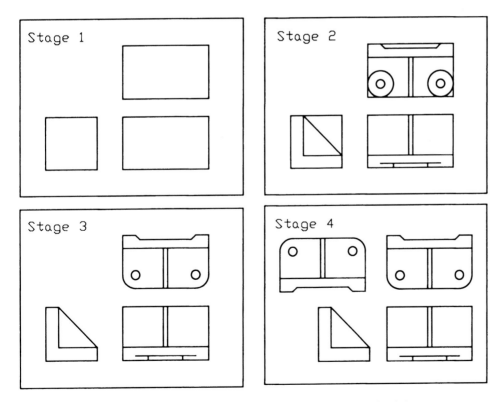

Fig. 6.5 *Stages in producing an orthographic projection of the bracket in Fig. 6.4.*

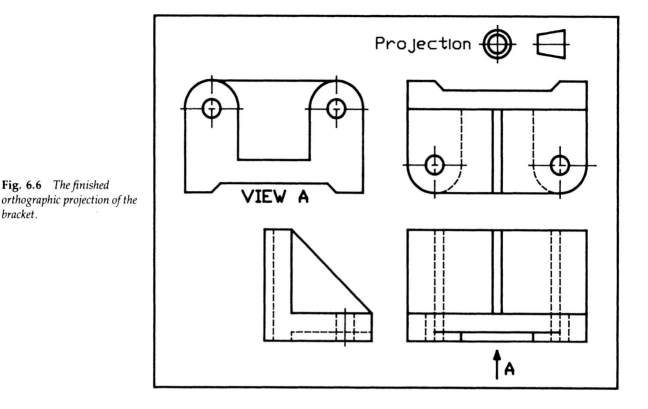

Fig. 6.6 *The finished orthographic projection of the bracket.*

1. Layer 1: outline lines, black;
2. Layer 2: hidden detail lines, red;
3. Layer 3: centre lines, green;
4. Grid: set at 10 mm each way;
5. Snap: set to 5 mm each way.

Stage 1: Draw the outlines of the rectangles which will contain the three views, relying upon the 5 mm snap points to obtain accurate sizes.

Stage 2: Add details of the three views within these rectangle outlines. Note that in this example, instead of using fillets at the bottom corners of the plan, circles have been drawn. It depends on the software being used.

Stage 3: **ERASE** and **BREAK** unwanted lines.

Stage 4: To obtain VIEW A, copy the plan view to a new position and rotate it through 180°. Move the four views to new positions to give a better layout on the drawing sheet.

Stage 5 (Fig. 6.6): Complete the drawing by adding:

1. amendments to VIEW A (outline layer);
2. text;
3. projection symbol.
4. hidden detail (hidden lines layer);
5. centre lines (centre lines layer).

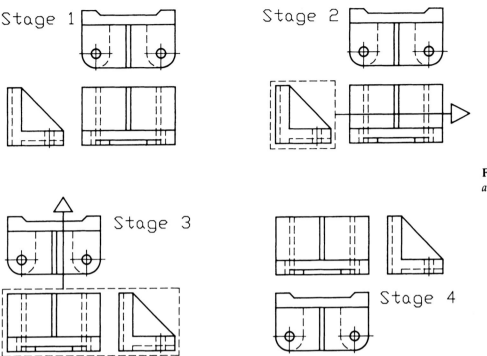

Stage 1

Stage 2

Stage 3

Stage 4

Fig. 6.7 *Converting a third angle projection to first angle.*

Figure 6.7 shows how, by **MOVE**ing front and end views and plan of Fig. 6.6 a Third Angle projection can be changed to a First Angle projection.

Stage 1: The VIEW A has been erased (deleted).

Stage 2: **MOVE** the end view to the right of the front view.

Stage 3: **MOVE** front and end views to above the plan.

Stage 4: The First Angle projection is completed.

Note: Figures 6.5 to 6.7 have been drawn from computer drawing files with the aid of a plotter using two pens, one of 0.6 mm and the other of 0.3 mm thicknesses. When using AutoCAD, such drawings can be printed on a printer with thick outline lines and thin centre and hidden detail lines to conform with the appropriate British Standard. This can be achieved by plotting outline lines on screen using the **PLINE** command (Polyline), with outline lines of width 0.6.

6.4 DIMENSIONING

All CAD software will draw dimensions automatically, although the methods by which they are included in drawings vary between packages. Once again comparisons can be made between our three selected packages. Taking that which provides the most comprehensive system, AutoCAD first, we get the following.

Figure 6.8 shows aligned, angular, circle, horizontal, radius and vertical dimensions obtained by selecting the command **DIM**, after setting zero (0) digits after the decimal point of units by the **UNITS** commands, so that only integers

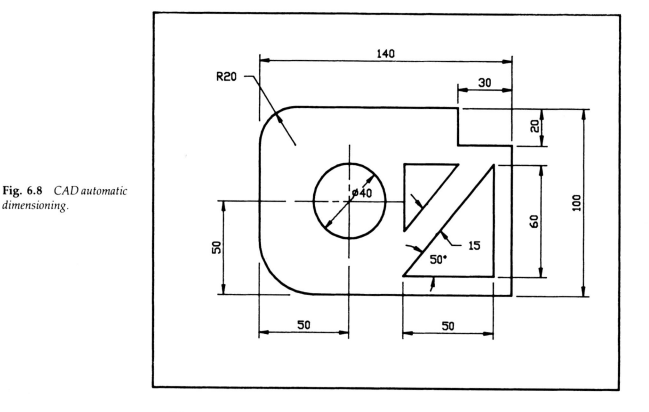

Fig. 6.8 *CAD automatic dimensioning.*

will be displayed. To draw the dimensions of Fig. 6.7 the dimensioning status of DIM had to be set to the following:

1. **DIMASZ** – 5   (arrow length);
2. **DIMDLI** – 3   (dimension line extension);
3. **DIMEXE** – 3   (extension above dimension line);
4. **DIMTP** – off   (add + tolerances);
5. **DIMTM** – off   (add − tolerances);
6. **DIMTOL** – off   (generate tolerances);
7. **DIMTAD** – on   (dimensions above dimension line);
8. **DIMEXO** – 3   (extension line offset);
9. **DIMTIH** – off   (dimensions inside dimension lines).

In addition the text height was set to 4 by the **STYLE** command.

This series of dimension status settings needs only to be completed once. The set of dimension settings can then be saved with the sheet file. When the sheet file is again loaded, the above settings will be the default settings for that file.

Figure 6.9 Shows tolerances included with dimensions after setting the digits after decimal point at 2 by using the UNITS command and altering some DIM status conditions:

1. **DIMTP** – 0.05;
2. **DIMTM** – 0.05;
3. **DIMTOL** – on.

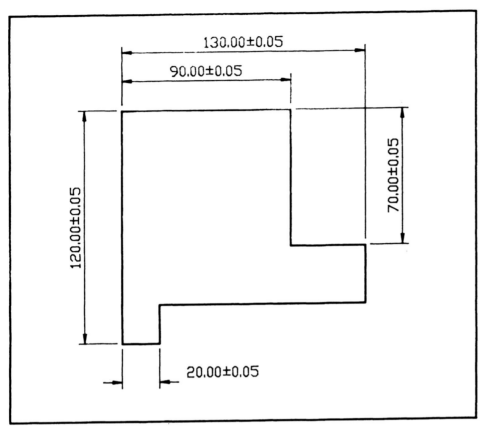

Fig. 6.9 *CAD automatic tolerance dimensioning.*

When using AutoSketch, aligned, horizontal and vertical dimensions can be drawn automatically. The height of dimension figures is controlled by text height selection. Dimension line and projection line extensions are preset.

When using Techsoft Designer the variables associated with dimensioning can be changed, i.e. arrow sizes, projection gaps, text size and slope, and whether figures are placed in automatically or keyed in when requested. Aligned, parallel and vertical dimensions are possible, as is the placing of arrowheads automatically at the ends of lines for the dimensioning of angle, arcs and circles.

Note: When including dimensions in drawings, remember to draw them on a new LAYER (or the equivalent), in order that line thicknesses (or colour) can be changed by a change of pens in the plotter used for producing hardcopy.

6.5 TEXT STYLES

In AutoCAD and in AutoSketch a variety of text **STYLE**s are available. Figure 6.10 shows some of these. Each style of text can be drawn at different heights, slopes and widths. The command **STYLE** (AutoCAD) with its prompts allows

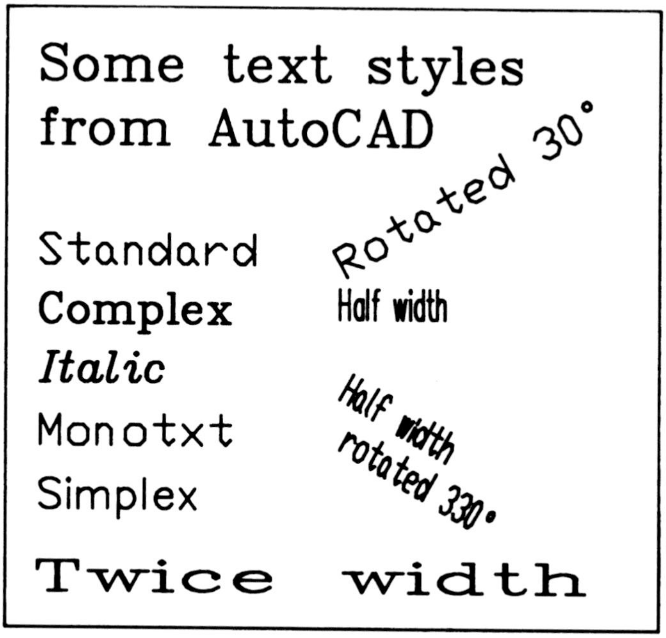

Fig. 6.10 *Example of CAD text styles.*

the user to make these changes. Other software packages also allow changes of style, height and slope of text.

Figure 6.11 is an example of an orthographic drawing produced with the aid of CAD software. Details about features such as sections and surface finish symbols used in this drawing are given in later pages in this book. The drawing entailed the following LAYERs. The background colour for the screen drawing area was blue:

1. Layer 0: borders only, colour white:
2. Layer Outline: all outlines, colour white;
3. Layer Centre: all centre lines, colour green;
4. Layer Hidden: all hidden detail, colour red;
5. Layer hatch: hatching lines in sectional view, also dimensions, colour magenta;
6. Layer text: all text, colour cyan.

6.5.1 VIEWS SHOWING TRUE SHAPE

A type of view frequently found in orthographic drawings is that which shows the true shapes of surfaces. These can be added to CAD drawings by taking advantage of the **ROTATE** command common to most CAD software. Figure

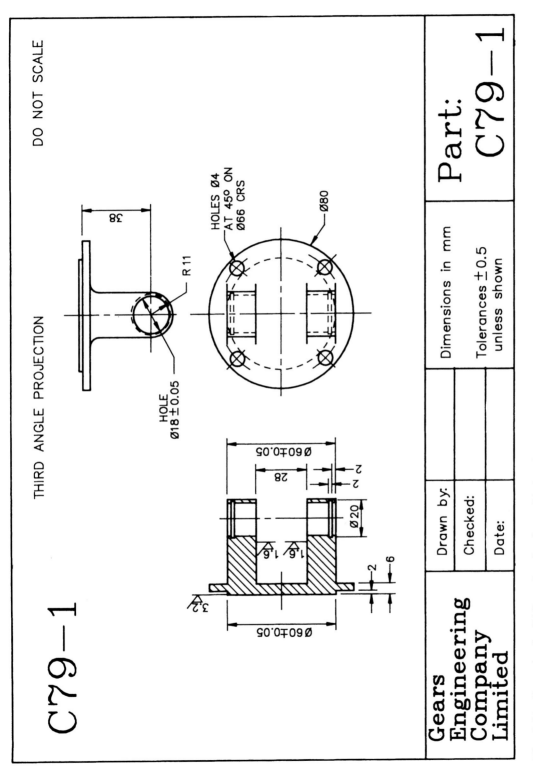

C79-1

DO NOT SCALE

THIRD ANGLE PROJECTION

35

R 11

HOLE
Ø18±0.05

HOLES Ø4
AT 45° ON
Ø66 CRS

Ø80

Ø60±0.05

28

2

2

Ø20

1.6

1.6

2

6

3.2

Ø60±0.05

Gears Engineering Company Limited	Drawn by:	Dimensions in mm	Part:
	Checked:	Tolerances ±0.5 unless shown	C79−1
	Date:		

Fig. 6.11 *Example of a CAD produced orthographic drawing.*

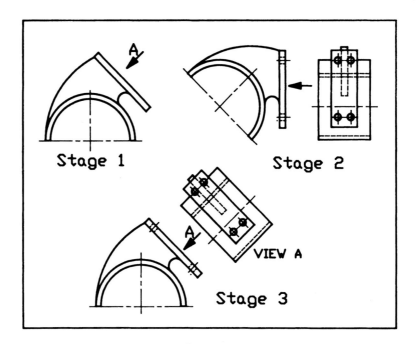

Fig. 6.12 *Stages in drawing a new view.*

6.12 shows stages by which this command could be used for producing true shape views.

Stage 1: Draw the view from which the true shape is to be derived.

Stage 2: Rotate this view so that the edge of the surface from which the true shape is to be projected is either vertical or horizontal. While the view is in this position it is easy to project the required true shape from the view.

Stage 3: When the true shape view has been drawn, **ROTATE** the original view and the new view back into the original position.

Note: Care must be taken when **ROTATE**ing to ensure that the surface from which the new view is to be projected is truly vertical or horizontal. This means that the centre of **ROTATE**ion must be chosen with some care.

Figure 6.13 is an example of a CAD drawing where the true shapes taken from two directions are included.

Figure 6.14 shows how the main view was **ROTATE**d into a new position to allow one of the true shape views to be taken while the surface from which the true shape was taken was horizontal.

When a drawing includes details of parts showing fine details, which do not show up clearly at the scale at which an orthographic projection has been drawn, it is a common practice to include an enlarged partial view as shown in Fig. 6.15.

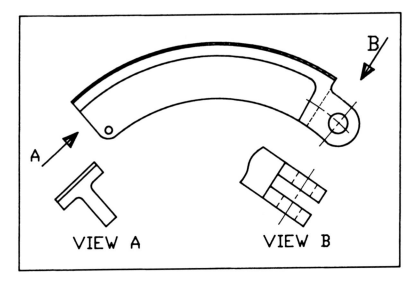

Fig. 6.13 *Example of a CAD drawing with a new view.*

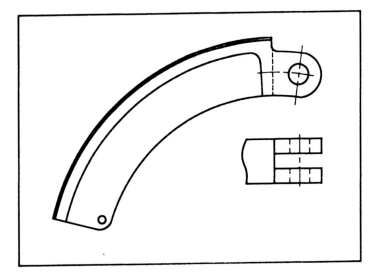

Fig. 6.14 *One stage in drawing the new view of Fig. 6.13.*

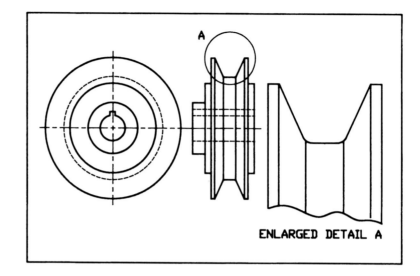

ENLARGED DETAIL A

Fig. 6.15 *An enlarged detail drawing.*

When using CAD, such views are very easy to add into an orthographic projection, by **COPY**ing part of the required view, then **SCALE**ing the copied part to a larger size.

6.6 SECTIONAL VIEWS

Cross hatching is a relatively simple activity when drawing manually, the computer however often finds hatching difficult and the result can be a lengthy procedure in building up the views or in having to duplicate lines, apparently unnecessarily. The problem is that if the computer sees an area which is not closed most systems will draw hatch lines apparently at random. This is known as leaking. Often when leaking occurs, a **ZOOM** will reveal lines which do not accurately intersect and so a closed area is not available for hatching. In some systems, it is necessary to construct areas to be hatched as separate regions with a series of lines drawn around them to produce a closed region. Specific examples are given on p. 157.

6.6.1 SECTION HATCHING LINES

Many CAD software packages include provision for drawing hatching lines automatically in sectional views. The systems of commands and prompts vary between packages, but provision is usually made for altering angles and spacings at which hatch lines are drawn. In engineering drawings hatching lines in sections are usually at 45° in either direction at a spacing of 4 mm, with other angles and spacings occasionally being required. Other forms of drawing may require different patterns of hatching. Some of the more advanced software will allow for this. Once again a comparison between our three specimen CAD software packages shows the variety of methods involved for hatching.

Section Hatching from AutoCAD

Note that the HATCH command will produce hatching in a variety of patterns if the response to the **Pattern**: prompt is 'style' or 's'. The answer '?' will list the styles of patterns available. Hatch lines should be drawn in their own **colour** to allow for a correct thickness of pen to be allocated when plotting a drawing.

To draw hatching lines with AutoCAD the prompts are as follows:

> **Command:** hatch [typed at keyboard or selected with pointer] Return
> **Pattern (? or name, U, style):** u [typed at keyboard] Return
> **Angle for crosshatch lines** $\langle 0 \rangle$: 45 [typed at keyboard] Return
> **Spacing between lines** $\langle 1.0000 \rangle$: 4 [typed at keyboard] Return
> **Double hatch area?** $\langle N \rangle$: Return
> **Select objects:** [select a line, etc., by pointing]
> **Select objects:** [select second line, etc.]
> **Select objects:** [Return when last line, etc., has been selected]

Lines and arcs etc. (objects) must be selected all around the area to be hatched. When the final object has been selected, hatching will automatically be drawn when the Return key (or pointer button) is pressed.

Section Hatching from Techsoft Designer

Provision is not made in this package for drawing a variety of pattern styles when hatching. Hatching over the same area several times with hatch lines at different angles and spacings will, however, produce a variety of patterns if required.

A system of layers as such is not available in this software, but hatch lines should be drawn on their own ELEMENT and with a specified pen thickness.

When HATCH is selected from MENU 2 by pointing with mouse, trackerball or cursor keys, etc., the following prompts appear in four stages at top and bottom of the screen drawing area.

1. Top of screen:

   Select (1–2)

   Bottom of screen:

   1 Enclosed area
   2 Elements

2. Select 1 (say). The following appear on screen. Top of screen:

   Hatching angle (in deg): 45 [typed at keyboard]
   Spacing: 4 [typed at keyboard]

3. After which the following appears bottom screen:

Hatching angle 45
Spacing 4

and at the top of screen:

Is this correct Y [typed at keyboard]

4. Then at the top of the screen:

Locate an edge (Locating point must lie within hatching area)

When a point within an area to be hatched is located by mouse, etc., hatching lines are automatically drawn within the area.

Section Hatching from AutoSketch

Provision is not made in this package for automatic hatching, so hatch lines have to be added one at a time within a sectional view. By careful setting of GRID and SNAP spacings, lines can accurately be drawn at 45° angles and with regular spacings. Hatch lines should be drawn in a separate colour.

With AutoSketch, use the **BREAK** command to erase the ends of hatch lines drawn beyond an outline caused by **SNAP**ping on to snap points outside the section outline.

6.6.2 PROBLEMS WITH AUTOMATIC HATCHING

Each CAD automatic hatch system gives rise to some problems. These can be highlighted by comparing hatching with AutoCAD and with Techsoft Designer.

Figure 6.16 is a Third Angle orthographic projection of a part, in which one view, the plan, is in section. The four drawings of Figure 6.17 show problems which can occur when drawing sectional view with these two software programs. Similar problems may also occur with other CAD software.

AutoCAD Hatching

If the outline of the plan, before hatching, is constructed as in Drawing 1 and all lines of the outline of the left hand end to be hatched are then selected as objects (shown by small marks on these lines) then the result will come out as in Drawing 2 when the hatching is completed. The software regards the upper and lower lines of the plan outline as objects.

This means that, when hatching with AutoCAD, the plan must be drawn as in Drawing 3, so that each part of the plan is completely surrounded only by lines which the software can clearly recognize as objects. There are no lines outside the plan which the software can regard as objects. When the hatching has been completed, the remaining lines of the plan can be added (Drawing 4).

The remaining lines can, of course be added as separate lines before the hatching starts, because the added lines will not be looked at by the software as selected objects, when the lines around the sectioned parts are selected. In all sectional drawings, those parts which are to be hatched must be drawn in this manner.

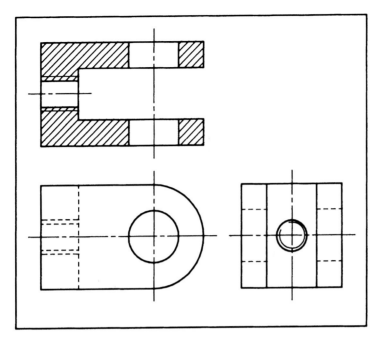

Fig. 6.16 *An orthographic drawing with section hatching.*

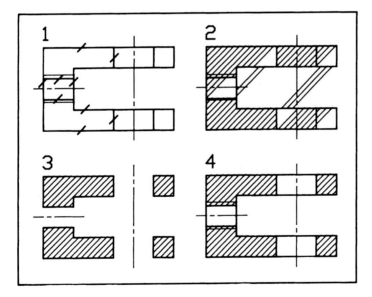

Fig. 6.17 *A method of overcoming leaking.*

Other Methods using AutoCAD

Outlines of Hatched Areas on a Separate Layer
Construct all outlines of areas of sections which are to be hatched on a separate layer, named say hatch01. When hatching has been completed layer hatch01 is turned OFF and thus does not appear either on screen or as part of a plotted drawing. The hatching however remains within the hatch01 closed area.

Using the BREAK Command

BREAK each intersection of an area to be hatched by selecting the intersection point twice as a break point. This effectively defines a closed area for hatching.

This problem does not arise when using Techsoft Designer.

Techsoft Designer Hatching

If there is the slightest gap between any two adjoining lines of the plan, the result will be as in Drawing 2: the hatching is said to have leaked out of the section. However, the problem of object recognition with AutoCAD does not arise with this software.

When constructing drawings which are to be hatched, use the **GRID LOCK** command to lock on to grid points. If there is any doubt, **ZOOM** to parts of the plan and look closely for any tiny gaps.

Fig. 6.18 *Five examples of sectional views drawn by CAD.*

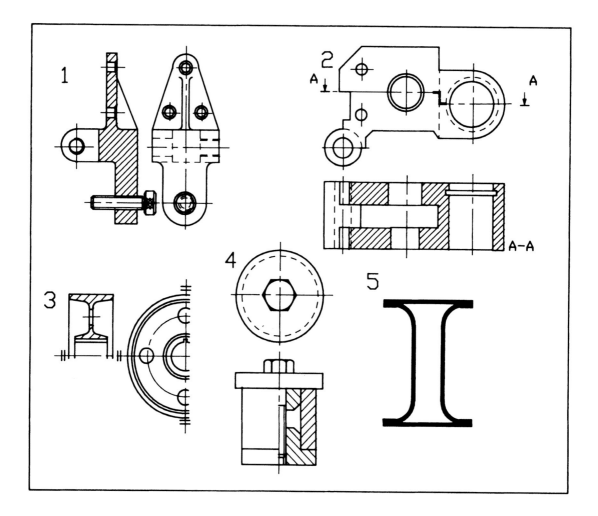

Examples of Section Hatching

Five examples of different types of sectional views drawn with the aid of CAD software are shown in Figure 6.18:

1. Drawing 1: an end view in section showing the principle that items such as ribs, webs and screwed parts are shown by outside view within sections;
2. Drawing 2: a plan in section showing the principle that a section taken from a staggered section plane is treated as if the section has been taken from a single plane;
3. Drawing 3: a section taken along symmetrical axes;
4. Drawing 4: a half section;
5. Drawing 5: a section through an object made from thick sheet material, drawn with the aid of the **PLINE** command.

Figure 6.19 is a further example of a CAD drawing which includes sectional views – a half section, a section showing a screwed part by an outside view and a removed section. Considerable use was made of **MIRROR**ing to obtain the required views in this example.

Fig. 6.19 *An example of a CAD drawing containing sectional views.*

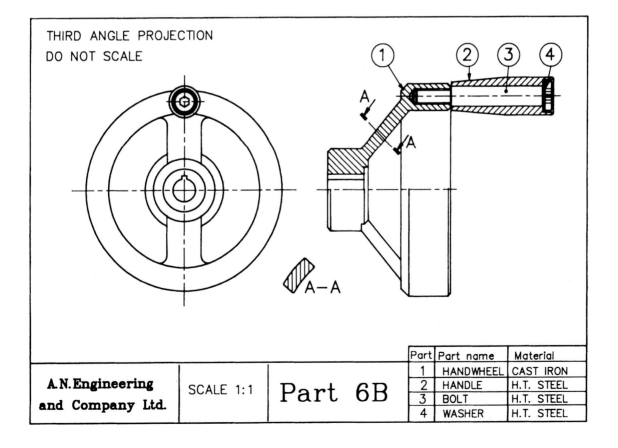

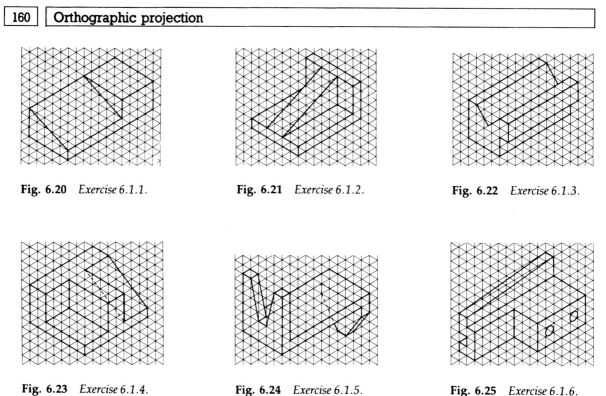

Fig. 6.20 *Exercise 6.1.1.*   **Fig. 6.21** *Exercise 6.1.2.*   **Fig. 6.22** *Exercise 6.1.3.*

Fig. 6.23 *Exercise 6.1.4.*   **Fig. 6.24** *Exercise 6.1.5.*   **Fig. 6.25** *Exercise 6.1.6.*

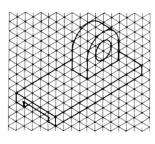

Fig. 6.26 *Exercise 6.1.7.*

Fig. 6.27 *Exercise 6.1.8.*

EXERCISES

Exercises 6.1

Ten pictorial drawings are given in Figs. 6.20 to 6.29. Most are drawn on isometric grids from which sizes can be judged. One includes dimensions. These are included here to allow the reader to practice the use of his/her CAD software by producing orthographic projections of simple objects with the aid of the most simple of the CAD commands. The required orthographic views can all be drawn on a screen which has been loaded with an A4 sheet file. When attempting these exercises:

1. determine how many orthographic views will show clearly the form of the block without ambiguity;
2. work in either First on Third Angle projection (you are advised to attempt some of the exercises in First Angle and some in Third Angle);
3. work full size and when you have drawn the required views **MOVE** them into positions to show a good layout for each drawing when it is printed or plotted;
4. you may find it advisable first to plan the views freehand on scrap paper before attempting to draw on the screen.

Exercise 6.2

Draw the following orthographic drawings, which include sectional views, with the aid of CAD. Work in either First or Third Angle projection.

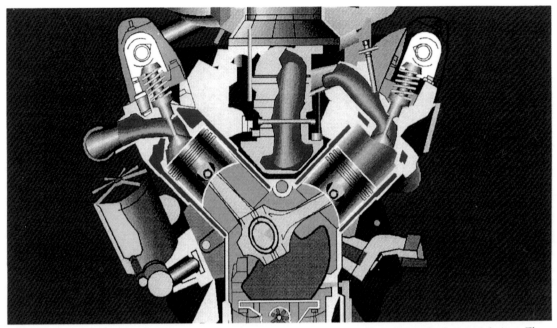

Plate 1 *A cross-sectional view of an internal combustion engine constructed using a pixel painting technique. The colour hardcopy was produced using a Tektronix 4693D thermal printer (courtesy of Tektronix).*

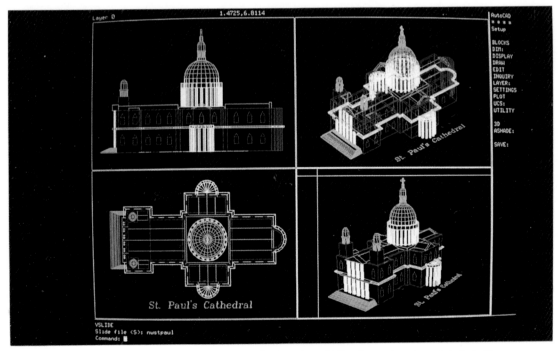

Plate 2 *Four views of St Paul's Cathedral constructed using AutoCAD software (courtesy of Autodesk).*

Plates 3 to 5 *The three illustrations on this page show a building constructed with the aid of AutoCAD software, working with a Tandon PC. The illustrations are:*

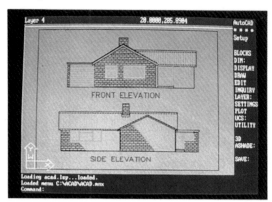

Plate 4 *A pull-down menu showing some of the commands used to construct the drawing.*

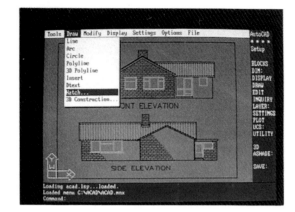

Plate 3 *The two elevations of a bungalow, drawn in several colours as the drawing appeared on the computer screen.*

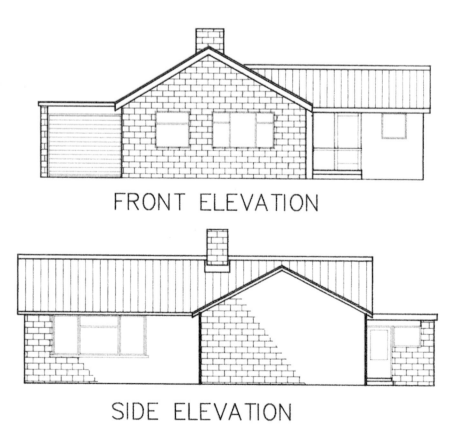

FRONT ELEVATION

SIDE ELEVATION

Plate 5 *A plot of the drawing.*

Plates 6 to 8 *The three illustrations on this page were constructed with the aid of AutoCAD software, working wth a Nimbus PC. The illustrations show an exploded orthographic projection drawn in a variety of colours. The illustrations are:*

Plate 6 *The screen of the microcomputer when the drawing had been completed.*

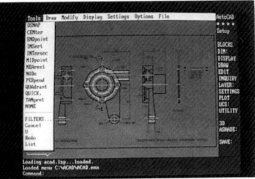

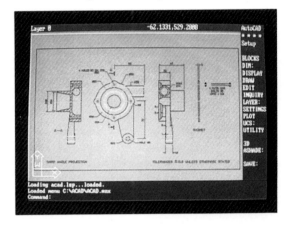

Plate 7 *A pull-down menu showing OSNAP settings, used to obtain an accurate drawing on the screen.*

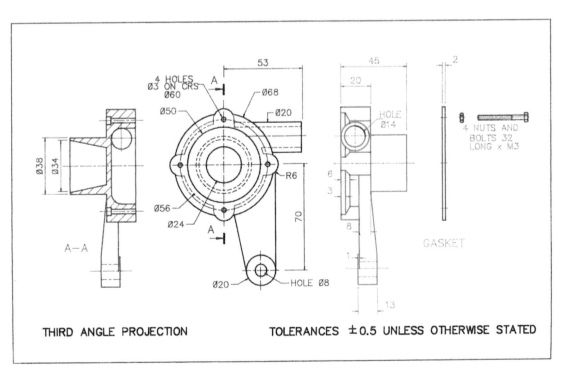

Plate 8 *Hardcopy produced with the aid of a Roland 880A plotter.*

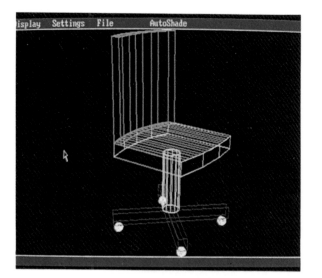

Plate 9 *A 3-D wire-frame model of a chair constructed in AutoCAD and displayed as a scene in AutoSHADE.*

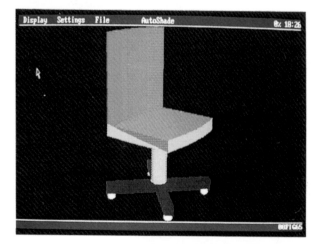

Plate 10 *The chair after being full-shaded in AutoSHADE.*

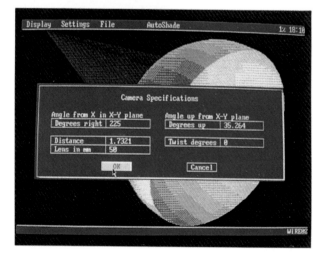

Plate 11 *A dialogue box for camera settings in AutoSHADE.*

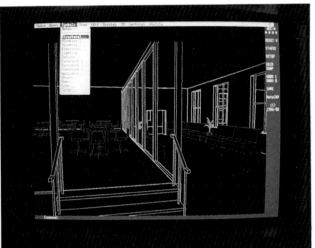

Plate 12 *An interior view of a building constructed using AutoCAD AEC Architectural (courtesy of Autodesk).*

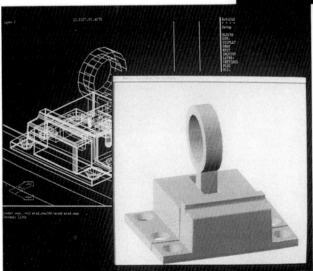

Plate 13 *An assembly of items created using AutoCAD and AutoSolid (courtesy of Autodesk).*

Plate 14 *A pulley and hook assembly colour rendered using AutoSHADE (courtesy of Autodesk).*

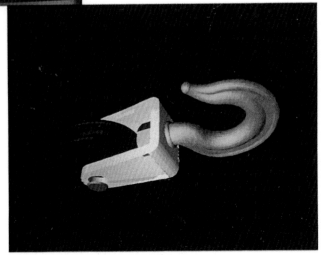

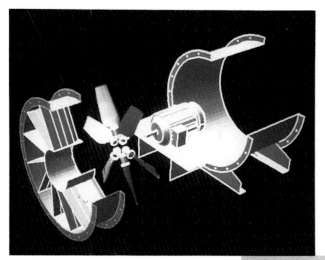

Plate 15 *An exploded view of an axial fan modelled in DOGS 3D (courtesy of PAFEC).*

Plate 16 *The body of a water pump from a domestic washing machine modelled using the BOXER solid modelling software. The original hardcopy was made with a four colour ink jet printer linked to the graphics display. Compare the quality of this image to the others in this section which have been photographed directly from the screen.*

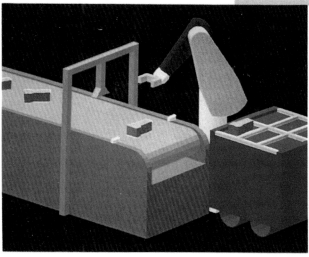

Plate 17 *A robot workstation simulated using GRASP (courtesy of BYG Systems).*

Plate 18 *A CIM workstation that shows a robotic manipulator (yellow) inserting a windscreen (yellow) into a motor car (white). This picture illustrates how a complex wireframe image can be enhanced by the use of colour to provide a meaningful picture for a low computational cost (courtesy of Prime).*

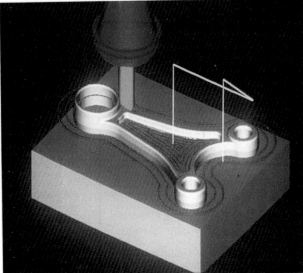

Plate 19 *CNC machine tool path simulation with both the machine tool and the workpiece solid modelled. The cutter path is indicated in red and rapid tool movements to and from the start position are indicated in yellow (courtesy of Intergraph).*

Plate 20 *A solid model of a printed circuit board showing the layout of electronic components and the joining electrical connections (courtesy of Intergraph).*

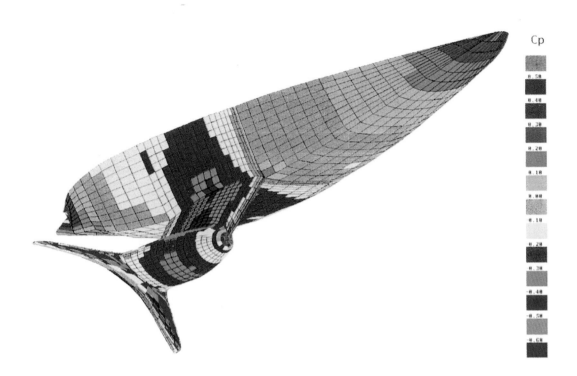

Plate 21 *The distribution of static pressure coefficient across the surface of a 12-metre yacht calculated by analytical methods (courtesy of Tektronix).*

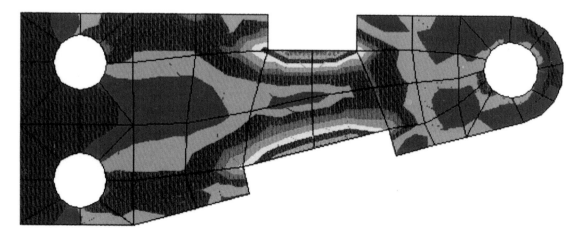

Plate 22 *Stress contours generated by a finite element post-processor.*

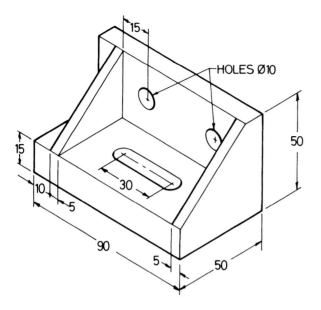

Fig. 6.28 *Exercise 6.1.9.*

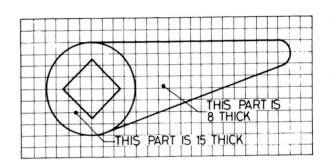

Fig. 6.29 *Exercise 6.1.10.*

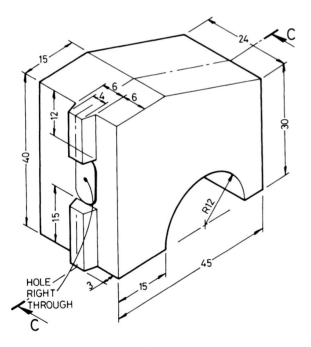

Fig. 6.30 *Slide block exercise.*

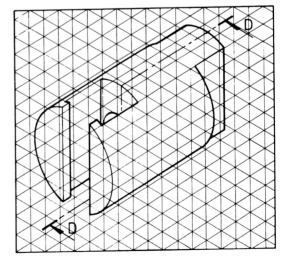

Fig. 6.31 *Gear clutch link exercise.*

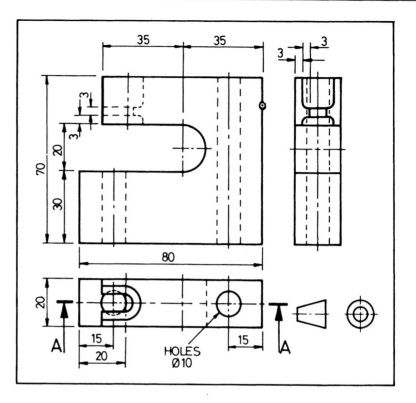

Fig. 6.32 *Gudgeon pin removal tool exercise.*

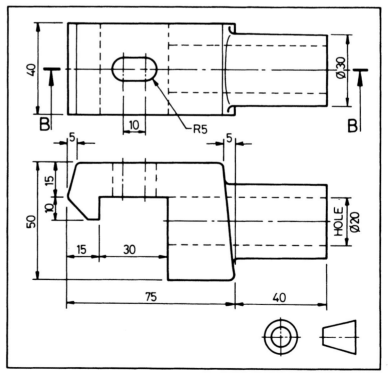

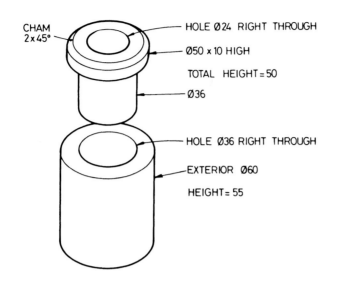

CHAM
2 x 45°

HOLE Ø24 RIGHT THROUGH

Ø50 x 10 HIGH

TOTAL HEIGHT = 50

Ø36

HOLE Ø36 RIGHT THROUGH

EXTERIOR Ø60

HEIGHT = 55

Fig. 6.34 *Sealing cap exercise.*

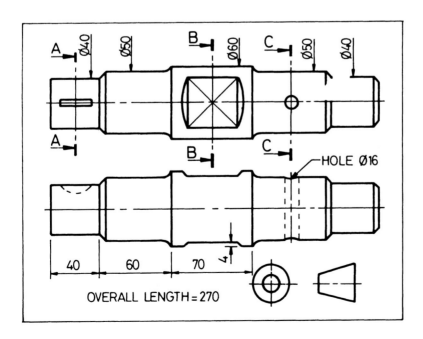

HOLE Ø16

OVERALL LENGTH = 270

Fig. 6.35 *Axle shaft exercise.*

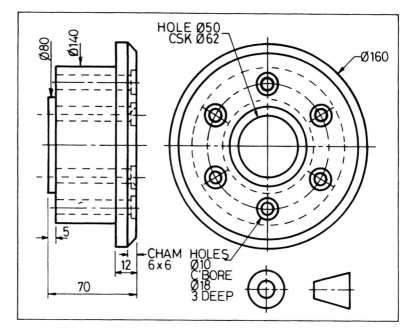

Fig. 6.36 *Seal removal tool exercise.*

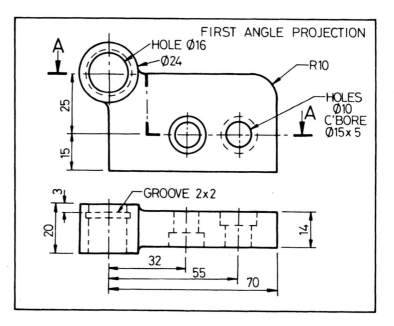

Fig. 6.37 *Lever change plate exercise.*

1. Draw the front sectional view C–C, an end view and a plan of the slide block shown in Fig. 6.30.
2. Draw (Fig. 6.31):
   (a) the front sectional view on DD;
   (b) an end view;

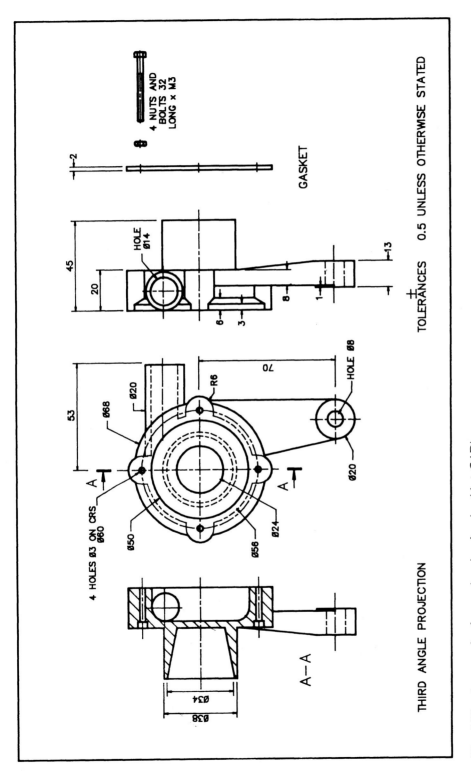

Fig. 6.38 *An example of an engineering drawing (AutoCAD).*

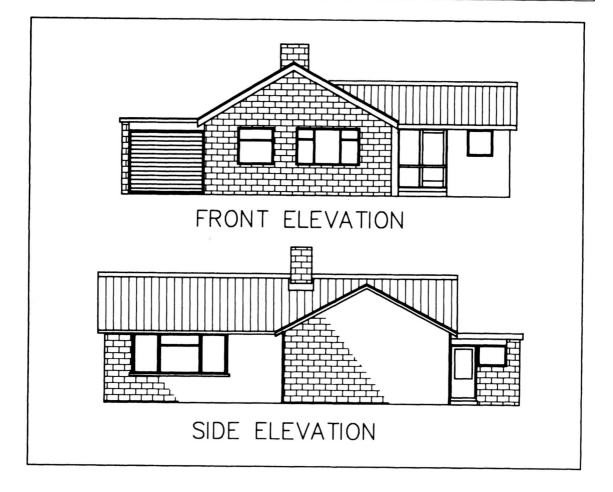

FRONT ELEVATION

SIDE ELEVATION

Fig. 6.39 *A building drawing in which roof tiles and brickwork have been added by HATCHing (AutoCAD).*

(c) a plan;
of the gear clutch link shown.

3. A pictorial drawing of a gudgeon pin removal tool is given in Fig. 6.32. Draw three views of the tool to include the sectional view A–A.

4. Draw three views of the taper turning guide shown by Fig. 6.33. The section B–B should be one of your views.

5. Draw the two views of a sealing cap shown in Fig. 6.34, but with the left-hand view in section, taken along the centre line of the right-hand view.

6. Copy the upper view of the axle shaft of Fig. 6.35. Add the three removed sections A–A, B–B and C–C.

7. The drawing of Fig. 6.36 shows a seal removal tool. Draw a half sectional view through the tool.

8. Figure 6.37 shows a lever change plate taken from gear box of a lorry. Copy the given front view (the upper view in Fig. 6.37) and add a section taken along A–A.

Libraries of symbols and parts drawings

One of the most valuable facilities offered by CAD software is the option of being able to store files of drawing entities. When required any of these entity files can be recalled to be included in drawings. Sets of such files are known as libraries. The use of library files saves a great deal of time. A detail or symbol can be added to a drawing merely by calling up the necessary entity file from its library disk.

7.1   NOTES ON LIBRARY FILES

1. Using libraries allows very fast production of those drawings which contain large numbers of symbols or repetitive items. Because of this, the methods by which libraries of parts and symbols are built up and used are described in some detail in the pages which follow.
2. When using CAD software it should never be necessary to draw the same item twice – either a single item can be copied, or it can be inserted into a drawing from a library of symbols or parts drawings.
3. Some of the systems employed for using such libraries may seem rather complex, but if the prompts given on screen are carefully read and followed, the compiling of and use of files from libraries is not very difficult. If in doubt refer to the software manual.
4. Some software firms supply disks of libraries of symbols files for use with some CAD software (e.g. AutoCAD).
5. Users of CAD can build up their own libraries of symbol files as and when the need for them arises. There is no limit to the number of files that can be accumulated for this purpose.
6. If your CAD system includes a graphics tablet, it can be configured to include a variety of symbols. If it is, symbols will appear on screen when selected from the tablet with its puck or stylus pointing device.
7. AutoCAD contains a programming language **AutoLisp**, which has been developed from the original **Lisp** language. AutoLisp can be used to program **macros**, which can be stored on disk as library files. A standard AutoCAD setup would usually have a number of AutoLisp files available for use.
8. **Parametric** files are computer files of drawings which can have variable dimensions applied to the entities they load onto screen – e.g. a file of a

British Standards drawing of a bolt from a parametric file can be drawn on screen to a variety of input dimensions (length, diameter, etc.) Parametric drawings can be programmed using AutoLisp.

7.2 EXAMPLES OF LIBRARIES

Some of the types of files found in libraries are given below. Note that these can be in parametric form, to be scaled, stretched or rotated to their required size when positioned in a drawing.

1. electrical symbols for circuit drawing;
2. electronics symbols for circuit drawing;
3. pneumatic symbols for circuit drawing;
4. hydraulic symbols for circuit drawing;
5. gate logic symbols for drawing computer gate circuits;
6. building drawing symbols for building drawings;
7. architectural symbols for inclusion in architectural drawings;
8. parts drawings for fastenings such as bolts, nuts, washers and rivets for engineering drawings; these can often be stored in parametric form, to be scaled or stretched to their required size when positioned in a drawing;
9. dimension tolerance symbols and geometrical tolerance symbols for adding to engineering drawings;
10. surface finish symbols for adding to engineering drawings;
11. dimensioning symbols for assisting the dimensioning of architectural, building or engineering drawings;
12. sheet size files with borders and with a variety of settings such as GRID, SNAP, DIM sizes;
13. title blocks for insertion in a variety of sheet sizes.

7.3 COMPILING LIBRARY FILES

When compiling one's own sets of libraries, some precautions will be necessary.

1. Draw each symbol or part on the correct sheet size. The symbols can however be enlarged or reduced by scaling.
2. Suitable names for the files should be chosen.
   (a) Avoid using the same name twice. In fact most CAD software packages will warn against this happening or even prevent it from happening.
   (b) Ensure that each symbol is sensibly named. If sensible names are not used, difficulties can arise when sorting out and referencing library files.
   (c) Some may prefer numbers for file names within their respective libraries. This is particularly useful if the symbols are selected by keying in the file names – it is much quicker to type say 01 than say 5-port_6. There is however, a danger when using numbers that the file title may not be clearly understood.
3. Make hardcopy prints which include all the symbols within each of your libraries. These can then be used as reference sheets when adding details from libraries to drawings.

7.4 PRODUCING FILES

7.4.1 AUTOCAD

Two commands are available for producing drawing files for libraries in AutoCAD: **WBLOCK** and **BLOCK**.

WBLOCK

The methods of using the two commands **WBLOCK** and **BLOCK** are similar, so only the steps involved in the WBLOCK system are given below.

Before saving a drawing of a symbol (say) as a WBLOCK, it must first be drawn. It can then be saved as a WBLOCK for insertion into other drawings as and when needed. It should be noted here that a WBLOCK file is a standard drawing file with the extension .dwg. In fact any drawing file with the extension .dwg can be inserted into another drawing using the **INSERT** command. The WBLOCK is written (hence the W) to its own drawing file.

To Save a WBLOCK

Command: wblock [typed at keyboard or selected with pointer] Return
File name: 3-port [typed at keyboard] Return
Block name: Return
Insertion base point: [select by pointing]
Select objects: w [typed at keyboard] Return
First corner: [point] **Other corner:** [point]
Select objects: Return

And the WBLOCK is saved to disk under its file name. The extension .dwg is automatically added to the file name.

To INSERT a WBLOCK into a Drawing
Again note that any drawing file with the .dwg extension can be inserted into another drawing using the **INSERT** command.

Command: insert [typed at keyboard or selected with pointer] Return
Block name (or ?): 3-port [typed at keyboard] Return
Insertion point: [point] **X scale factor** ⟨1⟩/**corner/XYZ:** Return
Y scale factor(default=X): Return
Rotation angle ⟨0⟩: Return

The block is inserted at the position selected by the insertion point. Note that the inserted drawing can be scaled in both (or either) x and y directions.

Notes
1. WBLOCKs and BLOCKs are filed as complete entities and can be **MOVE**ed, **COPY**ed, **MIRROR**ed, **ERASE**d, or **ROTATE**d as single units. The block entities can be converted back into their original elements with the **EXPLODE** command.
2. WBLOCKs or BLOCKs can be scaled by stating a required scaling factor at the

X scale: and/or Y scale: prompts, or rotated through any angle at the **Rotation angle**: prompt. The rotation angle is usually through a rotation anti-clock-wise, although this can be amended if required.

3. After inserting a block, it can be **MOVEd, COPYed MIRRORed** or **ROTATEd** as a single unit to replace it exactly where required.

4. When inserting, moving or copying blocks, exact positions on ends of circuit lines can be achieved by making use of the various **OSNAP** commands.

5. Whole drawings can be saved to file as WBLOCKs or BLOCKs. This can be a convenient device on occasions.

6. A block is saved as a complete unit. If it becomes necessary to amend a part of a WBLOCK after it is inserted into a drawing, its elements (objects) must first be exploded apart with the EXPLODE command.

7. If the ? key is pressed in response to the **INSERT** command, a list of available BLOCKs will appear on screen. The does not apply when using WBLOCKs. Only those WBLOCKs which have been **INSERT**ed in the current drawing will be listed.

BLOCK

When a symbol (say), is defined by the **BLOCK** command it is saved in the same file as that within which the drawing in which it occurs is saved. The block file can only be inserted back into a drawing within that file. If you are drawing a circuit which contains only electrical or electronics symbols, then a file of blocks all held on the same file can be formed to draw the required circuit. When the circuit has been drawn it can then be saved under a new filename. The file containing the symbols as BLOCKs can then be used on another occasion. In this way a series of drawing files containing BLOCKs can be built up for drawings such as:

1. electrical and electronics circuits;
2. building drawings;
3. gate logic circuits;
4. pneumatic and hydraulics circuits.

Figure 7.1 shows the **BLOCK** command in use for drawing the block file of a bolt.

7.4.2 AUTOSKETCH

Part

In AutoSketch the library facility is called Part. The files in AutoSketch libraries are held in a Parts directory.

The method of drawing a file in the Parts directory follows the sequence.

1. Draw the required symbol.
2. Select **Group** from the Change menu. Window the symbol and select **Group** again. This ensures that the part can be **MOVEd, COPYed, SCALEd**, etc., as a single unit.

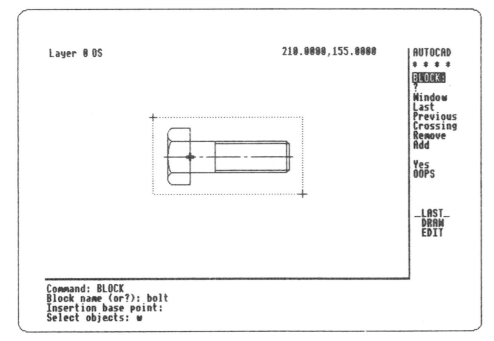

Fig. 7.1 *The BLOCK command (AutoCAD).*

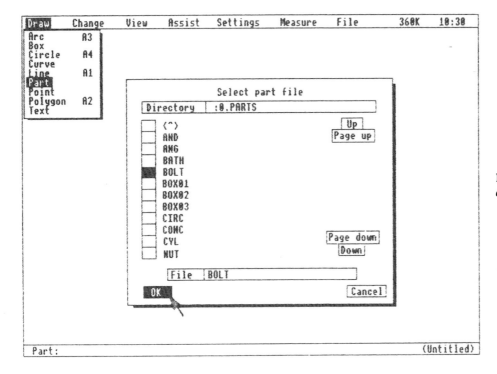

Fig. 7.2 *The PART command (AutoSketch).*

3. Select the command **Part base** from the Settings menu and point to the required insertion point on the symbol.
4. **SAVE** the part drawn in a Parts directory.
5. When the part is required to be added into a drawing, select **Part** from the Draw menu and further select the required part by its filename from the menu which appears on screen (Fig. 7.2).
6. The symbol will appear on screen as a Part attached to the screen pointer at the selected insertion point. The Part can be **MOVE**d to where it is required by moving the pointer with the mouse (or cursor keys). The part can also be **SCALE**d, **COPY**ed, **MOVE**d or **ROTATE**d again as required.
7. The **Attach** command can be called into play to assist in positioning a Part exactly at, say, the end or at the centre of a line.
8. Note that a whole drawing can be saved as a Part. The drawing must first be **Group**ed, otherwise its various members will not be moved as one unit if required.
9. Parts can be ungrouped into their various elements by the use of the **Ungroup** command.

7.4.3   TECHSOFT DESIGNER

NEW ELEMENTS

In Techsoft Designer each library file must be held as an element. Each file must have its own ELEMENT number.

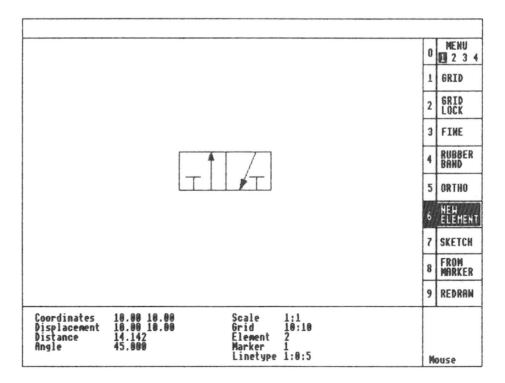

Fig. 7.3 *The NEW ELEMENT command (Techsoft Designer).*

1. Each symbol which is to be SAVEd to a library file, must be drawn on a NEW ELEMENT.
2. Draw the required symbol and then **SAVE** it after its First element and Last element numbers and its file name.
3. The symbol can be added to a drawing by:
   (a) selecting a **NEW ELEMENT** for it to be called on;
   (b) using the **ADD FILE** command to add the symbol to the drawing.
4. The symbol can be moved to its position in the drawing by using the **MOVE** command and stating its element number(s).

Notes
1. When a symbol is brought back to screen by using the **ADD FILE** command, it must be added on to a NEW ELEMENT. In the Techsoft Designer software systems, parts of a drawing can only be MOVEd or ROTATEd as numbered ELEMENTs.
2. When using Techsoft Designer a symbol is added to a drawing, in the position on the screen in which it was originally drawn. This needs to be remembered when calling symbols from library files.
3. A whole drawing can be saved as an element or as a number of consecutive elements if required.

Note
As can be seen from the above, each CAD package has its own system of saving, filing and using libraries of symbols in drawings. Note the differences between our three packages: in AutoCAD library files are WBLOCKs or BLOCKs; in AutoSketch they are Parts; in Techsoft Designer they are ELEMENTs. Despite these differences in command names and in their method of use, they are similar in their effect – of having a method within the software by which details, such as circuit symbols can easily and quickly be inserted into drawings from libraries.

7.5 EXAMPLES OF LIBRARY APPLICATIONS

7.5.1 NUTS, BOLTS AND WASHERS IN ENGINEERING DRAWINGS

Figure 7.4 shows some fastenings from an engineering drawing library. A full library for say, AutoCAD, would include hundreds of such drawings. The insertion point for each fastening is marked with a cross in Fig. 7.4. Figure 7.5 shows how the single drawing file BOLT from the library can be SCALEd and ROTATEd to give a range of bolt drawing of different scales and positions for inclusion in drawings.

Figure 7.6. shows drawings of a BOLT from a library using AutoSketch. With this software, a drawing can be STRETCHed as well as SCALEd or ROTATEd. Each of the various drawings in Fig. 7.6 is produced by different SCALEs, STRETCHes or ROTATEions of the same BOLT AutoSketch part file.

Figure 7.7 is a sectional drawing in which the bolts, nut and washers have been added from library files. Some amendment was needed to the drawing of

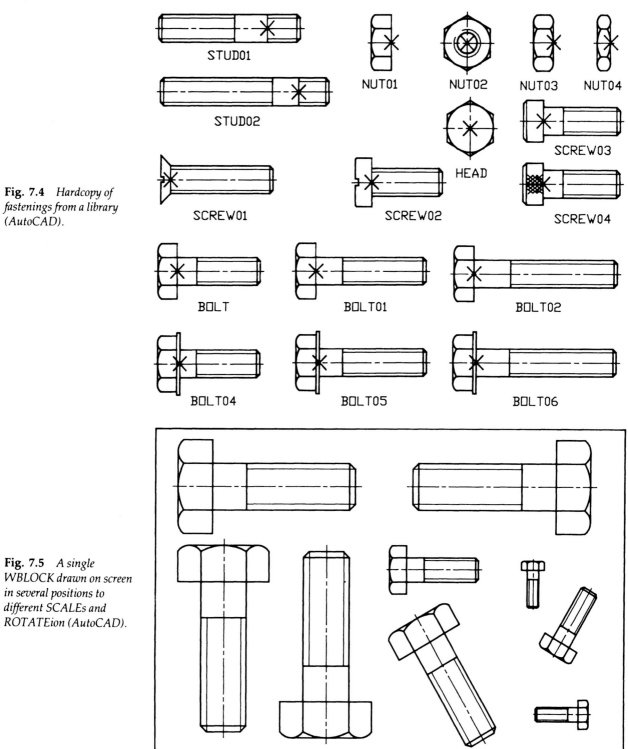

Fig. 7.4 *Hardcopy of fastenings from a library (AutoCAD).*

Fig. 7.5 *A single WBLOCK drawn on screen in several positions to different SCALEs and ROTATEion (AutoCAD).*

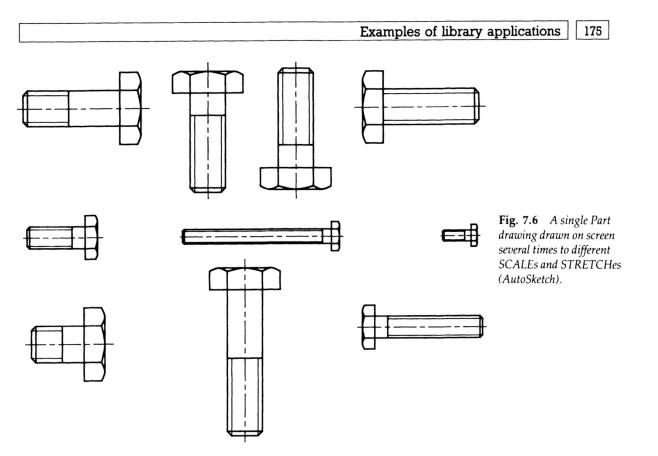

Fig. 7.6 *A single Part drawing drawn on screen several times to different SCALEs and STRETCHes (AutoSketch).*

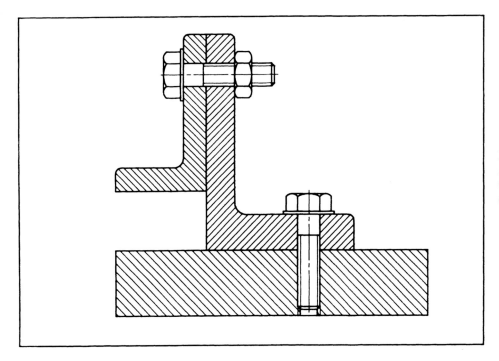

Fig. 7.7 *A sectional view in which bolts, nuts and washers have been INSERTed (AutoCAD).*

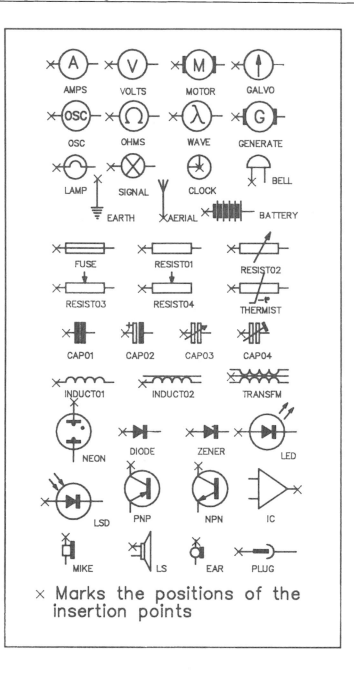

Fig. 7.8 *Hardcopy of a group of electronics and electrical symbols (AutoCAD).*

the nut, because it was inserted over the bolt. Lines from the bolt through the nut had to be erased. Before they could be erased the bolt drawing had to be EXPLODEd. It was then reduced to its elements from its state as a BLOCK entity.

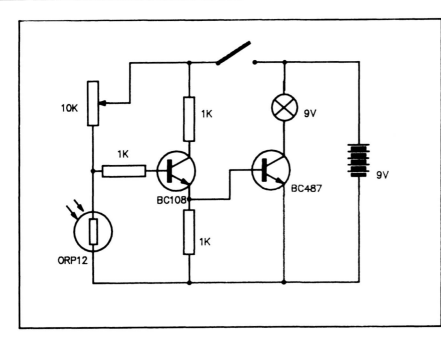

Fig. 7.9 *An electronic circuit drawn by INSERTing BLOCKs (AutoCAD).*

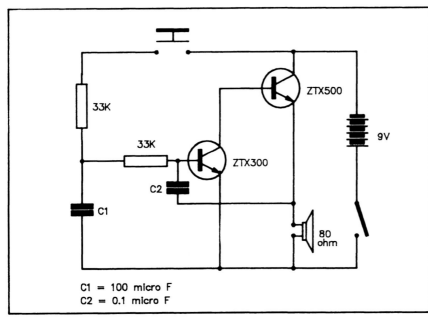

Fig. 7.10 *An electronic circuit from PARTS (AutoSketch).*

7.5.2 ELECTRICAL AND ELECTRONICS CIRCUIT DRAWINGS

Figure 7.8 shows some electrical/electronics symbols from a library. Each of the insertion points is again indicated by a cross. Figures 7.9 and 7.10 are simple electronics circuit drawings constructed by INSERTion from this library. The

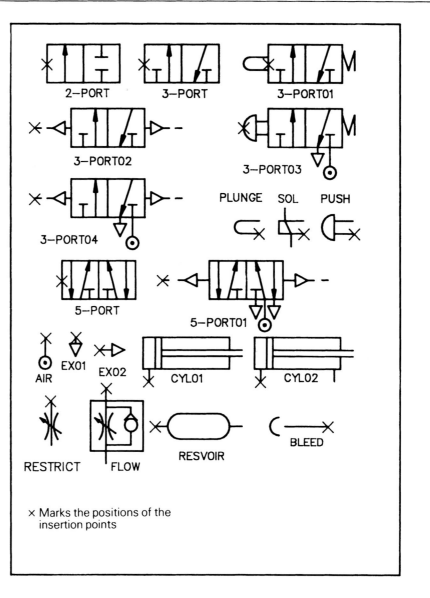

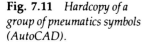

Fig. 7.11 *Hardcopy of a group of pneumatics symbols (AutoCAD).*

conductor lines were added after the symbols had been inserted. When drawing such circuits GRID and SNAP (or equivalent) should be on and also the OSNAP or ATTACH commands should be in operation. This allows conductor lines to be added in their exact positions relative to the symbols.

7.5.3 PNEUMATICS CIRCUIT DRAWINGS

Figure 7.11 shows a representative group of pneumatic (hydraulics) symbols from a pneumatics circuit library. Two simple pneumatics circuits drawn with

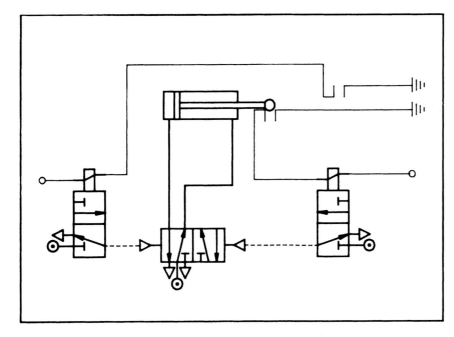

Fig. 7.12 *A pneumatics circuit drawn by INSERTing BLOCKs (AutoCAD).*

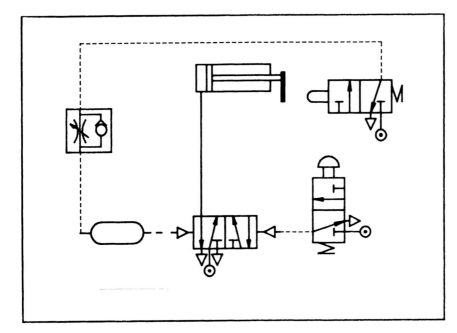

Fig. 7.13 *A pneumatics circuit drawn from a PARTS library (AutoSketch).*

the aid of symbols from this library are given in Fig. 7.12 and 7.13. Air (continuous) and exhaust (broken) lines were added after the symbols had been positioned on the screen. Again GRID and SNAP were operating to allow correct positioning of features from the library.

7.5.4 LOGIC GATE CIRCUIT DRAWINGS

The six common logic gates forming a six-symbol library are shown in Fig. 7.14. Note that there are a variety of different types of symbols used for logic gate circuits. Those shown are in common use. A circuit formed from this library is given in Fig. 7.15.

7.5.5 BUILDING DRAWING

A representative group of symbol files from a building drawing library is shown in Fig. 7.16. The two-storey house drawing of Fig. 7.17 was constructed from

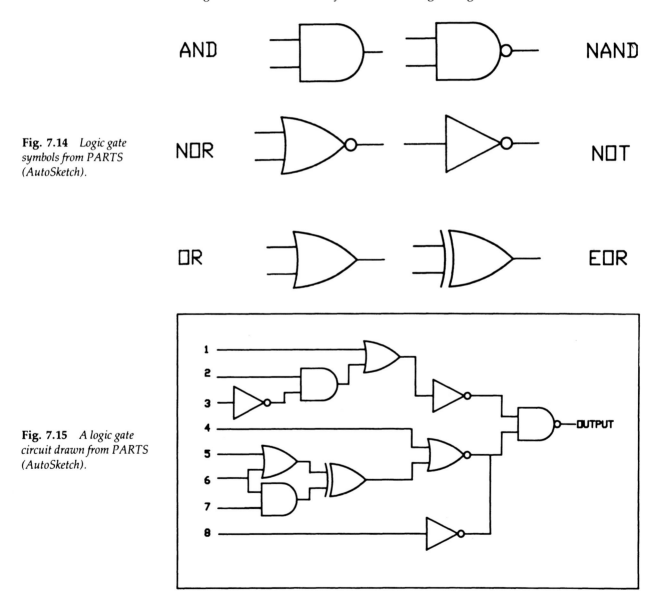

Fig. 7.14 *Logic gate symbols from PARTS (AutoSketch).*

Fig. 7.15 *A logic gate circuit drawn from PARTS (AutoSketch).*

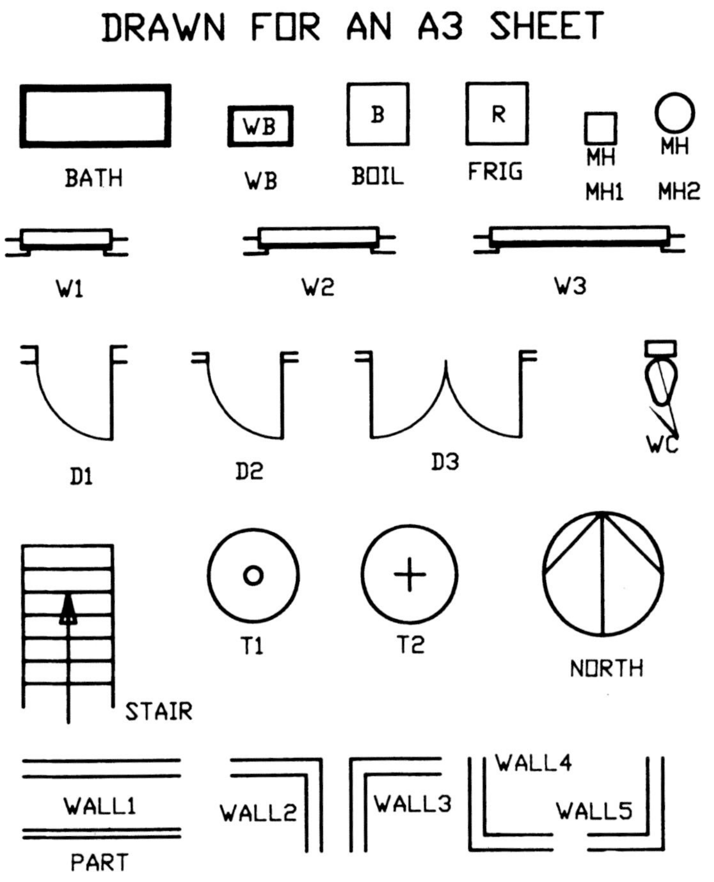

DRAWN FOR AN A3 SHEET

Fig. 7.16 *Building drawing symbols (AutoSketch).*

Fig. 7.17 *Plans of the two floors of a house drawn from a PARTS library (AutoSketch).*

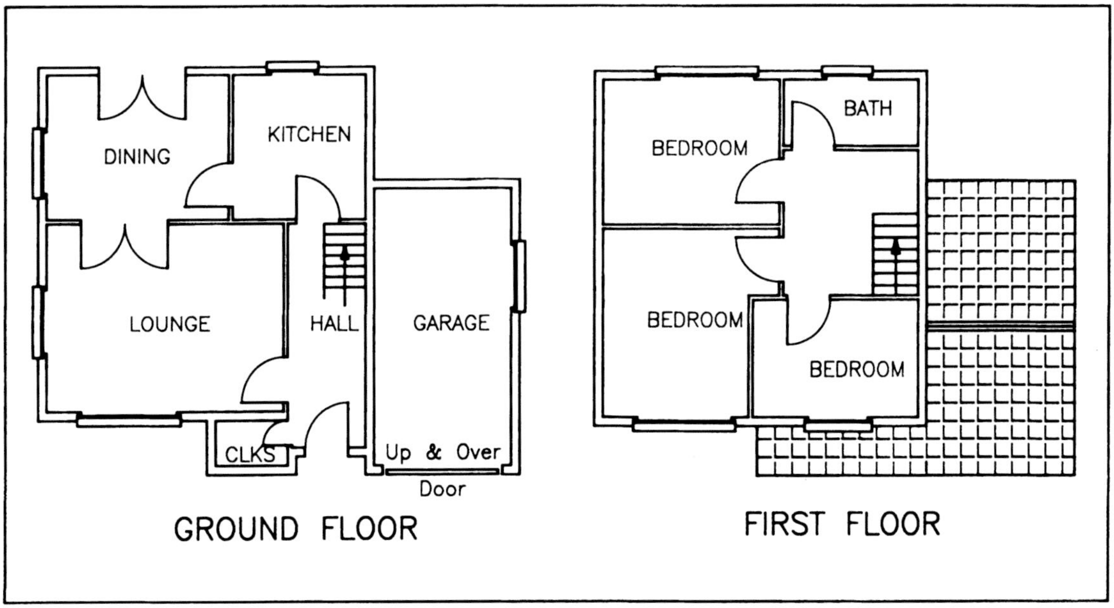

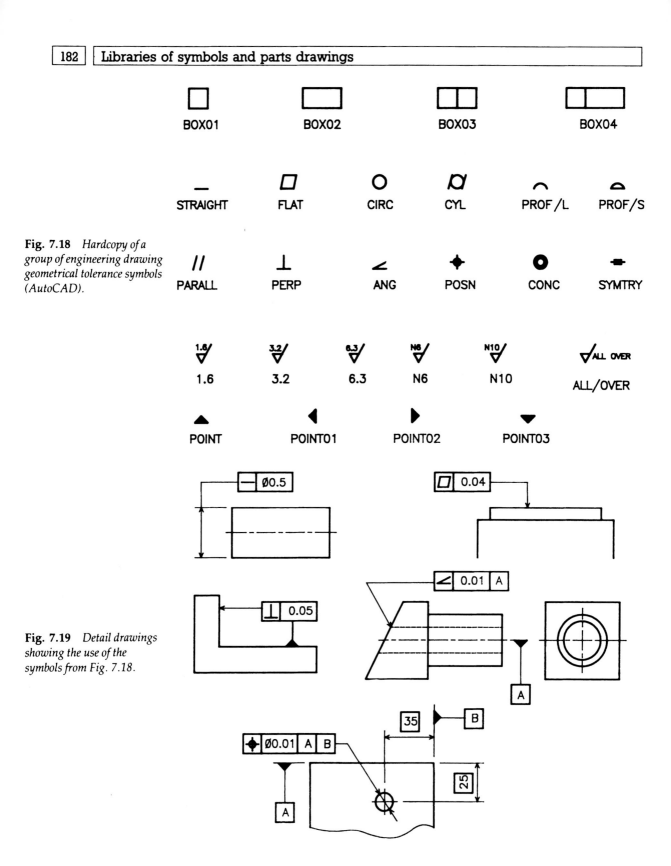

Fig. 7.18 *Hardcopy of a group of engineering drawing geometrical tolerance symbols (AutoCAD).*

Fig. 7.19 *Detail drawings showing the use of the symbols from Fig. 7.18.*

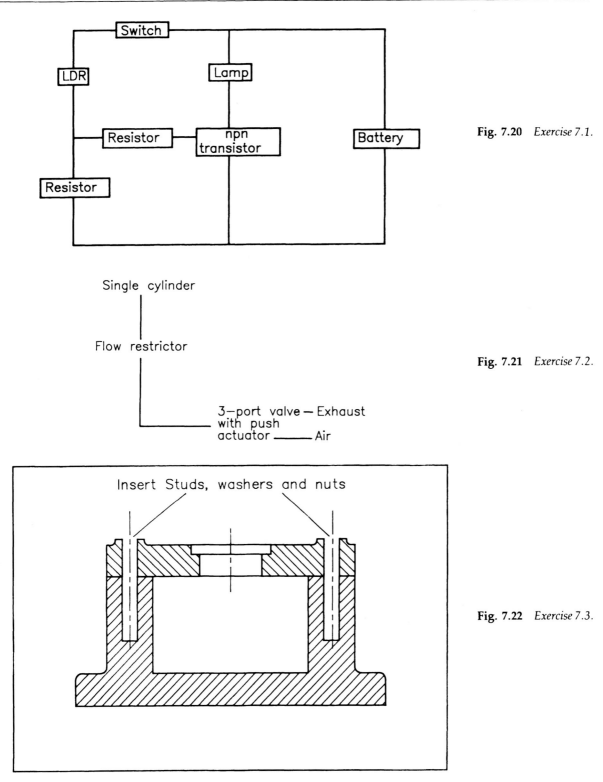

Fig. 7.20   *Exercise 7.1.*

Fig. 7.21   *Exercise 7.2.*

Fig. 7.22   *Exercise 7.3.*

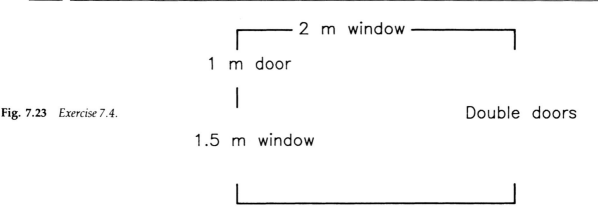

Fig. 7.23 *Exercise 7.4.*

symbols in this library. The roof tiles of the lower storey were added by COPYing a single tile, then groups of tiles over the roof.

7.5.6 GEOMETRICAL TOLERANCE AND SURFACE FINISH SYMBOLS

A group of geometrical tolerance and surface finish symbols from an engineering drawing library is shown in Figure 7.18. A number of small-detail drawings showing the use of the geometrical tolerance symbols can be seen in Fig. 7.19.

EXERCISES

Before attempting to draw more complex circuits or drawings involving libraries, practice with your software to be able to do the following.
(a) Draw a small number of symbol files and save them in a library. There are sufficient examples of suitable symbols in the illustrations already included in this Chapter.
(b) Insert symbols from your library to complete the required drawings in the exercises given below.

1. In the electronics circuit (Fig. 7.20) replace the names in the boxes with symbols.
2. In the pneumatics circuit (Fig. 7.21) replace the named components with symbols to complete the circuit.
3. Copy Fig. 7.22. Add suitable studs with washers and nuts in the positions indicated from your library file.
4. Draw a building plan of the brick-built garage shown in the outline drawing of Fig. 7.23, by insertion of building drawing symbols from your library.

Three-dimensional (3-D) drawing | 8

8.1 INTRODUCTION

Of the three CAD packages with which we have been dealing in Chapters 5, 6 and 7, only AutoCAD offers both isometric and true 3-D drawing and modelling facilities. AutoSketch does not have an isometric facility, although isometric drawings can be produced by setting the grid and snap points to different x and y sizes (approximately $x = 5.0$ and $y = 2.9$). However like much of the inexpensive software of this type, AutoSketch cannot produce isometric circles (ellipses), isometric drawing is thus mostly restricted to straight lines. Techsoft Designer possesses an isometric capability – GRID and SNAP can be set isometrically by stating the angles required for the x and y grids (30° and 150°) when setting grid points on screen. This software also allows ellipses to be drawn. Examples of isometric drawings created using these three CAD packages are shown in Figs. 8.1, 8.2 and 8.3.

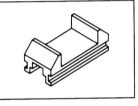

Fig. 8.1 *An isometric drawing (AutoSketch).*

8.2 ISOMETRIC DRAWING WITH AUTOCAD

Stages:
1. Set GRID.
2. Set SNAP:

> **Command:** snap [typed at keyboard] Return
> **Snap spacing or ON/OFF/Rotate/Style** ⟨**10.0000**⟩: s [Typed at keyboard] Return
> **Standard/Isometric** ⟨**S**⟩: i [typed at keyboard] Return
> **Vertical spacing** ⟨**10.0000**⟩: Return

3. Set isoplane:

> **Command:** isoplane [typed at keyboard] Return
> **Left/Top/Right** ⟨**Toggle**⟩: Return
> **Current Isometric plane is:** Top [typed at keyboard] Return (toggles between isoplanes)

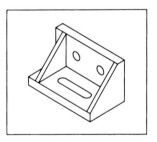

Fig. 8.2 *An isometric drawing (Techsoft Designer).*

4. Draw isometric ellipse:

> **Command:** ellipse [typed at keyboard] Return
> ⟨**Axis endpoint 1**⟩/**Centre/Isocircle:** i [typed at keyboard] Return

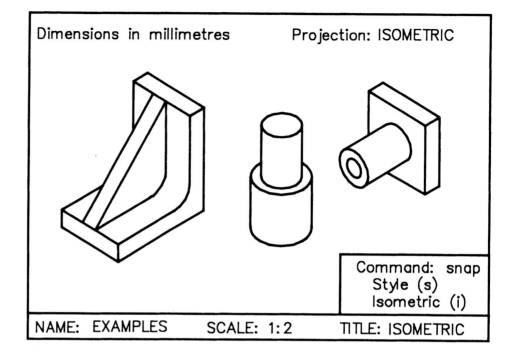

Dimensions in millimetres   Projection: ISOMETRIC

Command: snap
Style (s)
Isometric (i)

NAME: EXAMPLES   SCALE: 1:2   TITLE: ISOMETRIC

Fig. 8.3 *An isometric drawing (AutoCAD).*

Centre of circle: [point]
⟨**Circle radius**⟩**/Diameter:** d Return
Circle diameter: 10 [Return]
and the isometric circle (ellipse) is drawn on the stated isoplane.

8.2.1 ISOMETRIC DRAWING IS NOT A TRUE 3-D METHOD

Note that isometric drawing is not a true 3-D method of producing 3-D models. An isometric drawing is a 2-D drawing, produced on a flat plane (i.e. in the *x*, *y* plane). With AutoCAD true 3-D drawings can be constructed in an *x*, *y*, and *z* co-ordinate system and models produced from them. This is in addition to AutoCAD's isometric drawing facility. Note that even in AutoCAD isometric drawing is only a 2-D method. Isometric drawings in AutoCAD cannot be transferred to the 3-D systems available in this software.

It must also be noted that the sophisticated 3-D modelling systems of packages such as AutoCAD, PAFEC and IDEAS (explained in Chapter 9) must be balanced against their being considerably more expensive to purchase than AutoSketch, Techsoft Designer and other inexpensive CAD packages.

In AutoCAD, drawings can be constructed in a 3-D environment based on an *x*, *y* and *z* co-ordinate system. The *x*, *y*, *z* co-ordinate system is similar to the *x*, *y* system, except that if the *x*, *y* plane is regarded as a horizontal plane, then the *z* co-ordinate produces the 'height' or the vertical planes *x*, *z* and *y*, *z*.

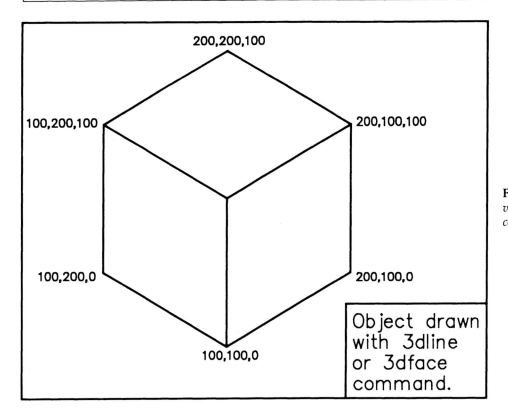

200,200,100

100,200,100

200,100,100

100,200,0

200,100,0

100,100,0

Object drawn with 3dline or 3dface command.

Fig. 8.4 *Three-dimensional view drawn using* x,y,z *co-ordinates.*

8.3 THREE-DIMENSIONAL DRAWING AND MODELLING IN AUTOCAD

The following details apply to Version 10, or later, of AutoCAD. Earlier versions do not possess some of the 3-D facilities described here.

AutoCAD is unique in the PC-based software systems in that it allows 3-D models to be constructed in several ways, giving true 3-D representation.

1. Key in x, y, z co-ordinates of points in response to the commands **3DLINE** or **3DFACE** (Fig. 8.4).
2. Use the **ELEV** command system, in which objects such as lines, arcs, circles, polylines, etc., from 2-D drawings, can be extruded for height above stated ELEVations (Fig. 8.5). **ELEV** will not be available in Version 11.
3. Use the user co-ordinate system (UCS) command system, in which faces of a 3-D object being drawn can be positioned as if lying on the surface of the monitor screen. The UCS system allows the drawing of details on sloping faces of 3-D objects (Fig. 8.6).
4. Build up wire-frame objects using the 3-D objects which can be loaded into the AutoCAD drawing editor from the AutoLisp file 3d.lsp. The main 3-D objects found in this AutoLisp file are shown in Fig. 8.7.

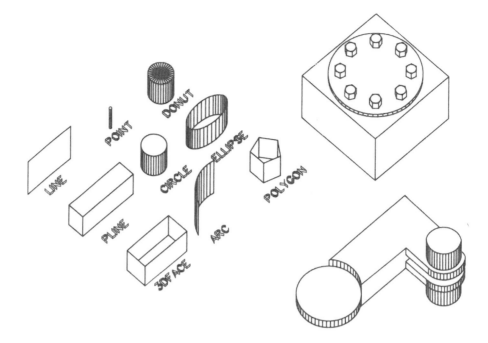

Fig. 8.5 *Three-dimensional view drawn using ELEVation commands.*

Note
AutoCAD will automatically load a file acad.lsp if the computer being used is configured to do so. This file controls the use of AutoLisp files held in the system. AutoLisp is a computing language based on an original language Lisp and developed specifically for use with AutoCAD. The use of AutoLisp allows designers to write special-purpose programs to enhance the capabilities of AutoCAD. Such programs can be for the purpose of calculation (e.g. the strength of simple objects that have been drawn) and for creating special graphics routines. A number of AutoLisp files are included in the Version 10 3-D menu systems. The 3-D objects cubes, pyramids, domes and dishes, toruses, spheres and wedges shown in Fig. 8.7 are called from such files.

5. Use the 3-D commands **EDGSURF, REVSURF, RULSURF** and **TABSURF**. These commands can be used to draw surfaces which are made up from 3DFACEs and which when the **HIDE** command is called will HIDE hidden lines behind the surfaces (Fig. 8.8 to 8.10). Other surface shapes can be developed in 3-D using the commands **3dface, 3dmesh** and **3dpoly**.

Note
Some of the models produced by AutoCAD 3-D methods are wire frames. This must be borne in mind when constructing 3-D models with the aid of this

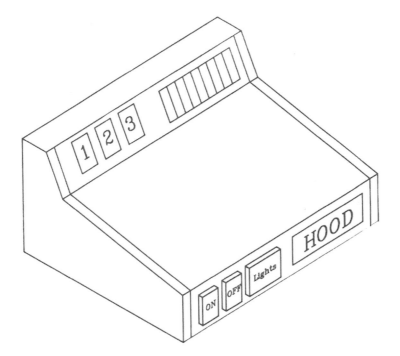

Fig. 8.6 *Three-dimensional view drawn in the user co-ordinate system.*

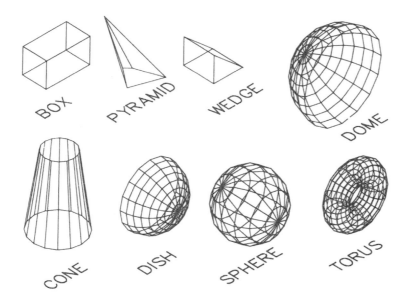

Fig. 8.7 *Objects from a 3d. 1sp AutoLisp file.*

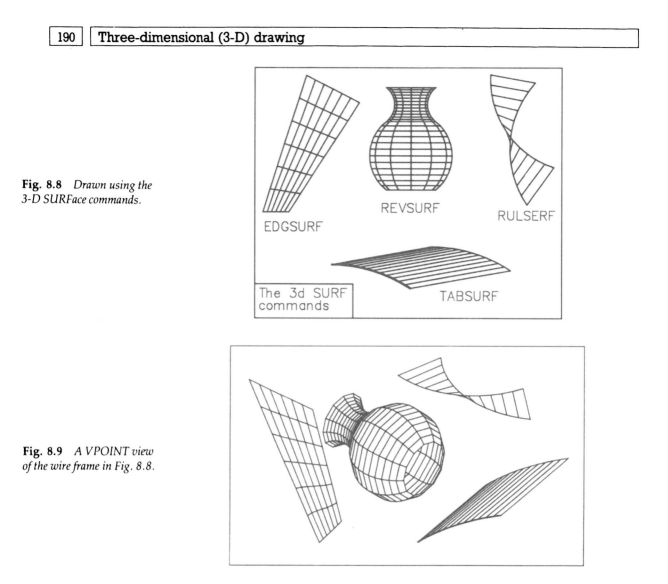

Fig. 8.8 *Drawn using the 3-D SURFace commands.*

Fig. 8.9 *A VPOINT view of the wire frame in Fig. 8.8.*

software. Some (but not all) of the lines behind faces in 3-D models can be removed by using the HIDE command of the 3-D systems. It must also be remembered that 3-D wire-frame models of any degree of complexity require large amounts of disk space, running into many Kb or even Mb. Such complex 3-D wire-frame models also require a fair amount of time to be generated on the screen when transferred from disk.

The 3-D models constructed with the aid of these systems can be viewed in a variety of directions, from any angle and from below or from above, by using the following command systems of AutoCAD.

8.3.1 VPOINT

Three-dimensional drawings can be viewed from a variety of positions with the aid of the VPOINT command. When **VPOINT** is called, the following appears at the command line:

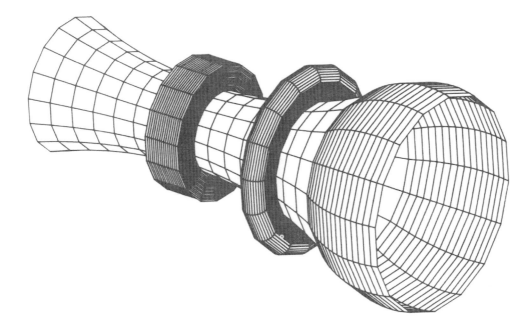

Command: vpoint [typed at keyboard] Return
Rotate/⟨View point⟩: ⟨0.0000, 0.0000, 1.0000⟩:

Fig. 8.10 *Wire frame from several SURF commands.*

The *x*, *y*, *z* co-ordinate figures given in this response are for viewing the plan view (usually just drawn).

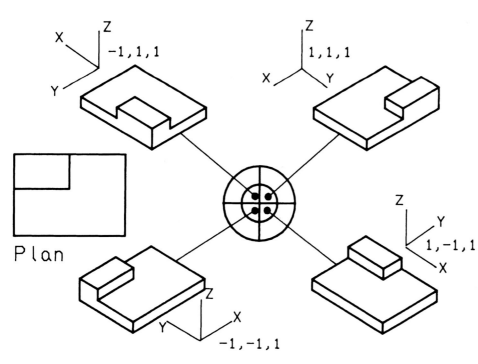

Fig. 8.11 *The VPOINT icon. Note the icon appears on screen separate from the objects being drawn.*

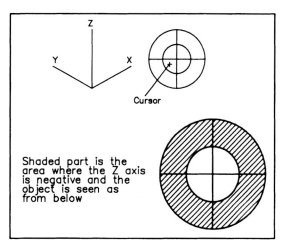

Fig. 8.12 *The VPOINT icon as it appears on screen. Enlarged view is underneath.*

If the ROTATE response is called by typing r, an icon appears (Figs. 8.11 and 8.12) to assist in obtaining a good viewing position, selected from the icon with a pointing device. Figure 8.11 shows four views obtained from selecting by pointing at the icon. Or, as an alternative, a viewing position can be selected by giving *x, y, z* numbers typed at the keyboard, as also indicated in Fig. 8.11. The ROTATE response allows the object to be rotated inside the *x, y, z* frame; rotating the reference frame, also rotates *x, y, z*.

8.3.2   USER CO-ORDINATE SYSTEM (UCS)

With the aid of AutoCAD's UCS any face (vertical, horizontal or sloping) can be viewed as if it that face were a plan view, resting on the horizontal plane. This allows drawing of details directly on to any face of a 3-D model. The process follows the procedure outlined below.

When UCS is called the following prompt appear at the command line position:

Command: ucs [typed at keyboard] Return
Origin/ZAxis/3point/Entity/View/X/Y/Z/Prev/Restore/Save/Del/?/⟨World⟩:
To use this system of commands and options follow the sequence below.

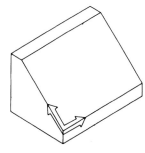

Fig. 8.13 *The UCS icon positioned on a sloping face. When Return is pressed the face appears as if flat on screen surface.*

1. The outline of the required 3-D model is constructed, with the aid of the **3DLINE, 3DFACE** command systems.
2. The UCS icon is placed in an appropriate position on the drawing (Fig. 8.13).
3. The 3-D drawing is rotated into its new UCS position using the **3point** option from the series of options under the UCS command line. This places the object in a position with the result that the selected, inclined face is viewed 'flat on' as if the face was flat on the monitor screen.
4. The required details can easily be drawn on this view (Fig. 8.14).

5. The 3-D model is then rotated under UCS into its previous (normally **World**) position, ready to be moved to a new position if required.

8.3.3 DVIEW

This command allows dynamic viewing of a 3-D drawing. When a 3-D object has been drawn and the **DVIEW** command called, the operator is asked to select the object he wishes to view. Then a set of commands appears at the command line of the screen as follows:

> **Command:** dview [typed at keyboard] Return
> **CAmera/TArget/Distance/POinter/PAn/Zoom/TWist/CLip/Hide/Off/ Undo/⟨eXit⟩:**

By keying in the required response, the object can, for example, be viewed as if from a camera, the lens of which can be adjusted as to focal length; its distance from the camera can be adjusted; the object can be moved around on the screen; part of the object can be clipped to allow internal views to be generated; the ZOOM option allows perspective views to be obtained. All these options can

Fig. 8.14 *Drawn in the user co-ordinate system.*

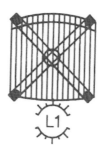

Fig. 8.15 *Detail of scene as it appears on screen when constructed under ASHADE.*

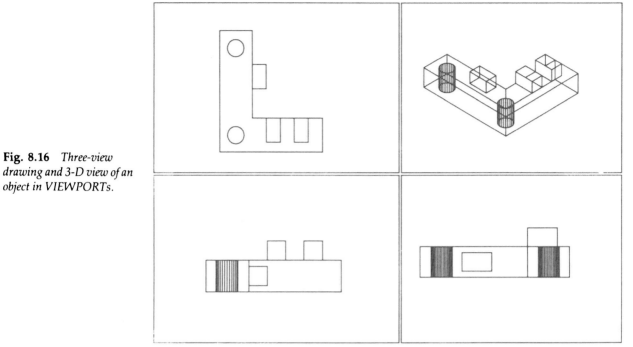

Fig. 8.16 *Three-view drawing and 3-D view of an object in VIEWPORTs.*

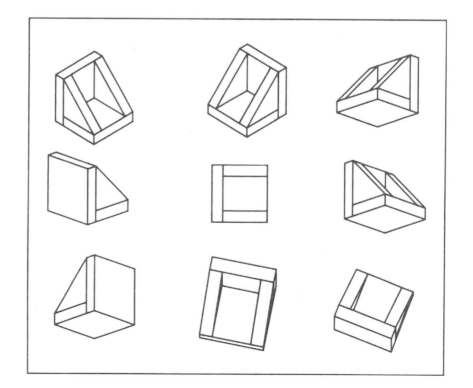

Fig. 8.17 *An example of a use of VPOINT.*

be controlled dynamically by the operator's selection pointing device. As the selection device is moved, the view rotates in synchronization on the screen.

8.3.4 AUTOSHADE

When a 3-D drawing has been constructed in AutoCAD, a shaded, coloured, 3-D view of it can be constructed on screen by transferring the file to another program called AutoShade (a stand-alone program for use with Version 10 of AutoCAD). AutoShade can be used in conjunction with the command system ASHADE (an AutoLisp program), by which an object can be viewed from various positions as if lit by a number of lights. When ASHADE is loaded, a **scene** can be set up in which a **camera** is targeted on the object, which can be lit by lights either pointed or directed at the object. The commands for this scene preparation are:

LIGHTS, CAMERA and **ACTION** (**SCENE** and **FILMROLL**).

A filmroll of a number of scenes so formed can be saved as a file for loading into AutoShade. Figure 8.15 shows how a scene is displayed on screen, when **ASHADE** is used to prepare a filmroll, a camera can be positioned (x, y, z position) in relation to the object being filmed. Lights (L1, L2, L3, etc.) can then be positioned as if illuminating the object from various points (also x, y, z positions). A colour shot of the scene portrayed in Fig. 8.15 is shown in the plate section between p. 160–1.

8.3.5 VIEWPORTS

Another feature recently introduced in Version 10 is the ability to place 3-D drawings into viewports, in which, for example, a front view, an end view, a plan and a 3-D view can be shown and worked with at the same time. See Chapter 3, p.72, for an introduction to viewpoints. Figure 8.16 shows front, end and plan views, together with a 3-D view in four viewports. Some computer systems allow as many as 16 ports to appear on screen at any one time. AutoCAD, on PC-compatible type computer systems, will only allow up to four viewports on screen at any one time. The views in each port can be controlled with the **UCS** or the **VPOINT** command systems. Viewports are only suitable for use with 3-D drawings and models. It is possible to work in either a single viewport, in two viewports in three viewports or in four viewports showing on the screen at any one time. The viewport being worked in is selected with the operator's pointing device.

8.4 EXAMPLES OF 3-D DRAWINGS FROM AUTOCAD

Figures 8.17 to 8.20 show further examples of 3-D objects drawn with the aid of AutoCAD software. In these examples:

1. Fig. 8.17 – each view was selected using the **VPOINT** command;
2. Fig. 8.18 – is a a 3-D view drawn with the aid of the **UCS** system;
3. Fig. 8.19 was drawn with the aid of the **ELEV** system, the ball feet were included from an AutoLisp 3-D objects file;

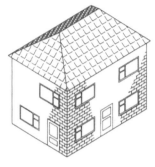

Fig. 8.18 *Drawn in the user co-ordinate system.*

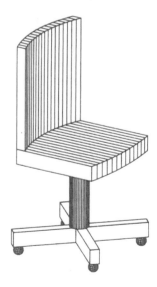

Fig. 8.19 *Drawn with the aid of the ELEVation command.*

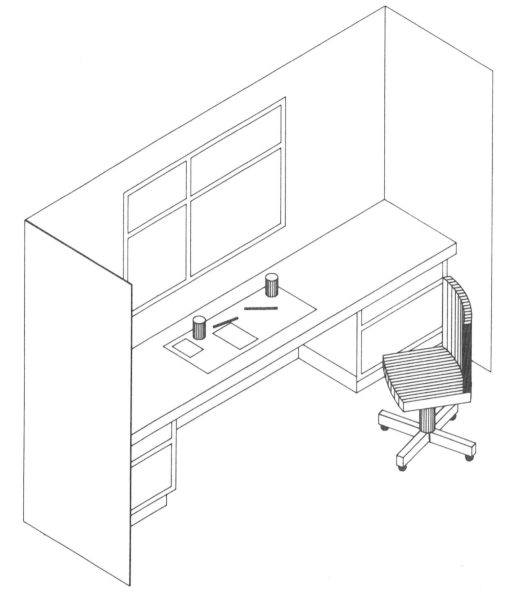

Fig. 8.20 *Drawn with the aid of the ELEVation command.*

4. Fig. 8.20 was drawn with the aid of the **3Dfaces, 3Dlines** and **ELEV** command systems. The chair was included as a WBLOCK from the file of the drawing shown in Fig. 8.19. The completed drawing was then placed in a viewing position with the **VPOINT** command.

Towards integration: draughting and 3-D modelling

9.1 INTRODUCTION

In Chapters 5 to 7 we have considered in some depth 2-D draughting using just PC-based CAD systems. In Chapter 8 we have seen for the first time how the 2-D draughting approach can be extended into 3-D wire-frame modelling. This model can be used to create pictorial views of the object and, as the examples created with AutoShade illustrate, provide colour shaded images of the 3-D model using a facetted surface representation. In this way, it is hoped that we have demonstrated adequately the capabilities of the PC-based CAD systems. In this chapter, we will begin to look at draughting and 3-D modelling using a minicomputer-based CAD system.

In recent years, the trend towards cheaper and more powerful computer hardware has meant that we have already seen the gap between PC-based CAD systems and those based on minicomputers or intelligent workstations starting to close. Also software that historically was devised for PC-based CAD (e.g. AutoCAD) systems has been adapted for use with the larger computer systems. Similarly, software devised for intelligent workstations or minicomputers (e.g. DOGS) is being adapted for use with PC-based CAD systems. Consequently, it is now possible to link draughting with analysis and manufacture using PC-based versions of software (e.g. ANSYS finite element analysis) previously only available on minicomputer systems. This software provides the individual user or small company with a very powerful and wide-ranging CAD tool. As a result, the dividing line between the two levels of CAD system has become increasingly blurred.

Moreover, it is now easier for the move from PC-based CAD to minicomputer-based CAD to be made, which is important for the user whose needs can no longer be accommodated by the PC-based systems. This is necessary where the information stored on the CAD system database is shared amongst many users who are then able to use the same data for a variety of tasks besides draughting. In large organizations, where many different engineering specialists will contribute to the design and manufacture of a product, it is most useful fully to integrate draughting with modelling, analysis, manufacture, etc., in which case a minicomputer-based CAE system is more appropriate for these activities. DOGS is a 2-D draughting package that is part of a minicomputer-based integrated CAE system. We will be using DOGS in this chapter to illustrate how the first steps towards full integration of the CAE activity can be made.

9.2 DOGS

DOGS (Drawing Office Graphics System) is a comprehensive draughting system from PAFEC Ltd, and is just one element of their integrated CAE system. However, as we will soon see, DOGS plays a key role in the integration of the various design, analysis, manufacture and management activities supported by PAFEC's software. DOGS actually incorporates a number of these CAE activities within the bounds of the same package, and is not just a 2-D draughting system. However, the acronym is commonly used to refer just to the draughting part of this package. To be more precise, DOGS 2D is the 2-D draughting part of this system. DOGS 3D, DOGS NC, DOGS MAPPING, DOGS ARCHITECTURE and DOGS RC are extensions to the core draughting program for 3-D modelling, numerical machine control simulation, digitization of drawings, architectural draughting and reinforced concrete draughting.

DOGS can be used on most 32-bit computer systems and occupies at least 50 Mbyte of storage space on the hard disk. The software has been developed continually over a number of years, during which time a number of different versions of the DOGS software have been released by PAFEC Limited. The Level number indicates which version of the software is being used; DOGS Level 4.1 was released in 1989. The previous version, DOGS Level 3.2, could be used with a variety of different graphics terminal types including direct-view storage displays such as the Tektronix 4014 (see Chapter 2). However, DOGS Level 4.1 uses drop-down menus for inputting instructions during the drawing activity and so can only be used with raster scan type devices. The latest version of DOGs also includes a major reorganization of the draughting instructions to provide a larger selection of facilities and options. This has required experienced DOGS users to learn new instruction codes, though the fundamental operating principles of DOGS Level 3.2 have not been changed.

A PC version of DOGS, PC DOGS, is in wide use. PC DOGS is a 2-D draughting package, suitable for PCs fitted with at least 10 Mbyte of hard disk storage capacity. The draughting facilities supplied with PC DOGS are a subset of those supplied with the full version of DOGS Level 3.2. Drawings created using PC DOGS can be used by DOGS 2D, provided the data files can be moved between the two CAD systems. Consequently, PC DOGS provides a good low-entry route into the PAFEC CAE system, and users who are familiar with the PC version will have no difficulties using DOGS Level 3.2 for 2-D draughting.

9.3 DRAUGHTING WITH DOGS 2D

We will now consider briefly the draughting facilities provided by DOGS 2D operating on a minicomputer-based CAD system. To operate the DOGS package, you must be logged on to your CAD system before you can start up the DOGS software. This procedure will vary between systems, so ask your local system manager for specific details. You will need to use a graphics terminal,

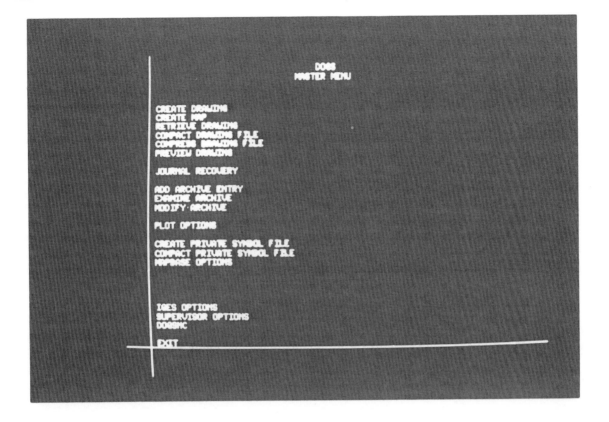

Fig. 9.1 *The DOGS MASTER MENU.*

and for speed and ease of operation, a digitizer tablet or other cursor-control device is useful. DOGS is a large program, so there is a short delay while the software is loaded. A series of prompts will appear and your responses will again be specific to the CAD system you are using and the manner in which data files and information have been organized on the system. Once the initial responses have been made, the DOGS MASTER MENU will be displayed, Fig. 9.1. This menu of options provides access to the different DOGS facilities, of which 2-D draughting is one. At this point, however, we will not consider the DOGS MASTER MENU in any further detail, though each option will be discussed later in the text at an appropriate opportunity.

To begin 2-D draughting, we must select CREATE DRAWING from the DOGS MASTER MENU using the screen cursor or other pick device. DOGS will prompt you for the name of the data file in which all drawing information will be stored. The size and style of filename allowed are dependent upon the CAD system being used. However, a meaningful name should be given so that at a later date you are able immediately to identify which file in your directory holds the drawing of interest. When a new drawing is created, the INITIALISE MENU appears. This menu of options provides, amongst other things, information about the size of the drawing paper, A0, A1, etc., the active drawing units, mm, cm, etc., and the scale to be used, 1:1, 1:2, etc. Each option has a default setting which is dependent upon the CAD system being used. If the default settings satisfy your own needs, than selecting START with the screen cursor will activate the 2-D draughting activity. If they are not suitable, each may be altered as appropriate before selecting START.

The procedure for creating a drawing involves many steps which can seem quite tedious to the beginner. However, it is important to appreciate that this initialization process is carried out by any industrial draughtsman, whether he uses a CAD system or not. Before he can put pen to paper, a draughtsman will decide what size of paper to use, what dimension units to use, what scale, what projection system, how the views are to be organized on the sheet, what the drawing title should be, etc. Many of these decisions are made subconsciously by the experienced draughtsman, but when using a CAD system this type of drawing information is requested as a formal procedure that can often appear very pedantic.

Once a drawing has been initialized, the DOGS 2D screen menu and drawing area will be displayed on the graphics screen. DOGS 2D provides a large range of drawing options which can be selected in a number of ways. The DOGS 2D menu card lists all the available drawing options and is designed to be fixed to the surface of a digitizer tablet, so that the selection device can be used to select the option by pointing to its position on the menu card. Alternatively, the option may be selected from the screen menu using the screen cursor (or cross-hairs). With DOGS Level 3.2, each option is identified by the heading in the first

Fig. 9.2 *DOGS Level 3.2 screen menu.*

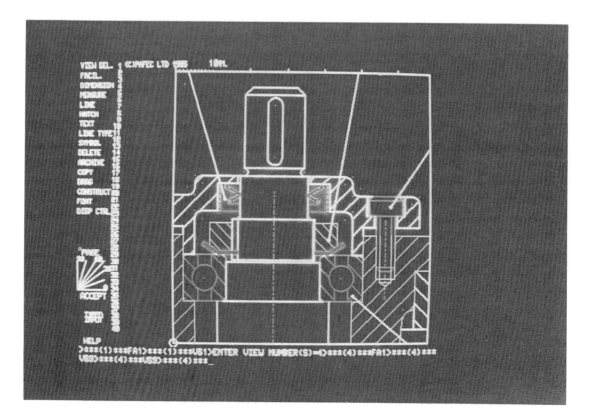

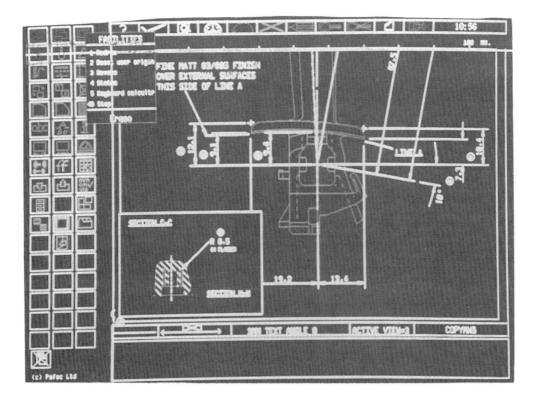

Fig. 9.3 *DOGS Level 4.1 screen menu.*

column and its number in the second column, Fig. 9.2. However, with DOGS Level 4.1, the screen menu consists of small icons for each heading. Selecting an icon invokes the display of a pull-down menu from which the specific option can be selected, Fig. 9.3. Finally, the option code can be input using typed input. The code consists of a two- or three-character string to identify the option heading, plus the number of the option itself.

DOGS 2D uses either Cartesian (X,Y), e.g. X20, Y30, or polar (L,A) coordinates, e.g. L50, A30, to define the position of a point, Fig. 9.4. These coordinate systems can be mixed, e.g. X30, A15, provided that an unambiguous definition of the position of the point is made. The position of a point on the screen can be defined using the screen cursor, but if the cursor is near an existing point or intersection of lines, the cursor will automatically SNAP to the coordinates of this point. Where precise control of position is required, typed input is preferred. However, where a point is already defined on the drawing, e.g. the end of an existing line, it is better practice to select this point using the screen cursor. This is a quicker and more precise method than inputting the co-ordinates once more, using typed input. DOGS 2D also allows the position of a single point to be defined using both typed and cursor input, e.g. one ordinate is defined by typed input, the other using the cursor.

The LINE option enables only straight lines and circular arcs to be constructed in DOGS 2D. Other curve types, e.g. ellipses, must be created as series of line segments joined together to form an estimate of the curve shape. A single

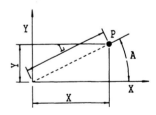

Fig. 9.4 *Single point construction.*

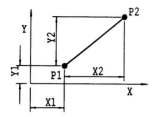

Fig. 9.5 *Single line construction.*

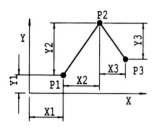

Fig. 9.6 *Continuous line construction.*

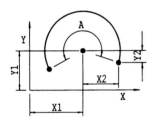

Fig. 9.7 *Circular arc construction.*

straight line is defined by the positions of its two endpoints, Fig. 9.5. The position of the first point is defined with respect to the drawing origin, and the position of the second with respect to the first. Lines may be created singularly, as a continuous series of straight lines (Fig. 9.6) where each is joined to the previous line in the sequence, or as multiple copies of an existing line with user-defined separations. The orientation of a line may be controlled to be either parallel, tangent, perpendicular or normal to an existing line or circular arc.

A circular arc is generally defined by the position of its centre of radius with respect to the drawing origin, the position of the start point with respect to the centre, and position of the endpoint with respect to the start, Fig. 9.7. The sense of the arc, i.e. clockwise or anticlockwise, is determined by which arc construction option is chosen. This method of construction allows the radius of curvature to be controlled precisely. Alternatively, DOGS 2D can construct a circular arc through three points on the arc, calculating the radius of curvature required to draw an arc through all three points. Full circles are generated by defining the position of the centre of radius with respect to the drawing origin and the position of a point on the circumference with respect to the centre.

Additional DOGS 2D drawing options include those for creating fillets (Fig. 9.8) and chamfers (Fig. 9.9). The FILLET option is particularly useful when the position of the fillet centre of curvature is unknown. If the basic outline of the item is drawn using straight lines and circular arcs, the corner features can quickly be defined using these two options, and drawing construction times can consequently be reduced significantly. Closed boundaries may be HATCHed using a variety of hatching patterns. The hatch area can be defined by pointing to a position within the hatch area or to a line on the boundary. DOGS 2D will fully define the hatch boundary and fill the area with a hatching pattern, Fig. 9.10. If a complex drawing is being hatched, the user may have to define the boundary manually to ensure that a closed boundary is obtained and that the correct area is filled with the hatch pattern.

A COPY facility allows areas of the drawing to be copied to other parts of the drawing page. The position and orientation of the copy are controlled by the new positions of up to three control points defined in the original. The size of

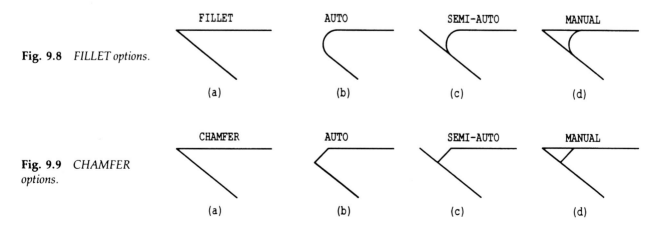

Fig. 9.8 *FILLET options.*

Fig. 9.9 *CHAMFER options.*

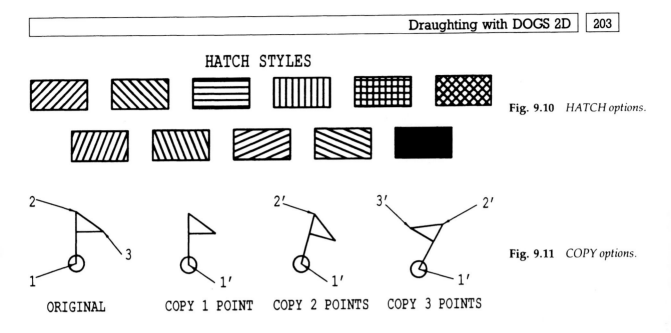

HATCH STYLES

Fig. 9.10 *HATCH options.*

ORIGINAL   COPY 1 POINT   COPY 2 POINTS   COPY 3 POINTS

Fig. 9.11 *COPY options.*

the copy can be controlled by specifying a scaling factor or is calculated from the new positions of the control points, Fig. 9.11. Copies may be mirrored about an existing line, or rotated through a fixed angle about a predefined point. If a number of copies are created simultaneously, the displacement and reorientation that occurs between the original and the first copy will be repeated between the first copy and the second, the second and the third, etc. This is particularly useful for revolved parts where repeated features, e.g. holes in a flange, can be generated very quickly by copying just one original. Areas of the drawing may be repositioned using a DRAG option. This option works in a similar way to the COPY option, enabling the drawing to be modified in size or orientation in the same operation. Individual lines or points can be DRAGged, allowing discrete modifications to the drawing to be made.

The LINE style option provides a large variety of line types, (solid, dashed, chain dashed, etc.) and line intensities, i.e. colour or thickness. It is usual to use colour to help differentiate between different features on the drawing. This is especially useful for assembly drawings, where each item may be drawn using a different colour intensity. When a DOGS drawing is plotted, to create a hard copy, different coloured pens will automatically be selected to reproduce the colour definition of the drawing. Since a colour change invokes a pen change in the DOGS plotting procedure, it is possible to use different colour intensities to represent the different line thicknesses used in drawing, and to replace the selection of pens in the plotter with ones of different nib thicknesses.

The different line thicknesses may also be displayed on the graphics screen, Fig. 9.12. However, it is more usual to use a single line thickness to ensure that a sharp screen image is achieved.

Leader lines and dimension lines are generated automatically by DOGS 2D when features are being DIMENSIONed using either linear, angular or radial dimensioning options. The value of the dimension is calculated and displayed in various formats that are controlled by the DIMENSION TEXT option. In this

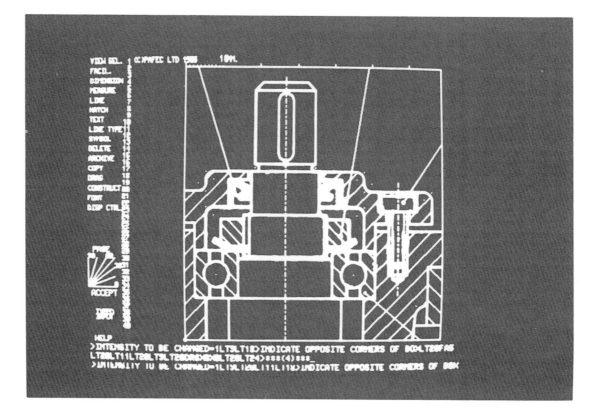

Fig. 9.12 *Line thickness displayed on the screen.*

option, tolerances can be predefined and included in the dimension text, the dimension value can be prefixed or appended by additional notes, M42×1.5, 2.5×45°, etc., or the angle of the dimension can be controlled, e.g. to allow dimensions to be organized into horizontal or vertical groups.

Notes and other written information can be added to the drawing using the TEXT option. Multiple line text ensures that where several lines of text are required, the lines are equally spaced out on the page. Typing errors can be corrected using a text editor, obviating the need for the whole of the note to be redefined. The orientation of the text can be controlled by its angle to the drawing page or to existing lines or circles. The TEXT STYLE option presents the user with a large variety of text styles, sizes and typescript fonts.

A DOGS 2D drawing can be constructed from a series of views (c.f. AutoCAD layers discussed in Chapter 6), each created using the VIEW MANAGE option. Each view can be considered to be a separate drawing drawn on clear acetate film, thus it is possible to see the information from a number of views when displayed simultaneously. However, it is only possible to draw on the active view, e.g. the top piece of acetate film, but features seen on the other views can be used for construction purposes. Views are most useful where information is to be displayed selectively, or where different view scales are being used. Distributing drawing information amongst different views allows DOGS 2D to operate faster because only certain areas of the drawing database need be examined or displayed at any one time. A drawing might be typically organized as follows:

1. View 0: Company drawing sheet with logo;
2. View 1: Front elevation of item;
3. View 2: Plan elevation;
4. View 3: Side elevation;
5. View 4: Dimensions;
6. View 5: Notes.

Information can be copied between views using the ARCHIVE option. A special view, View C, contains construction geometry that is only displayed on the screen; it does not form part of the drawing when plotted.

The CONSTRUCTION option provides a number of construction geometry features, e.g. for projecting a line across the whole page, which can be used to assist drawing construction. This facility is most useful for defining the position of points, for example, defined by the intersections of construction lines projected from two views of the item. Included in the CONSTRUCTION option are facilities for dissecting lines and arcs into segments, and to create a snap grid.

An area of the drawing can be used to define a symbol or shape using the SYMBOL option. A symbol is treated by DOGS 2D as an entity in itself. When a symbol is retrieved and placed on the drawing, its constituent lines will, in general, be ignored by DOGS 2D during drawing construction. When a shape is retrieved, however, its constituent lines immediately become part of the drawing. DOGS 2D will treat these lines like any others on the drawing. The SYMBOL option provides several facilities for controlling the properties of a symbol so that the way the symbol can be used in future applications is controlled, though these are of little interest here. More importantly, though, is the source of a symbol. A symbol can be retrieved from two sources: the private or public symbol files. Both are libraries of symbols that can be used by the DOGS 2D user. The private symbol file is a library of symbols created by the owner, e.g. the DOGS 2D user, which are stored in his own file space on the CAD system. Their use is restricted to the owner alone. In contrast, the public symbol file is shared by all users of the CAD system. Therefore, this library of files tends to contain standard drawing symbols. Additions to the list of symbols in this file can only be made by the CAD system manager, therefore symbols created by an individual must be stored in his own private symbol file. Symbols provide a quick and easy means of generating drawings of standard features, but they also provide a means of transferring drawing information into DOGS 2D from an external source.

The GENERAL SETTINGS, DISPLAY CONTROL, FACILITIES and WINDOW options provide the DOGS user with various facilities for controlling the way a drawing is displayed on the graphic screen and the way DOGS responds during the draughting activity. The MANAGEMENT option provides a **safe update** facility to enable drawing information to be stored in a data file while construction continues. A **plot** facility enables a plot file to be created. This file will contain the information required by a plotter to generate a hard copy of the drawing. Finally, when the draughting is complete, the STOP option will terminate the draughting activity, save all the drawing information into the drawing data file, and return the user to the DOGS MASTER MENU. The DOGS activity can be completely terminated at this point by selecting EXIT from the DOGS MASTER MENU. The user is then returned to the control of the CAD operating system.

The techniques of drawing construction using DOGS have not been discussed in great depth, since it is not appropriate to consider any further the precise syntax of the commands or the exact details of each variation of a command in this text. These are best described in the DOGS user manual which is extensive in its description of each DOGS option. However, it is hoped that the brief description of DOGS 2D given here will suffice to show that the fundamental 2-D draughting techniques for a minicomputer-based CAD system like DOGS do not differ from those of a PC-based CAD system like AutoCAD. In both cases, the drawing is merely a collection of lines, circular arcs, circles, text, dimensions, hatch patterns and standard symbols. The DOGS draughtsman, like the AutoCAD draughtsman, uses his knowledge of conventional drawing methods to create a series of views of a component. These must be organized on the drawing page according to the rules of First or Third Angle projection if a full understanding of the drawing is to be gained by others. The 2-D draughting CAD system provides many facilities to simplify this process and reduce the tedium of repetitive tasks, but on the whole, the computer is being used merely as an electronic replacement of the conventional drawing board. In this respect alone, many CAD users might be able to justify the expense of the PC based CAD system using AutoCAD. It is unlikely, though, that the expense of a larger CAD system with DOGS could be justified in the same way unless the other features offered by DOGS are utilized. Most notable of all these being its 3-D modelling capability.

9.4 OBJECT MODELLING WITH DOGS 3D

DOGS 3D is a 3-D modelling system that is incorporated into the DOGS program and is accessible via the DOGS 2D menu. The drawing construction principles of the 2-D system are extended into 3-D to allow the creation of wireframe models of objects. Each vertex and edge of the model must be defined in 3-D space. This is simple enough using typed input, but where the screen cursor is required to select existing entities its use is complicated by the additional modelling dimension. To assist with the construction process, DOGS 3D provides several facilities that are extensions of their 2-D counterparts into 3-D space. A limited set of surface types can be used to add surface detail to the model, enabling hidden-line removed and colour-shaded images of the object to be displayed.

To get DOGS 3D started, a drawing must be created in the usual way using DOGS. When the DOGS 2D screen is displayed, DOGS 3D is invoked by selecting the PAGE 3 option. DOGS will prompt for the size of the 3-D workspace to be defined in terms of its x, y and z limits. The modelling scale must also be defined. At this stage, the DOGS 2D screen will clear, and is replaced by the DOGS 3D workspace, Fig. 9.13. The graphics screen shows four viewports, each

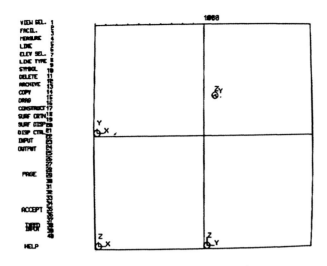

Fig. 9.13 *DOGS 3D graphics screen showing four viewports and screen menu.*

giving a different view elevation of the workspace. In three of the elevations, the workspace is viewed along one of the x, y and z axes. Thus in these views only two of the three dimensions can be seen, e.g. yz, xz, xy. The fourth viewport provides a perspective view of the workspace in which all three dimensions can be seen simultaneously. Inspection of the menu card shows that the number of construction options available in DOGS 3D is significantly smaller than the number available in DOGS 2D. Despite this, DOGS 3D provides some useful construction facilities for aiding the modelling process. These options are selected using the same methods employed in DOGS 2D.

The position of a point in the 3-D workspace can be defined by typed input using Cartesian co-ordinates (X, Y, Z) e.g. X30, Y40, Z70. In this case the values for all three dimensions are known. The screen position of a point can be defined using the cursor. Unlike DOGS 2D, a single cursor 'hit' is not sufficient to define all three dimensions. In DOGS 3D, two 'hits' of the cursor in two of the three orthographic elevations is required to define fully the position of a point in the 3-D workspace. For example, if the first cursor hit is made in the YZ elevation, the second hit must be made in either the ZX or XY elevations to ensure the point is fully defined. If the cursor position is in close proximity to an existing point or intersection of edges, the cursor position will snap to that point. DOGS 3D provides **advanced typed input** methods that enable the position of a point, which cannot easily be defined using Cartesian co-ordinates, to be defined by the intersection of three surfaces. Four generic surface types can be defined by typed input:

1. angled plane;
2. cylindrical;

3. conical; and
4. spherical.

The angled plane is a flat planar surface specified by a code (XA60, YA45, ZA10, etc.). For example, a YA45 planar surface will pass through the y axis rotated by 45° in the positive sense from the z=0 plane. A positive rotation is a clockwise rotation about the axis when looking down it from the origin. A cylindrical surface is specified by a code (e.g. XL40, YL120, ZL70), where the axis of the cylinder is denoted by the first letter of the code, and its radius by the number. Thus XL40 defines a cylindrical surface with its axis along the x axis and a radius of 40 units. A conical surface is specified by a code (e.g. XD40, YD15, ZD-30), where the first letter of the code specifies the axis of the half cone, and the external angle of the cone by the number. A negative number defines the half cone along the negative axis.

A spherical surface is defined by its radius, e.g. L100. The position of a point in space can be defined by mixing these typed input formats, e.g. L20, YA30, XD15 defines a point positioned at the intersection of a sphere radius 20 units, an angled plane passing through the y axis at an angle of 30°, and a cone whose axis coincides with the x axis with an external cone angle of 15°.

The LINE option in DOGS 3D provides facilities for defining straight lines and circular arcs in 3-D space. A straight line is defined by the positions of its end-points using the point-construction techniques described above. Often a series of lines will be constructed with, e.g. the same z co-ordinate, in which case DOGS 3D allows this dimension to be fixed. The construction effort is then restricted to a 2-D plane, and so only two of the three co-ordinates need to be specified, e.g. x and y co-ordinates, to define fully the point. Separate and continuous line construction options are provided. Circular arcs are defined using three control points. It is usual to define the positions of the arc centre and two endpoints, though defining the positions of three points on the arc is a satisfactory alternative. The circular arc is constructed so that it lies in the same plane as the three control points. Full circles can be constructed using just two control points, but the plane of the circle must be specified before DOGS 3D is able to generate the curve. If the circle lies in one of the planes of projection, e.g. the yz plane, pointing to the view of this plane on the graphics screen with the cursor will provide DOGS 3D with sufficient information fully to construct the circle. Alternatively, if none of the three projections planes are appropriate, the surface must be defined fully by typed input or similar, e.g. to define a third point in the plane.

The COPY and DRAG options in DOGS 3D provide several techniques for assisting creation and modification of the 3-D model. In DOGS 3D, however, the COPY and DRAG options act upon a volume of the model contained within the bounds of a cuboid, rather than an area of the drawing as in DOGS 2D. The DRAG option enables the position, size and orientation of the model, or part of the model, to be modified using translation, rotation, scaling or mirror operators. The modifications made to the model using a DRAG operation are controlled by the new positions of up to three control points in much the same way as they are in DOGS 2D. The COPY option provides facilities for copying

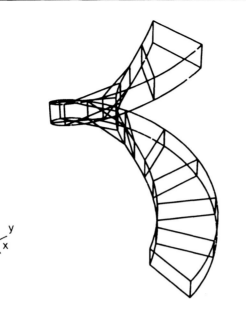

Fig. 9.14 *A facetted helix created using SPIRAL COPY extended with circular arcs.*

the whole, or part of, the model using the same translation, rotation, scaling or mirror operators. In addition to making single copies of the model, multiple copies can be generated during one operation which significantly improves the speed with which complex models can be constructed. To aid further the speed of model construction, DOGS 3D provides an EXTEND facility for joining each vertex in the original to its corresponding vertex in the copy using either straight lines or circular arcs. This is extremely useful for 2½-D objects where a 2-D profile is given depth or revolved about an axis to generate a fully defined 3-D wire-frame model. Finally, when using the SPIRAL COPY option, the copy of the model is rotated and translated along the axis of rotation (the displacement defined by the **glide length**) in a single operation. Figure 9.14 shows the result of a 2-D rectangular block being copied twelve times using a SPIRAL COPY. Each copy is rotated 30° and displaced along the axis of rotation. The EXTEND option was selected, so each copy has been joined to the previous copy with, for example, circular arcs. Thus, in one COPY operation, a facetted model of a helix has been created, and the size of the model has been quickly increased by an additional 48 straight edges and 48 circular arcs. Clearly, the COPY options must be fully exploited when constructing 3-D models to minimize the effort needed to define repeated features in 3-D space.

Figure 9.15 shows a perspective view of a 3-D wire-frame model created using DOGS 3D. This model is constructed from 15 straight lines, 2 circular arcs and 2 full circles. The sequence of modelling operations required to model this object begins with the creation of the base of the cube using the LINE option (Fig. 9.16). The full cube was created by COPYing and EXTENDing with straight lines the base of the cube (Fig. 9.17). Two circular arcs were created separately and the WINDOW option was used to enlarge the size of the screen image in each viewport (Fig. 9.18). The two circular arcs are joined by three straight lines in a

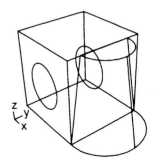

Fig. 9.15 *perspective view of an object created in DOGS 3D.*

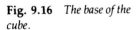

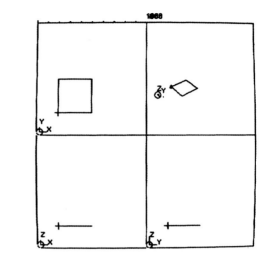

Fig. 9.16 *The base of the cube.*

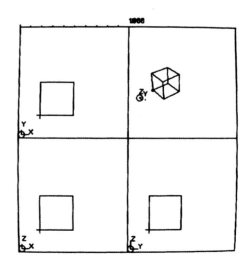

Fig. 9.17 *Full cube created using COPY and EXTEND.*

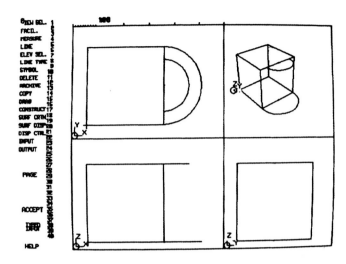

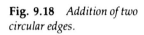

Fig. 9.18 *Addition of two circular edges.*

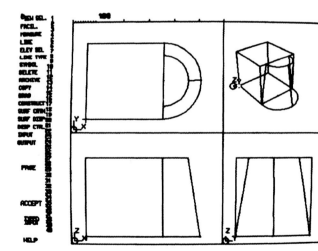

Fig. 9.19 *Addition of three connecting straight edges.*

separate operation (Fig. 9.19), although the COPY and EXTEND option could have been used again for these features. A hole is represented by two full circles (Fig. 9.20), yet there are no connecting lines between them to assist in visualizing this relationship. Although it is possible to display just one of the viewports so that the screen is filled by a single image of the model, all four views must be displayed during model construction so that points, lines, arcs and planes in 3-D space can be readily defined by cursor input. Having created the 3-D model, we are only able to display wire-frame images in each of the viewports. The shape of the object is reasonably well defined by the three orthographic views, but is is not possible to discern which edges are seen, hidden or partially hidden with the present state of the model.

Surface geometry can be defined using the SURFACE CREATION option. Only three surface types can be defined with DOGS 3D, namely planar, cylindrical or conical surfaces. In each case the boundary edges for each surface patch must be identified. The perspective view can be used for indicating boundary edges using the cursor, though the other views need to be displayed because sometimes the identification of the edge needs to be clarified by a pick in another view. Figure 9.21 shows the hole being defined using a cylindrical surface that is bounded by the two full circular edges. Figure 9.22 shows the use of a conical surface to define the surface between the two circular edges. The limits of the surface patch are bounded by the straight edges that join the end points of each circular edge. In Fig. 9.23, the front face of the object has been defined using a planar surface, where its outer boundary is defined by four straight edges. An internal boundary has also been specified, i.e. the edge of the hole, by indicating the circular arc. The other faces of the cube are defined using planar surfaces,

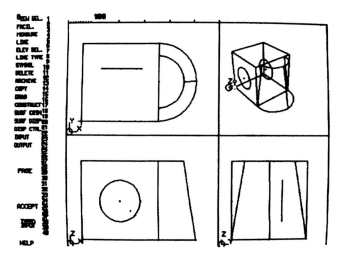

Fig. 9.20 *Two circular edges used to define ends of a hole.*

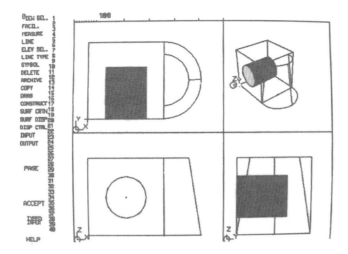

Fig. 9.21 *A cylindrical surface used to define the hole.*

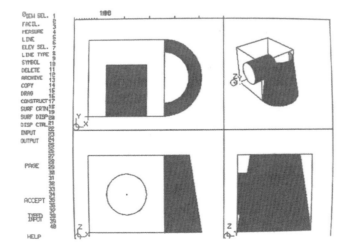

Fig. 9.22 *A conical surface used to define end feature.*

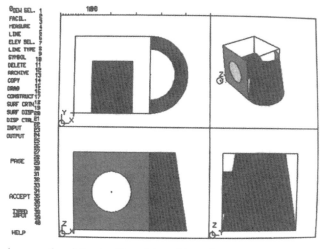

Fig. 9.23 *A planar surface defined with an internal boundary.*

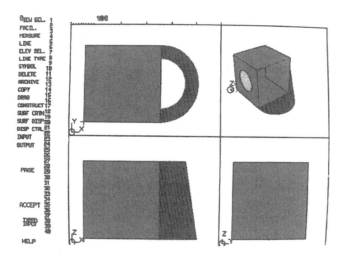

Fig. 9.24 *Planar surfaces used to define other faces.*

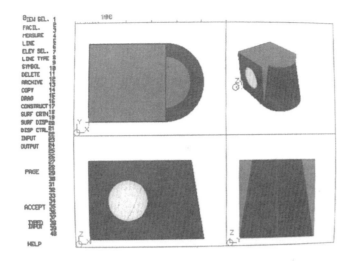

Fig. 9.25 *The complete model with surfaces displayed precisely.*

Fig. 9.24, which shows that the newly formed faces obscure some of the other surfaces, yet in reality they are further away from the observer than those faces obscured. This is not a fault of the model, but a consequence of DOGS 3D displaying the surfaces in the order of their creation. This ensures a rapid display response during the building of the model. However, when the model is complete, a precise display of the surfaces can be generated (Fig. 9.25). This clearly shows the object as if it were solid, but the length of time taken to generate such images is often unacceptable during routine display tasks.

Once a 3-D model has been created and its surface geometry specified, DOGS 3D allows the model to be viewed in several different ways. The graphics screen can be used to display one, two, three or four elevations simultaneously using either First or Third Angle projection. The object can be observed from a fixed or roving viewpoint from which a pictorial view of the object can be generated using either perspective or parallel projection. Full-colour shaded images of the object can be generated with the intensities of the ambient and the point light sources specified by the user. In the colour section, the 'exploded view' of an extractor fan shows each part of the assembly modelled as separate items using DOGS 3D.

When the DOGS 3D modelling activity has been completed, the user may return to DOGS 2D to continue with draughting work simply by selecting the PAGE 1 option, though the geometric data representing the item(s) modelled in DOG 3D is not lost when control reverts back to DOGS 2D. When the STOP command is invoked, either during DOGS 3D or DOGS 2D activity, all the 3-D information is stored automatically in the DOGS drawing file. Thus a DOGS drawing file will contain both DOGS 2D and DOGS 3D data and information.

When this file is retrieved, the user may continue draughting with DOGS 2D or modelling with DOGS 3D. However, although a DOGS data file may contain both 2-D and 3-D data and information, these do not necessarily have to be related in any way; the DOGS 3D model may represent a different item to that drawn using DOGS 2D, though this is not a particularly good way to organize a drawing and 3-D model database. It is better to arrange that the DOGS drawing file contains information related to the same item in both the 2-D and the 3-D databases, thereby integrating the draughting and 3-D modelling activities by means of this file.

9.5 THE INTEGRATION OF DOGS 2-D DRAUGHTING AND 3-D MODELLING

The DOGS 3D modelling system allows a full 3-D geometric representation of an object to be generated. This process is, by comparison to the solid modelling techniques we will consider in the next chapter, tedious and lengthy. It requires the designer to have prepared a detailed numerical description of the item prior to the modelling activity, requiring each edge and vertex to be defined in 3-D space, and the boundary edges of each surface patch to be identified to ensure the faces of the item are defined correctly. While DOGS 3D provides a number of facilities to assist the designer with the construction of the model, the time required to create an accurate 3-D representation of an item must be rewarded with a use of the model beyond just the visualization tasks we have considered so far. If the 3-D model data created with DOGS 3D is to be used with the other computer-aided tasks supported by the PAFEC CAE system, including draughting with DOGS 2D, a means of transferring information and data between these activities is required. In DOGS this is provided by the ARCHIVE option.

The ARCHIVE option is available in both DOGS 2D and DOGS 3D. In both cases this option enables drawing information or 3-D model data to be transferred between one view to another in the same drawing file. This information may also be transferred from one drawing file to another, which is particularly useful for retrieving information about a number of different components from separate drawing files and collecting them in one file to create an assembly drawing. The ARCHIVE option in DOGS 3D has an additional facility that enables information to be transferred from the 3-D workspace to the 2-D workspace of DOGS 2D. Graphical information, from either a single elevation or all four views, can be transferred in a single operation. Using this option, a 3-D model can be used as the basis for generating quickly the basic drawing information of a DOGS 2D drawing organized to conform to First or Third Angle projection systems. Often the transferred views will require modification, e.g. where hidden detail needs to be displayed using a dashed line style, so the designer must use DOGS 2D to complete the drawing in full, adding dimensions and text as appropriate. Despite this limitation, however, we can see that the ARCHIVE option provides a mechanism for integrating the 3-D modelling activity with the 2-D draughting activity within the DOGS system.

Graphical information can be transferred from the 2-D workspace to the 3-D workspace using the COPY option in DOGS 2D. This transfer requires a destination plane to be defined in 3-D space on to which the drawing information from DOGS 2D will be copied. The exact position of the drawing on this plane is controlled by defining the target locations of up to three control points specified during the COPY process. Often it is convenient to use the *xy*, *yz* or *zx* planes for receiving 2-D information, though a general plane in space can be defined by the target locations of the three control points. The COPY option is particularly useful for transferring edge profiles of 2½-D objects drawn in DOGS 2D to DOGS 3D where they can be used to generate 3-D representations of the item. Figure 9.26 shows a 2-D edge profile drawn in DOGS 2D. This profile has been copied to the *zx* plane in DOGS 3D, Fig. 9.27, where it has subsequently been copied and extended with arcs to form the revolved object shown in Fig. 9.29. Surface information has not been generated automatically, so this must be defined in the usual manner in DOGS 3D (Fig. 9.29).

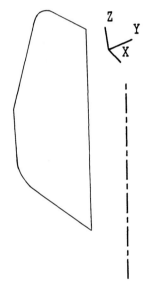

Fig. 9.26 *A 2-D profile created in DOGS 2D.*

9.6 THE INTEGRATION OF DOGS WITH OTHER CAE ACTIVITIES

In this chapter we have only discussed the integration of DOGS 2D and DOGS 3D. The process of transferring graphical information between these two systems is controlled by the DOGS system using an approach that is, in its detail, unique to the PAFEC CAE system, i.e. the ARCHIVE option is only suitable for use with DOGS-generated drawing files. The 2-D and 3-D data stored in a DOGS drawing file provides a full geometric representation of an object that can be the basis of all other CAE tasks (analysis, manufacture, etc.). Where these tasks can be undertaken by software from the PAFEC CAE system, DOGS provides various other information transfer facilities to ensure information is

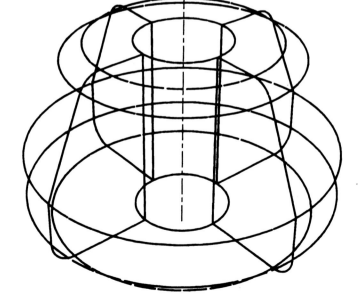

Fig. 9.27 *The 2-D profile copied to the zx plane in DOGS 3D.*

Fig. 9.28 *The 2-D profile revolved using COPY and EXTEND.*

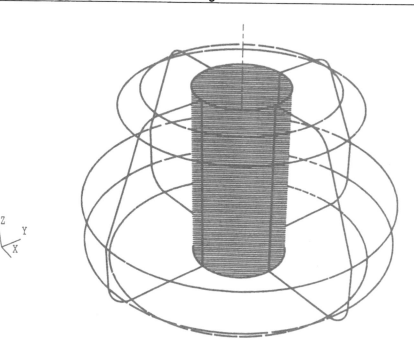

Fig. 9.29 *A cylindrical surface used to define the central bore of the revolved object.*

translated directly into a format suitable for the receiving package, e.g. symbols. However, where information is required by another CAE system, then DOGS data and information must be translated into a neutral format file, e.g. using an IGES format. The IGES option can be selected from the DOGS MASTER MENU and provides facilities for generating both 2-D and 3-D IGES format files. The IGES option also provides a facility to read an IGES file and create a DOGS format drawing file. This facility allows the exchange of data and information between the DOGS draughting and modelling systems and any other CAE system supporting IGES neutral format files. However, neutral format files are large in size because the data is stored in an ASCII format, and so they tend to occupy large amounts of storage space compared with the specialist file formats devised by each software manufacturer. Therefore, once the exchange of data and information has been successfully completed and verified, it is advisable to delete the IGES drawing files from the drawing database and use just the local version of this file. A further problem with IGES files is that the transfer systems are not all equally robust. With some software suppliers, if a file is transferred a few times using IGES, parts of the drawing become corrupted or lost.

SUMMARY

In this chapter we have briefly considered the draughting capabilities of a minicomputer based 2-D draughting and 3-D modelling system. We have seen that the fundamental operating principles of DOGS 2D do not differ very much from those of AutoCAD. Each system provides a wide variety of drawing construction and display facilities to allow industrial quality drawings to be produced to any relevant drawing standard and plotted onto a hard copy medium. We have also considered 3-D modelling using DOGS 3D. This system allows a wire-frame model of an object to be generated independently of the 2-D draughting activity. The wire-frame model can be enhanced by specifying surface features, though the variety of surface types provided by DOGS 3D is somewhat limited, restricting the scope of the surface modelling activity to planar, cylindrical and conical surfaces forms. The DOGS 3D and DOGS 2D systems have facilities for exchanging data between the 3-D and 2-D work-spaces, and so for the first time in this text we have seen a two-way exchange of information and data between different CAE activities. This theme is continued in the next chapter in which we will consider 3-D solid modelling systems.

10 Towards integration: solid modelling

10.1 INTRODUCTION

Solid modelling is the most advanced technique available to the designer for generating a 3-D representation of an item on a CAD system. The solid model represents both the full surface geometry of the item and the interior volume bounded by the surface faces. Consequently, an unambiguous representation of an item can be generated using this technique. The Boolean operators allow 'material' simply to be added to, or subtracted from, the item currently modelled on the CAD system. Any new edges or surfaces created by a Boolean operation are calculated immediately by the modelling software and incorporated into the object model. Once an item has been solid modelled, its 3-D representation can be used to integrate the design activity with other CAE activities. The importance of this approach to 3-D modelling can be gauged by its increasing frequency of use in industry for a range of diverse engineering applications. Also the importance of the 2-D database as the basis of an integrated CAE system has declined in preference to the 3-D solid model database.

We briefly discussed in Chapter 4 some of the solid modelling techniques currently in use, but in this chapter we will concentrate on the application of two specific packages and the use of just two techniques: constructive solid geometry (CSG) and boundary representation (B-Rep). These two methods form the basis of the majority of industrial-quality solid modelling systems, of which BOXER (PAFEC) and GEOMOD (SDRC) are good examples. We will be using these two CAD packages to illustrate solid modelling methods and to contrast the difference between the CSG and B-Rep approaches. We will also continue to see how various computer-aided engineering (CAE) activities can be integrated using geometric information and data generated by these two systems.

10.2 BOXER: A CONSTRUCTIVE SOLID GEOMETRY SOLID MODELLING SYSTEM

The BOXER solid modelling system is part of PAFEC's integrated CAE system. It has undergone a lengthy development history before achieving commercial maturity in the PAFEC CAE system. A rudimentary version of the BOXER solid modelling system was first developed in the USA under the acronym PADL-1 during the 1970s. Development continued at Leeds University in the UK where the modelling software was known by the acronym NONAME. NONAME provided the fundamental operating principles of the solid modelling software adapted by PAFEC for use in their integrated CAE system, which was subsequently known as BOXER. BOXER operates independently of any other package in the PAFEC CAE system. Whilst links to other packages within the system exist, it is possible to operate BOXER without having DOGS 2D, DOGS 3D, etc., available for use. However, many of the display and data- management facilities provided by the software are similar to those found in DOGS 2D and DOGS 3D. The screen menu and the BOXER menu card are used in exactly the same way as they are used in DOGS. Thus the PAFEC user will find a great deal of similarity in the way information is input to the system for all these different packages.

To operate the BOXER package, you must be logged on to a minicomputer-based CAD system (PC-based systems generally do not have adequate power to run packages of this complexity). As with DOGS, you will need to use a graphics terminal, and for speed and ease of operation, a digitizer tablet or other cursor control device is useful, together with a printed menu card, for inputting data. When you invoke BOXER, you will be prompted for a **session code** and a **graphics terminal identifier**. The latter is specific to your CAD system, and depending upon your reply, may invoke BOXER to prompt you for more information about your system set-up. The session code, however plays a vital role in the organization of the 3-D solid model database, but it is difficult for the reader to appreciate fully its significance at this stage. Suffice to say, the session code is a three-letter identifier, e.g. ABC, that is appended to object names created by BOXER during the modelling activity. Once the initialization process is complete, the BOXER graphics screen will be displayed, Fig. 10.1. This figure shows the graphics viewport, the screen menu to its left and the typed input **scratchpad** at the bottom of the screen. The screen cursor can be used to select modelling options from the screen menu or for identifying features displayed in the viewport, e.g. object names. If a digitizing tablet is connected, the puck can be used to pick modelling commands from the BOXER menu card. Alternatively, typed input may be used to select commands and input information into the system. Once the graphics screen is displayed, BOXER is ready to begin the modelling activity.

10.2.1 SOLID MODEL CONSTRUCTION USING BOXER

BOXER is a constructive solid geometry type solid modelling system. An object model is created by combining basic solid model forms using the Boolean operations union, difference and intersection. The results of these basic solid modelling operations were discussed in Chapter 4, and illustrated by Figs. 4.15 and 4.16. Figure 10.2 shows the five basic solid model forms provided by BOXER, which are:

1. Block;
2. Cylinder;
3. Cone;

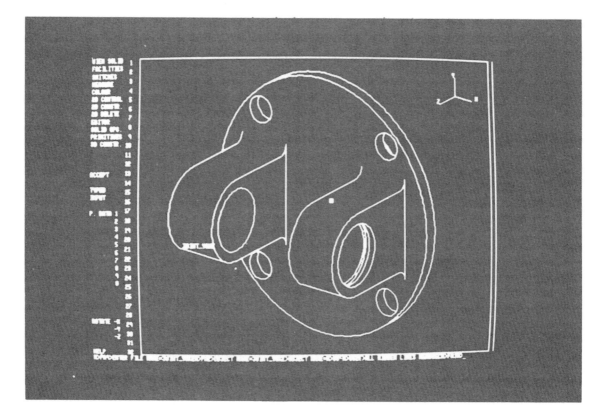

Fig. 10.1 *BOXER graphics screen showing screen menu.*

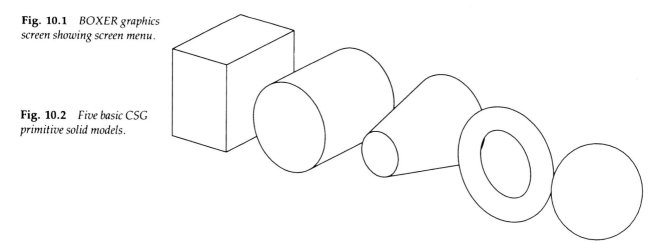

Fig. 10.2 *Five basic CSG primitive solid models.*

4. Torus;
5. Sphere.

These basic solid model forms are known as the primitives, and it is from these five primitives that all other solid models must be derived.

Table 10.1 A summary of the input variables required to define the BOXER primitives

	Block	Cylinder	Cone	Torus	Sphere
Primitive					
PT	1	2	3	4	5
Geometry					
LG	√	√	√	–	–
R1	–	√	√	√	√
R2	–	–	√	√	–
AN	–	–	√	–	–
Position					
CE	√	√	√	√	√
E1	–	√	√	–	–
E2	–	√	√	–	–
CR	√	–	–	–	–
MF	√	–	–	–	–
Orientation					
MX	√	√	√	√	√
MY	√	√	√	√	√
MZ	√	√	√	√	√
RX	√	√	√	√	√
RY	√	√	√	√	√
RZ	√	√	√	√	√
Accept					
AC	√	√	√	√	√

PT = Primitive option   LG = Length(s)
R1 = Minor radius   R2 = Major radius
AN = Angle   CE = Centroid position
E1 = Mid-face position   E2 = Mid-face position
CR = Corner position   MF = Mid-face position
MX = Move in x direction   RX = Rotate about x axis
MY = Move in y direction   RY = Rotate about y axis
MZ = Move in z direction   RZ = Rotate about z axis

The procedure for creating a primitive solid model is quite simple and can be completed very quickly. At the beginning of a modelling session when there are no solid models in the 3-D workspace, typed input must be used to input the basic information required to describe the geometry, position and orientation of the primitive solid model. A primitive is created using the PRIMITIVE option, selecting PRIMITIVE 1 (PT1) enables a block to be created, selecting PRIMITIVE 2 (PT2) enables a cylinder to be created, etc. Once the primitive type has been selected, the user must identify which describing parameter is going to be specified next before entering any numerical values. The type of data required to define fully each primitive solid model is summarized in Table 10.1 and illustrated in Fig. 10.3. For example, this table shows that the geometry of a block is defined solely by its lengths (LG) in the x, y and z directions. The position of the block can be controlled by defining the positions of its centroid (CE), a mid-face point (MF), or a corner point (CR). The orientation of the block can be

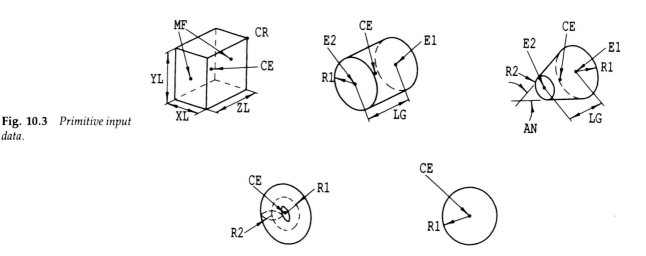

Fig. 10.3 *Primitive input data.*

defined by translation (MX, MY, MZ) vectors and rotation (RX, RY, RZ) angles in each direction. Similarly, the geometry of a cone is defined by any three of its four descriptive parameters: z-length (LG), major radius (R1), minor radius (R2), or cone angle (AN). Its overall position can be controlled by specifying the positions of the centroid (CE), or the mid-face points of the the two end faces (E1, E2). The orientation of the cone can be defined by translation (MX, MY, MZ) vectors and rotation (RX, RY, RZ) angles in each direction. The geometry and position variables do not have to be defined in any particular order. However, it is essential that the orientation transformations be defined in their correct sequence to ensure the overall desired transformation is achieved. When the designer has finished defining the primitive data, the accept (AC) command is used to indicate to BOXER that the data input sequence is complete. Using the information provided, BOXER will then create a solid model of the primitive. The model will be assigned a name by which it can be identified, and an isometric wire-frame image of the object will be displayed on the graphics screen.

It should be noted that the wire frame is displayed for speed and convenience only. All the data necessary for the full solid model is available, if required, to generate a hidden-line removed image of the object. However, the hidden-line removed image will take some time to be generated from the solid model database, and therefore its continual use will inhibit the speed at which this activity can be carried out.

When creating a primitive solid model, it is not essential to provide data for each variable indicated in Table 10.1. Provided sufficient data has been input for BOXER to determine the size and shape of the primitive, the solid model can be created when the ACCEPT command is given. Default position and orientation values are defined in the software, and therefore the definition of these variables during the primitive definition phase is optional.

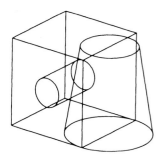

Fig. 10.4 *Three primitive solid models correctly positioned prior to being combined as a whole.*

The method used by BOXER to define primitive solid models is, in principle, no different from that in other CSG solid modelling packages. Unlike the other 3-D modelling approaches, however, the solid modeller is capable of defining the full geometric properties of the object from basic overall dimensions. The position of the object can initially be controlled by defining the positions of a few keypoints (centroid, mid-face points, etc.), and its orientation defined by a sequence of transformations applied to the whole model. Using this information and data, the solid modeller is capable of determining automatically the edge and surface properties of the solid model, allowing wire-frame images of the model to be displayed, with or without hidden edges shown.

Once a primitive solid model has been created, it can be shown on the graphics screen with vertices, mid-edge and mid-face points displayed. During the creation of subsequent primitive solid models, these keypoints can be indicated with the screen cursor to define specific position or vector data. This is particularly useful where, for example, the mid-faces of two primitive solid models need to coincide. (This particular use of keypoints in solid modelling is analogous to the SNAP facility in 2-D draughting.) Thus, once a point in 3-D space has been defined by some entity, it can be used time and time again during the modelling phase, without the designer needing to state its specific x, y, z co-ordinates.

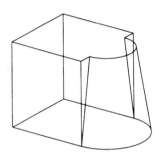

Figure 10.4 shows the three primitive solid models required to create a solid model of the object first shown in Chapter 9, Fig. 9.15, and subsequently surface modelled using DOGS 3D. The object can be solid modelled using a block, a cylinder and a cone positioned as shown. A mid-face keypoint on the block was used to define the position of one of the mid-faces of the cylinder (E2), and two mid-edge keypoints were used to define the positions of the two mid-faces of the cone (E1, E2). The dimensions of all other variables have been defined by typed input.

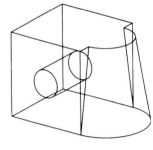

Fig. 10.5 *Intermediate solid model resulting from a union operation.*

The primitive solid models can be combined using the SOLID OPERATIONS option. This option provides the Boolean operations union, difference and intersection. Figures 10.5 and 10.6 show the sequence of operations required to define fully the object using the three primitives, and involves just two Boolean operations. The first combines the block and cone using a union operation, the second creates a hole in the united object by subtracting the cylinder using a difference operation. As a consequence of this sequence of solid modelling operations, BOXER creates two new objects. The first is the intermediate object resulting from the union operation, the second is the final object resulting from the difference operation. A total of five objects exist in the solid model database, each uniquely identified by an object name assigned by BOXER. Three of these objects are primitive solid models, and two are **compound** solid models. The solid model database contains the definition data for the three primitive solid models, from which the size, position and orientation of each can be determined directly. The two compound solid models, however, are not defined in the same way. The size and shape of the compound solid models can be determined only by inspection of the CSG **tree**. This records the sequence of solid modelling operations required to create each object. The outcome of these operations must be calculated each time a compound solid model is retrieved.

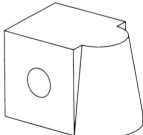

Each time a compound solid model is displayed, the CSG tree is searched to find the primitives used during the modelling process. The current definitions for these primitives are used to generate the final object form using the sequence

Fig. 10.6 *Final solid model resulting from a difference operation (wire frame and hidden line removed).*

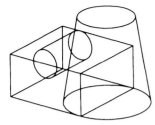

Fig. 10.7 *The three primitive solid models with the height of the block modified.*

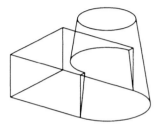

Fig. 10.8 *The modified intermediate solid model.*

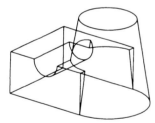

Fig. 10.9 *The modified final solid model (wire frame and hidden line removed).*

of modelling operations recorded in the CSG tree. If the size, position or orientation of one of the primitives has been modified since the time the compound model was first created, the original form of the compound model will be modified in some way too. Thus, the final size and shape of the compound solid model depends upon the current state of primitive definition data.

Figure 10.7 shows the three primitives of Fig. 10.4 once more, except in this case the height of the block has been halved. Figures 10.8 and 10.9 show how the two compound models are modified as a result of changing the size of the original block. A quite different object form results in both cases. The two solid models shown in Figs. 10.8 and 10.9 are not newly defined models, but merely the present state of the original compound models based upon the present state of their constituent primitives. Clearly the definition of a compound solid model does not retain the information describing its geometric, position and orientation attributes at the time of its creation. For this reason, CSG solid models are said to be **unevaluated**.

The characteristics of unevaluated CSG modelling systems differ to those of evaluated modelling systems, e.g. B-rep solid modellers or surface modellers like DOGS 3D (Chapter 9). The CSG approach is particularly useful during initial design studies when an object definition may require modification. If the size, position and orientation of one or more of the primitives are changed, when the compound solid model is retrieved, the modifications made to the primitives will also be made to the compound solid model definition. This provides the designer with the scope to invoke easily a change to the solid model database. However, the boundary definition of the object, used to create the wire-frame screen image, must be calculated each time the object definition is retrieved from the database. This is a tedious and slow process when compared to an evaluated system where the boundary definition forms part of the database, allowing the screen image of the object to be displayed very quickly.

The universal joint yoke shown in Fig. 10.1 is the result of several modelling operations using a number of primitive solid models. Figures 10.10 to 10.20 show the sequence of operations required to form this model. The basic shape of the yoke is formed from four primitive solid models, Figs. 10.10 to 10.13. When these primitives are united, the compound solid model illustrated in Fig.

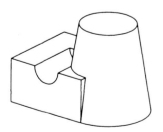

Fig. 10.9 *The modified final solid model (wire frame and hidden line removed).*

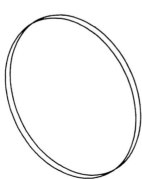

Fig. 10.10 *Cylinder A.*

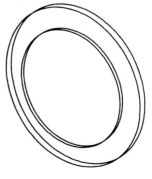

Fig. 10.11 *Cylinders A and B.*

Fig. 10.12 *Cylinders A and B, block C.*

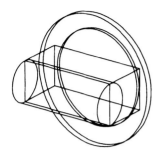

Fig. 10.13 *Cylinders A, B and D, block C.*

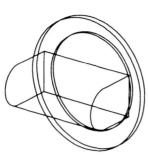

Fig. 10.14 *Union E = A ∪ B ∪ C ∪ D.*

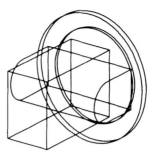

Fig. 10.15 *Union E, block F.*

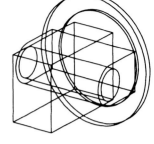

Fig. 10.16 *Union E, block F, cylinder G.*

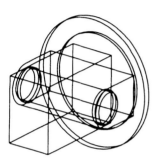

Fig. 10.17 *Union E, F, cylinders G, H and I.*

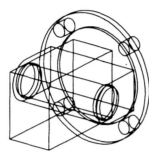

Fig. 10.18 *Union E, block F, cylinder G, H, I, J, K, L and M.*

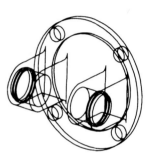

Fig. 10.19 *Difference N = E − F − G − H − I − J − K − L − M.*

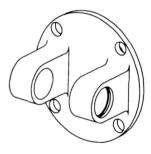

Fig. 10.20 *Difference N with filleted edges.*

10.14 results. A further eight primitive solid models are created. Figs. 10.15 to 10.18, before a difference operation is used to create the object illustrated in Fig. 10.19. Finally, the fillets are modelled using the fillet operation. This must be repeated four times, once for each edge, before an accurate representation of the yoke is created, Figs. 10.20 and 10.21. A total of twelve primitives are required for this model, combined using just two Boolean operations plus four fillet modelling operations.

A number of features of the universal joint yoke are identical and have been created using the COPY operation. For example, the recesses in each bore of the yoke are created using two narrow cylinders, Fig. 10.17. However, since the recesses are identical in width and diameter, rather than create two independently defined cylinders, only one cylinder was defined as a primitive. The other has been created using the COPY operation. This operation enables several copies of an existing solid model to be generated automatically by BOXER, each displaced from the original by a translation and/or rotation transformation. Thus, the second recess is formed using a cylinder that is a copy of the cylinder used for the first recess. The copy has been translated along the axis of the hole to its correct position. This ensures that the geometric attributes of the second cylinder will always be identical to those of the first. Similarly, three

Fig. 10.21 *Hidden line removed image of universal joint yoke.*

of the four cylinders used to create the holes in the flange of the yoke are copies of the cylinder used for the first hole, Fig. 10.18. Each copy has been rotated by 90°, ensuring the holes are equispaced around the flange. If the diameters of the holes need to be modified, it is only necessary to modify the diameter of the original cylinder used to cut the first hole. The diameters of the three copies will be adjusted automatically, and the final model of the yoke will show all the holes in the flange modified in the same way. Thus, the copy option does not generate a separate primitive for each copy, but creates an entry in the CSG tree as if it were a compound solid model. The CSG tree entry shows the primitive from which the copy is derived and specifies the transformation required to place it in its correct position.

The SOLID OPERATIONS option provides several other modelling operations that can be used to combine solid models or modify them in some way. We have already seen the results of the FILLET operation in Fig. 10.20. A similar modelling operation is the CHAMFER operation. In both cases the geometry of an edge is modified either to a concave fillet or a planar chamfer. These local modelling operations involve BOXER-defined solid models that are largely invisible to the designer. For instance, on straight edges a fillet is modelled using a difference operation between a square sectioned block and a cylinder; this feature is then unified with the original solid model. Similarly, a chamfer on a straight edge is created by a difference operation between the original solid model and a block positioned at an angle across the edge. In both cases, all the designer has to do is use the screen cursor to indicate which edge is to be modified and specify the size of the feature, i.e. the fillet radius or chamfer depth.

The MIRROR operation enables a copy of a solid model (or part of one) to be made that is a mirror image of the original. This is particularly useful where an item has symmetric features, e.g. the universal joint yoke. The constructions for many of the features in Fig. 10.20 could have been simplified if the MIRROR command had been used and would have saved many of the COPY commands. The mirror plane is generally defined by the positions of three points lying in the plane, though the $x = 0$, $y = 0$ and $z = 0$ planes are often suitable for such operations.

The DRAG operation enables the position and orientation of a solid model to be modified. The translation (MX, MY, MZ) and rotation (RX, RY, RZ) operations must be specified for the three principal dimensions separately. All rotations occur about the global Ox, Oy and Oz axes, so the sequence in which they are defined must be planned carefully to ensure the desired overall transformation result is achieved. A **local** rotation operation allows the rotation axis to be defined anywhere in 3-D space. Keypoints displayed on the graphics screen can be used to define the positions of two points on the axis of rotation. The position and orientation of the solid model can then be modified by defining a rotation about this axis.

The SECTION operation enables the designer to cut away parts of an object as if using a difference operation. The resultant object shows the cut faces of the model hatched in the plane of the cut face. The SECTIONing with plane operation creates a full half section model by cutting the original solid model with a planar surface. Again, cut faces are hatched, Fig. 10.22. The objects that result from these section operations cannot be used in any subsequent modelling operations, and so are only useful for display purposes.

The ASSEMBLY operation allows several items which have been modelled separately to be combined to form a single solid model. The ASSEMBLY operation does not modify the separate solid models, but merely records that these items can be considered as a whole when the assembled object is recalled. Figure 10.23 shows a water pump from a domestic washing machine, and Fig. 10.24 shows a solid model of the same created using BOXER. The solid model of the water pump has been created from nine separate solid models assembled together. This is shown in Fig. 10.25 in which a cut-away model of the water pump illustrates the complexity of the solid models involved.

The ASSEMBLY operation allows the designer to develop quite complex solid models that consist of many separate parts. In these cases, each individual item should be modelled separately and brought together only when each solid model is complete. If the assembly operation is to be successful, it is imperative that the object names of the primitives and compound solid models are unique. When the object names have been allocated automatically by BOXER during the modelling activity, it is good practice to ensure that a unique session code is used for each item. The reader may recall that when BOXER is initialized, the user must input a session code. This code is appended to all the object names created by BOXER during that modelling session. Thus, to ensure each solid model is named uniquely, each individual item of the assembly should be created during different BOXER modelling sessions.

The 2-D control option enables 2½-D objects to be solid modelled using SPIN (i.e. rotation) and LIFT (i.e. linear translation) modelling operations. In both cases, the 2-D profile of the object is created in a 2-D workspace that is provided by the BOXER package. The profile is created using a limited set of 2-D construction facilities from which a **spin boundary** or **lift boundary** is defined. Before the solid model can be generated, the spin axis of a revolved item must be defined in 3-D space, while for prismatic items, a lift point, a lift direction and depth dimension must be defined. The boundary can then be spun or lifted in the 3-D workspace to create the 2½-D solid model as required. This method of

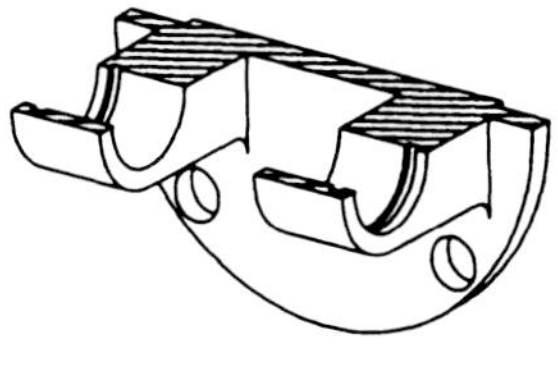

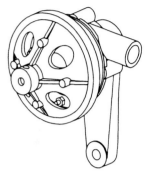

Fig. 10.22 *Half section of universal joint yoke.*

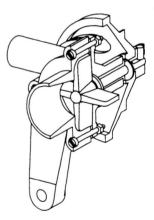

Fig. 10.24 *BOXER solid model of water pump.*

Fig. 10.25 *Cut-away solid model of water pump.*

Fig. 10.23 *Water pump from domestic washing machine.*

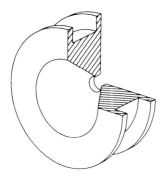

Fig. 10.26 *Revolved solid created using SPIN command.*

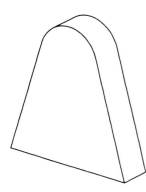

Fig. 10.27 *Prismatic solid created using LIFT command.*

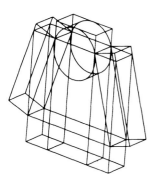

Fig. 10.28 *Primitives used to create prismatic solid.*

solid model construction is convenient for 2½-D items which the designer finds difficult to define using a conventional modelling approach based upon primitive solid models. Figure 10.26 shows a revolved solid model which has been sectioned to show its 2-D profile. Figure 10.27 shows a prismatic item constructed using the lift operation. This particular object has two surfaces that are tangent to the rounded edge. The place of tangency in 3-D space would have been known by the designer before he could position the primitives required to model this object using conventional modelling methods. This position cannot be determined easily without resorting to calculation. However, the 2-D workspace provides a construction facility to draw tangency lines to a circle. Thus, the profile of the object can be drawn easily in the 2-D workspace. The lift construction method, therefore, seems to be a most reasonable approach to adopt. However, the solid model shown in Fig. 10.26 does not differ in any way from the other solid models illustrated in this section. It is a compound solid model constructed from many different primitives generated automatically by BOXER during the lift operation. These are shown in Fig. 10.28. Therefore, while it is convenient to use a lift operation to model a 2½-D item, the resulting object requires several primitive solid models to define its size and shape. If possible, a more conventional modelling approach should be sought first.

The information required to define a solid model can be archived at any time during the BOXER modelling activity. The definition file is an ASCII format file that contains just the primitive solid model definitions and the CSG tree records of each compound solid model, consequently the size of a BOXER definition file is very small compared to even a 2-D drawing file, e.g. the definition file for the water pump assembly illustrated in Fig. 10.25 is less than 2 Kb in size. The solid modelling procedure described above is normally performed interactively. However, an experienced user of BOXER, who fully understands the format of the definition file, should be able to modify the data using a file editor. This allows the definition file to be modified without having to interact with BOXER. Alterations to the numerical database can be done very quickly, but BOXER will have to be invoked if the results of the modifications need to be seen. When the solid model data is retrieved from the archive data file, the modifications to the model definition will be implemented immediately, since the CSG models are unevaluated.

The VIEW SOLID option allows the solid model to be displayed in several different ways. Normally the object would be displayed as a wire-frame model showing all its edges in a single isometric view, Fig. 10.20. However, since the surface geometry of the object is represented by the solid model, hidden edges can be displayed as dashed lines or completely removed from the screen image, Fig. 10.21. This process involves significant calculation, and is generally used only to clarify the finalized representation of the object. The isometric view type can be replaced by a perspective view, or by three orthographic views arranged in either first or third angle projection systems. In the latter case, all three views are displayed simultaneously on the graphics screen and provide front, side and plan elevations of the object. This type of view is to be preferred when the position and orientation of the solid model needs to be checked visually before continuing with the modelling process. Screen images of the solid model can be archived in a **picture file** or used to create **plotfiles** from which a hard copy of the image can be generated. Picture files are useful for rapid display of solid models and require only enough memory to specify the colour or grey shade for each pixel.

The COLOUR option provides facilities for generating coloured shaded images of the solid model (see colour section). The number, position, intensity, etc., of the light sources can be specified by the designer to achieve a high-quality coloured image of the model. The generation of these coloured images requires a large amount of computer time, and even on a large CAD system several minutes would elapse before an image of even the simplest of solid models would appear. It is good practice to run BOXER in batch mode overnight if colour images of a complex object are required, when these images can be generated off-line and the bit-mapped data archived to picture files.

The MEASURE option allows geometric properties of the solid model to be evaluated. Thus it is possible to verify the co-ordinates of a keypoint, measure the length of an edge, etc. The solid modeller is also able to determine the volume of a model, the position of its centroid and calculate moments about the principal Ox, Oy and Oz axes. If the mass properties of a solid model are defined by the designer, the solid modeller is capable of determining the total mass of an object and its principal moments of inertia.

When the user has completed the solid modelling activity, he may either QUIT, in which case all solid model definitions will be lost, or he may EXIT and SAVE, whereby all solid model definitions will be archived into a data file for retrieval at a later date. Where data has been stored in a definition file during the BOXER activity, or where data has been retrieved from a previously defined file, it is possible to have that file updated rather than a new file created for each BOXER session. When BOXER has been terminated in this way, the user is returned to the control of the CAD operating system.

10.3 THE INTEGRATION OF BOXER AND DOGS

The BOXER solid modelling system allows a full 3-D geometric representation of an object to be generated very quickly. Unlike the DOGS 3D approach to 3-D modelling, the solid modelling system does not require the designer to prepare a detailed numerical description of the item prior to the modelling activity. When using BOXER, the designer need only prepare basic dimension data. His challenge, though, is to plan a modelling approach that minimizes the use of primitives and avoids, if possible, the use of LIFT and SPIN modelling operations. An experienced solid model designer will consider many alternative ways of constructing the solid model, and will look for an approach that minimizes the number of operations in this process. From the basic primitive data, the solid modelling system will generate all the information required to represent accurately the edge and surface geometries of the object. The item may be viewed in several different ways, ranging from the simplicity of a wire-frame representation to the complexity of a shaded colour image using multiple light sources.

Even though the BOXER approach to 3-D modelling is more straightforward than the DOGS 3D approach, the effort required to generate the solid model must be rewarded with a use of the model beyond just visualization tasks. The solid modelling system is capable of measuring and calculating many geometric attributes of the model that are important to a designer (volume of item, mass of item, moments of inertia, etc.). But even this use of the solid model data is quite limited, and cannot justify the expense of the system alone. As with DOGS 3D, it is the integration of BOXER with other computer-aided tasks supported by the PAFEC CAE system that justifies the usefulness of generating a solid model description of a single item or assembly of parts. The integration of BOXER with DOGS is the link that most concerns the designer.

Once a single item has been modelled on the BOXER system, it is likely that a fully dimensioned detail drawing of the item will be required. Similarly, if an assembly of parts has been modelled using BOXER, a general assembly drawing with a parts list is likely to be required. In both cases, the drawing must be created using DOGS 2D. Any view of a solid model generated by BOXER can be transferred to the DOGS 2D system as a symbol. The procedure in BOXER for creating this file involves three simple tasks: opening a parametric symbol file; re-displaying the view of the model required to be transferred; and closing the parametric symbol file. In DOGS 2D the contents of the symbol file can be displayed on the drawing sheet using the retrieve symbol option.

The parametric symbol file is a special data file type unique to the PAFEC system. The file contains a list of 2-D draughting commands which, when executed in DOGS 2D, recreate the view of the solid model by drawing a sequence of lines and circular arcs. The dimensions of the solid model are preserved and drawn to the scale of the DOGS 2D drawing. Difficulties can arise where the units used in the solid modelling activity are different to those used for the DOGS drawing. In this case, it is imperative that the size of paper, the active units and the view scale are chosen in DOGS to ensure that the full sized view of the solid model can fit on to the drawing sheet.

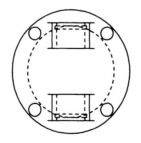
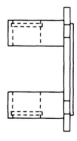

Fig. 10.29 *Third angle orthographic views of the universal joint yoke created using BOXER and transferred to DOGS.*

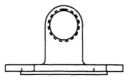

A typical BOXER to DOGS 2D transfer sequence is illustrated in Figs. 10.29 to 10.32. Figure 10.29 shows a third angle orthographic view of the universal joint yoke which has been generated in a dashed hidden line style using BOXER. All three elevations are transferred simultaneously to DOGS 2D as a single view. A sectioned drawing can be created if the side elevation is deleted and replaced by a half section view. The half section view is also created using BOXER and transferred to DOGS 2D. Figure 10.30 shows the DOGS 2D drawing with the side elevation deleted and the half section view retrieved from the symbol file. When the symbol is first retrieved, it is not possible to place the half section view in its correct position on the drawing sheet. This is not important, because the DOGS 2D DRAG option can be used to move the view to its rightful place,

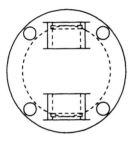

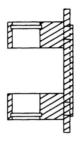

Fig. 10.30 *Half section view of the universal joint yoke transferred from BOXER to DOGS.*

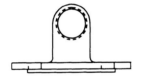

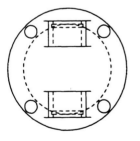

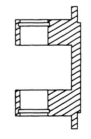

Fig. 10.31 *The three views correctly arranged on a drawing sheet.*

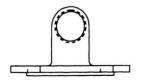

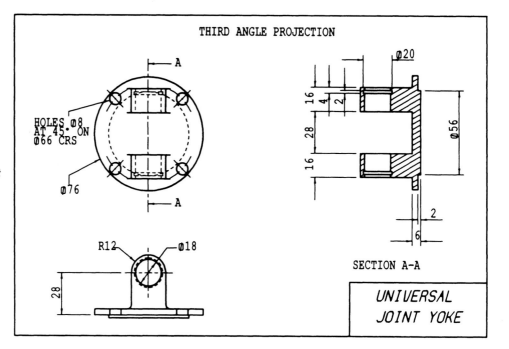

THIRD ANGLE PROJECTION

HOLES Ø8
AT 45° ON
Ø66 CRS

Ø76

R12   Ø18

28

Ø20

16
4
2

28

16

Ø56

2

6

SECTION A-A

UNIVERSAL
JOINT YOKE

Fig. 10.32 *A DOGS drawing of the universal joint yoke.*

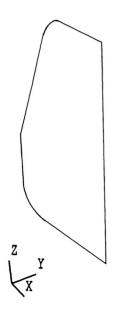

Z
Y
X

Fig. 10.33 *A 2-D profile created in DOGS and transferred to BOXER.*

Fig. 10.31. Figure 10.32 shows the drawing dimensioned and annotated with notes.

Information can also be transferred from DOGS 2D to BOXER, but unlike the transfer of information from DOGS 2D to DOGS 3D, the exchange cannot be completed in a single operation. A 2-D profile can only be transferred to BOXER if it is a closed boundary. This is true for the item illustrated in Fig. 10.33, which was first seen in Chapter 9, Fig. 9.26, and subsequently used in DOGS 3D to create a revolved body. To start the transfer process, the NC (numerical control) output option must be used in DOGS 2D to create a **boundary file**. In this data file the geometric properties of the closed boundary are stored. The NC output option is more normally used for transferring information from DOGS 2D to numerically controlled machine-tool simulation systems (DOGS NC, GNC, etc.), though the specific detail of this approach will not be considered any further here, because it is the subject of more detailed discussion in the next chapter. Information from the boundary file can be retrieved in BOXER using the READ DOGS boundary option. This option places the boundary into the BOXER 2-D workspace from which a revolved or prismatic solid model can be created using the SPIN or LIFT modelling operations. Figure 10.34 shows a sectioned solid model created in BOXER using the 2-D profile of Fig. 10.33 and spun to form a revolved body.

Transfer of information between BOXER and DOGS 3D is restricted to one direction only, i.e. BOXER to DOGS 3D. This restriction on data exchange results from the different ways in which 3-D geometric data is represented in each modelling system. A BOXER CSG solid model cannot be generated automatically from the edge and surface information that would be provided by

DOGS 3D, therefore geometric information cannot be passed to the solid model-ling system from the surface modelling system. However, the CSG solid model can be used to generate a boundary representation of an item (BOXER already performs this task to display the wire-frame image of the model). This boundary information can be transferred from BOXER to DOGS 3D, and other 3-D model-ling systems, using the IGES option. This option generates an IGES neutral format data file to be created from the BOXER solid model. However, even though a BOXER solid model provides a full geometric representation of an item, the IGES file created by BOXER only contains edge geometry information. Information about the surface geometry of the item is not, at present, rep-resented in the neutral file. Consequently the exchange of 3-D information from BOXER to DOGS 3D only results in a wire-frame model of the item being transferred.

Fig. 10.34 *The result of spinning the 2-D profile (sectioned for clarity).*

10.4 GEOMOD: A CSG AND BOUNDARY REPRESENTATION SOLID MODELLING SYSTEM

A commonly available CAE package called I-DEAS by Structural Dynamics Research Corporation (SDRC) includes the solid modelling package GEOMOD. The whole I-DEAS package can be run on an intelligent workstation with, for a single user, about 2 Mb of memory and a 71 Mb hard disk. The GEOMOD solid modeller provides a facility for the designer to try out a number of design ideas speedily and compare their relative merits. In order that the solid modeller can deal with the numerous objects commonly met with in engineering and can quickly model them on a wide range of hardware, the following features were built into the GEOMOD program.

1. The programs are written in a language which can be applied to a wide range of computers and have a general-purpose interface program which allows a large number of display devices to be used.
2. To allow for quick display, curved surfaces can be readily approximated by facets. The precise geometry is available for surfaces and intersections to be calculated and displayed, should these be required.
3. Boolean set operations are provided for joining (c.f. BOXER union) and cutting (c.f. BOXER difference) primitives in a CSG approach.
4. In addition to the CSG approach, a boundary representation file is used which stores a description of the final object by using its orientated surface geometry. This allows objects to be stored very efficiently.
5. To provide speed of display and flexibility for various levels of realism, objects can be displayed in a combination of wire frames, hidden detail and colour shaded images.
6. Surfaces can be either precisely or approximately represented in a mathe-matical form that minimizes the calculations and data storage for surface intersections, orientations, displays and features such as the determination of tangents and normals to surfaces. This reduces the size of the programs to allow them to be most easily developed, run and stored.
7. The data can handle objects which are not closed and which have a zero-thickness structure.

8. Objects and surfaces can be deformed by standard operations (bending, stretching, warping, filleting, etc.).
9. Two-dimensional curves may be generated which can be extruded (c.f. BOXER lift), revolved (c.f. BOXER spin) or skinned together to create a continuous surface.
10. Two-dimensional and 3-D properties may be calculated (volume, centre of gravity, moment of inertia, principal axes, surface areas, etc.).
11. Component models can be assembled into an overall system by specifying connecting points, lines, planes, curves, surfaces, etc.
12. Interference between adjacent components or systems can be detected automatically.
13. The kinematic relationship between objects can be stored so that performance cycles can be animated.

Several of these features are similar to features provided by the BOXER solid modelling system. However, since GEOMOD is also a B-Rep solid modeller, there are many features provided by the software that are special to this solid modelling approach. It is to these special features which we will now turn our attention.

10.4.1   SOLID MODEL CONSTRUCTION USING GEOMOD

GEOMOD is a boundary representation type solid modelling system, yet object models can be combined using Boolean operations. To support this method of model construction, GEOMOD provides several primitive solid model shapes:

1. block;
2. cylinder;
3. cone;
4. sphere;
5. quadilateral;
6. hexahedron;
7. tube.

These primitives can be combined using the GEOMOD Boolean operations JOIN, CUT and INTERSECT, Fig. 10.35. The results of these operations are exactly the same as the BOXER Boolean operations UNION, DIFFERENCE and INTERSECTION. Additional modelling operations include ADD, which enables two objects with overlapping volumes to be defined in the same 3-D workspace, PLANE CUT, which intersects a solid model with a plane, and INTERFERENCE CHECKING, whereby the common volume of two objects can be identified.

Non-uniform rational B-splines (NURBS, see Chapter 4) lie at the heart of the solid model geometrical definition. Planar, cylindrical, conical, spherical and bi-cubic surface patches are all represented parametrically using just one surface patch type. Surface intersections are fully represented by splines too. The B-Rep data file maintains a dual structure in which the solid model is defined using both facetted and precise representations, Fig. 10.36, with all surfaces and curves of intersection precisely evaluated. Since the solid model has a fully

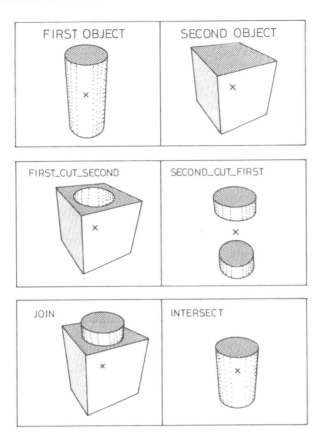

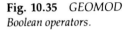

Fig. 10.35 *GEOMOD Boolean operators.*

evaluated data structure, a primitive may be used many times during the modelling process. For instance, a single cylinder may be used repeatedly to create a set of holes in an object. Unlike BOXER, where a separate primitive needs to be created for each hole, GEOMOD can use the same cylinder to define each hole, though a separate Boolean operation is required to make each cut. This use of the cylinder is analogous to the use of a tool, e.g. a drill bit, that is used to create holes of the same size. Also, since the geometry of the solid model is fully evaluated, the boundary structure definition is calculated only once, i.e. when it is first created. Thus, when the model definition is retrieved from the archive file, it can be displayed immediately as a wire frame.

Like BOXER, GEOMOD has the ability to create solid model definitions from 2-D profile boundaries. The boundaries can be created in a separate 2-D work-space or in a work plane defined in 3-D space. The boundary, which is a composite curve composed of sequential segments of straight lines, circles and splines, can be extruded (c.f. BOXER LIFT), or revolved (c.f. BOXER SPIN). Furthermore, the profile may be extruded with a twist, or revolved with an axial and/or radial offset. The profile may be open or closed and include interior holes.

The SKINning operation allows sculptured solid models to be generated from

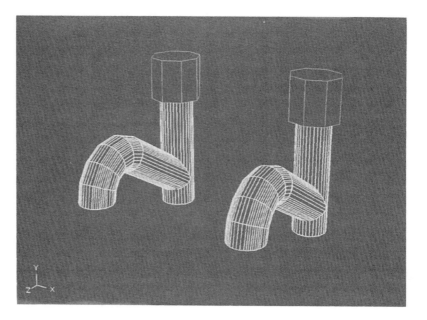

Fig. 10.36 *Facetted and precise GEOMOD solid models.*

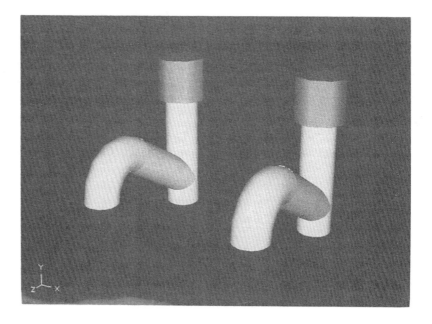

a series of cross sections organized in 3-D space, Fig. 10.37. A smooth skin that covers the cross sections is generated automatically by GEOMOD, Fig. 10.38. This is particularly useful for irregular shapes such as are found in motor cars and in aircraft.

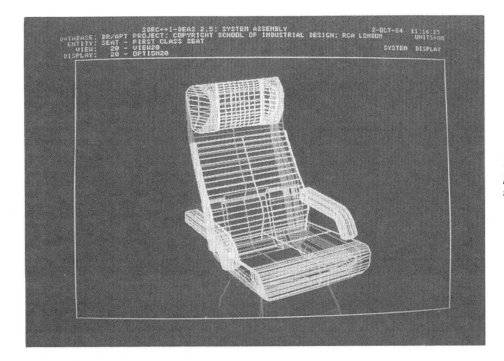

Fig. 10.37 *A series of 2-D profiles arranged for skinning.*

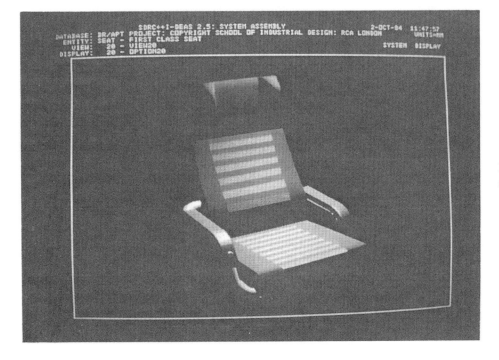

Fig. 10.38 *The resultant skinned surface.*

The orientation operators allow the solid model to be positioned in a desired location using translation, rotation and axis positioning transformations.

Shaping operations allow local modifications to be made to the geometry of the solid model. These local operations include BEND, BLEND, TWEAK, STRETCH, THICK, REFLECT, WARP and SCALE.

1. The BEND operation allows a component model to be bent into a new shape by defining an original skeleton of an object and then repositioning it to a new desired skeleton. The geometry of the object is also modified to incorporate the changed shape of the skeleton. As an example, a duct could be defined by a series of cross-sections along a straight centre line. The centre line could then be bent into a final shape with the profile of the duct being transformed automatically.
2. The BLEND operation smooths out specified regions of an object. It is of especial value for providing a fillet between two surfaces or for rounding sharp corners and edges.
3. TWEAKing allows the designer to access the geometry of an object. Small changes may then be implemented by modifying the geometry of a point or the merging of two lines.
4. The STRETCH operation elongates the object in any specified direction.
5. A specified thickness can be added to an object using the THICK operation. This can be useful for checking if the addition of manufacture tolerances on a thickness will cause the part to overlap with another.
6. REFLECT mirrors an object about an axis to allow the designer to take advantage of any symmetry which an object may possess.
7. WARP allows the designer to push or pull the part at a point to deform it in a controlled manner.
8. The SCALE operation is used for shrinking or enlarging an object.

Assembly modelling allows large models with an unlimited number of components to be created as an assembly with multi-level sub-assemblies. The use of instances enables a component or sub-assembly to be represented in an assembly more than once without the need to copy the solid model definition. One of the most time-consuming processes in building up a CAD assembly is in ensuring parts are correctly orientated, particularly where the components do not fit precisely, e.g. with clearance fits. GEOMOD has a feature which automatically ensures a coincidence or alignment of geometric primitives, e.g. points, lines, planes, space curves and surfaces, in a manner designated by the designer. This avoids the necessity of the user having to check visually that objects are correctly positioned. Automatic interference detection allows the user to check interference between one component and all others in the assembly, or with all the components outside the assembly, or each component with every other in two assemblies.

The geometric data of the solid model can be used to generate any required display, e.g. wire frame, hidden lines, shaded image. The user can scale or rotate, call for perspective views and use a series of multiple viewports to display several images on the screen at the same time. Colour, reflectivity and shadows can be added to provide images of great realism, Fig. 10.39. Parts of the

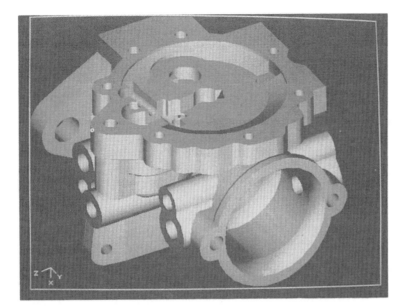

Fig. 10.39 *A shaded image of a carburettor.*

Fig. 10.40 *Exploded view of hair dryer solid model.*

picture can be selectively blanked out, e.g. dimensions and text to emphasize a component's relationship. Alternatively a series of layers of views can be blanked out to give a part sectional view of component assemblies under a front surface, or parts can be shown as exploded views as in Fig. 10.40.

It is often desirable to store views and display them at another time on other graphics devices. Thus, in addition to the geometry, annotation and configuration of the parts, it is necessary also to store information about the views and display parameters to enable views to be displayed automatically from the graphics display data. This is carried out with a pictorial layout package which can also be used directly to create sectioned or exploded views or to use general cutting volumes to reveal internal geometrical detail.

These display features, together with text annotation, are of value not only for concept design and presentation, but also for advertizing and marketing. With the aid of these techniques, computer-generated artwork can be produced at a fraction of the time and cost of artwork produced by conventional methods.

10.5 THE INTEGRATION OF GEOMOD AND GEODRAW

GEODRAW is the 2-D draughting module associated with the I-DEAS CAE system and has a comprehensive range of facilities similar to those of DOGS and AutoCAD. There are two possible ways in which GEOMOD can be integrated with GEODRAW. Either the solid model geometry of an object can be created in GEOMOD and the geometry files transferred to GEODRAW for automatic dimensioning, sectioning, plotting, etc., or a new object can be created afresh using GEODRAW. The latter method generates a 3-D geometry file in GEO-DRAW which can, in turn, be passed back to the solid modeller for further manipulation. The close integration of these two modules in the the I-DEAS CAE system reflect the same close relationship held between DOGS and BOXER and is a further example of the considerable advantages gained when designing components using solid modelling systems. While most modellers can pass their geometry to most draughting packages through the medium of an IGES file, the process can be slow, cumbersome and subject to error. The closely integrated nature of packages such as GEOMOD and GEODRAW or of BOXER and DOGS permits a much faster, easier transfer of geometry than is possible using IGES.

SUMMARY

In this chapter we have considered the process of solid modelling and seen how solid model data can be used to integrate the 3-D modelling activity with 2-D draughting. We have also seen how geometric information can be passed from a 2-D draughting system and used to create revolved or prismatic solid models. The full integration of the solid modelling and 2-D draughting activities has, in the most part, been illustrated using the BOXER and DOGS packages. However, we have considered briefly another solid modeller, GEOMOD. This solid modelling system has a number of special modelling features that are not available in the BOXER system. Consequently, the solid model definitions created using the GEOMOD system can be significantly more complex in their shape, e.g. sculptured shapes, and local geometric detail. However, despite the differences between the CSG and B-Rep modelling approaches, the use of the solid model database is much the same for both systems. In the next chapter, we will discuss how the geometric definition of an object created using a solid modeller can be put to further use in other computer-aided activities besides the preliminary definition of the solid model.

11.1 INTRODUCTION

We shall consider in this chapter the integration of CAD with other computer-aided engineering tasks (analysis, manufacture, etc.). We have seen in previous chapters the advantages to be gained from a two-way exchange of data and information in CAD. For example, if a 3-D model of an item is created using a solid modelling system, orthographic views of the item can be generated automatically from the geometric information archived in the solid modelling system database. If the solid modeller is integrated with a 2-D draughting system, then geometric information about the size and shape of the item can be exchanged between the two activities, e.g. the orthographic views of the component can be passed to the 2-D draughting package to produce a fully dimensioned detail drawing of the component. The advantage of this approach is that the integration of these two activities prevents the designer from having to specify the geometric characteristics of an item more than once on the CAD system. This not only saves time, e.g. because the designer does not have to construct the orthographic views of the item from scratch, but ensures that the geometry of a component is represented accurately in both systems. Similarly, if the CAD packages are linked to CAE packages, the same benefits will accrue because the exchange of data can occur across the whole CAE system. Once the geometric characteristics of an item have been defined on the CAD system, in a fully integrated CAE system, that data can be used as the basis for all other tasks where the precise geometry of the item needs to be defined. The PAFEC CAE suite of programs and SDRC's I-DEAS software package are both examples of integrated CAE systems. Not only do these systems include CAD software for 2-D draughting and 3-D modelling, but also packages for analysis and manufacture.

11.2 THE ROLE OF SOLID MODELLING IN AN INTEGRATED CAE SYSTEM

Solid modelling is the only technique currently available that allows the designer to create unambiguous 3-D representations of items on a computer system. The application of solid modelling techniques to computer-aided engineering has increased steadily in recent years. It is clear that this growth will continue in the foreseeable future, and that the solid model database will be at the heart of all integrated CAE systems. Consequently, it is important that the links between the solid modeller and other packages in the CAE system should allow data to be transferred with ease to and from each package and not require the user to reformulate the data into a new structure each time a new set of software is to be used. In systems where this occurs, the designer will be able to create a solid model representation of an item with full knowledge that the geometric data created by this process can be used for other CAE activities.

Of an integrated CAE system of this type, it is often said that engineering drawings are not required because the solid model database provides all the geometric data about the item for its complete manufacture. Certainly the solid modeller provides all the relevant geometric data to define its size and shape, but the engineering drawing is still the medium through which the designer specifies tolerances, surface texture, welding details, heat treatment processes, material type, etc. So while the use of solid modelling may increase, the engineering drawing will still provide a record of all the information relevant for the correctness of the manufactured item to be checked by inspection. Hence, the strong links between solid modelling and draughting must be maintained if all manufacturing information is to be recorded on the CAE system. However, except where 2-D profiles can be used to define 2½-D solid models, it will be future common practice to first use solid modelling as the means for generating an object definition on the CAD database. Also, the engineering drawing may not necessarily be plotted out on to paper. It will become more common for everyone to have access to a graphics display so that the drawing can be displayed directly on the screen. Similarly, it will no longer be necessary to keep a record of the drawing on paper since it can be archived on to disk or tape or alternatively stored on microfiche in a very small space.

As we have seen in Chapter 10, solid modellers provide several features that enable quite complex object definitions to be built from basic geometrical information provided by the designer. The designer may work with 3-D primitives and generate the final solid model by a series of Boolean operations, or he may use 2-D profiles originally drawn on a 2-D draughting system to generate 2½-D solid models, or he may use a mixture of techniques to develop his final solid model definition. An experienced solid model designer will use a combination of techniques chosen to develop the most efficient solid model definition with a minimum of effort and time. When using a CSG solid modeller, e.g. BOXER, a good measure of modelling efficiency is the number of primitives used, the challenge being to devise a sequence of modelling operations that minimizes the use of primitives. However, since it is always possible to devise several alternative approaches to solid modelling of the same item, it is highly likely that different designers will develop different model solutions. It is also highly likely that an individual designer will use different modelling solutions when defining an item a second or third time. Although, once the most effective modelling solution has been devised for a particular item, it is good practice to use the same procedure for repeat models of the same item (or for models of items that have the same physical features, but the relative size or number of which are different, Fig. 11.1). For these items, parametric solid models provide the designer

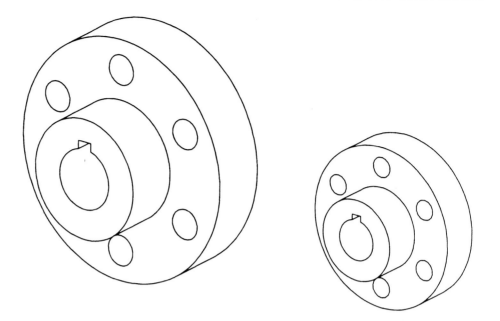

Fig. 11.1 *Parametric solid models of a shaft coupling.*

with a quick means of generating an object definition by specifying a few key dimensions without needing to consider the detail of the modelling sequence.

Figure 11.1 shows two examples of a shaft coupling created with BOXER using the user defined primitive facility. This facility provides the designer with a means of recalling a sequence of modelling operations previously defined and verified by the user. The user defined primitive is created in the same way as the standard primitives, in that the designer must specify a few key dimensions, e.g. diameter of shaft. From these key dimensions a sequence of modelling actions is completed automatically, creating a solid model definition that can be used in exactly the same way as any other solid model definition. Those dimensions not specified by the designer must be calculated during the modelling sequence. The shaft couplings in Fig. 11.1 are fully defined by the shaft diameter. The sizes of the boss, flange and holes are proportional to the shaft diameter, and the number of holes is fixed. Thus from one single dimension, all dimensions are defined.

The BOXER package also includes sixteen predefined parametric solid model definitions (straight pipe, curved pipe, pyramid, hemisphere, nut, etc.). These are referred to as primitives by BOXER, yet each is truly a compound primitive modelled using a combination of the five basic primitives. Again, a limited number of key dimensions allows these objects to be defined fully. A CAD system that has a large library of parametric model definitions will be similar to a 2-D draughting package with a large library of symbols. Items that are in common use will be modelled more quickly, more efficiently and more accurately, if they are created using a parametric model definition.

Once the solid model of an item has been created, the modelling system can be used to determine a number of physical characteristics (volume, mass, moments of inertia, surface area, etc.). The item may also be viewed in several different ways (wire frame, hidden line removed, colour shaded, etc.), or from different viewpoints, or using different projection systems (isometric, perspective, third angle orthographic, etc.). Not only do these images assist the designer in validating the model, but they can be used for several applications besides concept validation. It is common practice to use the screen images created by solid modelling systems for advertizing, product brochures and product documentation. It is also possible to provide pictorial views of more complex assemblies or items to supplement the orthographic views on an engineering drawing. Whilst the view will not be used for defining the item, the pictorial view may assist the recipient of the drawing to comprehend the item of interest.

An additional feature of GEOMOD is a kinematic simulation facility. If a system, composed from a number of objects has parts which can move relative to each other, the parts are said to have **kinematic motion**. The study of kinematics involves the geometry of the parts, their range and direction of movement, together with the position and nature of their axes, rotational or linear. Because the solid modeller contains the complete geometry of the parts, it is possible to derive information, e.g. about the path which a point follows. Thus the sequence of configurations that a kinematic system passes through as it moves can be calculated, stored and displayed. The sequence of motion can be displayed forward or reverse or at a single step at a time to give the overall envelope of operation and automatically check for potential collision of parts. The sequence of movement can be animated if required to run at real operating speeds and the result stored on film or video tape. This avoids the need for the building of expensive physical models to study the kinematics of a part.

When the solid model has been created to the initial satisfaction of the designer, he may wish to have the in-service performance of the solid model analysed using, e.g. finite element analysis (FEA) techniques. This analysis technique allows a comprehensive range of tests to be performed, and often carried out by finite element analysis specialists. In an integrated CAE system, the geometric data required for finite element analysis can be provided directly by the designer to the finite element analysis specialist. The results of this analysis may require a modification to the design of the item, in which case the solid model will need to be modified to implement any changes into the geometric database. The finite element analysis will have to be repeated to ensure that the change has overcome the weaknesses of the original design solution before the designer can be completely satisfied with the validity of his design solution.

The solid model may also be integrated with a specialist modelling system like SAMMIE, Fig. 11.2. SAMMIE allows the designer to represent human forms using solid models that are sized according to standard **anthropomorphic** data. Thereby allowing the designer to consider fully the **ergonomic** aspects of the design solution.

Once the designer is satisfied with his final solution, the solid model data becomes the sole source of information describing the physical geometry of the item. Engineering drawings can be generated directly from the solid model database as we have already seen in Chapter 9. However, linking with manu-

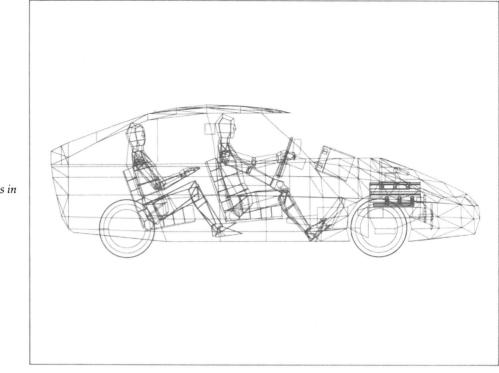

Fig. 11.2 *SAMMIE – a modelling system for representing human beings in ergonomic design studies.*

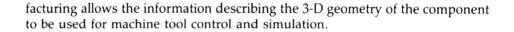

facturing allows the information describing the 3-D geometry of the component to be used for machine tool control and simulation.

11.3 FINITE ELEMENT ANALYSIS

In finite element analysis, a component is broken down into a series of polygons to form a mesh. The applied forces are then recalculated to form component forces at the nodes of the particular meshes which result in stresses. These stresses are then applied to the appropriate nodes of the next mesh element and the resultant stresses at the adjacent nodes are calculated. This process is continued until the stresses have been calculated at every node point right across the object. The production of finite element programs tends to be a specialist business, with different programs available for different geometries and types of problem. Thus finite element analysis programs are provided by specialist software houses, e.g. PAFEC.

PAFEC FE is the finite element analysis program associated with PAFEC's integrated CAE system. It is capable of treating linear, non-linear, static and dynamic load cases. The use of this program for finite element analysis is particularly common in universities and colleges in the UK. The PAFEC **data preparation file** is an ASCII format file that specifies the geometry and mechanical properties of the mesh, and defines the external loads acting on the body. The geometry of the mesh is defined by a list of node co-ordinates sequentially numbered for identification purposes. The topology of the mesh is defined by a list of elements. Each entry in this list specifies the identification numbers of the nodes that define the size, shape and position of each element. The number of elements required to define an object is dependent upon the type of element being used and the accuracy of the results required. The list of elements will also include information about the properties of the element (material type, cross-sectional area, second moments of area, etc.), though the amount of information required will depend upon the type of element being used. The information about the nodes, elements and properties is sufficient for PAFEC FE to define fully the geometric and mechanical characteristics of the mesh. The data preparation file will also contain information about the loads and restraints imposed upon the object. The load information is a list of the nodes to which the external forces and couples are being applied. The list specifies numerically the magnitude and direction of the forces acting at each point. The restraints specify which nodes are unable to move (at least one node must be restrained fully, or else the whole mesh would be free to move in space). PAFEC FE uses the data preparation file to analyse the mesh and determine the stresses that occur at each node. The number of calculations required is immense. For this reason, the normal procedure is to carry out the analysis in batch mode, i.e. not in real-time, but off-line, frequently overnight. This is a most convenient method of working, because there is no requirement for the user to interact with the program during its execution; the data preparation file should contain sufficient information for the analysis to be completed successfully. There are a number of phases in the sequence of analysis tasks performed by the PAFEC FE program. Once each phase is complete, an output data file is generated. These may be used to check the validity of the analysis. The output file from phases 7 and 9 provide all the numerical results for deformation and stress at each node. The stress levels within each element must be interpolated from the values of stress determined for each node defining its topology.

If the number of elements required to define the surface of an object is quite small, the process of dividing the object up into a mesh could be performed by hand and the resultant stresses could be plotted (also by hand) as stress levels or contour lines shown on the surface of the object. However, the majority of objects require large numbers of elements, typically several hundred, and thus a special mesh generation program (or pre-processor) is required. To plot out by hand the resultant stresses as contour lines would take far too long and so the results of a finite element analysis have to be converted back into a visual form using a post-processor.

The PAFEC pre- and post-processor is known as PIGS (PAFEC Interactive Graphics System). PIGS is fully integrated with DOGS 2D and DOGS 3D, allowing 2-D and 3-D geometries to be passed through to the finite element analysis pre-processor using a specialized data transfer file. PIGS can also receive 3-D geometric data from BOXER, and other modelling systems, using the IGES neutral file format. DOGS includes a limited facility for defining elements before the geometry is passed across to PIGS. However, since PIGS provides a wider variety of element types and mesh construction features, it is advisable to use DOGS merely for generating the geometric data defining the

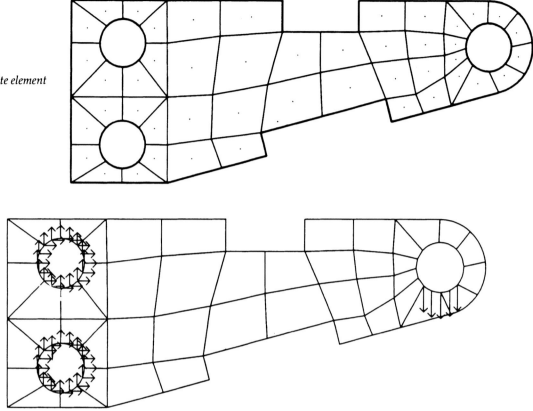

Fig. 11.3 *A finite element mesh.*

Fig. 11.4 *A finite element mesh with loads and restraints displayed.*

boundary of the object. Once in PIGS, the object boundary and the user may define interactively the mesh using a variety of meshing operations, Fig. 11.3. Loads and restraints may also be defined interactively, using the screen cursor to indicate the nodes to be loaded or restrained, Fig. 11.4. Using PIGS allows the validity of the mesh and the loadcase being analysed to be checked before the data preparation file is created. Once the pre-processing is sucessfully completed, PIGS will automatically organize all the user-defined information about nodes, element topologies, element properties, loads and constraints into the data preparation file ready for off-line analysis.

The advantage to the user of the integrated approach to finite element analysis and the use of interactive graphics at the pre-processing stage are twofold. First, if the geometry of the object is passed from, e.g. a 2-D draughting system or 3-D solid modelling system, the user will know that the geometry of the object will be correctly defined in the finite element analysis data preparation file. Second, when the resultant mesh is displayed on the graphics terminal, the experienced user will be able to examine the mesh and modify it appropriately, reducing the number of elements where stress is expected to be low and increasing them in regions where high stress is anticipated. Since a complex structure of elements will take a long time to analyse, there is a great incentive to minimize the number of elements required. For this reason, it may be that only a simple, approximate 3-D model of the geometry is generated initially to give a feel for where the problem area are likely to be encountered. When the designer has developed a satisfactory mesh, it can then be submitted to the finite element analysis program.

Having obtained results from the analysis program it is necessary to display these, superimposed upon the original mesh as a series of contour lines. The different stress levels can be shown on a monochrome display as a series of annotations on each line. However, for complex structures, this is difficult to interpret and it is of greater value to use colour displays where different colours can be used to represent particular stress levels. It then becomes easy to identify areas of stress concentration. PIGS, like most post-processors, provides a variety of mesh display and stress display options, Fig. 11.5, which allow the user to more easily interpret the results being displayed. Because the designer will generally wish to try out the effect of different loads or a variety of geometries, this procedure of pre-processing, analysing and post-processing may have to be repeated many times.

In the I-DEAS system, the finite elements package is called SUPERTAB and

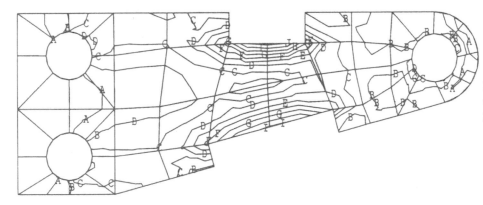

Fig. 11.5 *Stress contours shown using a finite element post-processor.*

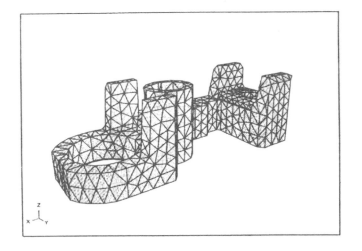

Fig. 11.6 *Automatic mesh generation of a component using a finite element pre-processor.*

consists of a pre-processor mesh generator which can generate automatically solid elements as well as surface meshes from the solid model database defined using GEOMOD, Fig. 11.6. Loads, restraints, couples and material properties can all be specified easily. The finite elements analysis program can be supplied by a specialist software house or a SUPERTAB version can be employed, which can treat both static and dynamic stresses. The results can then be displayed as stress levels using a post-processor. Colour animation may be used where dynamic stresses are present.

Finite element analysis has traditionally been carried out using minicomputers or large mainframe computers because of the immense number of calculations involved. However, as the power of the personal computer has increased so has its ability to undertake finite element analysis. The ANSYS PC/SOLID FEA system from Swanson Analysis Systems is a typical PC-based solid modelling system that provides pre- and post-processing for the PC version of the ANSYS finite element analysis program. Using this system, the designer is able to create 3-D solid models and provide a full 3-D analysis using several thousand elements in the mesh, all based on a PC CAD system. Alternatively, the object can be modelled in AutoCAD and the geometry passed to ANSYS PC in a similar way to PAFEC's DOGS and PIGS. Similar features are available in the SDRC suite of software in which components modelled in GEOMOD can be passed to the finite element program SUPERTAB which also contains pre- and post-processor routines.

In addition to modelling stresses, the finite element method can also be used to model any field effects such as fluid dynamics in determining pressure fields or thermodynamics to determine temperature distributions or in nuclear physics, to determine radiation fields in nuclear reactors.

11.4 COMPUTER-INTEGRATED MANUFACTURE

As discussed in Chapters 9 and 10, in addition to generating the geometry of a part for design purposes, the same geometric database can be used for manufacturing the object. The most usual computer-aided manufacture (CAM) activity is in the use of **numerical control** (NC) machine tools. In a large integrated CAE system, the geometric data from a solid model can be passed directly to the NC program code generator. However, rotational parts can be machined on an NC lathe using a profile of the part which is used to generate the 2½-D solid model by a rotation about the axis of the object. Similarly profiles of parts which are extruded in a 2½-D solid model may be machined using a numerically controlled milling machine. Hence the area of NC machining can often be implemented with a relatively simple 2½-D modelling system. There are a number of specialized NC machining systems commercially available which both design the part profile, allow the cutter tool path and sequence of cuts to be decided upon and then displayed on the graphics screen. From this information, with a minimum of help from the user, the computer can generate the series of coded instructions which the NC machine requires to give the correct machining instructions.

Figure 11.7 shows an example of a PC-based NC system called PATHTRACE.

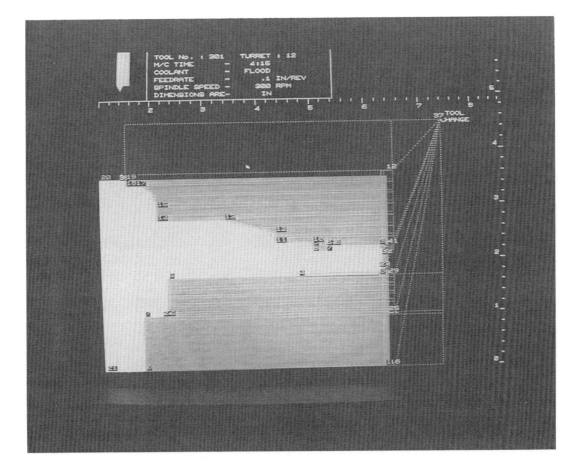

Fig. 11.7 *Tool path simulation of a part to be machined on a numerically controlled lathe.*

The example shows a part displayed on a display screen. The part is to be turned on a NC lathe. The lower horizontal edge represents the centre of rotation. The outer rectangle represents the bar of material from which the part is to be machined. The inner lighter toned shape is the part which is to be machined. The straight lines are the representation of the tool path while it is cutting, while the dotted lines show the rapid traverse of the tool. An information window at the top of the screen displays information about the machine tool program, such as feed rates, spindle speeds, coolant state, the correct position and a machining time estimate. The lathe turning tool can be selected from a library of up to 1800 tools. A representation of the tool currently being used is displayed in the top left-hand corner of the screen. The geometry of the component profile can be first defined using a separate program which has additional commands to make the display easier, such as mirror, add chamfers, blend radii. The geometry of the profile can then be loaded into the appropriate NC program for manufacture on a lathe or mill. Fixtures and clamps can also be shown. The tool path for milled components can be offset automatically from the geometry of the component once the tool diameter is specified, Fig. 11.8.

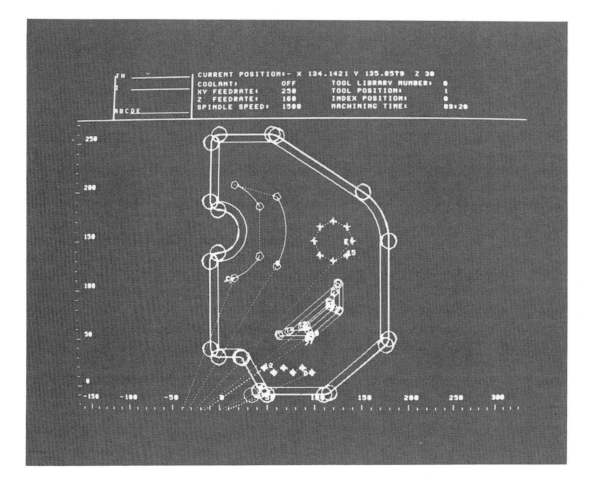

Fig. 11.8 *Tool path simulation of a part to be machined on a numerically controlled milling machine.*

The examples shown in Figs. 11.7 and 11.8 are typical 2½-D components that may be represented on a PC-based CAD system using a 2-D draughting package, e.g. AutoCAD. The geometry of the component profiles can be transferred from the draughting package to PATHTRACE using either IGES or DXF neutral data file standards. Where the component is turned, often only one profile is required to fully define the internal and external shape of the item. Milled components, however, require several profile definitions, allowing external profiles and internal pockets to be machined. In the latter case, each profile is usually machined at preset z heights above the machine table; the orientation of the cutter to the workpiece will remain fixed during the machining cycle. Consequently, the milled surfaces will always have a flat planar form. Where the profile defines the boundary of a pocket, the **area clearance** facility automatically generates in a single command the machine tool paths required to remove all the material within the pocket, Fig. 11.8. Pockets may be cleared with or without **islands**. Figure 11.8 also shows two standard machining cycles, e.g. drilling, tapping, boring, where the positions of the hole centres are marked by crosses. These locations will be used several times during a standard machining cycle to position the tool during each operation. For example, a tapping cycle will usually involve three operations to centre drill, drill and tap each hole. Thus, when using NC machining packages such as PATHTRACE, it is possible to generate machining routines for quite complex 3-D component geometries from a series of relatively simple 2-D profiles. This level of NC machining technology is suitable for the majority of engineering applications, so a fully integrated CAD/CAM system can be built around PC-based CAD/CAM software linked to basic NC lathes and milling machines.

The PAFEC CAE system has its own NC machining system known as DOGS NC. This system is linked directly to DOGS 2D using a specialized exchange data file. The file contains a series of 2-D profiles that are defined separately using DOGS 2D. Each profile is a closed boundary of straight line and circular arc segments that are identified either manually using the screen cursor, or automatically by DOGS using boundary search routines. When the exchange datafile is being generated, the z heights of each 2-D profile must be specified. In this way, DOGS NC receives information about the 3-D nature of the component being represented and is able to organize the profiles with respect to z depth in its 3-D database. The NC machining facilities provided by DOGS NC enable machining routines to be generated and displayed on the graphics screen in a manner similar to PATHTRACE. Once the machining routines have been devised and simulated using DOGS NC, the coded instructions required to control numerically the appropriate machine tool (e.g. rotate cutter, turn coolant on) are automatically generated by the software.

Components that have sculptured surfaces, must be manufactured using multi-axis machine tools. These machines provide full x, y, z position control of the tool and orientate the machining head to ensure that the axis of the cutting tool remains normal to the sculptured surface at all times. This necessarily requires the component to be modelled using a 3-D surface or solid modelling system, an NC machining system that is able to generate machine tool paths from 3-D surface geometry, and a five-axis milling machine. The level of technology involved is significantly more complex and expensive to implement than the systems considered above, therefore the use of such integrated CAD/CAM systems is restricted to specialized engineering applications, e.g. tooling for dies, moulds, forgings, where the full 3-D surface machining capability of the system is fully exploited.

PATHTRACE has the capability to generate machining routines for ruled surfaces, surfaces of revolution, Coons patches, B-spline and Bezier spline surfaces, and non-rational B-spline surfaces which can be generated within the PATHTRACE system or received from other CAD systems using the IGES neutral data file system. The PAFEC CAE system, however, must be linked directly, or via IGES, to a specialist NC machining system known as GNC (graphic numerical control) for these complex surface forms, Fig. 11.9. In 3-D NC machining systems, the machine tool, fixtures, clamps, vices, headstock, and workpiece are all represented in the 3-D workspace. Figure 11.10 shows an example generated using Schlumberger Technologies BravoNC package. Thus machining routines can be visually tested for clashes between, e.g. the tool and the fixtures.

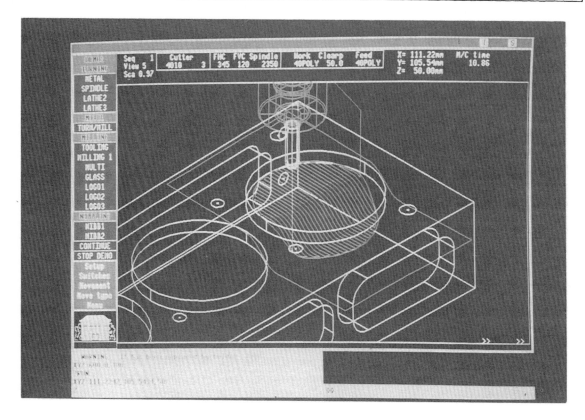

Fig. 11.9 *Tool path simulation for a 3-D surface machined on a numerically controlled milling machine. (GNC)*

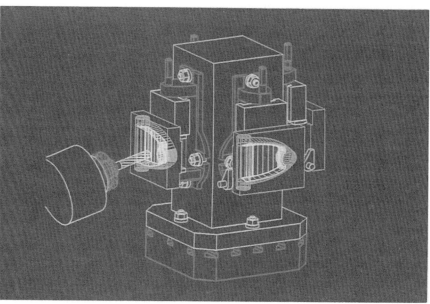

Fig. 11.10 *Modelling of fixtures and clamps to check for possible tool collisons during the machining cycle. (BravoNC)*

NC machining packages allow the user to generate machining routines from geometrical data created using 2-D or 3-D CAD systems. Integration with CAD ensures that the geometric representation of the component is the same in both systems. The simulation of machining cycles on the graphics screen allows the sequence of operation to be thoroughly checked, reducing the likelihood of, for example hitting fixtures, machining clamps, during the machining cycle, before the coded instructions are transferred to the NC machine tool itself.

11.5 SIMULATION

In addition to the above simulation on the graphics screen of the NC machine showing the cutting tool moving around the part, it is possible to simulate other activities graphically as an aid to manufacture.

11.5.1 MACHINE TOOL LAYOUTS

One of the more usual applications of graphical simulation as an aid to manufacture is in the motion of machine tools. A typical example is shown in Fig. 11.11. Here the physical motions of a robot are simulated together with those of

Fig. 11.11 *Simulation of a robot and machine tool cell. (GRASP)*

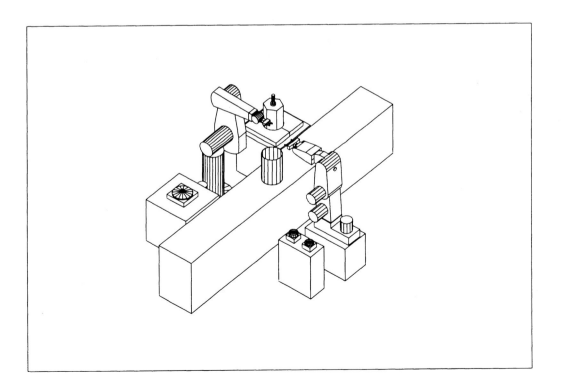

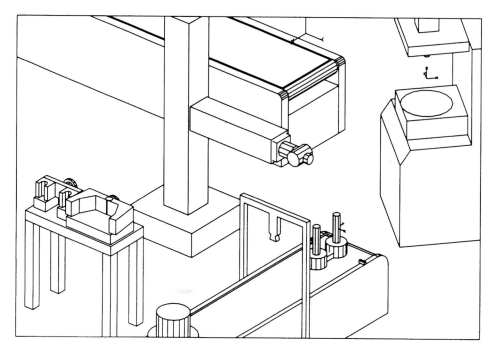

Fig. 11.12 *Simulation of a robot and manufacturing cell.*

adjacent machine tools, conveyors, etc. The individual motions are built up using a specially designed program called GRASP (BYG Systems), which facilitates the display of the outlines of various machines and their relative motions. Using this approach it is possible to select the robot structure which is the most appropriate for a task, and then to try out various movements in relation to the machine tool to ensure it can carry out the required tasks.

If the robot and machine tool dimensions are sufficiently accurate it is possible to decide on the sequence and range of motions which the robot must have to carry out the task. Figure 11.12 shows another example of a manufacturing cell modelled using GRASP. In the foreground is the **inward-conveyor** that brings components to the workplace for machining. To the right is a vertical drilling machine, and in the background is the **outward-conveyor**. There are two different components that require machining on the conveyor. The robot in the centre of screen has to pick each item from the inward-conveyor, transport it to the drilling machine, before finally placing it on the outward-conveyor. To pick up the component, the robot must first select the appropriate gripper from the table on the left. Figures 11.13 to 11.19 show the sequence of motions required to carry out this task. This sequence is animated on the graphics screen so that the robot motion can be visualized by the user. All the items are modelled in GRASP using a 3-D surface modeller, thus GRASP is able to detect clashes between items by testing whether any surfaces intersect. The user must modify the sequence of robot motions if the clash is to be avoided. Since the items are modelled in 3-D, wire frame, hidden line removed and colour shaded images of the workplace can be generated, Fig. 11.20.

The robot simulation can then be employed to produce a program of robot

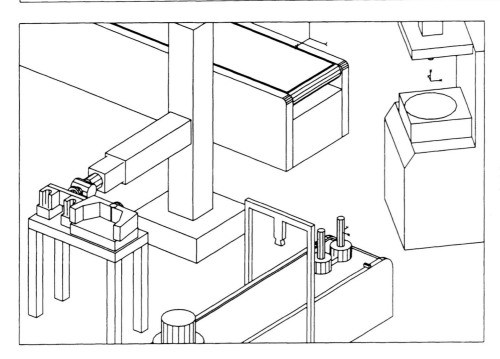

Fig. 11.13 *Robot moves towards gripper.*

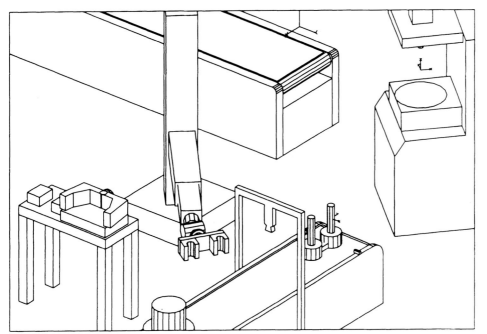

Fig. 11.14 *Gripper selected.*

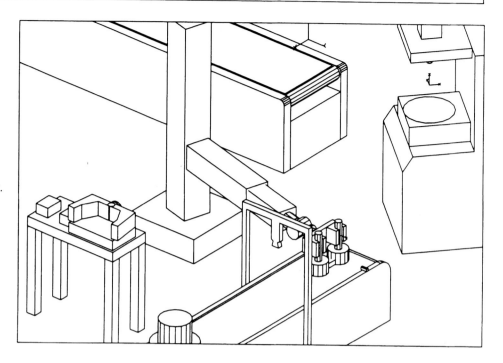

Fig. 11.15 *Component picked from inward conveyor.*

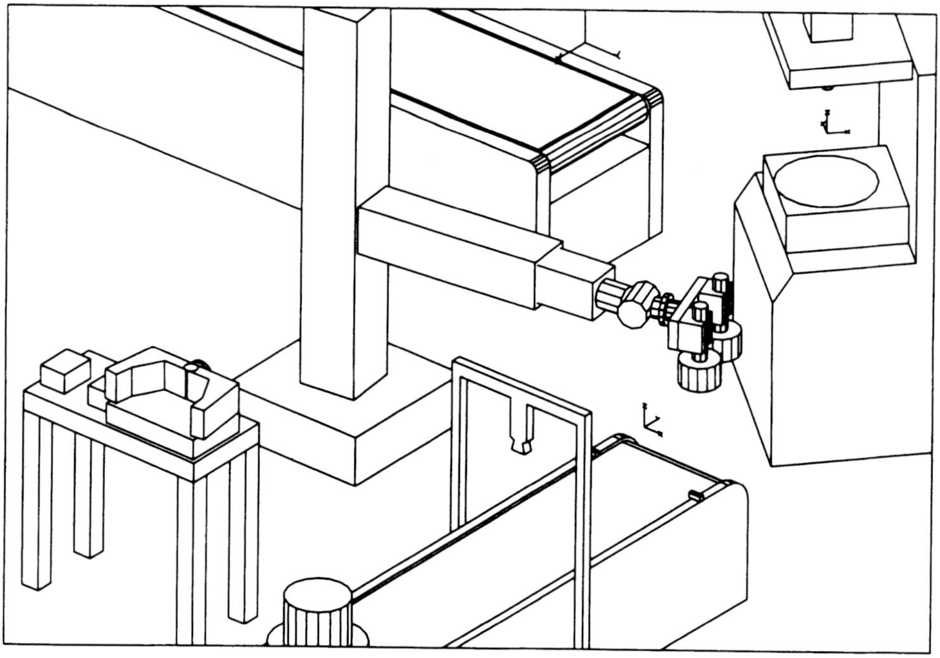

Fig. 11.16 *Component moved to vertical drill.*

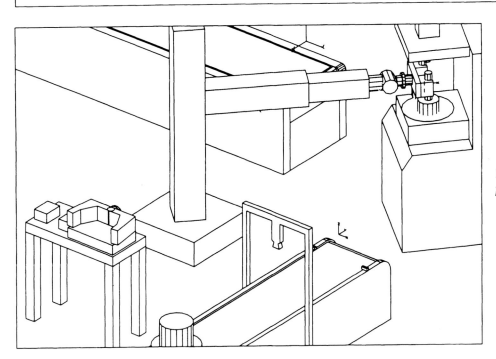

Fig. 11.17 *Component placed on vertical drill.*

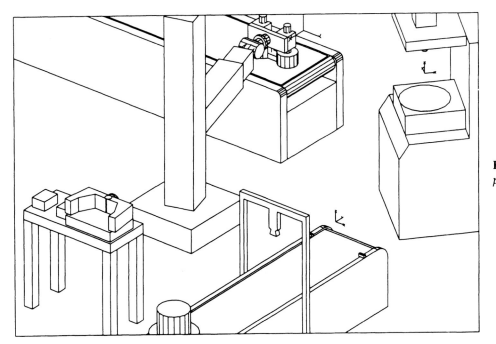

Fig. 11.18 *Component placed on outward conveyor.*

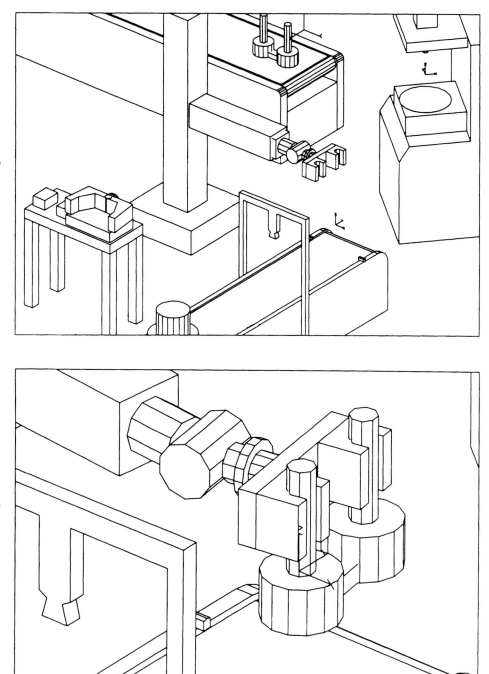

Fig. 11.19 *Robot returns to start position.*

Fig. 11.20 *Detailed view of component being held by robot.*

motions which can be sent direct to the robot controller. Thus the robot can be programmed for a new task off-line so that it can switch directly from the task to another. This avoids the robot and associated machines being out of use, often for long periods of time while the robot is taught a new sequence of motions by leading through by hand. The use of graphic simulation for off-line programming of robots, machine tools and automatically guided vehicles can lead to considerable improvements in manufacturing efficiency.

11.5.2 PROCESS PLANNING

A further use for graphical simulation is as an adjunct to the manufacture planning process. As an aid to planning the layout of a manufacture activity, computers have for some time been employed to simulate a series of manufacture processes. Thus the time to order a part to be made, the time for the material to be drawn from stores and the time to manufacture on a variety of machines can all be simulated as a process in the computer. The planning department can then decide on whether to bring in additional lathes, milling machines, etc., to improve the production rate in order to meet required delivery dates. The effects of the additional machines can then be judged by running the computer model of the manufacture process in a speeded up time. The buildup of a queue of parts at various stages of manufacture can be used to assess the necessity of speeding up machining cycles or of introducing new machine tools at various stages. Traditionally the throughput, individual cycle times and other data were given as a large sequence of numbers which required considerable skill to interpret. The advent of cheap graphical display systems enables the processes to be displayed on a screen in a form which can be understood easily.

The workshop foreman can now use a package with graphical display to determine the best machine utilization given the current availability of machine tools at any given time. Figure 11.21 shows the simulation of a flexible manufacture cell displayed using a graphical simulation program called DRAFT. The cell consists of two lathes, a grinding machine and gauging station. The input of orders, selection of raw materials from stores and the final packaging of the parts is also simulated. With a known distribution of frequency of orders, together with machine performance, the likely production can be displayed dynamically with a full day's production being simulated in a few minutes, with various bottleneck stages identified. Figure 11.22 shows the same cell simulated with an additional packer to reduce the bottleneck which was occurring at the final packing stage.

11.6 ELECTRONIC CIRCUIT DESIGN

Electronic circuit design is a specialized activity that utilizes computer graphics for many of its tasks. The design of an electronic circuit has two distinct phases. In the first phase, the structure of the circuit is devised using various logic devices that are connected together to form the required operational performance. The logic circuit can be drawn using a 2-D draughting system with a li-

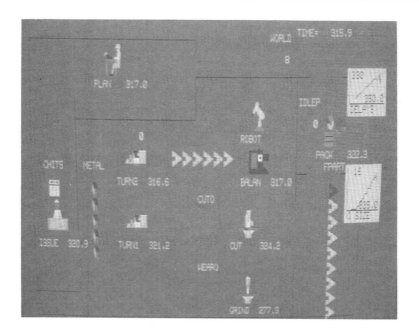

Fig. 11.21 *Simulation of the production capabilities of a flexible manufacture cell, showing bottleneck at packing station.*

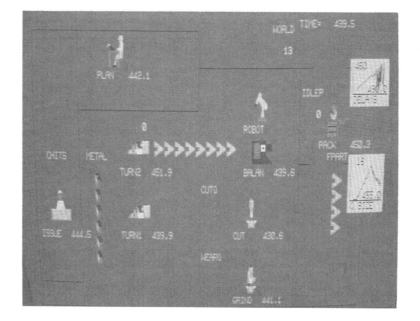

Fig. 11.22 *Simulation of a flexible manufacture cell showing effect of an additional packer.*

brary of logic device symbols (a simple logic circuit has been drawn in Chapter 7, Fig. 7.15). However, this graphical information can be used by the computer to test the logic of the circuit, in which case, the resulting output of the circuit is determined for every possible state that the input channels might take. Once the

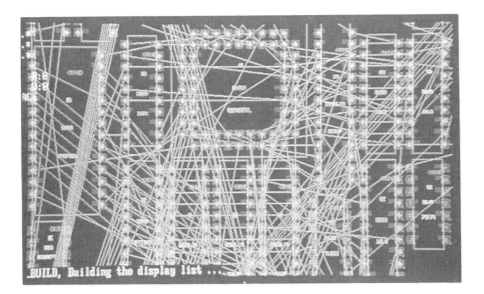

Fig. 11.23 *A printed circuit board displayed as a 'ratsnest' of connections.*

designer is satisfied that the logic of the circuit provides the desired results, the physical design of the circuit can commence.

In this second phase of circuit design, the logic circuit is transformed into an electronic circuit layout in which electronic components are positioned on a printed circuit board (PCB), or silicon chip, and the connections between the various logic devices made. Since a single electronic component may contain

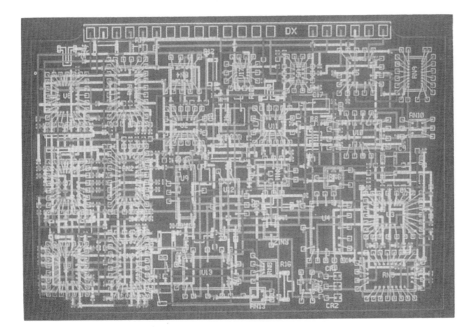

Fig. 11.24 *A multi-layered printed circuit board with all connections organized to avoid short circuits.*

several logic devices, many circuit connections will need to be made to that component. At first the connections between the devices are linked directly by straight lines, a form of display known as 'ratsnesting', Fig. 11.23. The electronic components can be moved interactively to new positions on the PCB to mini-

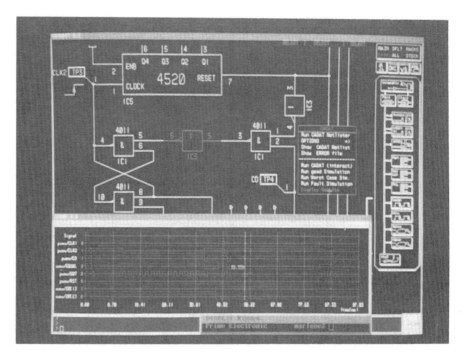

Fig. 11.25 *Simulation of the dynamic performance of the electronic circuit.*

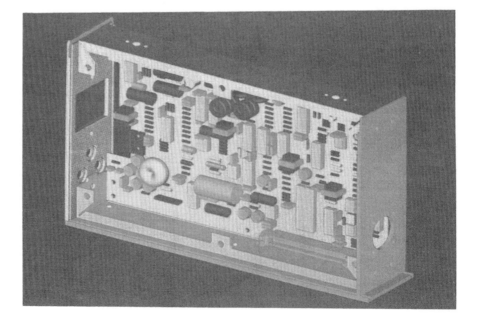

Fig. 11.26 *A solid model of a printed circuit board.*

mize the congestion of the ratsnest. However, many of the connections will overlap and so must be re-routed to avoid short circuits.

The layout of the PCB connections is a task that can be carried out manually or automatically, depending upon the sophistication of the electronic design software. Modern PCBs have multiple layers on which the circuit connections can be organized, Fig. 11.24. For such boards, a colour graphics display is essential for the layour activity, because the connections on each layer need to be displayed in different colours.

Once the layout of the PCB has been finalized, the dynamic performance of the electronic circuit may be simulated, e.g. the speed of response of the circuit will depend upon the total length of the connections between various components, Fig. 11.25. The layout can be used to generate a solid model of the PCB for testing the mechanical properties of the design, Fig. 11.26, and to provide information suitable for computer-aided manufacture of the PCB.

11.7 TWO EXAMPLES OF THE APPLICATION OF AN INTEGRATED CAE SYSTEM

Example 11.1

An example of an application of the GEOMOD solid modelling system in operation is shown in Figs. 11.27 to 11.41. This shows the design of a robotic manipulator. The overall final assembly is shown in Fig. 11.27. The first step is to lay out the overall configuration of joints and drives using a mechanism synthesis program for determining initial sizes of links and pulleys, as shown in Fig. 11.28. The geometry of new parts can be defined as shown in Figs. 11.29 to 11.32, which give details of the shoulder rotation joint and the associated upper arm link. Figure 11.29 shows the buildup of the exterior shape using construction geometry, while Fig. 11.30 shows the desired profile. Figure 11.31 shows the profile extruded to the desired thickness to create a solid object. The recess and holes are created by subtracting features.

So far no interior surfaces have been designed and thus the object is assumed by the computer to be solid. As the robot is to be fabricated from plate material, the thickness of the main block is specified to define an interior surface. The two plate lugs are also joined at this stage, Fig. 11.32. Note the facetted construction of circles as an approximation for speed of display, although the full, precise geometry is also held in the database for exact display tasks such as interference checks. The structural integrity of the upper arm can now be analysed using the SUPERTAB finite element analysis package. The results of this analysis can be displayed on the structure for ease of interpretation, Fig. 11.33, and appropriate modifications made to the design of the upper arm before the process continues.

The remainder of the parts are specified together with their connections as in Fig. 11.34. The arm is then put together, Fig. 11.35, and different configurations of the design tested to check the range of movements. Structural interference and packaging restraints can also be investigated. A potential interference zone between the waist and the forearm can be seen in Fig. 11.36 which leads to the need for an additional extension to the waist joint which can be tested in Fig.

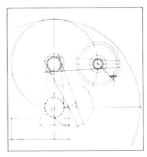

Fig. 11.27 *Final assembly of a robotic arm.*

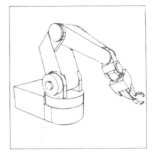

Fig. 11.28 *Kinematic layout of the arm.*

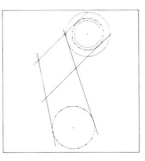

Fig. 11.29 *Definition of the upper arm shape.*

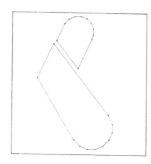

Fig. 11.30 *Profile of the upper arm side piece.*

Fig. 11.31 *Pieces for the upper arm.*

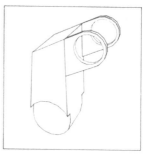

Fig. 11.32 *Completed upper arm.*

Fig. 11.33 *Strain distribution in the upper arm shown using a finite element post-processor.*

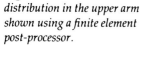

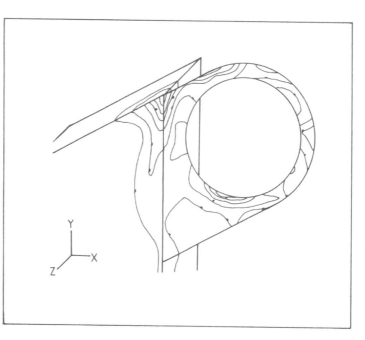

Fig. 11.34 *Exploded view of the components which make up the robot.*

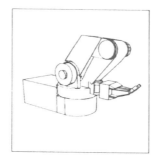

Fig. 11.35 *A different position of the robot.*

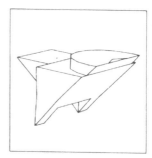

Fig. 11.36 *Interference zone between the robot wrist and forearm.*

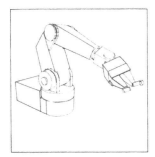

Fig. 11.37 *A modified design of the robot wrist.*

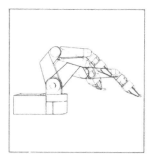

Fig. 11.38 *Robot trajectory using kinematic analysis.*

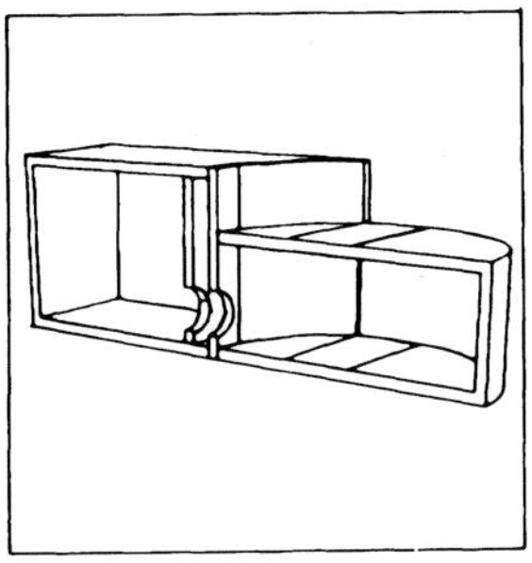

Fig. 11.39 *Sectioned view of the base platform.*

11.37. A check on the possible trajectories is carried out using the kinematics analysis package, Fig. 11.38. Detailed design of individual components is aided by the ability to take sectional views from such assemblies and exploded views. Figure 11.39 shows a sectional view of the base, while a complete subassembly of a drive joint is sectioned in Fig. 11.40. The drive joint is also shown as an exploded view in Fig. 11.41.

Example 11.2

This example shows an application of a 3-D surface modelling system know as DUCT (from Deltacam Systems Limited) which has been used by subcontractors of the Ford Motor Company to manufacture an exhaust manifold casting, Fig. 11.42. Using DUCT, a designer is able to construct complex surface shapes from a series of cross-sections placed on spines, Fig. 11.43. This initial data may be created within DUCT itself, or as in this example, transferred from Ford's Computervision CAD system into DUCT using the IGES data exchange system. From this initial profile data, DUCT automatically creates the 3-D surface geometry of each manifold tract, blending the surfaces where they intersect, Fig. 11.44. The internal shape of the exhaust manifold is also represented. This design data was used by the foundery and patternmaker to create the final DUCT model, Fig. 11.45, from which the outside pattern and core box patterns could be made. Figs. 11.46 to 11.48 show the stages in manufacture of the core, and Figs. 11.49 to 11.51 show the stages in manufacture of the pattern. In both cases the surface geometry of the DUCT models have been used to generate NC milling routines for the manufacture of the casting patterns, models of which are shown in Fig. 11.52.

The exchange of design data between the Ford Motor company and its subcontractors occurred entirely using the IGES exchange standard. At no time were paper drawings used to exchange information. Thus integration occurred between different organizations with specialist knowledge and skills in each CAE activity. This broader approach to the integration of CAE is being keenly pursued by several manufacturing organizations.

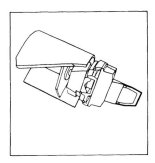

Fig. 11.40 *Sectioned view of the joint drive.*

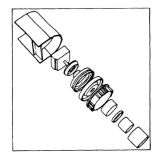

Fig. 11.41 *Exploded view of the joint drive.*

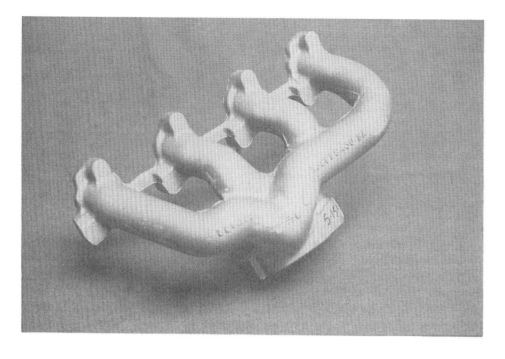

Fig. 11.42 *An engine exhaust manifold casting*

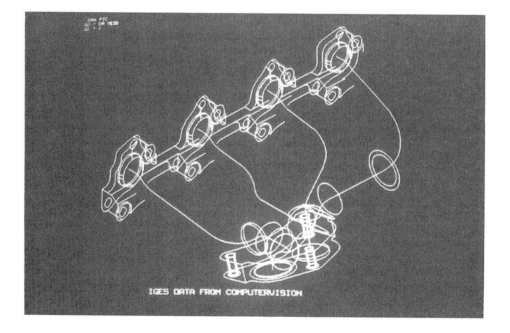

Fig. 11.43 *Initial geometric data input via IGES.*

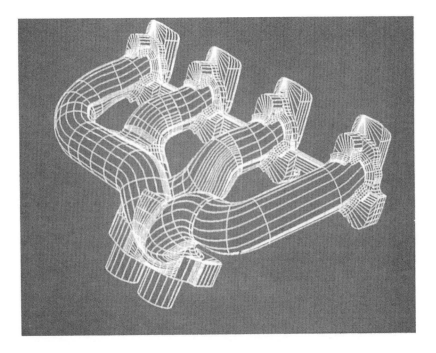

Fig. 11.44 *Surface model of an exhaust manifold.*

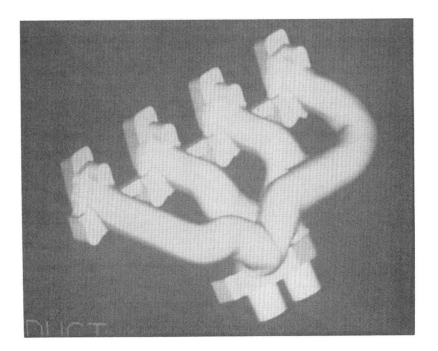

Fig. 11.45 *Shaded image of the exhaust manifold showing the internal casting core.*

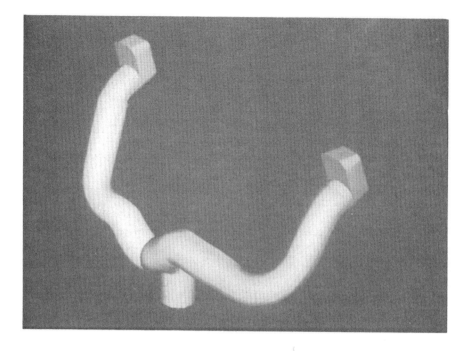

Fig. 11.46 *Computer model of the outer core.*

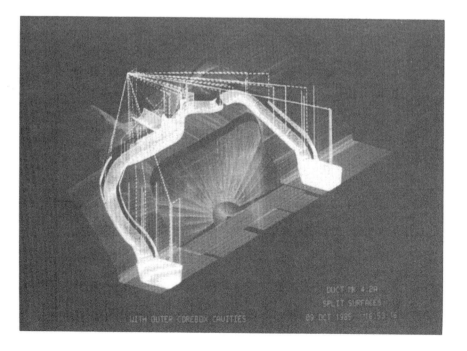

Fig. 11.47 *Tool path simulation for the manufacture of the outer core box using a numerically controlled milling machine.*

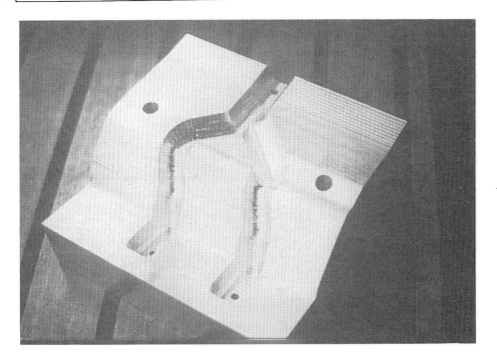

Fig. 11.48 *One half of the finished outer core box.*

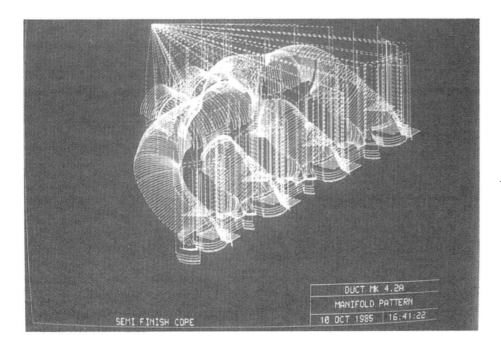

Fig. 11.49 *Tool path simulation for the manufacture of the exhaust manifold pattern.*

Fig. 11.50 *Rough machining of the pattern using a numerically controlled milling machine.*

Fig. 11.51 *Finished exhaust manifold pattern.*

Fig. 11.52 *Pattern and core modelled in resin.*

11.8 THE IMPLEMENTATION OF A FULLY INTEGRATED CAE SYSTEM

The computer-based activities considered in this text have traditionally been carried out in isolation from the other activities using specialist applications packages. In each case, the use of the computer can often be justified by identifying specific benefits gained by this approach. For example using a simple draughting system may reduce drawing production times, result in higher quality hard copies, reduce drawing retrieval times, simplify drawing archiving, etc. Similarly, the use of finite element analysis allows the designer to assess quickly, for example, the load-bearing capability of an item, implement a design change if necessary and re-appraise the performance of the modified part. In this chapter, and Chapters 9 and 10, we have seen how these different activities may be linked by the use of a common database of information from which geometric data can be transferred between the different computer application packages. In this way design, analysis and manufacture become fully integrated in a single CAE system.

The benefits of a fully integrated CAE system are much broader than the specific benefits that can be identified for each applications package. For example, an organization that invests in a fully integrated CAE system might seek to design better products, bring the product to the market more quickly and do so with more profit. To achieve these goals, however, the specific benefits of each part of the CAE system must be realized, e.g. the time taken to produce a detailed engineering drawing can be significantly reduced if all the item is modelled fully using a solid modelling system, orthographic views passed to the draughting system where the auto-dimensioning facility, the symbols library, etc., should be utilized to complete the drawing quickly.

Therefore, not only is it important to understand fully the specific benefits of each applications package, and ensure that these are realized, but it is important to develop an overall strategy of approach that identifies what type of information needs to be exchanged and how the individual elements of the whole CAE system are to be linked together. The implementation of a fully integrated CAE system will necessarily require fundamental changes to existing work practices and procedures, e.g. 3-D solid modelling may become the core design activity for design conception and evaluation, therefore these changes must be introduced gradually and the workforce retrained as appropriate.

The implementation of a fully integrated CAE system cannot be undertaken lightly; it is an expensive and important strategic change for any company to make. If the broader benefits of such a system are to be achieved fully, a great deal of effort must be made in the early planning stages before specific equipment or software is purchased. This necessarily involves several stages of work, which if carried out thoroughly, will indicate clearly the likely success of the fully integrated CAE approach within the company.

To begin with, the operating and trading objectives of the company should be reviewed and future goals and objectives identified. A long-term plan should be devised from which an idealized model of how the company will operate in the future can be developed. This model should not be constrained by present work methods, practices or technology, but should define the desired *modus operandi*, e.g. how information is to be transferred within the company and between customers and subcontractors. The specific details of how this is to be achieved, though, should not be considered at this stage.

Next, the present structure and organization of the company should be reviewed to ensure that all the activities within the company are understood fully. The nature of, and use of information should be examined in detail, identifying where information is first generated and how it is used subsequently. The changes that must be made to achieve the future goals can then be identified. An individual person must be identified who has a complete understanding of the newly defined goals and objectives of the company, and who appreciates the benefits that a fully integrated CAE system will bring to the company. He should be made responsible for developing the implementation plan and guiding the company through its changeover period to a fully integrated CAE approach to product design and manufacture.

A review of present CAE technologies will allow an assessment to be made of what is currently feasible and at what price. An awareness of future changes or improvements in the technology must also be gained. With this information, a short-term implementation plan can be devised. In the short term, concentrate on the tasks that are most crucial to the success of the new system. If these can be implemented successfully, it is more likely that the long-term plan, too, will be successful. In devising a short-term strategy, however, the objectives of the long-term plan should not be jeopardized by a poor choice of equipment or software that prevents the development of the CAE system from continuing in future years. A detailed specification of the fully integrated CAE system must be prepared. This document should clearly and precisely define the required characteristics of the hardware and software, the technical support required, and the operating procedures by which information will be stored and exchanged between the various CAE activities.

At this stage, a clear and concise definition of the hardware and software characteristics of the CAE system will have emerged. A strategy of system operation, that specifies how data and information are to be used, will also have been defined fully. The selection and purchase of equipment and software can now commence. As we have seen in this chapter, a fully integrated CAE system can be based upon personal computers, intelligent workstations or minicomputers, with design data generated using 3-D or 2-D modelling systems. The choice of technology most appropriate to the company's needs can only be judged by comparing the facilities of each system with the capabilities demanded by the CAE system specification. If the demands of the specification are satisfied by the hardware and software mix chosen, a fully integrated CAE system will emerge that should provide the means to satisfy the long-term goals of the company. However, these goals are not going to be achieved immediately. The in-house development of the system may take many years, during which time a gradual change between traditional work practices and new work practices will take place. It should also be remembered that a continuing investment will be required, not just in puchasing equipment, but also in annual maintenance charges for both hardware and software. Software maintenance implies that the new release of software will be available automatically together with the support, advice and documentation from the supplying company. However, the purchaser must also be prepared for the new software release to require more disk space and memory to run the enhanced, updated software. This can cause problems for a company's plans for expansion as well as requiring in-house investment in new documentation and training.

With the CAE system installed, an individual or group of people will be required to manage the everyday operation of the system. New operators will have to be trained to use the various packages and equipment, which necessitates time away from current production work. Operators must be selected who are keen and eager to learn. Training should begin with the basic tasks, and only when these tasks have been mastered, should the training be extended to more demanding tasks. Good work practices should be developed from the outset, with standard work procedures devised for all to follow. These procedures must be tried and tested and recorded in a suitable document that has been prepared in-house. This will ensure that all users will operate the CAE system in the same way, so that the database of information they generate can be fully understood and utilized by any user at a later date. During the initial period of use, the development of the system must progress at a controlled rate. Short-term goals must be specified, so that the success of the new system can be measured at an early stage. Speed of operation is not a good measure of success at this stage, though reliability and efficient work practice is. It is essential to demonstrate these successes and identify the specific benefits gained by operation of the system to other people in the company. Their confidence and support must be gained as early as possible if the system is to be implemented fully.

Once the system has been established firmly, seek new opportunities to expand the use of the system both inside and outside the company. Continue to demonstrate the capabilities of the system and educate people about the benefits of a fully integrated CAE approach. Be prepared to exchange information with customers or clients. Determine the features of the CAE system that are common to their systems, and establish reliable links between the systems. In the main, continue to develop more efficient work practices that exploit fully the capabilities of the whole system, maintaining an awareness of technological developments that may further enhance the speed and efficiency of the system. Continue to review whether the broader benefits of the system, identified at the very start of the project, are being realized. However, if the implementation procedure described has been thoroughly executed, there is no reason why any company cannot benefit in many aspects by the installation of a fully integrated CAE system.

SUMMARY

In this chapter we have considered various specialized CAE tasks. The use of computer graphics enables these activities to be linked directly with the design activity, allowing the full integration of design, analysis and manufacture in a single CAE system. A procedure for implementing a CAE system has been described. All of the most common applications of computer graphics in the engineering process have now been described, and although a limited number of software packages have been described, it is hoped that the fundamental principles of the CAE approach have been demonstrated adequately. In the next chapter are some exercises for you to experiment with this approach using your own CAE system.

Exercises 12

Exercise 12.1
Using a 2-D draughting system, construct a file of a standard drawing sheet which can then be retrieved from the library for use in drawing exercises. The standard drawing sheet should provide the following information:

1. title;
2. drawing number;
3. draughtsman name;
4. projection system symbol;
5. drawing scale;
6. dimension units;
7. date;
8. organization name/logo;
9. standard tolerances and surface textures;
10. warning messages, e.g. DO NOT SCALE.

Exercise 12.2
Figure 12.1 shows four blocks drawn in Third Angle projection. Use a 2-D draughting system to construct a three-view First Angle projection of each block including a sectioned view to show the hidden details. Add a representative selection of dimensions.

What facilities would you use in your draughting software to rearrange the views to create a Third Angle projection drawing?

Exercise 12.3
Using a 2-D draughting system, draw isometric drawings of the four blocks shown in Fig. 12.1.

Exercise 12.4
Figure 12.2 is a bar chart giving comparisons between the production by a manufacturing firm in tonnes for the past nine years. The chart was drawn with the aid of a CAD system. Use your CAD system to construct a bar chart for the following set of figures. These figures show the variations in the share price of a firm during the past year.

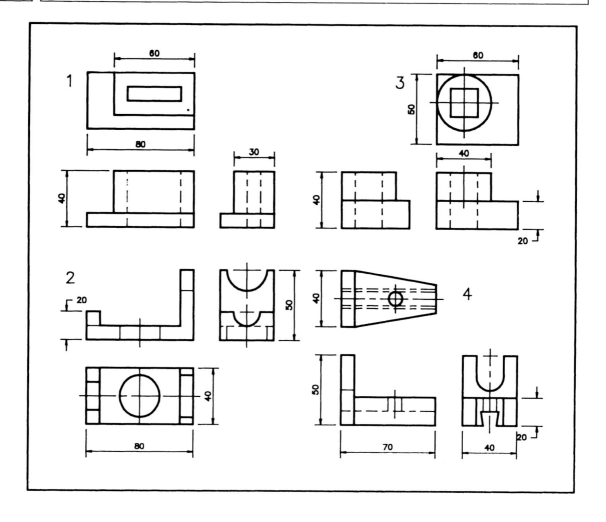

Fig. 12.1 *Four blocks.*

January	100p	July	124p
February	112p	August	108p
March	120p	September	104p
April	135p	October	96p
May	150p	November	104p
June	140p	December	110p

You could also construct a line graph for the same set of figures. Which type of graph do you think shows up the rise and fall in the share value to the best advantage?

Exercise 12.5
Figure 12.3 is a graph showing three sine waves superimposed on each other. Use your CAD system to construct a similar graph for a 10 Hz sine wave during a time period of 1 second.

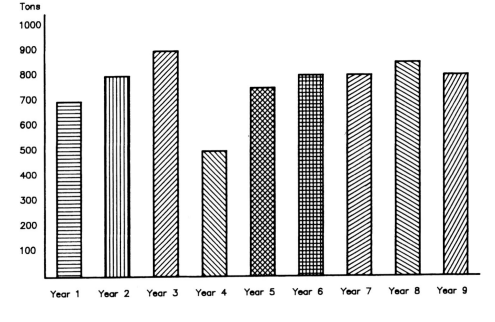

Fig. 12.2 *Bar chart showing annual production output.*

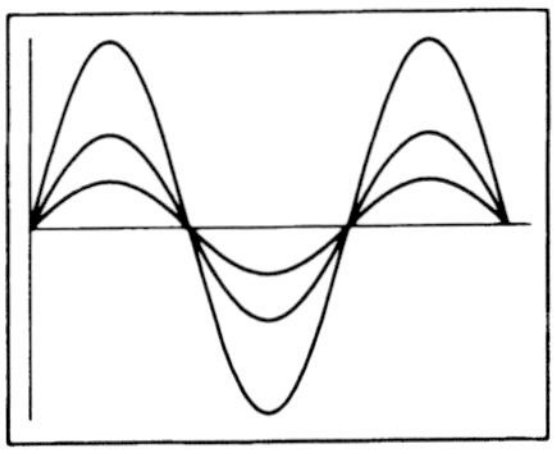

Exercise 12.6

Figure 12.4 shows an outline plan of a small bungalow. Construct a full plan view using the building drawing symbols shown on p.181. You may have to build up a small set of library symbol files on your CAD system before attempting this exercise.

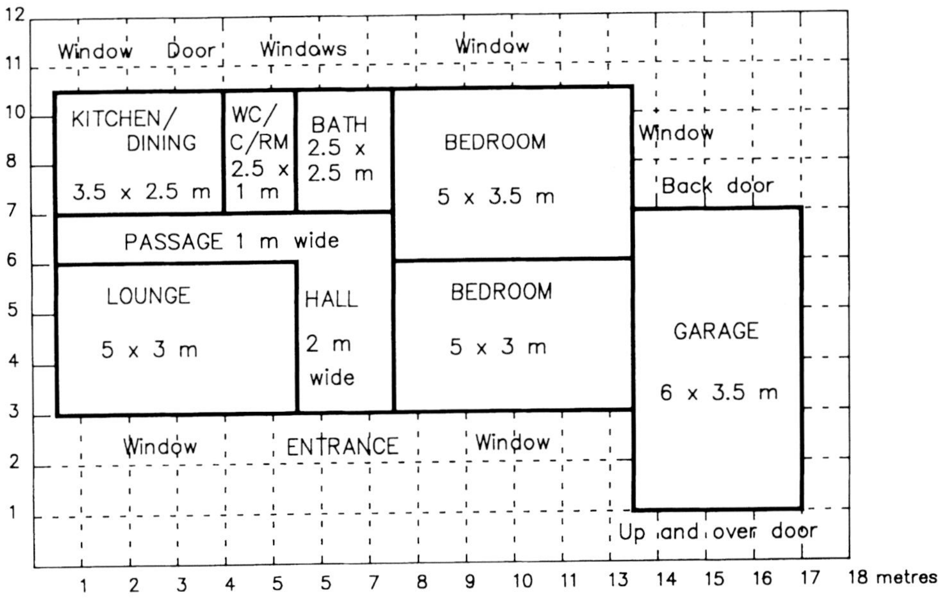

Fig. 12.3 *Three sine waves.*

Fig. 12.4 *Plan of a bungalow.*

Exercise 12.7
Use a 2-D draughting system to create a Third Angle projection of the universal joint yoke detailed in Fig. 6.11, p.151. The drawing should be fully dimensioned with appropriate tolerances.

Exercise 12.8
Use a 2-D draughting system to draw an isometric view of the universal joint yoke shown in Fig. 6.11.

Discuss how a 3-D solid model of the yoke could be used to aid the generation of the drawing in an integrated CAD system.

Exercise 12.9
Create a library of drawing symbol files for standard parts (nuts, bolts, washers, etc.).

Discuss the merits of parametric symbols whereby a few key dimensions are used to define automatically all the other dimensions of the symbol.

Exercise 12.10
Figure 12.5 is an exploded orthographic view of a tailstock clamp from a screw cutting lathe (drawn with the aid of AutoCAD). The clamp is assembled as follows.

1. Part 1 fits into the 10 mm diameter hole in Part 2 and is held in position with an M5 grub screw.
2. Part 2 fits into the 10 mm diameter hole in Part 3.
3. Part 3 fits into the slot in Part 5 and is prevented from dropping out of the slot by the nut Part 4.

When the five parts are assembled, they can be slid into the bed of the lathe and by turning the handle (Part 1) through about 20°, the assembly is locked onto the lathe bed by the cam action of the movement of the spindle of Part 2.

Draw in Third Angle projection, to include the sectional view A–A, an assembled drawing of the tailstock clamp.

Exercise 12.11
Figures 12.6 and 12.7 show details of the various parts of a water pump from a domestic washing machine. The pump is driven by a friction wheel which engages on a patterned rubber ring fitting over Part 5 of the pump. The rubber ring is not included in the detail drawings and should not be included in the drawing produced as an answer to this exercise.

Using a 2-D draughting system, draw a sectioned view taken centrally through the assembled water pump at a scale of 2:1.

NOTE: Parts 1, 2, 3, 4 and 5 are assembled together and held by Part 6. This subassembly is then held in Part 7 with a gasket between Parts 3 and 7 by four nuts and bolts (Part 9).

Exercise 12.12
Use a 2-D draughting system to construct orthographic views of the objects shown in Figs. 12.8. and 12.9. From these views, create 2-D profiles of each

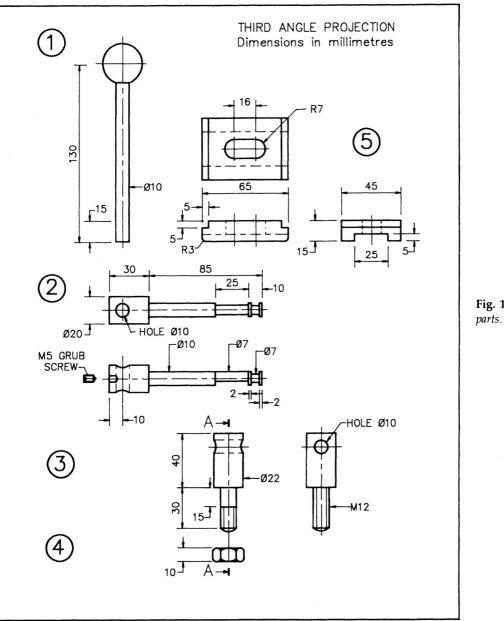

Fig. 12.5 *Tailstock clamp parts.*

object and use these to generate 2½-D extrusions of each using a modelling system.

If possible, use the modeller to calculate the volume of material in each object, and list any geometric properties your CAD system is able to calculate from the 3-D database.

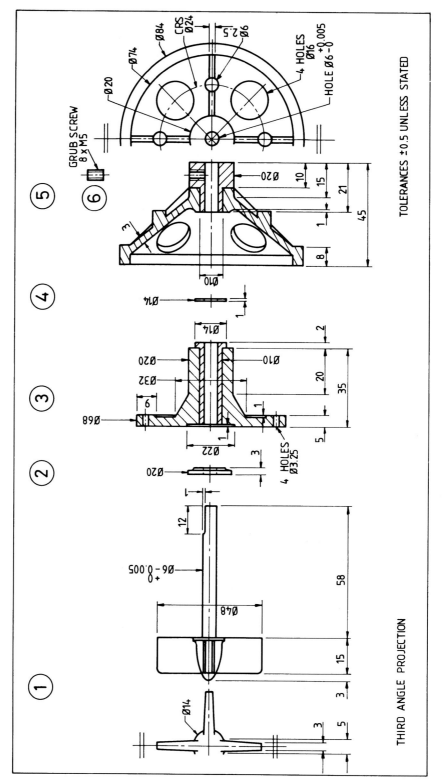

Fig. 12.6 Water pump parts.

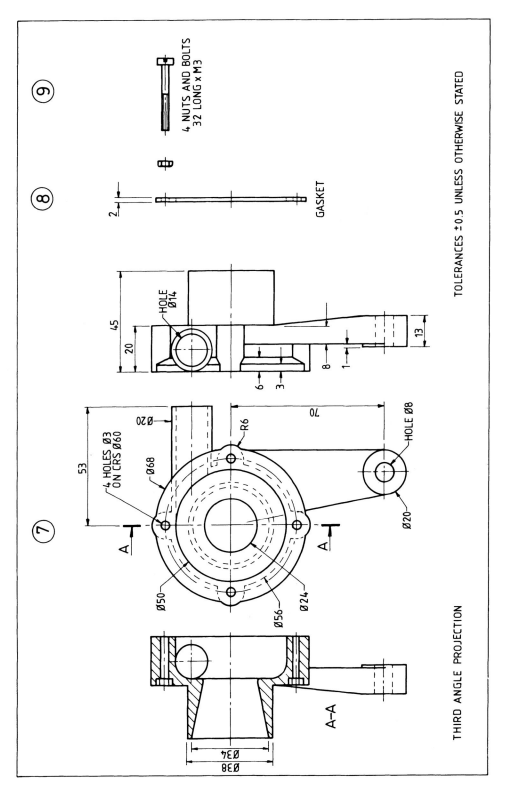

Fig. 12.7 *Water pump parts.*

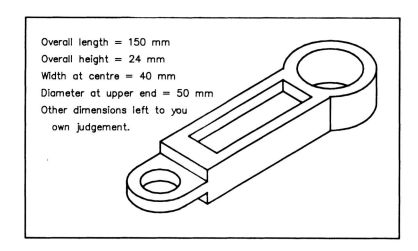

Overall length = 150 mm
Overall height = 24 mm
Width at centre = 40 mm
Diameter at upper end = 50 mm
Other dimensions left to you
    own judgement.

Fig. 12.10   *Clip.*

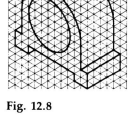

Fig. 12.8

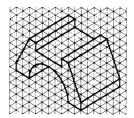

Fig. 12.9

Exercise 12.13
Figure 12.10 shows an isometric drawing of a clip. Construct a 3-D model of the clip using a surface modelling system. Create both wire frame and hidden line removed images of the clip.

Exercise 12.14
Figure 12.11 is a three-view orthographic projection of a small garden tool shed. Construct a 3-D model of the shed using a modelling system. If possible, create a colour shaded image of the shed using different surface colours to highlight individual features.

Exercise 12.15
Figure 12.12 shows a design for a swimming pool to be built in the garden of a house. Construct a 3-D model of the swimming pool, including its concrete bed and diving stand.
   List, and determine if possible, the geometric properties of the design that may be calculated from the 3-D database which will be of particular interest to the designer.

Exercise 12.16
Construct a face–edge–vertex listing for the objects shown in Figs. 12.13 to 12.16. Use the isometric grid to determine the positions of each vertex assuming a right-hand Cartesian co-ordinate system is used, the objects are located in positive (x, y, z) space, and the isometric grid spacing is 5 mm.

Exercise 12.17
Describe and sketch the sequence of modelling activities required in Figs. 12.17 to 12.22 using the constructive solid geometry primitives of a rectangular block

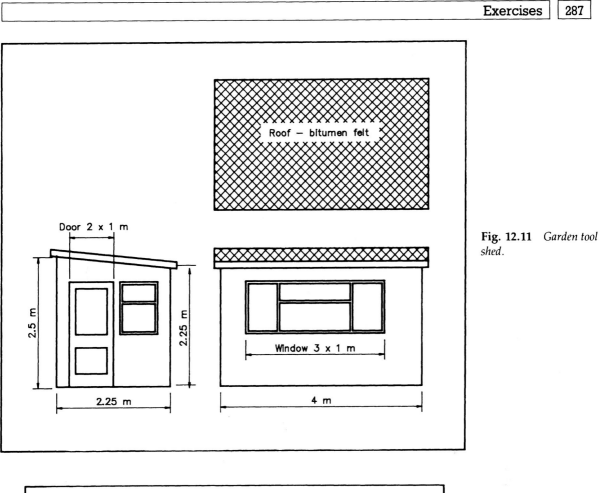

Fig. 12.11 *Garden tool shed.*

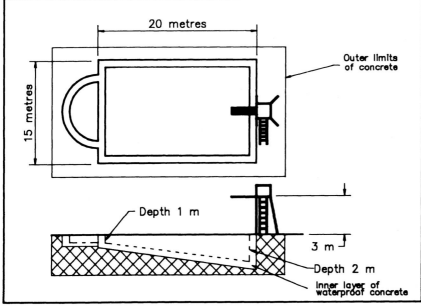

Fig. 12.12 *Swimming pool.*

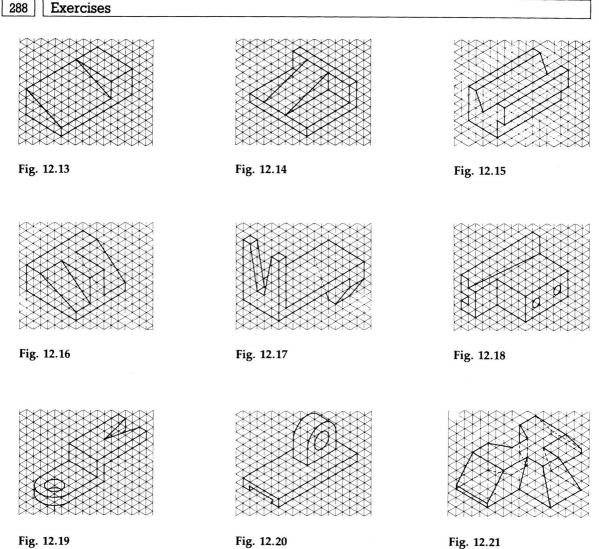

Fig. 12.13

Fig. 12.14

Fig. 12.15

Fig. 12.16

Fig. 12.17

Fig. 12.18

Fig. 12.19

Fig. 12.20

Fig. 12.21

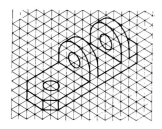

Fig. 12.22

and cylinder, together with the Boolean operators of intersection, union and difference. Sketch the resulting intersections.

Discuss alternative modelling sequences and contrast the merits of each approach.

Use a solid modelling system to generate models of each item using the most effective modelling sequence.

Exercise 12.18

Describe and sketch the sequence of modelling activities required to generate a solid model of the brake shoe shown in Fig. 12.23 using the constructive solid geometry primitives of a rectangular block and cylinder, together with the Boolean operators of intersection, union and difference. Sketch the resulting intersections.

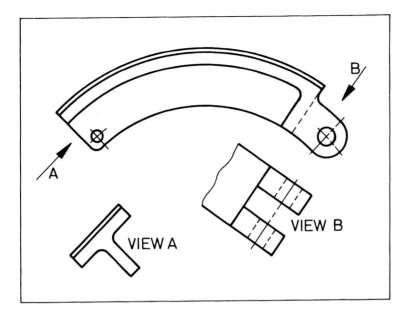

Fig. 12.23 *Brake shoe.*

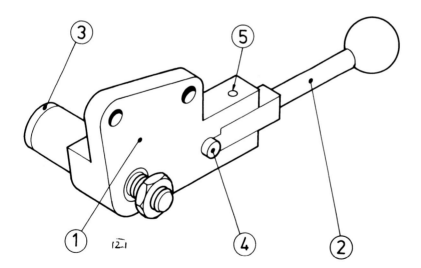

Fig. 12.24 *Gear change lever assembly.*

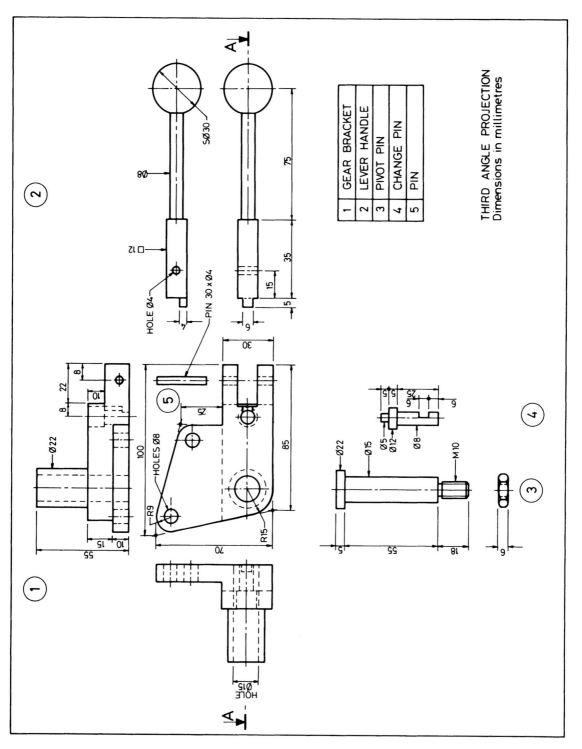

1	GEAR BRACKET
2	LEVER HANDLE
3	PIVOT PIN
4	CHANGE PIN
5	PIN

THIRD ANGLE PROJECTION
Dimensions in millimetres

Fig. 12.25 *Gear change lever parts.*

Describe, with the aid of sketches, an alternative sequence of modelling tasks using a boundary representation modeller that combines a profile sweep (spin) with constructive solid geometry primitives using the Boolean operators. Sketch the resulting intersections.

Use a solid modelling system to generate models of the brake shoe, using the most effective of these modelling methods that are available to you.

Exercise 12.19
Describe and sketch the sequence of modelling activities necessary to generate a solid model of the tailstock clamp assembly described in Exercise 12.10.

Discuss how the solid model of the tailstock clamp may be used to aid the draughting activity demanded in Exercise 12.10.

Use a solid modelling system to create a hidden line removed image of the tailstock clamp.

Exercise 12.20
The pictorial drawing Fig. 12.24 shows the assembled parts of a gear change lever from an engineering lathe. Details of the parts of the assembly are shown in Fig. 12.26.

Using a 3-D modelling system, create models of each item and use these to create an assembled model of the gear change lever with each part positioned in its correct location. Produce a pictorial view of the assembled gear change lever using hidden line removed and colour shaded styles.

Create an orthographic view of the gear change lever. Transfer this view to a 2-D draughting system where a general assembly drawing, with dimensions and parts list, should be produced.

Exercise 12.21
Figures 12.6 and 12.7 show details of the various parts of a water pump from a domestic washing machine. This pump is fully described in Exercise 12.11.

Use a solid modelling system to create models of each part and use these to create a solid model of the assembled water pump. Produce a pictorial view of the assembled water pump like that shown in Fig. 10.24.

Half section Parts 3, 5, 7 and 8 and use these to create a cut-away model of the assembly like that shown in Fig. 10.25.

Discuss how the solid model data created during this exercise might be used in a fully integrated CAE system.

Exercise 12.22
The body (Part 7) of the water pump described in Exercise 12.11 (and solid modelled in Exercise 12.21) is manufactured as a cast item, with its mating surfaces and clearance holes machined to finish.

Describe how the solid model database that represents the water pump body might be used in an integrated CAE system to aid these manufacturing processes. Sketch the form of the solid model used during these two processes.

Matrix notation for graphical transformations

This appendix is not intended as an introduction to matrix notation but serves to supplement the principles given in Chapters 3 and 4 concerning transformations by using the shorthand of matrix notations.

A.1 TWO-DIMENSIONAL TRANSFORMATIONS

A generalized point in 2-D can be represented by its x and y co-ordinates as

$$P = [x_1, y_1],$$

where $[x_1, y_1]$ is a 1×2 matrix. Similarly a line in 2-D can be represented by its end points as a 2×2 matrix:

$$L = \begin{bmatrix} x_1 & y_1 \\ x_2 & y_2 \end{bmatrix}.$$

The general 2-D point (x, y) can be transferred into the point (x_1, y_1) as

$$\begin{align} x_1 &= ax + by \\ y_1 &= cx + dy, \end{align} \tag{A.1}$$

where the transform T can be expressed in matrix form as:

$$T = \begin{bmatrix} a & c \\ b & d \end{bmatrix}.$$

Equation (A.1) can now be expressed in matrix form as

$$(x_1, y_1) = (x, y) \begin{bmatrix} a & c \\ b & d \end{bmatrix}, \tag{A.2}$$

i.e. x_1 can be found by multiplying the row vector (x, y) by the first column

$$\begin{bmatrix} a & \cdot \\ b & \cdot \end{bmatrix}$$

and y_1 by multiplying (x, y) by the second column

$$\begin{bmatrix} \cdot & c \\ \cdot & d \end{bmatrix}.$$

Similarly a pair of matrix transformations can be multiplied together to give one combined (or **concatenated**) form. Thus if

$$T_1 = \begin{bmatrix} a & c \\ b & d \end{bmatrix}$$

and

$$T_2 = \begin{bmatrix} e & g \\ f & h \end{bmatrix}$$

then the concatenated transform

$$T = T_1 \cdot T_2 = \begin{bmatrix} a & c \\ b & d \end{bmatrix} \begin{bmatrix} e & g \\ f & h \end{bmatrix}$$

or

$$T = \begin{bmatrix} (ae + cf) & (ag + ch) \\ (be + df) & (bg + dh) \end{bmatrix}$$

$$T = \begin{bmatrix} j & l \\ k & m \end{bmatrix},$$

where $j = ae + cf$, i.e. j is formed by taking the sum of the products of the first row of T_1 with the first column of T_2;
$k = be + df$, i.e. k is formed by taking the sum of the products of the second row of T_1 with the first column of T_2;
$l = ag + ch$, i.e. l is formed by taking the sum of the products of the first row of T_1 with the second row of T_2;
$m = bg + dh$, i.e. m is formed by taking the sum of the products of the second row of T_1 with the second column of T_2.

A.2 TRANSLATION

The expressions given in Chapter 3 for translation of a point are

$$x_1 = x + \Delta x, \; y_1 = y + \Delta y,$$

where x_1 and y_1 are co-ordinates of the translated point, i.e.

$$(x_1, y_1) = (x, y) + T$$

where

$$T = [\Delta x, \Delta y]$$

Similarly a line L can be translated as

$$\begin{bmatrix} x_1' & y_1' \\ x_2' & y_2' \end{bmatrix} = \begin{bmatrix} x_1 & y_1 \\ x_2 & y_2 \end{bmatrix} + T,$$

where $T = \begin{bmatrix} \Delta x_1 & \Delta y_1 \\ \Delta x_2 & \Delta y_2 \end{bmatrix}$,

i.e. $\begin{bmatrix} x_1' & y_1' \\ x_2' & y_2' \end{bmatrix} = \begin{bmatrix} x_1 & y_1 \\ x_2 & y_2 \end{bmatrix} + \begin{bmatrix} \Delta x_1 & \Delta y_1 \\ \Delta x_2 & \Delta y_2 \end{bmatrix}$

$$= \begin{bmatrix} (x_1 + \Delta x_1) & (y_1 + \Delta y_1) \\ (x_2 + \Delta x_2) & (y_2 + \Delta y_2) \end{bmatrix}. \qquad (A.3)$$

Thus in Fig. 3.17, the line

$$L = \begin{bmatrix} 1 & 1 \\ 2 & 3 \end{bmatrix}$$

which is translated by two units in x and one unit in y as

$$T = \begin{bmatrix} 2 & 1 \\ 2 & 1 \end{bmatrix}.$$

Hence from eqn (A.3), the transform is

$$L + T = \begin{bmatrix} 1 & 1 \\ 2 & 3 \end{bmatrix} + \begin{bmatrix} 2 & 1 \\ 2 & 1 \end{bmatrix} = \begin{bmatrix} 3 & 2 \\ 4 & 4 \end{bmatrix},$$

i.e. $(x_1, y_1) = (3, 2)$

$(x_2, y_2) = (4, 4)$ as in Fig. 3.17.

A.3 SCALING

Scaling involves enlarging or reducing size, e.g. the point

$$(x', y') = (x, y)\,\mathbf{S}$$

where

$$S = \begin{bmatrix} \Delta x & 0 \\ 0 & \Delta y \end{bmatrix}$$

the scaling matrix. This scales by Δx in the x direction and by Δy in the y direction. An enlargement (Δx, $\Delta y > 1$) also translates further from the origin, while a reduction (Δx, $\Delta y < 1$) translates nearer the origin.

In the example Fig. 3.18, the line

$$L = \begin{bmatrix} 1 & 1 \\ 2 & 3 \end{bmatrix}$$

is doubled in size, i.e.

$$S = \begin{bmatrix} 2 & 0 \\ 0 & 2 \end{bmatrix}$$

and

$$LS = \begin{bmatrix} (1 \times 2 + 1 \times 0) & (1 \times 0 + 1 \times 2) \\ (2 \times 2 + 3 \times 0) & (2 \times 0 + 3 \times 2) \end{bmatrix}$$

$$= \begin{bmatrix} 2 & 2 \\ 4 & 6 \end{bmatrix}$$

i.e. $(x_1, y_1) = (2, 2)$

$(x_2, y_2) = (4, 6)$ as in Fig. 3.18.

A.4 ROTATION

In a 2-D transformation, points are rotated about Oz in an anti-clockwise direction for positive values of θ, using a right-hand co-ordinate system, e.g. for a point (x_1, y_1)

$$x_1 = x \cos\theta + y \sin\theta$$
$$y_1 = y \cos\theta + x \sin\theta,$$

where x_1 and y_1 are the transformed co-ordinates of the point (x, y), or

$$(x_1, y_1) = (x, y)\mathbf{R}$$

where

$$R = \begin{bmatrix} \cos\theta & \sin\theta \\ -\sin\theta & \cos\theta \end{bmatrix}$$

the rotation matrix.

In the example given in Fig. 3.20 the line

$$L = \begin{bmatrix} 1 & 1 \\ 2 & 3 \end{bmatrix}$$

is rotated by $\theta = 60°$ about the origin, i.e.

$$R = \begin{bmatrix} \cos 60° & \sin 60° \\ -\sin 60° & \cos 60° \end{bmatrix}$$

and

$$LR = \begin{bmatrix} -0.366 & 1.366 \\ -1.598 & 3.232 \end{bmatrix}.$$

A.5 HOMOGENEOUS CO-ORDINATES

To achieve a pure rotation about the end $(1, 1)$ of a line, it would be necessary to translate the end $(1, 1)$ to the origin, perform the rotation and then retranslate the end of the line back to the position $(1, 1)$. The advantage and strength of matrix multiplication is that the successive processes of translation, rotation and translation can be combined into a single transformation matrix. However, the desire to combine the above 2×2 matrices into a single multiplication matrix gives rise to difficulties because the translation transform is an additive process, while rotation and scaling are multiplicative. To achieve a similar multiplicative form with translation, the concept of homogeneous co-ordinate transforms is introduced.

To treat all 2-D processes as multiplicative, the translation process must be turned into a dot product form. The transformations can then all be treated similarly (or homogeneously). This is carried out by considering the xy plane con-

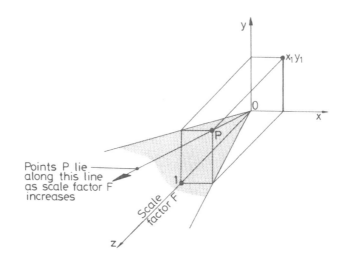

Fig. A.1 *Homogeneous co-ordinate representation of a point by use of a scale factor* F.

taining the line L to be scaled in the z direction. The xy plane is then only one of an infinite number of planes in the z direction. The z axis then represents a scaling factor F which ranges from 0 to ∞ as shown in Fig. A.1. A point $p(x_1, y_1)$ is now represented as $p(F \cdot x_1, F \cdot y_1, F)$ where scale factor $F \neq 0$ giving the homogeneous co-ordinate representation for a point as $P(XYF)$. The 2-D Cartesian co-ordinates are given by $x = X/F$, $y = Y/F$. In practice F is normally chosen as 1 and thus division by F is not required.

For 2-D representation in homogeneous form, a point now becomes a three element row vector $[x, y, 1]$ and a translation becomes the dot product

$$[x'\, y'\, 1] = [x\, y\, 1] \cdot T(\Delta x\, \Delta y),$$

where $[x'\, y'\, 1]$ is the transformed point at $F = 1$ and $[x\, y\, 1]$ is the original point at $F = 1$ and

$$T(\Delta x\, \Delta y) = \begin{bmatrix} 1 & 0 & 0 \\ 0 & 1 & 0 \\ \Delta x & \Delta y & 1 \end{bmatrix}$$

A series of translations one after the other, can be accomplished by first finding the dot products of all the translation matrices to give a concatenated form as a single translation matrix whose elements will be the sum of the individual elements.

A scaling is now

$$[x'\,y'\,1] = [x\,y\,1] \cdot \begin{bmatrix} \Delta x & 0 & 0 \\ 0 & \Delta y & 0 \\ 0 & 0 & 1 \end{bmatrix}.$$

The concatenated form of successive scalings one after the other will be the product of the individual elements.

A rotation is now

$$[x'\,y'\,1] = [x\,y\,1] \cdot \begin{bmatrix} \cos\theta & \sin\theta & 0 \\ -\sin\theta & \cos\theta & 0 \\ 0 & 0 & 1 \end{bmatrix}.$$

Concatenation of successive rotations will be the sum of individual elements.

Example A.1

Rotate a square about a corner P through an angle θ. Because transformations are with respect to the origin, this process has three parts:

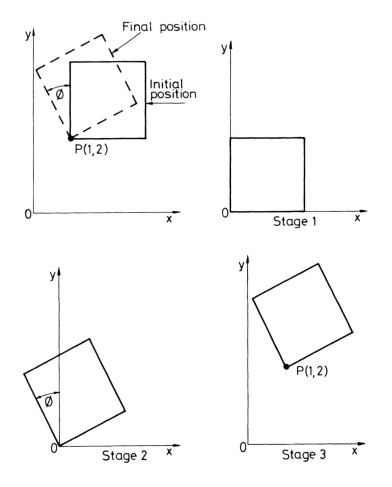

Fig. A.2 *Stages in the rotation of a square.*

1. translate P to the origin;
2. rotate through an angle θ;
3. re-translate back to the original position of P as shown in Fig. A.2.

The net transformation matrix is:

$$\begin{bmatrix} 1 & 0 & 0 \\ 0 & 1 & 0 \\ -x_1 & -y_1 & 1 \end{bmatrix} \cdot \begin{bmatrix} \cos\theta & \sin\theta & 0 \\ -\sin\theta & \cos\theta & 0 \\ 0 & 0 & 1 \end{bmatrix} \cdot \begin{bmatrix} 1 & 0 & 0 \\ 0 & 1 & 0 \\ x_1 & y_1 & 1 \end{bmatrix}$$

$$= \begin{bmatrix} \cos\theta & \sin\theta & 0 \\ -\sin\theta & \cos\theta & 0 \\ x_1(1 - \cos\theta) + y_1 \sin\theta & y_1(1 - \cos\theta) - x_1 \sin\theta & 1 \end{bmatrix}.$$

This single transformation matrix can then be applied to all four corners of the square to give their final co-ordinates. The order of the above steps is clearly vital. If a rotation about P were followed by two translations, the result would be quite different and thus matrices are not, in general, commutative. The only transforms in which order is unimportant are:

1. a series of translations;
2. successive scalings;
3. successive rotations;
4. when a scaling (with the same x and y scale factor) is followed by a rotation.

A.5.1 COMPUTATIONAL EFFICIENCY

Although the individual matrices need to be kept as a 3×3 matrix, the final transformation matrix can have the last column ignored. Thus the transformation of a 2-D point uses four multiplications and four additions, instead of nine multiplications and six additions. The resulting saving of computation time can be worth while for the transformation of complex items or where speed is important, as in dynamic displays.

A.6 THREE-DIMENSIONAL TRANSFORMATIONS

3-D transformations in homogeneous co-ordinates involve a 4×4 matrix.
A 3-D translation becomes

$$T(\Delta x, \Delta y, \Delta z) = \begin{bmatrix} 1 & 0 & 0 & 0 \\ 0 & 1 & 1 & 0 \\ 0 & 0 & 1 & 0 \\ \Delta x & \Delta y & \Delta z & 1 \end{bmatrix}.$$

A 3-D scaling becomes

$$S(\Delta x, \Delta y, \Delta z) = \begin{bmatrix} \Delta x & 0 & 0 & 0 \\ 0 & \Delta y & 0 & 0 \\ 0 & 0 & \Delta z & 0 \\ 0 & 0 & 0 & 1 \end{bmatrix}.$$

A 3-D rotation becomes:
rotation about the x axis

$$R_x = \begin{bmatrix} 1 & 0 & 0 & 0 \\ 0 & \cos\theta & \sin\theta & 0 \\ 0 & -\sin\theta & \cos\theta & 0 \\ 0 & 0 & 0 & 1 \end{bmatrix};$$

rotation about the y axis

$$R_y = \begin{bmatrix} \cos\theta & 0 & -\sin\theta & 0 \\ 0 & 1 & 0 & 0 \\ \sin\theta & 0 & \cos\theta & 0 \\ 0 & 0 & 0 & 1 \end{bmatrix};$$

rotation about the z axis

$$R_z = \begin{bmatrix} \cos\theta & \sin\theta & 0 & 0 \\ -\sin\theta & \cos\theta & 0 & 0 \\ 0 & 0 & 1 & 0 \\ 0 & 0 & 0 & 1 \end{bmatrix}.$$

The example given in Fig. 4.19, which involves a rotation of a triangle ABC, first about $0z$ by $+90°$ and then by $-60°$ about the $0x$ axis, is now considered.

Since corner A is placed at the origin, and always remains there, it can be ignored.

The matrix rotation for the two stages of rotation of B is

$$[x_B' \, y_B' \, z_B'] = [x_B \, y_B \, z_B] \cdot R_{0z}$$

$$= [x_B \, y_B \, z_B \, 1] \cdot \begin{bmatrix} \cos 90° & \sin 90° & 0 \\ -\sin 90° & \cos 90° & 0 \\ 0 & 0 & 0 \\ 0 & 0 & 1 \end{bmatrix}$$

and since

$$x_B = 2, \, y_B = 0, \, z_B = 0$$
$$[x_B' \, y_B' \, z_B'] = [0, \, 2, \, 0]$$

and

$$[x_B'' \, y_B'' \, z_B''] = [x_B' \, y_B' \, z_B' \, 1] \cdot R_{0x}$$

$$= [x_B' \, y_B' \, z_B' \, 1] \cdot \begin{bmatrix} 1 & 0 & 0 & 0 \\ 0 & \cos\theta & \sin\theta & 0 \\ 0 & -\sin\theta & \cos\theta & 0 \\ 0 & 0 & 0 & 1 \end{bmatrix}$$

$$= [0, 2, 0, 1] \cdot \begin{bmatrix} 1 & 0 & 0 & 0 \\ 0 & 0.5 & -0.866 & 0 \\ 0 & 0.866 & 0.5 & 0 \\ 0 & 0 & 0 & 1 \end{bmatrix}$$

$$= [0, 1.0, -1.732, 1]$$

More usually, the above two rotation matrices could be concatenated to produce a single transform as

$$T = \begin{bmatrix} \cos\theta & \sin\theta & 0 & 0 \\ -\sin\theta & \cos\theta & 0 & 0 \\ 0 & 0 & 1 & 0 \\ 0 & 0 & 0 & 1 \end{bmatrix} \cdot \begin{bmatrix} 1 & 0 & 0 & 0 \\ 0 & \cos\phi & \sin\phi & 0 \\ 0 & -\sin\phi & \cos\phi & 0 \\ 0 & 0 & 0 & 1 \end{bmatrix},$$

where $\theta = 90°$ and $\phi = -60°$

or

$$T = \begin{bmatrix} \cos\theta & \sin\theta\cos\phi & \sin\theta\sin\phi & 0 \\ -\sin\theta & \cos\theta\cos\phi & \cos\theta\sin\phi & 0 \\ 0 & \sin\phi & \cos\phi & 0 \\ 0 & 0 & 0 & 1 \end{bmatrix}$$

$$= \begin{bmatrix} 0 & 0.5 & -0.866 & 0 \\ -1 & 0 & 0 & 0 \\ 0 & 0.866 & 0.5 & 0 \\ 0 & 0 & 0 & 1 \end{bmatrix}.$$

Hence

$$[x\,y\,z\,1] \cdot T$$

$$= [2\,0\,0\,1] \cdot \begin{bmatrix} 0 & 0.5 & -0.866 & 0 \\ -1 & 0 & 0 & 0 \\ 0 & 0.866 & 0.5 & 0 \\ 0 & 0 & 0 & 1 \end{bmatrix}$$

$$= [0, 1, 0, -1.732, 1] \text{ as before.}$$

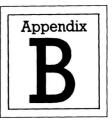

Graphs

Appendix

B

B.1 INTRODUCTION

Because graphs are a good pictorial way of representing information, they are often used by engineers and managers. The combination of the use of data and pictorial representation makes the computer ideal for use with graphs. For this reason a section on graphs has been included. Although a separate issue from computer-aided draughting, it is felt that the use of computer-generated graphs is of sufficient relevance to this text to warrant their inclusion, albeit in an appendix.

A brief introduction is given to the different types of conventional 2-D and 3-D graphs. This is followed by a review of the way that the use of computer generated graphics and **spreadsheets** has affected the use of graphs and charts.

Data and information expressed in the form of a series of numbers are very difficult to evaluate or to analyse for significant trends or for overall properties. If the data can be translated into a suitable graphical form (into a graph) the general relationships are much easier to understand. With the aid of a graph overall trends of one variable component in a series of data as compared with others can be seen clearly. Graphs, however, are not a good medium for the provision of precise information relating to data. Depending upon the scale adopted, graphs may provide adequate accuracy for many tasks, but if precise quantities are required, these must be obtained from the original data from which the graph was constructed. For this reason, original data should be provided with a graph.

The term chart is frequently used as having the same meaning as the word graph. However, it is more usual to consider a chart as a means of representing sequential or spatial relationships in symbolic or diagrammatic form. A map is an example of a chart in which terrain and features are represented by special symbols.

B.2 TWO-DIMENSIONAL GRAPHS

B.2.1 LINEAR CO-ORDINATE GRAPHS

Linear co-ordinate graphs are the most common form of graph to represent changes between two variables. They are plotted from points on a grid using

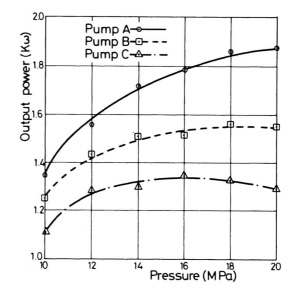

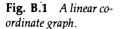
Fig. B.1 *A linear co-ordinate graph.*

two measurements called co-ordinates. The horizontal line represents one variable and is called the x axis (or **abscissa**). The vertical line represents the other variable and is called the y axis (or **ordinate**). Figure B.1 shows a typical graph of this type. This graph represents the output powers for three hydraulic pumps in terms of changing pressures. Each of the three curves is distinguished from the others by means of distinct symbols, e.g. a circle, square or cross and by different types of lines, e.g. full, dotted and dashed. Note that the tests carried out as indicated by the graphs are at discrete pressures as represented by the symbols, the points are joined by smooth curves. These curves imply that it

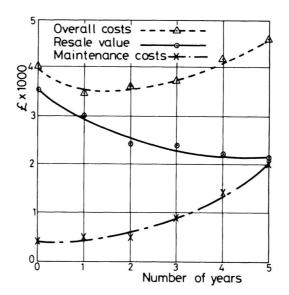

Fig. B.2 *A linear co-ordinate graph.*

should be possible to find the pressure and power relationship at points other than those tested from the graph, by estimation (or **interpolation**). As is shown by Fig. B.1, it is good practice to terminate the curve either side of the symbol to allow greater accuracy when reading at that point.

It is possible to employ graphs to determine information which may be difficult to determine mathematically. Figure B.2 shows the drop in the resale value of a machine tool and the cost of maintenance over a number of years. Because the cost of maintenance rises with the age of the machine, there is a minimum total cost at a particular age. This can be found by summing the ordinate values of the two curves to produce a graph of the total cost (shown dotted) from which the minimum cost can readily be found.

In the graph of Fig. B.2, a smooth curve has been drawn through a series of discrete points. This implies a continuity between the points. This may not always be the case. As an example, share quotations are given on the Stock Exchange at the end of each day as discrete values. These discrete values are usually joined together each day by straight line segments as shown in Fig. B.3. It would not be appropriate to join the points by a smooth curve, because a smooth curve would imply a continuity in between the daily readings, which in fact is not present. The reason for joining the points with straight lines is to emphasize an overall trend.

The interpretation of graphs must be carried out with care, because the choice of scale, origin and the data used can produce a misleading impression. Fig. B.4(a) shows a graph prepared by the sales department of a machine tool company giving the results of its sales campaign in a favourable light. The Managing Director, however, had the results plotted on a new range of time and a new scale (Fig. B.4(b)). The resulting graph displayed a much less impressive sales campaign.

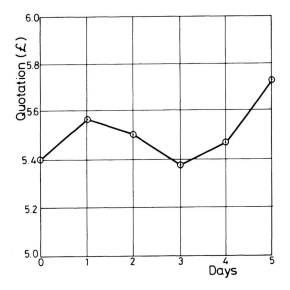

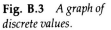

Fig. B.3 *A graph of discrete values.*

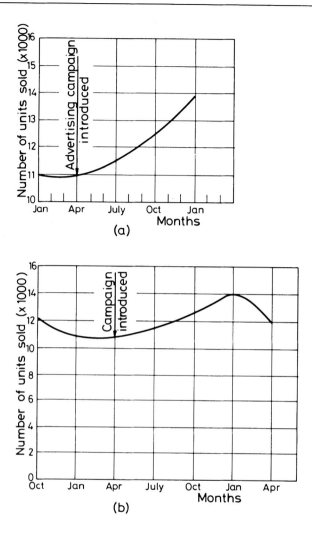

Fig. B.4 *Two viewpoints of the same data.*

B.2.2 STRAIGHT-LINE GRAPHS

A point P can be represented by its x and y co-ordinates as $P(x, y)$. Similarly a straight line can be described by two points lying on the graph as $P_1(x_1 y_1)$, $P_2(x_2 y_2)$. The generalized equation for a straight line is

$$y = mx + c,$$

where m is the tangent of the angle between the line and the horizontal, i.e. the slope of the line; and c is the intercept of the line with the y axis at $x=0$.

If an experiment is conducted in which data are produced and plotted as points which lie more or less on a straight line, then the equation of that line can be found from the above slope/intercept formula, as shown by Fig. B.5. In this example it is necessary to project back from the end of the line to intersect with the y axis to give $c=10$. The slope is found from:

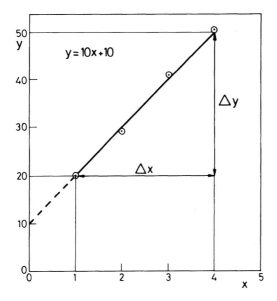

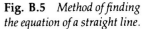

Fig. B.5 *Method of finding the equation of a straight line.*

$$m = \frac{\Delta y}{\Delta x} = \frac{50 - 20}{4 - 1} = 10.$$

Therefore the equation for the line is:

$$y = 10x + 10.$$

B.2.3 NON-LINEAR CO-ORDINATE GRAPHS

In engineering it is not unusual to find that a variable changes in an approximately logarithmic (or log) manner with respect to another. In such cases, it is appropriate to use a semi-log graph as shown in Fig. B.6. This shows the growth in sales of a product over a number of years. The y axis, representing the number of products sold, is to a log scale. The x axis, representing the year of sales, is to a linear scale. Semi-log graphs are very good for showing the relative rate of change. When both variables change in an approximately logarithmic way, a log/log plot is used, an example being given by Fig. B.7. This graph shows the variation of wind tunnel velocity against the distance from the wind tunnel wall.

If the variables vary in an exactly logarithmic manner the log/log plot will be a straight line. This is much easier to interpret than the curve resulting from plotting in linear co-ordinates. The equation of a log/log relationship is of the form

$$y = cx^{m}.$$

This can be expressed by taking logarithms of both sides as

$$\log y = \log c + m \log x.$$

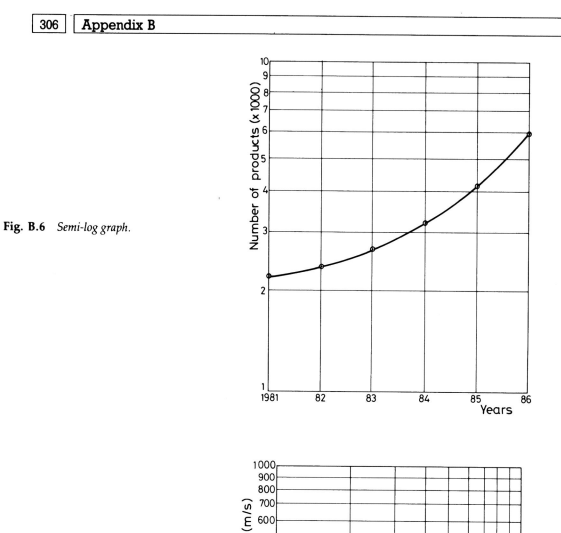

Fig. B.6 *Semi-log graph.*

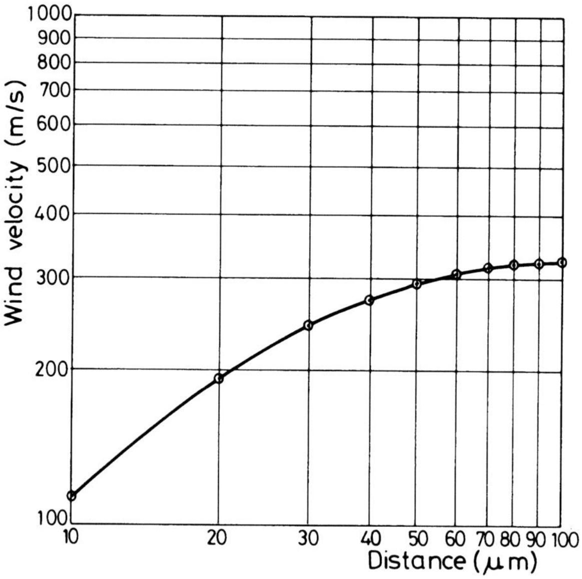

Fig. B.7 *A log/log graph.*

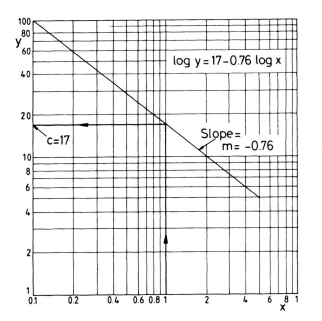

This is the equation for a straight line in which the slope is m and the intercept is log c, provided the axes are plotted as log x/log y. However, since log $1=0$, the intercept with the y axis must be taken at $x=1$.

Figure B.8 shows a log/log plot. Since the slope of the graph is downwards, the value of m is negative, i.e.

$$m = \frac{\Delta\log y}{\Delta\log x} = \frac{\log 5 - \log 100}{\log 5 - \log 0.1}$$
$$= \frac{0.7 - 2.0}{0.7 - (-1)} = \frac{-1.3}{1.7}$$
$$= -0.76.$$

Note: Since m is a slope, it may be evaluated by measuring directly from the graph. For this any horizontal or vertical scale of measurement may be taken as long as it is the same, e.g.

$$m = \frac{-7.6\,\text{cm}}{10\,\text{cm}} = -0.76 \text{ as before.}$$

The intercept at $x = 1.0$ is in the middle of the plot. Hence $c=17$ and the equation of the line is

$$\log y = 17 - 0.76 \log x.$$

B.2.4 BAR GRAPHS

Bar graphs provide an effective method of displaying discrete entities for comparison when there is no sense of continuity between entities. Figure B.9 shows a comparison of the production of a factory for three distinct periods. Not only

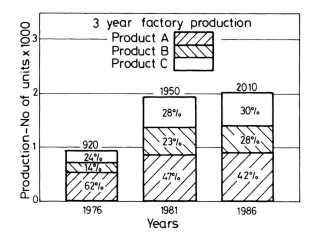

Fig. B.9 *A bar graph.*

is the total production shown in this bar graph, but also how the product mix varies as a proportion of total production. Showing the values as a percentage of the total often gives a better comparison between adjacent bars than using number values.

B.2.5 PIE GRAPHS

Pie graphs, like bar graphs, are well suited to showing discrete entities. Pie graphs are, however, also particularly good for showing the relationship of the parts to the whole – how the total pie is divided into parts. Figure B.10 is a pie graph showing the distribution of personnel in a company given the data in Table B.1.

The total of 1030 employees is represented by the full circle of 360°. Because it is the relative proportions which are of interest here, it is best to find first the individual percentages of the total and then find these as a proportion of the full circle. Pie graphs give no information graphically about absolute numbers and thus it is advisable to write them on the pie graph, to avoid the loss of valuable information. Note that the pie graph of Fig. B.10 is set out so that the

Table B.1

Personnel	No. of employees	% of total	Angle in degrees
Unskilled	510	48	173°
Skilled	120	12	43°
Research	83	8	29°
Administration	275	27	97°
Other	42	5	18°
Totals	1030	100	360°

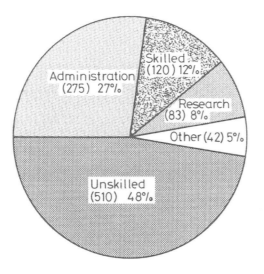

Fig. B.10 *A pie graph.*

smaller arc segments are horizontal in order to facilitate lettering. Pie graphs are most effective when the number of variables to be displayed is small. It is possible to use the diameter of the pie to represent, in proportion, the total quantity being displayed. Thus if the data shown in Fig. B.10 were to be shown for three separate years, to indicate changes in total personnel employed, three separate pie graphs could be drawn, the diameters of which represent in proportion to their diameters, the total number of personnel for each of the three years.

B.2.6 POLAR GRAPHS

In contrast to Cartesian axis graphs, polar graphs use polar co-ordinates, whose variables are plotted as a change in radius and angle. Figure B.11 shows a plot of the electrical response of the electrical control system illustrated by Fig. B.12. The relative amplitude of an output displacement x is compared with an input displacement y to form an amplitude ratio A. The magnitude of A is shown as a radial value on the polar plot. The value of A is a **modulus**, i.e. an absolute

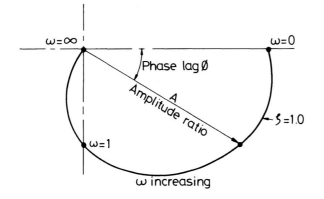

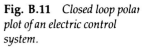

Fig. B.11 *Closed loop polar plot of an electric control system.*

Fig. B.12 *Electrical control system figured in Fig. B.11.*

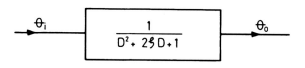

$$\theta_i \longrightarrow \boxed{\dfrac{1}{D^2 + 2\zeta D + 1}} \longrightarrow \theta_o$$

magnitude independent of sign, written as $|A|$. If the input signal varies in a sinusoidal manner, the difference in phase between sinusoid input signal (x) and the resultant sinusoid output signal (y), is shown as an angle (ϕ). The values of the disturbing frequency (ω) of the input signal are also plotted along the response curve for each modulus of amplitude ratio $|A|$ and phase angle ϕ. This type of polar plot is commonly used in electrical control systems and is called a closed-loop polar plot.

B.3 THREE-DIMENSIONAL GRAPHS

B.3.1 THREE-DIMENSIONAL LINE CO-ORDINATE GRAPHS

A 3-D line co-ordinate graph allows the representation of three interrelated variables together in one view. Fig. B.13 shows the growth of a factory in terms of a number of employees, size of site and number of years. Because of the nature of the plot the number of years is represented along the $-z$ axis. This 3-D graph could be represented by a pair of separate 2-D graphs showing, e.g. site area (as ordinate)/year (abscissa) and employees (ordinate)/year (abscissa). These two 2-D graphs would allow intermediate values to be interpolated more

Fig. B.13 *A 3-D graph.*

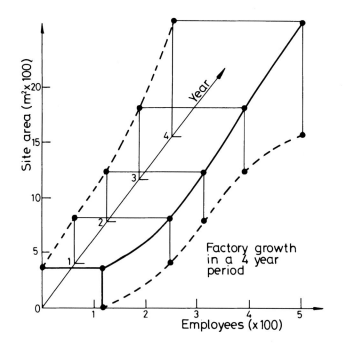

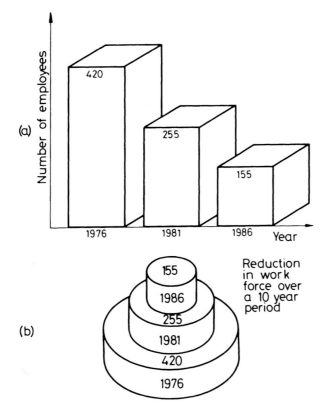

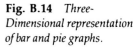

Fig. B.14 *Three-Dimensional representation of bar and pie graphs.*

accurately than when using the 3-D graph. However, the pictorial impact of the interrelated variables would be diminished. The relationship between a greater number than three variables can be expressed by using a series of 2-D and 3-D graphs to interrelate them.

B.3.2 THREE-DIMENSIONAL BAR AND PIE GRAPHS

These are frequently drawn for visual impact, as shown by Fig. B.14(a) and (b). While the third variable dimension could, in theory, be used to represent a third variable, in practice this is unusual.

B.4 USING THE COMPUTER TO DISPLAY GRAPHS

Where the computer has been used, for example, for analysis or for recording experimental measurements, the amount of data and information requiring evaluation is likely to be significantly larger than if the calculation or data capture tasks had been carried out using alternative methods. However, as we have already discussed, data that has been translated into a suitable graphical form is much easier to understand than if expressed as a series of numbers. If large volumes of data have to be translated from the computer database into a graphical form, it is sensible to use the computer for this task and to display the graphs on the graphics screen. This application of computer graphics is, in essence, straight-forward since the techniques for producing 2-D and 3-D co-ordinate graphs (linear and non-linear), bar graphs and pie graphs can be incorporated easily into computer programs, and the data can be displayed on the graphics screen using the same software principles considered in Chapters 3 and 4. Difficulties arise, though, where the relationships between the variables have to be determined, or where smooth curves must be drawn through discrete data. Generally, further numerical analysis of the whole database is required, before the data can be represented by a single straight line or curve.

Specialist computer programs for producing a variety of graph types are readily available for all computers, enabling data and information already stored on the computer system to be displayed in a graph form. These programs are often of a generalist nature so that they can be used with the user's own analysis or data capture programs, precluding the need for specialist graph plotting routines to be written. They are most commonly used with spreadsheet packages (SuperCalc, Lotus 1–2–3, etc.), where the relationships between any of the variables can be displayed quickly on the graphic screen or drawn on paper using a plotter.

B.4.1 TWO-DIMENSIONAL GRAPHS

To produce 2-D graphs, the computer uses the principles of 2-D draughting to display the data on the screen. The discrete values of the x and y variables are independently scaled to obtain their screen co-ordinates (x', y'), i.e.

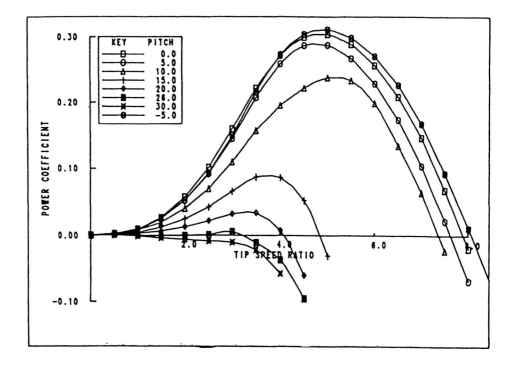

Fig. B.15 *A computer generated 2-D graph.*

$$x' = S_x x' + \Delta x$$
$$y' = S_y y' + \Delta y,$$

where Δx and Δy are the screen co-ordinates of the origin. The values of the scaling factors S_x and S_y are often determined automatically by the computer to ensure the graph fills the display area of the graphics screen, but where the limits of the axes need to remain fixed, e.g. so that data on separate graphs can be compared, the scaling factors must be fixed by the user. The position of discrete data points can be marked with symbols chosen from a set of standard software or hardware symbols. These points may be linked by straight lines drawn using the data to define the endpoints of each segment. Smooth curves can be generated by a variety of different methods which are discussed later.

Figure B.15 is an example of a graph plotted using a specialist graph-plotting program. The source data has been calculated by another computer program and retrieved from a series of different data files. The graph shows the variation of the power coefficient of a small wind turbine with respect to its tip speed ratio (a non-dimensional rotational speed) for several different blade pitch angles. Each data point is marked on the graph with a symbol. Results for each blade pitch angle are linked using a 'smooth' curve. In reality, the curve is made up of a series of straight line segments whose endpoints have been calculated by interpolation of the original data. The key identifies the symbol used for each blade pitch angle.

B.4.2 BAR AND PIE GRAPHS

These types of graph are created using parametric symbols for the bars or 'slices of pie', where the significant dimension is determined automatically from the data held in the computer. The area of the bar or pie is often block filled with colour to create a more vivid screen picture. Alternatively, a pictorial representation of the variable being displayed provides an additional emphasis to the significance of the data.

B.4.3 THREE-DIMENSIONAL GRAPHS

To produce 3-D graphs, the computer uses the principles of 3-D modelling to display the data on the screen. Each discrete data point can be considered as a point positioned in 3-D space. The screen image is a projection of the 3-D space data on to a projection plane that lies between the observer and the data. The data can be observed from any viewpoint, though isometric projections of the 3-D graph are suitable for most applications. If a single curve through the data points is to be shown, interpolation or curve fitting routines must be used to determine the screen position of intermediate points on the curve. However, one of the reasons for plotting 3-D graphs is that the dependent variable is a function of two independent variables. This function is not fully represented by a single curve, whereas a surface form can be used to represent all the possible values the dependent variable may be able to take. Thus, by using surface modelling techniques, the discrete values of the data set can be used to develop

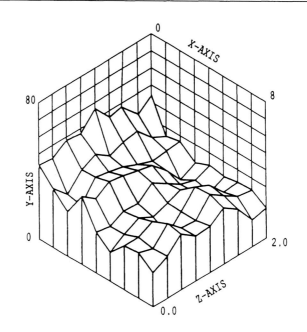

Fig. B.16 *A 3-D carpet plot.*

a 3-D surface model representation of the function. In its simplest form, the surface model can be made from planar facets to represent discrete surface segments. Each data point will define the corner position of at least four surface segments. Hidden line removed views of the surface allow the variation of the dependent variable to be easily interpreted and understood. This form of graph is often known as a **carpet plot**, Fig. B.16.

B.4.4 INTERPOLATION

Where discrete data points are joined by straight line segments, Fig. B.3, intermediate values of the curve are of little interest. The segmented curve is drawn to indicate an overall trend in the data. Computer-generated graphs of this type are plotted using 2-D draughting principles to draw the straight-line segments between each data point. If there is continuity between the discrete data points, a smooth curve is used to show the overall trend. A computer-generated graph of this type must use interpolation techniques to calculate the value of the function between data points if a smooth curve is to be plotted. Linear interpolation between two points will generate a straight-line curve. Therefore, if smooth curves are required, higher order polynomial interpolation algorithms must be used, e.g. quadratic or cubic interpolation.

Quadratic interpolation uses three data points to estimate the value of the function for a given value of the independent variable. A simple quadratic interpolation algorithm involves three estimates of the value of the function, two based upon the original data, the third based upon these two first-order estimates. The cubic interpolation technique uses four data points and six estimates of the function value are made, three based upon the original data,

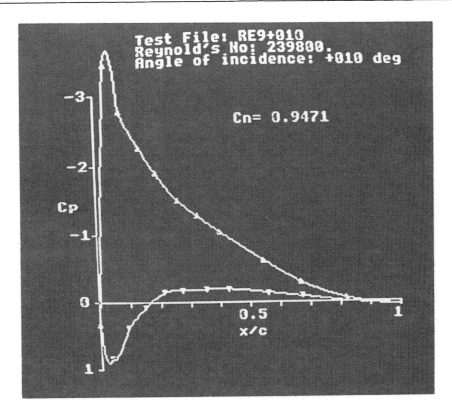

Fig. **B.17** *Curve generation using cubic interpolation.*

two based upon the three first-order estimates, and finally one based upon the two second-order estimates. In each case, the coefficients of a quadratic or cubic polynomial are being calculated for a curve defined in the locality of the inter-polating data points. Figure B.17 shows the variation of pressure coefficient around an aerofoil plotted with respect to chordwise position. Curves for the upper and lower surfaces are shown. These curves have been generated using a cubic interpolating polynomial which can been seen to give a smooth curve through the twenty discrete data points marked. The interpolation methods considered provide suitably smooth curves provided the order of the interpo-lating polynomial is not too large. The curve generally remains **stable** when plotted within the range of the interpolating data points, but often becomes **unstable** and highly inaccurate when extrapolated beyond this range.

B.4.5 CURVE FITTING

Where we need to determine the relationship between the dependent and independent variables, a straight-line graph provides a method for determining the equation of the function, Fig. B.5. Alternatively, we may just want a smooth curve to represent this function, Fig. B.2. The graphs in Figs. B.2 and B.5 show curves and lines that do not pass through every data point, but that shows the best fit to the data. The best-fit curve is drawn to minimize the differences

ASSUMPTIONS:
100% EQUITY 60% LOAN
0% GOVT.CAPITAL SUBSIDY
UNIT COST   £   250000
INSTALL/UNIT   £   48000
TOTAL COST (5)   £ 1490000
EFFECTIVE COST   £ 1490000
=======

YEAR	1990	1991	1992	1993	1994	1995	1996	1997	1998	1999	2000	2001	2002	2003	2004
REVENUE															
GROSS OUTPUT (GWh)	2.27	2.27	2.27	2.27	2.27	2.27	2.27	2.27	2.27	2.27	2.27	2.27	2.27	2.27	2.27
EFFICIENCY	.90	.90	.90	.90	.90	.90	.90	.90	.90	.90	.90	.90	.90	.90	.90
NETT OUTPUT (GWh)	2.04	2.04	2.04	2.04	2.04	2.04	2.04	2.04	2.04	2.04	2.04	2.04	2.04	2.04	2.04
DISPLACED ELECTRICITY (p/kWh)	4.30	4.60	4.92	5.27	5.64	6.03	6.45	6.90	7.39	7.91	8.46	9.05	9.68	10.36	11.09
OPERATING REVENUE (£ 000)	87.85	94.00	100.58	107.62	115.15	123.21	131.84	141.07	150.94	161.51	172.81	184.91	197.85	211.70	226.52
EXPENSES (£ 000)															
RATES	12.50	13.38	14.31	15.31	16.38	17.53	18.76	20.07	21.48	21.48	22.98	24.59	26.31	28.15	30.12
INSURANCE	2.98	3.19	3.41	3.65	3.91	4.18	4.47	4.79	5.12	5.48	5.86	6.27	6.71	7.18	7.68
MAINTENANCE & OPERATION	22.35	23.91	25.59	27.38	29.30	31.35	33.54	35.89	38.40	41.09	43.97	47.04	50.34	53.86	57.63
FINANCE COST	138.57	138.57	138.57	138.57	138.57	138.57	138.57	138.57	138.57	138.57	138.57	138.57	138.57	138.57	138.57
TOTAL EXPENSES	176.40	179.05	181.88	184.91	188.16	191.63	195.34	199.32	203.57	206.62	211.38	216.48	221.93	227.76	234.01
DEPRECIATION D	.08 119.20	109.66	100.89	92.82	85.39	78.56	72.28	66.50	61.18	56.28	51.78	47.64	43.83	40.32	37.09
EFFECTIVE COST - D	1370.80	1261.14	1160.25	1067.43	982.03	903.47	831.19	764.70	703.52	647.24	595.46	547.82	504.00	463.68	426.58
NET INFLOW C	-88.55	-85.05	-81.30	-77.29	-73.01	-68.42	-63.50	-58.25	-52.63	-45.11	-38.57	-31.57	-24.08	-16.06	-7.49
SURPLUS C-D (£ 000)	-207.75	-194.71	-182.19	-170.11	-158.40	-146.98	-135.78	-124.75	-113.80	-101.39	-90.35	-79.20	-67.90	-56.38	-44.58
CUMULATIVE SURPLUS (£ 000)	-207.75	-402.46	-584.66	-754.77	-913.17	-1060.15	-1195.93	-1320.68	-1434.48	-1535.87	-1626.22	-1705.42	-1773.32	-1829.70	-1874.28
PAYBACK NOT ACHIEVED															

Fig. B.18 *Spreadsheet data displayed on the graphics screen.*

between the curve and each data point for all values. In the manual process, it is the skill and experience of the person plotting the graph that determines how well the best-fit curve represents the data. Curve-fitting algorithms allow this procedure to be carried out by computer. A popular approach is the least squares fit. This curve-fitting method involves determining the coefficients of a polynomial equation by mathematically minimizing the cumulative error between the curve and the values of the data set. Once the coefficients of the equation are determined, the curve represents the whole data set. When this curve is plotted, it will show a best fit, but it is unlikely that the curve will pass exactly through any of the data points. This method involves additional analysis and manipulation of the data which for high-order polynomial curves can take a long time to complete. It also has a number of drawbacks, most notably the form of the equation of the curve must be assumed before the analysis can be performed. If a large number of data points are included in the analysis, the assumed form of the curve may be unrepresentative of local variations of the data. Selecting a higher-order polynomial for curve fitting may not always solve this problem. Finally, rogue data points may distort the data analysis so that the resulting curve is not truly representative of the valid data points.

B.4.6 SPREADSHEETS

Spreadsheets have been in common use for general business activities for several years, but it is only very recently that their use for engineering design and analysis has been more widely appreciated. A spreadsheet package allows data and information to be stored into a logically organized computer database. The basic data is displayed on the screen in rows and columns, Fig. B.18. This

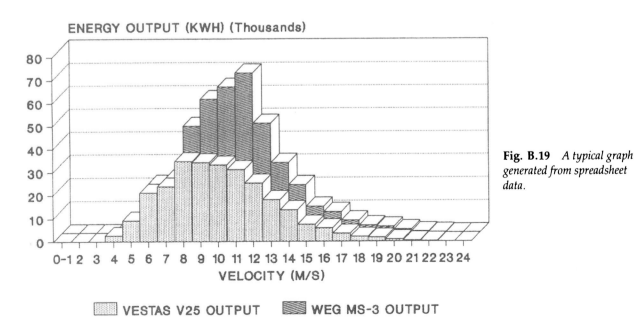

Fig. B.19 *A typical graph generated from spreadsheet data.*

data can be analysed by specifying mathematical relationships between the various columns or rows of data. The current results of these calculations are also displayed on the screen. The original data can be interactively modified by the user, and the consequence of the change can be immediately seen once all the calculation results have been updated. A spreadsheet is highly suitable for iterative design work where a number of intermediate solutions are devised before a satisfactory result is achieved. Spreadsheets are normally used in conjunction with graph plotting packages. Figure B.19 shows a typical graph generated automatically from a spreadsheet package.

Sources

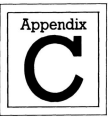

In this appendix the hardware and software used by the authors to produce the original illustrations in the text are listed. A list of useful addresses is also included.

C.1 HARDWARE AND SOFTWARE

AutoCAD: Tandon PAC 386SX and Nimbus PC
AutoSketch: Epson PCAX2 and Archimedes 310
BOXER: DEC MicroVAX cluster and Tektronix 4107 terminal
DOGS: DEC MicroVAX cluster and Tektronix 4107 terminal
GEOMOD: DEC MicroVAX cluster and Tektronix 4107 terminal
GRASP: DEC MicroVAX cluster and Tektronix 4107 terminal
OAK Parametric Design Tool: Archimedes 310
PIGS: DEC MicroVAX cluster and Tektronix 4107 terminal
Techsoft Designer: Acorn BBC Master 128
Techsoft Designer Intro: Archimedes 310

C.2 PLOTTING AND PRINTING

Hewlett Packard 33440A laser printer: to print single colour line drawings
Roland 880A: to plot single and multiple colour drawings with a variety of pen
    thicknesses.
Epson FX-800: to print text and desk edited illustrations.

C.3 WORD PROCESSING AND DESK EDITING

First Word +: word processing on Archimedes 310
Locoscript 2: word processing on Amstrad PCW8256
Locospell: spelling checker on Amstrad PCW8256
Pixel Perfect: screen illustrations on Archimedes 310 and Acorn BBC Master 128

C.4 USEFUL ADDRESSES

Apollo Computer (UK) Limited
Aegis Park
Bramley Road
Milton Keynes MK1 1PT

Autodesk (UK) Limited
Cross Lanes
Guildford
Surrey GU1 1UJ

Suppliers of: AutoCAD, AutoSketch, AutoShade, AutoSolid, AEC Architectural

Benson Electronics Limited
Techno House
Redcliffe Way
Bristol BS1 6NH

BYG Systems Limited
William Lee Building
Highfields Science Park
University Boulevard
Nottingham NG7 2RQ

Suppliers of: GRASP

Compaq Computer Limited
Hotham House
1 Heron Square
Richmond
Surrey TW9 1EJ

Deltacam Systems Limited
Aston Science Park
Birmingham B7 4AP

Suppliers of: DUCT

Digital Equipment Company Limited
Digital Park
POB 110 Imperial Way
Worton Grange
Reading
Berkshire RG2 OTR

Hewlett Packard limited
Cain Road
Bracknell
Berkshire RG12 1HN

IBM (UK) Limited
UK Graphics Marketing Centre
POB 31 Birmingham Road
Warwick
Warwickshire CV34 5JL

Intergraph (UK) Limited
Delta Business Park
Graet Western Way
Swindon
Wiltshire SN1 7XP

Pathtrace Engineering Systems
5 Frederick Sanger Road
The Surrey Research Park
Guildford
Surrey GU2 5YU

Suppliers of: Pathcam

PAFEC Limited
Strelley Hall
Main Street
Strelley
Nottingham NG8 6PE

Suppliers of: BOXER, DOGS, DOGS-PC, PAFEC-FE, PIGS, etc.

Prime Computer (UK) Limited
Beech House
373–399 London Road
Camberley
Surrey GU15 3HR

Suppliers of: SAMMIE

Roland Digital Group
Amalgamated Drive
West Cross Centre
Brentford
Middlesex TW8 9EZ

Schlumberger Technologies
CAD/CAM Division
Applicon Centre
Exchange Street
Stockport
Cheshire SK3 OEE

Suppliers of: BRAV03

Structural Dynamics Research Corporation
York House
Stevenage Road
Hitchin
Hertfordshire SG4 9DY

Suppliers of: I-DEAS, GEOMOD, GEODRAW, SUPERTAB, etc.

Tektronix (UK) Limited
Fourth Avenue
Globe Park
Marlow
Buckinghamshire SL7 1YD

Index